First and Second Language Acquisition

Infants and very young children develop almost miraculously the ability of speech, without apparent effort, without even being taught – as opposed to the teenager or the adult struggling without, it seems, ever being able to reach the same level of proficiency as five-year-olds in their first language. This useful textbook serves as a guide to different types of language acquisition: monolingual and bilingual first language development and child and adult second language acquisition. Unlike other books, it systematically compares first and second language acquisition, drawing on data from several languages. Research questions and findings from various subfields are helpfully summarized to show students how they are related and how they often complement each other. Specific facts about language, such as where the verb is placed, are used as examples to explain 'big questions' like the nature of the human Language Making Capacity. The essential guide to studying first and second language acquisition, it will be used on courses in linguistics, modern languages and developmental psychology.

JÜRGEN M. MEISEL is Professor Emeritus of Linguistics in the Department of Romance Languages and a member and former (1999–2006) Chair of the Research Center on Multilingualism at the University of Hamburg. He is also an Adjunct Professor in the Department of Linguistics and Distinguished Fellow in the Faculty of Humanities of the University of Calgary. He is one of the founding editors and current co-editor of the journal *Bilingualism: Language and Cognition*, published by Cambridge University Press.

CAMBRIDGE TEXTBOOKS IN LINGUISTICS

First and Second Language Acquisition

In this series

L. BAUER *English Word-Formation*
S.C. LEVINSON *Pragmatics*
G. BROWN and G. YULE *Discourse Analysis*
R. HUDDLESTON *Introduction to the Grammar of English*
R. LASS *Phonology*
B. COMRIE *Tense*
W. KLEIN *Second Language Acquisition*
A. J. WOODS, P. FLETCHER and A. HUGHES *Statistics in Language Studies*
D. A. CRUSE *Lexical Semantics*
A. RADFORD *Transformational Grammar*
M. GARMAN *Psycholinguistics*
G. G. CORBETT *Gender*
H. J. GIEGERICH *English Phonology*
R. CANN *Formal Semantics*
J. LAVER *Principles of Phonetics*
F. R. PALMER *Grammatical Roles and Relations*
M. A. JONES *Foundations of French Syntax*
A. RADFORD *Syntactic Theory and the Structure of English: A Minimalist Approach*
R. D. VAN VALIN, JR, and R. J. LAPOLLA *Syntax: Structure, Meaning and Function*
A. DURANTI *Linguistic Anthropology*
A. CRUTTENDEN *Intonation* Second edition
J. K. CHAMBERS and P. TRUDGILL *Dialectology* Second edition
C. LYONS *Definiteness*
R. KAGER *Optimality Theory*
J. A. HOLM *An Introduction to Pidgins and Creoles*
G. G. CORBETT *Number*
C. J. EWEN and H. VAN DER HULST *The Phonological Structure of Words*
F. R. PALMER *Mood and Modality* Second edition
B. J. BLAKE *Case* Second edition
E. GUSSMAN *Phonology: Analysis and Theory*
M. YIP *Tone*
W. CROFT *Typology and Universals* Second edition
F. COULMAS *Writing Systems: An Introduction to their Linguistic Analysis*
P. J. HOPPER and E. C. TRAUGOTT *Grammaticalization* Second edition
L. WHITE *Second Language Acquisition and Universal Grammar*
I. PLAG *Word-Formation in English*
W. CROFT and A. CRUSE *Cognitive Linguistics*
A. SIEWIERSKA *Person*
A. RADFORD *Minimalist Syntax: Exploring the Structure of English*
D. BÜRING *Binding Theory*
M. BUTT *Theories of Case*
N. HORNSTEIN, J. NUÑES and K. GROHMANN *Understanding Minimalism*
B. C. LUST *Child Language: Acquisition and Growth*
G. G. CORBETT *Agreement*
J. C. L. INGRAM *Neurolinguistics: An Introduction to Spoken Language Processing and its Disorders*
J. CLACKSON *Indo-European Linguistics: An Introduction*
M. ARIEL *Pragmatics and Grammar*
R. CANN, R. KEMPSON and E. GREGOROMICHELAKI *Semantics: An Introduction to Meaning in Language*
Y. MATRAS *Language Contact*
D. BIBER and S. CONRAD *Register, Genre and Style*
L. JEFFRIES and D. MCINTYRE *Stylistics*
R. HUDSON *An Introduction to Word Grammar*
M. L. MURPHY *Lexical Meaning*
J. M. MEISEL *First and Second Language Acquisition*

First and Second Language Acquisition

Parallels and Differences

JÜRGEN M. MEISEL

Universität Hamburg and University of Calgary

CAMBRIDGE UNIVERSITY PRESS
Cambridge, New York, Melbourne, Madrid, Cape Town,
Singapore, São Paulo, Delhi, Tokyo, Mexico City

Cambridge University Press
The Edinburgh Building, Cambridge CB2 8RU, UK

Published in the United States of America by Cambridge University Press, New York

www.cambridge.org
Information on this title: www.cambridge.org/9780521557641

First published 2011

Printed in the United Kingdom at the University Press, Cambridge

A catalogue record for this publication is available from the British Library

Library of Congress Cataloguing in Publication data
Meisel, Jürgen M., 1944–
First and Second Language Acquisition : Parallels and Differences / Jürgen M. Meisel.
p. cm. – (Cambridge Textbooks in Linguistics)
Includes bibliographical references and indexes.
ISBN 978-0-521-55294-3 (hardback) – ISBN 978-0-521-55764-1 (paperback)
1. Second language acquisition. 2. Language and languages – Study and
teaching. I. Title. II. Series.
P118.2.M45 2011
418.0071–dc22

2010051571

ISBN 978-0-521-55294-3 Hardback
ISBN 978-0-521-55764-1 Paperback

To Susanne

Contents

Figures

Tables

Preface

This is an introduction to the study of the human Language Making Capacity. More accurately, it is a textbook presenting research questions and research results referring to specific manifestations of this capacity in monolingual and bilingual first language acquisition and child and adult second language acquisition. A more comprehensive treatment of this subject would have to address other aspects as well, for example, the genesis and change of languages, creolization and pidginization, language attrition and loss, impaired acquisition, and so forth. However, such a comprehensive study of the Language Making Capacity is not yet an established discipline within the language sciences. Rather, its manifestations are usually investigated separately, with only limited interactions among the various domains of this field of research. This is true even for closely related domains like first and second language acquisition, or monolingual and bilingual first language acquisition – at best, the mutual interest can be characterized as one-sided, second language research being reasonably well informed about results of investigations into first language development, or bilingual studies about work on monolinguals – but not conversely. Assuming that the various types of acquisition are indeed strongly shaped by the Language Making Capacity – though to different degrees and in distinct ways – this is an unfortunate state of affairs, and I hope with this book to contribute to a change for the better.

I am convinced that grammar constitutes the core component of the language faculty, so the focus of this textbook lies on the acquisition of grammar, more specifically on the acquisition of syntax and morphology. It offers a linguistic approach to language acquisition, and although I adopt a psycholinguistic perspective, this particular focus on syntax and morphology is one of the limitations of this book. I do not pretend to cover all possible aspects of acquisition, perhaps not even all the major ones. Moreover, since I am also convinced that substantial results can only be obtained by theoretically guided analyses, I adopt the theory of Universal Grammar, as developed in the tradition of generative grammar. Given that every scientific theory defines which aspects of the object of study are of particular relevance – and which ones are not – this choice results in further limitations of the present text, but these are inevitable and indeed necessary ones. At any rate, this theoretical choice does not imply that only work carried out in this framework will be considered. In fact, one of the goals of this book is to resist the amnesia with which some acquisition studies seem to be afflicted. I acknowledge, firstly, that language acquisition research existed before the mid-1980s. The results of this early research should be discussed critically but not ignored. Secondly, the fact that controversial issues seem to disappear from the research agenda does not mean that the problems at stake have been solved. An example of this is the discussion of the initial state of second language acquisition which was hotly debated during the first half of the 1990s but much less so more recently, although no satisfactory consensus was reached.

My aim is to present a theoretically sophisticated approach to grammatical acquisition, while at the same time emphasizing the need for an empirically sound basis for its assessment. In doing so, I focus on a limited number of grammatical phenomena, trying to be as specific as possible with as few grammatical technicalities as possible. Although the focus lies on the development of grammatical competence, this textbook should be accessible not only to students of linguistics, but also to others in cognitive science, including psychologists who study L1 acquisition either experimentally or through naturalistic observation and those who study processes of induction through experiments with adults involving the learning of artificial L2 languages, provided they have a basic understanding of grammar, especially of syntax. If it is necessary to consult introductions to generative syntax, such books are readily available, e.g. Adger (2003); Hornstein, Nunes and Grohmann (2005) or Radford (2004).

I am indebted to many people who enabled me to write this book. The first one who I want to mention is Judith Ayling, then at Cambridge University Press, who invited me to write a textbook on this topic. I am also grateful to Pieter Musyken and the Netherlands Institute for Advanced Study in the Humanities and Social Sciences (NIAS) for inviting me to work at the NIAS in Wassenaar as a Fellow-in-Residence. This allowed me to start working on this text. Other commitments prevented me from working continuously on this project, which finally took me much longer to finish than initially envisaged. I therefore owe apologies for this delay to Andrew Winnard, also of Cambridge University Press, and thanks for his patience.

This work is based on several research projects which I directed over the past thirty-five years. It all started with the research group ZISA (Zweitspracherwerb italienischer, portugiesischer und spanischer Arbeiter – Second language acquisition by Italian, Portuguese and Spanish workers) at the University of Wuppertal. The ZISA team collected two corpora from 1977 through to 1981, first in a cross-sectional study for which I received funding by the Minister für Wissenschaft und Forschung des Landes Nordrhein-Westfalen (1977–1978), and subsequently in a longitudinal study funded by the Stiftung Volkswagenwerk (Volkswagen Foundation) (1978–1982). I gratefully acknowledge the support by both the Ministry and the Foundation.

I was very lucky to be supported in these endeavours by excellent collaborators, several of whom are today internationally renowned linguists and acquisition researchers. In fact, I could hardly have found better co-researchers than my then doctoral students Harald Clahsen and Manfred Pienemann, early members of the ZISA team in Wuppertal. When I moved to the University of Hamburg, Harald Clahsen joined me there as a member of the new ZISA team, together with Klaus-Michael Köpcke, Howard Nicholas and Maryse Vincent.

At the University of Hamburg, in 1980, I started working on (bilingual) first language acquisition and obtained funding for the research projects Deutsch und Französisch: Doppelter Erstspracherwerb (DuFDE, German and French: Bilingual First Language Acquisition, 1986–1992 and 1992–1995) and Baskisch und Spanisch: Doppelter Erstspracherwerb (BuSDE, Basque and Spanish: Simultaneous Acquisition of Two First Languages, 1990–1994), both supported by the Deutsche Forschungsgemeinschaft (DFG, German Research Foundation). The DFG also funded the research project Simultaner und sukzessiver Erwerb von Mehrsprachigkeit (Simultaneous and Successive Acquisition of Bilingualism, 1999–2009) as part of the Sonderforschungsbereich Mehrsprachigkeit (Research Center on Multilingualism). This continued financial support by the DFG is most gratefully acknowledged.

During this period, too, I had wonderful colleagues and co-researchers without whom the studies on which parts of the discussion in this textbook are based would not have been possible. The DuFDE team consisted of doctoral students Susanne Jekat, Georg A. Kaiser, Swantje Klinge, Caroline Koehn, Regina Köppe, Natascha Müller, Teresa Parodi, Ulrike Rohde-Hurpin, Achim Stenzel and of post-doctoral researcher Suzanne Schlyter. The BuSDE team comprised doctoral students Marijo Ezeizabarrena, Pilar Larrañaga and Axel Mahlau. In the Basque Country, a research team directed by Itziar Idiazabal carried out all of the data collection and part of the analysis. It consisted of Margareta Almgren, Andoni Barreña and Kristina Elosegi. The research group working with me in the Research Center on Multilingualism consisted of doctoral students Matthias Bonnesen, Marc-Olivier Hinzelin, Noemi Kintana, Robert Mensching, Barbara Miertsch, Anja Möhring, Cristina Pierantozzi, Susanne Rieckborn, Anne-Kathrin Riedel, Claudia Stöber, post-doctoral researcher Tessa Say and visiting researcher Aldona Sopata. Working together we all learned what we now know about bilingual first language acquisition. Many of the former students became colleagues, and some of the colleagues became friends. I am truly grateful to all of them.

The manuscript emanated from a number of lectures and seminars which I taught on the subject of this book, at the University of Hamburg, at the University of Leiden (LOT school), at the University of the Basque Country in Vitoria-Gasteiz, in the Department of Linguistics at the University of Salzburg, and in the Department of Linguistics and in the Language Research Center at the University of Calgary. I want to thank John Archibald (Calgary), Marijo Ezeizabarrena and Itziar Idiazabal (Vitoria-Gasteiz) and Hubert Haider (Salzburg) for making this possible, and the students in each of these places for their valuable feedback.

Finally, my deepest gratitude goes to those who read and commented on previous versions of several chapters of this volume: Matthias Bonnesen, Martin Elsig, Lynn Eubank, Galina Fix, Anne-Kathrin Riedel and Esther Rinke.

Susanne E. Carroll not only read the entire manuscript, commented on style and content, but she also shared with me her knowledge about language acquisition and about linguistics in general. It is impossible to determine her exact contribution, but I know that without her support, the book would not merely be different, it would be less interesting. In fact, without her, I would be different, poorer.

Abbreviations

A, AdjP	Adjective (Phrase)
Agr, AgrP	Agreement (Phrase)
aL2	adult second language
AOA	Age of Onset of Acquisition
Aux	Auxiliary
BA	Brodmann Area
C, Comp, CP	Complementizer (Phrase)
CA	Contrastive Analysis
cL2	child second language
CPH	Critical Period Hypothesis
CV	Consonant – Vowel
D, Det, DP	Determiner (Phrase)
DMTH	Developmentally Moderated Transfer Hypothesis
EA	Error Analysis
ECP	Empty Category Principle
EEG	Electroencephalography
EPP	Extended Projection Principle
ERP	Event-Related Brain Potentials
[±F]	Finiteness Feature
FC	Functional Category
FCH	Full Competence Hypothesis
FDH	Fundamental Difference Hypothesis
FFFH	Failed Functional Features Hypothesis
fMRI	functional Magnetic Resonance Imaging
FP	Functional Projection (underspecified)
FTFA	Full Transfer/Full Access to UG hypothesis
HPSG	Head-driven Phrase Structure Grammar
I, Infl, IP	Inflection (Phrase)
IL	Interlanguage
L1	First language
L2	Second language
LAD	Language Acquisition Device
LAN	Left Anterior Negativity
LF	Logical Form
LFG	Lexical Functional Grammar
LMC	Language Making Capacity
MP	Minimalist Program

MSIH	Missing Surface Inflection Hypothesis
MTH	Minimal Trees Hypothesis
N, NP	Noun (Phrase)
NEG, NEGP	Negation (Phrase)
NSP	Null-Subject Parameter
OV	Object – Verb
P	Preposition
PET	Positron Emission Tomography
PF	Phonetic Form
PLD	Primary Linguistic Data
PPT	Principles and Parameters Theory
PT	Processability Theory
SBH	Structure Building Hypothesis
SCH	Small Clause Hypothesis
SOV, SVO	Subject – Object – Verb, Subject – Verb – Object
SSH	Shallow Structure Hypothesis
T, TENSE, TP	Tense (Phrase)
TMA	Tense – Modality – Aspect
UG	Universal Grammar
V, VP	Verb (Phrase)
v, vP	Little Verb (Phrase)
V2	Verb-second
VFH	Valueless Features Hypothesis
VMP	Verb Movement Parameter
VO	Verb – Object

1 The quest for the LAD

1.1 Two types of language acquisition – One kind of language making capacity?

Learn a foreign language in your sleep! Language learning made easy by hypnosis! Lean back, relax and learn! Diverse methods of relaxation promise fast and (almost) unfailing success in adult foreign language learning, relying, for example, on exposure to Baroque music or on special breathing techniques, designed to activate underused cognitive resources of the brain, especially in the right hemisphere, to synchronize both brain hemispheres, to put conscious and subconscious into communication, and so forth. These as well as other advertised methods of language learning attract large numbers of people wishing to acquire a second language, people who may be frustrated by previous language learning experiences in school. They seem to believe or are easily convinced that they do have the capacity to acquire other languages, but that, somehow, access to this language making capacity is blocked and can be made accessible by removing some mental or psychological obstacles.

After all, toddlers quite obviously have this capacity. Infants and very young children develop almost miraculously the ability of speech, without apparent effort, without even being taught – as opposed to the teenager or the adult struggling in foreign language classrooms without, it seems, ever being able to reach the same level of proficiency as five-year-olds in their first language. On the other hand, blaming it on the teachers or on teaching methods does not seem to be fair, either, since learners in a naturalistic setting do not fare much better, frequently even worse, in fact, as is demonstrated by the limited success of many immigrants who have acquired their knowledge of their new linguistic environment in the process of everyday communication, without ever attending classes.

The suspicion thus is that whatever enables the child to acquire the mother tongue might not be lost forever, rather that it could be hidden somewhere among or underneath our other cognitive faculties. Assuming this to be true, the obvious question to ask is whether it is possible to reactivate this language making capacity available to the toddler, to access it again in other language acquisition contexts, in foreign language learning in the classroom, in naturalistic second language acquisition, in relearning languages once learned but later forgotten, and so on. Are these and other types of acquisition perhaps only different instantiations of one and the same process of language acquisition, the differences being caused by relatively superficial properties of the varying settings?

These are rather straightforward questions, it seems, and obvious ones to ask, once one begins to wonder why a task which is mastered so successfully by a child between, let us say, the ages of one and five, appears to be mission impossible for most teenagers and adults. And yet, the language sciences in general and language acquisition studies in particular cannot offer satisfactory answers. Not that there are no answers – there are many, but contradictory and frequently even mutually exclusive ones. This is all the more surprising since there is, indeed, consensus that children acquiring a first language develop it naturally, they need not be taught the necessary knowledge and the skills required to use it. Second language learners, on the other hand, apparently do need some guidance, although we do not know exactly how and to what extent these learners benefit from instruction. At any rate, to expect them to attain native or native-like competence after three, five or even eight years in the classroom appears to be an idea too unrealistic to be entertained seriously.

In view of the millions of students who – ever since the introduction of obligatory schooling in many countries in the nineteenth century – have been taught foreign languages through an almost countless variety of different teaching methods, one might have expected to find more definitive answers to the questions of what language teaching can possibly achieve and especially whether the child's language making capacity is, in principle, still accessible to the second language learner. And if one is inclined to give an affirmative answer to this question, how, then, can the obvious differences between child and adult learners be accounted for? If, on the other hand, one is to conclude that a negative answer is closer to the truth, how can the equally obvious similarities be explained? After all, in spite of the deplorable imperfections and limitations of second language learners' knowledge and skills, as compared to native learners, they fare infinitely better than chimpanzees and other primates coaxed into using different forms of communication mimicking human language.

These questions all relate to the core issues which will be discussed in the present volume. The story is primarily that of the LAD, the Language Acquisition Device (McNeill 1966; Chomsky 1981b) or the human language making capacity (LMC) as Slobin (1985) called it – its properties as they can be detected from studying child language development and its fate as it can be observed in the course of second language acquisition. A brief look at some lines of thought pursued in language acquisition research in the past may help us to understand why interest in such issues surged only fairly recently.

1.2 Relating first and second language acquisition

The question of whether or not different types of language acquisition share essential properties was not addressed in a systematic fashion until the late 1960s. Until then, it apparently seemed self-evident to most researchers that first (L1) and second language (L2) acquisition are fundamentally different. But this belief was not based on empirical research. In fact, L1 research did not pay much attention to L2 acquisition at all, and, surprisingly perhaps, this has not changed significantly since then. The idea that merely by contrasting different types of acquisition we can hope to gain a deeper understanding of the nature of the human language capacity began to spread only much later (cf. Wode 1981).

Until the 1960s, the research agenda of language acquisition studies, just like that of psychology and linguistics in general, was strongly determined by behaviourist learning theories. An explanation referring to mental capacities of the learner did not seem to make much sense in that context; it would, indeed, have been regarded as a non-scientific approach to the problem. Only after the constraints and restrictions of behaviourist psychology had been shaken off could the language sciences begin to understand language learning as a mental activity happening in the cognitive system of the individual. Chomsky's (1959) famous and influential review of Skinner's (1957) book *Verbal Behavior* is a milestone on this road to the *cognitive turn*. What this term is meant to convey is that it is the study of human cognition, which is now identified as the major task of linguistics, in close cooperation with other sciences, especially cognitive psychology and philosophy (see Chomsky 1968). With respect to the language faculty, the issues put on the research agenda by this change of perspective include, among other things, the problem of how to characterize the knowledge system represented in the mind of a person who speaks and understands a particular language, as well as to explain how this knowledge is used and, most importantly in the present context, how this linguistic knowledge and the ability to use it are acquired. The Language Acquisition Device, then, represents the initial state of the language faculty, that is, prior to any exposure to the language to be acquired (see Chomsky 1988). This new approach had an enormous impact on L1 research, and as early as in the early 1960s appeared the first of an ever increasing number of publications applying these ideas to the study of first language acquisition.

L2 research, on the other hand, took somewhat longer to liberate itself from the dominating influence of behaviourism. This is partly due, perhaps, to the fact that for a long time it had exclusively been occupied, and still continues to be primarily concerned, with foreign language learning in classroom settings, rather than with naturalistic L2 acquisition. The idea that learning crucially implies changing previously acquired behaviour seems to have been deeply rooted in language teaching. It is therefore not surprising that interference from L1 was, and in part still is, regarded as the major factor determining the shape of L2 speech. The research paradigm which elaborated this idea in considerable detail is Contrastive Analysis (CA).

Contrastive Analysis continued a line of thought which had been expressed quite clearly as early as 1945 by Charles C. Fries in the following frequently quoted statement:

> The most efficient materials are those that are based upon a scientific description of the language to be learned, carefully compared with a parallel description of the native language of the learner. (Fries 1945: 9)

The next step was taken by Robert Lado, a former student of Fries, in assuming that 'individuals tend to transfer forms and meanings, and the distribution of forms and meanings of their native language and culture to the foreign language and culture' (Lado 1957: 2). This assumption, which Lado as well as many others at the time regarded as an uncontroversial generalization based on empirical observation, was turned into a prediction, the perhaps major theoretical claim of CA, when Lado (1957) and Weinreich (1953) before him argued that 'those elements that are similar to his [i.e. the learner's, JMM] native language will be simple for him, and those elements that are different will be difficult' (Lado 1957: 2). I should hasten to add that CA researchers were not content with this somewhat naive one-to-one and yes-or-no formulation of the prediction but were able to make far more sophisticated suggestions; see Larsen-Freeman and Long (1991: 53) who present a summary of the proposal by Stockwell, Bowen and Martin (1965) distinguishing between structural and functional/semantic correspondence.

In spite of improvements made over the years, researchers became increasingly dissatisfied with CA. The arguments put forth against this approach are manifold; compare, for example, Whitman and Jackson 1972, Schachter and Celce-Murcia 1977, and Long and Sato 1984. But what ultimately led to profound disappointment was the fact that its prognostic powers turned out not to be satisfactory. After all, CA had been advertised as a scientific method, not just another intuitive way of dealing with language teaching and learning. It was based on a theoretical claim, the transfer hypothesis, and on a scientific description of the objects of its study, the native and the foreign language. Most importantly, this enabled researchers to formulate predictions about difficulty and ease of learning, not merely *post factum* 'explanations'. But it became increasingly obvious that, in spite of certain refinements in these claims, prognosticated errors were not found in the data, whereas learners clearly encountered difficulties where CA did not foresee any. An example of the latter case is presented by Hyltenstam (1977); the overprediction of transfer errors will be discussed in more detail in chapter 3 and in section 4.3.

Looking at it from today's perspective, Contrastive Analysis does not necessarily appear as fundamentally wrong. Its major shortcomings, direct consequences of its behaviourist descent, however, are such that it could not, in principle, lead to insights about what the learner has to know and do in order to acquire a second language successfully. This is primarily due to two problems.

First, the role of transfer was grossly overstated. The problem is neither the fact that two languages are contrasted nor the claim that transfer may occur. It would be absurd to ignore the fact that L2 learners, as opposed to monolingual and even bilingual children acquiring their first languages, have access to previously acquired linguistic knowledge and that, as a consequence, the L1 might interfere with the learning of the L2. But transfer from L1 occupied everybody's mind so much that other factors determining L2 acquisition were severely neglected or simply ignored, a point which is also stressed by Selinker (1992: 9). Why such undue stress was put on a single factor is difficult to assess. I believe, however, that it is, to a large part, caused by a notion of 'learning' defined primarily by habit formation. As Selinker (1992: 7) points out, Fries (1945) already saw the goal of the 'first stage of language learning' as 'the building up of a set of habits for the oral production of a language and for the receptive understanding of the language when it is spoken'. Since learners are claimed to transfer habits from the native to the foreign language, L2 learning must crucially imply changing some of these habits of learners (Lado 1957). Again, this is not in itself an unreasonable assumption. But the CA approach goes seriously wrong when learners' linguistic competence is equated with and reduced to sets of habits.

This brings us to the second point: the nature of linguistic knowledge. What Contrastive Analysis contrasts in order to predict difficulty and ease of learning are abstract linguistic systems, or rather grammars written by linguists. These researchers did not claim, however, that their grammatical descriptions captured some kind of psychological reality. In fact, mainstream linguistics, at the time, explicitly rejected mentalist considerations of this sort. Yet this inevitably leads to a paradox. CA claims that 'the grammatical structure of the native language tends to be transferred to the foreign language' (Lado 1957: 58).[1] The question, however, is not only from where and to where transfer could happen. The crucial issue is to determine the nature of what is transferred. In our understanding today, transfer must necessarily happen in the mind of the learner. The entire notion of transfer, therefore, does not make sense unless one is ready to claim that mental representations of the source as well as of the target system exist (Meisel 1983b, 1983c, 2000b). In other words, transfer cannot go from one abstract linguistic system to the other. If we want to postulate that it plays a part in the language learning process, we cannot avoid referring to psycholinguistically plausible entities. If the grammatical structures involved do not qualify as such, we should expect the above mentioned habits to do so. But this is a reasonable alternative only if one is ready to make strong psycholinguistic claims with respect to the parsing, processing and production mechanisms hidden behind the term 'habit' – a solution not available to an anti-mentalist theory of language and of learning.

An example may help to clarify the argument that linguistic structures cannot be used innocently in order to justify claims about second language learning without committing oneself to the hypothesis that they reflect mentally represented knowledge. German word order, especially the position of the verb, has frequently been observed to represent a major difficulty for second language learners. This problem will be discussed in more detail and in a more technical fashion in subsequent chapters of this volume. For the present purpose it suffices to look at the examples in (1).

(1) (i) Sie hat den Wein probiert.
She has the wine tasted
'She tasted the wine'
(ii) Sie will den Wein probieren.
She wants the wine to taste
'She wants to taste the wine'
(iii) Einen Chardonnay will sie probieren
A Chardonnay wants she to taste
'A Chardonnay she wants to taste'
(iv) . . . dass sie den Wein probiert.
that she the wine tastes
'. . . that she tastes the wine'
(v) . . . dass sie den Wein probieren will.
that she the wine to taste wants
'. . . that she wants to taste the wine'

What does a Contrastive Analysis approach predict, in this case, if the learners' first language is, for example, English or a Romance language, that is, an SVO language where both the finite and the non-finite verb normally follow the subject and precede the object in main as well as subordinate clauses? The prediction must be that English or Romance word order patterns, or habits of placing elements in this order, are transferred into the L2 German which would thus be analysed as an SVO language. Learners then have to discover that non-finite verbal elements must be placed in clause-final position, as in (1) (i) – (iii), and that in main clauses the order of the subject and the finite verb must be inverted in case an element other than the subject appears in initial position; see (1) (iii). In subordinate clauses, on the other hand, the finite verb too has to go to the end of the clause, as in (1) (iv), even following the non-finite one, see (1) (v). In other words, learners have to acquire the so-called rules of 'non-finite shift', 'subject–verb inversion' (in main clauses), and 'verb-end placement' (in subordinates). Note that if native German was analysed as an SVO language, as used to be assumed by traditional grammarians, children learning German as an L1 would face learning tasks identical to those of the L2 learners. The crucial point with respect to the argument to be made here is, however, that the definition of what kind of operations the learning tasks imply, for example 'inversion' and two kinds of 'verb movement', depends on one's grammatical analysis. The importance of this observation becomes evident if one considers the fact that native German is indeed commonly *not* analysed as an SVO language, that is, an alternative solution exists which is generally preferred. Most current treatments of German syntax agree that its canonical or underlying word order is SOV. Under this analysis, it can be argued that non-finite verbs need not change their position; rather, they remain in their original position, and only finite verbs have to move. And since these may go as far as to a position preceding the subject, a special operation (or rule) of subject–verb inversion is not needed, either. This is, in fact, the most widely accepted hypothesis about what kind of grammatical knowledge German (L1) children need to acquire. If, however, this is correct, that is, if in L1 development children treat German as an SOV language whereas in L2 acquisition SVO order may be transferred from the L1 to L2 German, as predicted by a CA approach, we are claiming that L1 and L2 learners face radically different learning tasks. Irrespective of whether or not this is indeed the case, it should be obvious now that contrastive analyses as a tool of language acquisition studies only make sense if one is prepared to interpret linguistic structures as representing the implicit knowledge of the learner about the target language – 'implicit' because learners are normally not aware of this knowledge and do not have direct access to it by simple introspection.

Returning to our point of departure, we can sum up by saying that second language research suffered longer than first language research from its behaviourist heritage. By focusing on the comparison of linguistic structures justified exclusively in grammatical terms rather than with respect to their psycholinguistic plausibility, and, moreover, by defining learning primarily in terms of habit formation and changing of habits, questions relating to the possibility of a common underlying language making capacity for the various types of language acquisition could not even be formulated. As a result, the role of the native language in second language acquisition was seen exclusively as a possible source of transfer.

Let me emphasize, once again, that this is not to say that CA did not make a significant contribution to our understanding of second language acquisition or that contrastive analyses could not be used as a tool for second language research. In fact, later developments in this field tend to incorporate previous hypotheses, methods and findings; they do not really stand in sharp contrast to earlier ones. One might, in fact, argue that more recent approaches to L2 acquisition, according to which parameters of the L1 grammar are transferred to early L2 grammars (see, e.g., White 1985), follow research strategies resembling those of classic CA, for example, contrasting structures from both languages and exploring the transfer hypothesis (see chapter 4). The crucial difference, however, is that in this theoretical context, grammatical structures are indeed interpreted as hypotheses about mental representations of the implicit linguistic knowledge of the learner.

An explicitly cognitive orientation of second language acquisition research was initiated in the late 1960s. Here is not the place to write a history of L2 research; the only point of interest, in the present context, is to see how language acquisition studies came to be interested in parallels and differences between first and second language acquisition.

The change is best illustrated by the seminal paper by Pit Corder (1967). He refers to the child's 'innate predisposition to acquire language' and the 'internal mechanism' which makes the acquisition of grammar possible, and then raises the question of whether the child's language making capacity remains available to second language learners. Although he is careful about the conclusions to be drawn from these assumptions, he leaves no doubt about the fact that he favours a positive answer, postulating 'the same mechanism' for both L1 and L2 acquisition, and proposes (p. 164)

> as a working hypothesis that some at least of the *strategies* adopted by the learner of a second language are substantially the same as those by which a first language is acquired. Such a proposal does not imply that the course or *sequence* of learning is the same in both cases.

What exactly Corder means by 'strategies' is not entirely clear, nor does he elaborate on the last point, that is, what might cause the emergence of different learning sequences in spite of the claim that the underlying mechanisms are the same. He does, however, list what he sees as differences between the two acquisition types, namely that (1) children acquiring their L1, as opposed to L2 learners, are inevitably successful, (2) L1 development is part of the child's maturational process, (3) at the onset of second language acquisition, another language is already present, and (4) the motivation for language acquisition is quite different in the two cases. Corder suspects that this last factor, motivation, is the principal one distinguishing first and second language acquisition. In order to gain insights into the nature of the underlying mechanism and of the strategies used in second language acquisition, Corder suggests studying the errors found in L2 speech. He distinguishes between random *mistakes* and systematic *errors*. The latter, he claims (p. 166), 'reveal his [the learner's, JMM] underlying knowledge of the language to date, or, as we may call it his *transitional competence*'. If, for example, learners use the form *thinked*, this suggests that they have acquired knowledge about tense marking in English, even if this particular form is an *error*, deviating from the target norm.

The study of errors has attracted the attention of L2 researchers ever since and continues to do so. In view of the rather limited success of error prognostications based on contrastive analyses, researchers concentrate on actually occurring errors, attempting to work their way back to the sources of such errors. As should be obvious, however, this type of Error Analysis (EA) lacks the predictive power of CA, unless error sources other than L1 transfer are identified which can be shown to lead to new predictions about possible learning difficulties. Yet since in EA transfer continues to be the single most frequently studied source of errors, little is gained and much is lost. Furthermore, by concentrating on errors, EA tends to underestimate learner achievements; on the other hand, in cases where learners avoid difficult structures, EA is likely not to detect this lack of knowledge or of skills and overestimates the knowledge of learners; see Larsen-Freeman and Long (1991: 61) for a critique of EA.

The truly stimulating ideas in Corder (1967), with respect to the present discussion, are that he explicitly suggested the same underlying mechanism for L1 and L2 acquisition, introduced the notion of 'transitional competence', and demanded that the focus of L2 research should be on the learner, rather than on learners' productions. This can only be achieved if acquisition studies strive for psycholinguistically plausible grammatical analyses of learner utterances. In other words, L2 learners are assumed to acquire systematic knowledge about the L2; a 'third system in addition to the NL [native language, JMM] of learners and the TL [target language, JMM] to be learned' is introduced, to use Selinker's (1992: 18) words. Note, however, that assuming a kind of transitional competence does not oblige us to subscribe to the idea of one and the same mechanism underlying L1 and L2 acquisition. The L2 competence might still be the product of some other cognitive capacities – whether this is indeed the case will be discussed in some detail in chapters 3 to 5.

Suggestions similar to the 'transitional competence' were indeed made by a number of authors, proposing 'approximative systems' (Nemser 1971), 'idiosyncratic dialects' (Corder 1971) or 'interlanguages' (Selinker 1972). These terms are not synonymous, but they coincide in so far as they postulate a structured transitional knowledge base in the L2 learner. It contains elements of the target grammar, possibly also elements of the L1 grammar ('interlingual errors', Richards 1971), and, most importantly, elements different from both source and target systems, 'developmental errors' ('intralingual errors', Richards 1971) which prove that the learner is actively and creatively participating in the acquisitional process. The term most generally adopted is Selinker's (1972) 'interlanguage' (IL),[2] and I will therefore also use it in this volume, although it is somewhat misleading since it refers to the product of language use, in spite of the fact that it is intended to capture properties of the learner's linguistic competence. 'Approximative system' renders the intended idea better but is perhaps not as elegant an expression and is less commonly used in the more recent L2 literature.

1.3 Searching for the questions to ask

Conceptualizing language acquisition, first or second, as a sequence of approximative systems represented in the learners' minds only became possible as a consequence of the cognitive turn in the language sciences. It is this perspective which will determine the route to be followed in the quest for the LAD undertaken in this volume, shaping the questions to be asked and therefore also the kinds of answers to be expected. One important consequence is that the parallels and differences to be studied are ultimately those *underlying* the ones to be observed in language use. The crucial question is whether the tacit knowledge guiding second language acquisition is in fundamental ways different from that available to first language learners, and whether the mechanisms of language use differ in significant ways. In addition, we must consider factors which might influence language acquisition or use in a way that leads perhaps to observable differences in spite of fundamental commonalities.

The most obvious fact in which the two types of acquisition differ is, of course, that in one case more than one language is present in the learners' environment and in their minds. The other obvious difference between these acquisition types is the age of onset of acquisition (AOA). In order to be able to disentangle the roles of these and other potentially intervening factors, it should be useful to contrast L2 and monolingual L1 with a third type of acquisition, the simultaneous acquisition of two or more languages (2L1). It resembles L1 in that both are acquired from birth, and it resembles L2 in that more than one language is acquired. On the other hand, 2L1 differs from L2 because the two languages develop simultaneously in 2L1 whereas they are acquired successively in L2. If we were to find significant differences between these acquisition types, the central issue of this debate is which causal factors can explain these differences. My assumption is that the ones just alluded to qualify as the most plausible and promising candidates: the need to acquire, process and store more than a single grammatical system, possible interaction between the newly acquired and simultaneously or previously acquired linguistic knowledge, and possible alterations of the language making capacity as a result of maturation and age. Concerning the latter, another problem arises, namely the identification of the developmental phase or age range during which such changes happen. Perhaps the most practicable way to proceed is to first focus on adult second language learners, that is, learners of approximately twelve years of age and older at the onset of acquisition, and to contrast them with monolingual as well as bilingual children. Subsequently, the results of this analysis can be compared to those obtained with child second language learners (cL2) (see especially chapter 6). In this fashion, the role of both age and bilingualism can be assessed. The age range for what counts as child second language acquisition, however, still needs to be justified. For the time being, I will simply assume that it covers approximately the period between ages four and eight (see Meisel 2008b).

One consequence of the cognitive turn in linguistics is that one asks questions about cognitive systems. It therefore makes sense to examine one such system, namely grammar, and to focus on the underlying principles and mechanisms of language acquisition. This is why this book is concerned almost exclusively with the acquisition of grammar. In fact, reflecting research concerns over the past decades in the area of second language acquisition, this amounts to saying that it will primarily deal with the acquisition of morphology and syntax. Second language acquisition will indeed be discussed in more detail than first language development, for there is a broad although not total consensus among language acquisition researchers that children are equipped with a species-specific language making capacity. The role, however, which this capacity might play in L2 acquisition is quite controversial and requires more attention.

In recent years, a considerable amount of research has been devoted to the study of similarities and differences between various types of language acquisition, enhancing our knowledge on this issue significantly, as compared to the time when Corder (1967) speculated about the availability of the child's language making capacity to second language learners. The goal of this volume, then, is to suggest at least a tentative solution to this puzzle by assembling pieces of available knowledge and by filling some of the gaps with additional facts, reflections and speculations.

1.4 Suggested readings and topics for discussion

When language acquisition research began to ask questions concerning parallels and differences between first and second language acquisition, answers initially favoured what has been called the 'identity hypothesis', claiming that the same type of 'psycholinguistic strategies and processes' are shared by both types of acquisition. Differences were attributed to 'non-linguistic factors such as motivation, memory span, general maturity, etc.' (Felix 1978: 470). Since this is how the current debate originated, it should be useful to look at some of these early works.

Suggested readings

Corder, S. P. 1967. 'The significance of learner's errors', *International Review of Applied Linguistics* 5: 161–70.

Ervin-Tripp, S. M. 1974. 'Is second language learning like the first?', *TESOL Quarterly* 8: 111–27.

Hatch, E. 1974. 'Second language learning – universals?', *Working Papers on Bilingualism* 3: 1–17.

Selinker, L. 1972. 'Interlanguage', *International Review of Applied Linguistics* 10: 209–31.

Topics for discussion

- Error Analysis is based on the assumption that one can distinguish between random *mistakes* and systematic *errors*. The latter should help us to gain insights into the learners' *transitional competence* (see Corder 1967). Draw up a list of criteria by which one can distinguish errors from mistakes when analysing L2 learners' speech production. Try to explain the kind of inferences one can draw about L2 learners' transitional grammars, based on what specific errors can tell us. After having read Corder (1967) and/or Selinker (1972), compare your list of criteria defining developmental errors and your hypotheses about L2 grammars with what these authors write.
- Contrastive Analysis, as well as Error Analysis, assumes that transfer of grammatical knowledge from the first language is the single most important factor shaping L2 grammars. Test the plausibility of this assumption by contrasting German as an L1, as described in the discussion of the examples in (1), with an L2 of your choice (preferably not English). Focusing on word order phenomena, which word order patterns should we expect native speakers of German to use when learning the target language which you selected, if transfer is the most important factor determining L2 learners' acquisition of syntax? Which arguments would speak in support of or against a strong

transfer hypothesis if one abandoned the idea of transfer of 'habits' in favour of a notion of L2 acquisition as a sequence of mental grammars which are gradually restructured, i.e. as approximative systems? Keep your notes and re-examine them after having read chapter 4. How do your ideas compare to those discussed in chapter 4?

- It has been argued in this chapter that predictions about the nature and the course of L2 acquisition depend in significant ways on the particular grammatical analysis adopted by the researcher. Although this is inevitably the case, it is important to be aware of this fact when interpreting one's findings. Examine again the examples given in (1) and spell out in more detail the kind of grammatical operations ('rules') which learners have to acquire and apply if German were an SVO language as compared to German as an SOV language. Which of the two underlying orders requires more learning efforts, according to your analysis? Keep your notes on this question and re-examine them after having read chapter 4. How do your ideas compare to those discussed in chapter 4?

2 First language development: Universal Grammar as the centrepiece of the human language making capacity

2.1 Universal Grammar and the LAD

The gift for language which manifests itself in the effortless acquisition of language by toddlers can safely be qualified as a species-specific endowment of humans. In fact, it enables children to develop a full grammatical competence of the languages they are exposed to, independently of individual properties like intelligence, personality, strength of memory and so on, or of particularities of the learning environment, for example social settings, whether the child is an only child or has siblings, birth order among siblings, whether the child has one or more primary caregivers, communicative styles of parents or caregivers, and so forth. These specific characteristics of the individual and of the setting in which language acquisition happens may determine the extent of the linguistic skills that enable people to express themselves in more or less elaborate ways when using language. But, except for pathological cases, for example children who suffer from brain damage, one will never find native speakers who acquired incomplete grammatical knowledge of their language. For example, we do not find individuals unable to use passive constructions because their intelligence is below average, or individuals who do not comprehend embedded clauses because their parents did not use enough embedded clauses when speaking to them.

These observations should be uncontroversial. Yet as soon as one sets out to describe more specifically the nature of the language capacity common to all humans, it becomes immediately obvious that many of the issues arising in this discussion are the object of much controversy. For a study which aims to explore the similarities and differences between first and second language acquisition, this is a rather unfortunate situation. After all, probably the most promising way to proceed in this investigation is to establish L1 development as the point of reference and ask to what extent second language acquisition is like first language development and how it differs from it, since, given the uniform success of L1 acquisition under considerable variation in learning environments, there can hardly be any doubt that children come equipped with the LAD. The availability of the same kind of language making capacity in L2 acquisition is, however, very much an open question. If, on the one hand, the nature of the language faculty attributed to children developing a first language cannot be captured adequately, it will be all the more difficult to determine whether the principles and mechanisms guiding second language acquisition are essentially identical to those underlying L1 development. On the other hand, the magnitude and complexity of the issues at stake in this discussion should not come as a surprise, for we are trying to understand the human language making capacity and thus ultimately the language faculty. To the extent that we are successful in this enterprise, we may hope to contribute in important ways to a better understanding of the human mind – certainly no small feat. In fact, it is difficult to imagine a more significant task for research in the humanities than one which promises to shed light on those mental faculties which distinguish humans from other living beings.

Meaningful answers to big questions such as the one about the nature of the human mind can only be obtained if such large problems are broken down into smaller ones and if answers are put to the test by scrutinizing specific and falsifiable hypotheses which refer to particular issues and which can be interpreted within a well-articulated theoretical framework. For the present purpose, the necessary research guidelines can be developed by referring to a theory of language or, more specifically, a theory of grammar. This focus on grammatical development follows from the fact that, although the human language making capacity comprises much more than grammatical competence, it is the mental grammar which is specific to the human language 'instinct' (Pinker 1994) and which distinguishes it from communicative abilities of other species. Grammatical theory therefore plays an essential role in defining the objects of our study. Equally importantly, it imposes constraints on possible solutions, thus helping us to avoid ad hoc suggestions and contributing to coherency within descriptions of particular languages, across linguistic systems, and in comparison with other cognitive capacities with which mental grammars interact in language use.

In most areas of scientific research, the necessity of embedding a discussion like the one we are about to undertake into a particular theoretical framework would appear as self-evident. In some branches of the humanities, including the language sciences, this is, however, not always the case. It may therefore be useful to briefly comment on this point. The most basic and principled argument is provided by philosophy of science, which has demonstrated that the perspective on the object of research necessarily directs the focus of one's attention, determines which issues are perceived as central, marginal or irrelevant, and shapes the nature of the insights one can hope to gain. Importantly, this perspective is inevitably determined by the assumptions one makes and by the beliefs one holds when approaching the object of study. Formulated more plainly, one always works within a theoretical framework, either an explicit one or an implicit folk theory. In all likelihood, it is preferable to follow an explicit theoretical approach, for, although it will necessarily highlight certain aspects of the topic one is interested in and conceal others, this choice is at least made explicit and can therefore be called into question. If one attempts to work without the constraints of a specific theory, or if one decides to combine fragments of different theories in an eclectic fashion, as has frequently been the case in language acquisition research, theoretically motivated biases are also operative, but the fact that they are concealed almost inevitably leads to serious problems of interpretation. One such problem is that it is extremely difficult to question implicit assumptions, and one may end up being guided by them without being aware of their nature. Moreover and perhaps more importantly, in dealing with a complex problem area and in studying a large number of questions, one runs the risk of proposing mutually contradicting solutions without even noticing that the optimal solution for a specific problem rests on assumptions which are in conflict with those underlying the preferred solution for a different problem. Similarly, hypotheses developed for a given language must conform to assumptions which need to be made for other languages and, of course, they should not conflict with what is known about the nature of human language in general. In other words, it is precisely the constraints imposed by a coherent theoretical model which force us to be consistent in our analyses and which help us to avoid proposing ad hoc solutions. These considerations are all the more pertinent in the present case where we set out to compare results from diverse research traditions, monolingual and bilingual first language development, naturalistic second language acquisition, and foreign language teaching, which, in the past, typically did not cooperate closely but followed quite different research agendas.

The theoretical framework adopted here as the theory about the human language making capacity is that of Universal Grammar (UG), as it has been developed by Chomsky (1981a, 1986, 1995, 2000a, among others) and his colleagues. This choice is motivated by the fact that it is part of a paradigm which includes a variety of elaborate grammatical theories, for example Head-driven Phrase Structure Grammar (HPSG), Lexical Functional Grammar (LFG) or Simpler Syntax (Culicover and Jackendoff 2005), which, importantly, refer explicitly to language development in defining their research interests. Although these theories assume diverse models of the lexicon, of the relationship between syntax and semantics, and between syntax and sound systems, there exists a large body of research on first and second language acquisition carried out within these frameworks on which we can draw. This is, of course, not the place to present in any detail the complex network of ideas which constitutes the theory of generative grammar in its different versions, let alone the reasons which justify the choice of this particular approach to language. Adequate introductory texts are available to the more technical aspects of generative grammar. For recent versions of the paradigm, see, for example, Adger 2003 or Hornstein, Nunes and Grohmann 2005, or Smith 1999 for the philosophical underpinnings of this line of thought. In the present context, a few general statements must suffice.

A central aspect of the theory of UG is that it views the human language faculty as comprising a priori knowledge about the structure of language. Importantly, knowledge of language is understood as being internal to the human mind/brain, and the object of linguistic theory is therefore the mental grammar or competence of the individual which Chomsky (1986) refers to as I-language, an internal entity of the individual, as opposed to E-language, 'E' suggesting 'external', that is, the overt products in language use.

The genetically transmitted or innate implicit linguistic knowledge which UG attempts to capture is formulated in this theory in terms of abstract principles determining the set of possible human languages. They are universal in the sense that it is predicted that no grammar of a natural language, that is, no I-language, will violate these principles. Note that this allows for the possibility that principles may simply not be manifest in a given language. If, for example, UG contains principles explaining properties of prepositions, these will not be exhibited in languages without prepositions. They are nevertheless universal in the intended meaning of the term, namely wherever prepositions occur, they are constrained by the relevant UG principles. To sum up this point, UG is designed to capture all and only those properties which human languages have in common and thus to explain the nature of this species-specific faculty, but not every property present in a grammar must conform to principles of UG. In fact, many grammatical phenomena are *language-specific*, representing particularities of individual languages, and UG has nothing to say about them. Take, for example, the fact that French interrogative words *qui/que* 'who/what' can both refer to objects, but only *qui* can question subjects. Although this is undoubtedly a property of French grammar which needs to be represented in the mental grammars of speakers of this language, it is rather unlikely that it follows from a constraint imposed by UG. In other words, the grammar of a particular language is characterized by universal as well as language-specific features. Both reflect properties of the language faculty, but the latter must be acquired and will be contingent on properties of the learner and the learning environment. It is thus conceivable that a learner might not cognize that **que vient?* 'what is coming?' is ungrammatical.

However, the range of grammatical possibilities is not exhausted by invariant universal characteristics on the one hand and idiosyncratic ones on the other. Rather, grammatical theory must also offer explanations for cross-linguistic variation. The challenge for every grammatical theory is to relate universal and particular features of languages within one theoretical system, rather than limiting the scope of the theory to what can be assumed to be universal and dismissing variation as a marginal phenomenon resulting from accidental diachronic developments, hardly worth serious theorizing. After all, core properties of grammars, too, vary across languages. An example is the placement of verbs. As was illustrated by example (1) in the first chapter (1.2), most Germanic languages differ from almost all Romance languages in that they are verb-second (V2) languages, that is, subjects follow the finite verb if another element is placed sentence-initially. Some of these languages differ moreover in that non-finite verbs either follow or precede objects, that is, in the OV/VO option. What matters here is that these are central features of the respective grammars which are subject to more general regularities than the above-mentioned property of French interrogatives; at the same time, they seem to reflect systemic variation across languages. In order to account for this tension between what is universal and what is particular, the theory of UG offers the notion of parameter. The idea is that principles of UG do not always account exhaustively for the grammatical properties to which they refer; instead, these parameterized principles offer several options, that is, parameters are left unspecified by UG and must be set to one of the possible values in each individual grammar. It is important to note that the principles as well as the parameterized options are given by UG. This can be illustrated by the most frequently discussed example, the Null-Subject Parameter. A principle of UG states that a sentence necessarily contains a structural subject, a fact captured by the Extended Projection Principle (EPP). Languages differ, however, in whether they require that this structural position be lexically filled or not. This option, namely the possibility of grammatically licensing a lexically empty subject position, distinguishes null-subject from non-null-subject languages and can be thought of as the result of a syntactic parameterization. This is to say that in each grammar the parameter determining the null-subject versus non-null-subject characteristics of a language needs to be fixed to its corresponding value. In sum, the theory of grammar makes a distinction between non-parameterized and parameterized universal principles of UG.

Now we can finally return to our question concerning the role of UG in explaining the human language making capacity. Or, to put it plainly, we must ask how all this can possibly be relevant for language development. The basic idea is that since UG is conceived of as representing the initial state of the language faculty, it can also be understood as a crucial component of the LAD, the Language Acquisition Device. The claim that UG indeed represents the initial state of the child's linguistic development has, in fact, long been a fundamental assumption of generative theorizing and continues to be a defining property of UG in that Universal Grammar is understood as a theory about what the child brings to the task of language acquisition – or 'growth', as Chomsky prefers to say, comparing language development to the growth of organs – before any experience with the target language. To quote only one instance where he explains this idea, Chomsky (2000a: 4) suggests that we

> think of the initial state as a 'language acquisition device' that takes experience as 'input' and gives the language as an 'output' – an 'output' that is internally represented in the mind/brain.

This amounts to saying that UG determines the form of grammars at every point of development; developing grammars must consequently conform to the principles of UG. As plausible as this may be, this assumption is by no means a logical necessity to which one has to subscribe if one adopts UG as the theory about the human language faculty. In principle, it is not implausible to assume that only the initial and the ultimately attained steady state of a grammar are constrained by UG. Under such a view, the developmental paths leading from the initial to the final state are not necessarily determined by UG. Instead, other mental faculties, in addition to the domain-specific linguistic module, would be attributed important roles in shaping the course of acquisition. Postulating UG as the centrepiece of the LAD is, however, a stronger and therefore more interesting hypothesis. It certainly represents the null hypothesis in that it assumes that the acquisition of grammar can be explained in grammatical terms alone, without having to refer to additional cognitive devices. Perhaps most importantly, under the perspective suggested by Chomsky, this is equivalent to claiming that the theory of UG attains explanatory adequacy. According to Chomsky (2000a: 7), a theory of human language satisfies the condition of descriptive adequacy if it accounts for the properties of the language which a speaker knows; but it satisfies the condition of explanatory adequacy only if it demonstrates 'how each particular language can be derived from a uniform initial state under the "boundary conditions" set by experience'. To be explicit on this point, adopting this view implies the assumption that grammatical development is a continuous process in so far as child grammars, during every phase from the point onwards when UG becomes accessible, contain only structures and operations which do not violate principles of UG. At the same time, this also implies that children in developing the knowledge of their target languages may well explore all the options offered by UG. Their mental grammars may thus differ from the mature target grammar in ways permitted by UG. Finally, just as universal principles need not be instantiated in all natural languages, developing grammars may temporarily not exhibit the full set of principles shaping the respective adult grammars, for if they lack the lexical or structural material to which a given principle applies, we should not expect their grammars to conform to this principle.

In sum, I will adopt the idea according to which UG as the theory of the human language faculty not only defines the initial state of first language development, but also determines essential properties of developing grammars at every moment of the acquisition process. In this sense, UG is a crucial part of the Language Acquisition Device. In fact, as becomes obvious from the above quote from Chomsky, UG is frequently equated with the LAD. In my view, this is too strong a reduction, limiting language acquisition studies to the analysis of only those phenomena which can be accounted for in terms of UG principles; see Carroll (2001: 113) for a similar and more detailed criticism of this view. In my opinion, if the LAD is supposed to be a theory about what enables the child to develop a grammatical competence, it must account for much more than universal properties of language, even if one only considers grammatical competence, that is, defining I-language as the object of our investigation. At the very least, the LAD must comprise the principles and mechanisms guiding children towards the relevant cues which enable them to discover formal properties of languages, as described in the following section, 2.2. In addition to these discovery principles, bootstrapping children into formal grammatical systems, the LAD must also provide them with the kind of learning mechanisms which allow them to acquire those structural features of their target grammars which are not within the realm of UG. Note that these principles and mechanisms, independently of whether they address universal or particular properties of languages, have in common that they are domain-specific in nature, that is, they refer to abstract formal properties of grammars. This justifies the assumption that they are all part of the LAD – with UG as the centrepiece.

These remarks must suffice as an explanation of the claim that, from a developmental perspective, Universal Grammar can be regarded as the crucial component of the human Language Acquisition Device. As such, it defines the initial state of grammatical development in first language acquisition, and it shapes mature as well as developing grammars. In order to be able to address the question of whether UG may be expected to also serve these functions in L2 acquisition, a number of fine points and technical details implied by this assumption need to be made explicit and be explicated. I will try to accomplish this in the remaining sections of this chapter. At this point, I only want to draw attention to one issue which has not been addressed here so far, namely what Felix (1984) called the *developmental problem*. What this alludes to is the observation that even if we may assume that UG indeed determines essential properties of the various states of grammars in L1 acquisition, this does not provide an answer to the question of how the transition from one state to another can be accounted for. Yet without a solution to this problem, one cannot claim to have offered an explanation of language acquisition, not even of how I-language develops. As for L2 acquisition, Gregg (1996: 50) argues quite convincingly, I believe, that one needs a 'transition theory' dealing with the problem of why a system changes from one state to another, as well as a 'property theory', that is, a theory of mental grammars concerned with the kind of knowledge instantiated in a system. The same applies to L1 acquisition and other types of language development, and UG only seems to provide the necessary property theory. Whether a transition theory needs to be part of the LAD is of course an entirely different issue. But a theory of language acquisition which has nothing to say about the developmental problem clearly misses its point and cannot really count as such; I will return to this issue in sections 2.3 and 2.4. And although by focusing on I-language we put property and transition theories at the centre of attention, Carroll (2001: 37) is certainly right when she argues that we also need a processing and a learning theory in order to explain language acquisition; see 6.3, below.

Before concluding this section, I would like to add a few observations on the relationship between studies on mature as opposed to developing grammars. A large part of the literature on language acquisition focuses exclusively on problems related to what has been called property theory – a quite unsatisfactory state of affairs. After all, the goal of this entire enterprise is to shed some light on the problem of how to explain grammatical development, and although it has been argued that a coherent treatment of acquisition problems is only possible if it is couched within a theory of grammar, an adequate theory of language acquisition does not fall out automatically, not even if the optimal grammatical theory was available. A number of consequences follow from this observation, and I want to mention at least two of them. First of all, since child language and learners' interlanguage are the objects of research in first and second language acquisition, it follows that a much larger territory must be covered than what is covered by UG, as has already been suggested above. Secondly, acquisition research must determine its own research agenda and should not limit its epistemological ambitions to being the testing ground for hypotheses generated by grammatical theory.

As for this latter point, the principal consideration is that the relationship between the two types of research should be reciprocal, if research on linguistic development is to be understood as part of theoretical linguistics. This is to say that even when dealing with issues which fall within the realm of grammatical theory and specifically within UG theory, analyses of developing grammars are likely to encounter problems and raise questions which have previously not been addressed by work on mature grammars or for which current theorizing has no satisfactory solutions to offer. These should then be put on the agenda of linguistic theory. On the other hand, findings from acquisition research can contribute to the advancement of grammatical theory by demonstrating, in cases of competing hypotheses about structural properties of mature grammars, that one of them can account in a more satisfactory fashion than others for developmental facts. In this case, one can argue that the solution which is more successful in explaining grammatical development should also be preferred for the adult grammar. But this does not mean that the ultimate goal of acquisition research is to corroborate or falsify hypotheses developed by linguistic (or psychological) theories. Its focus should rather be child language and its development, or interlanguage and approximative systems, respectively. In cases where this leads to the identification of phenomena about which current theorizing has little or nothing to say, they should nevertheless be the object of careful analyses and not be ignored. This is to say that guidance by a sophisticated theory need not lead to total dependence on theoretical debates. Consequently, the issues at stake are not artefacts of the respective theory. Rather, they are problems defined by theoretically informed observations and have to be dealt with by any adequate theory of language development.

This brings me to a last point: the commitment to one specific version of the theory of Universal Grammar. Grammatical theorizing within the generative framework is a dynamic process. As a result, there exist not only competing models (e.g. Principles and Parameters Theory, Lexical Functional Grammar, Head-driven Phrase Structure Grammar, or Simpler Syntax), but also different versions of each of them. Such dynamic developments in theorizing, however, confront researchers engaged in large-scale empirical studies with specific problems. It is, for example, not uncommon in language acquisition research that longitudinal studies require a data collection period of several months or even years. Preliminary treatment of the data and subsequent analysis will take even longer. The design of the empirical work as well as the choice of the appropriate tools for the analysis and the interpretation of the data gathered are necessarily determined by specific research interests, which, in turn, depend on theoretical considerations. Yet it is almost inevitable that significant theoretical changes will happen during the period necessary to complete such a project. Consequently, it is not always possible to adopt the most recent theoretical proposal in these analyses. Quite obviously, a textbook like the present one, dealing with broader issues and attempting to summarize the state-of-the-art for at least some of the topics dealt with, is subject to similar constraints. Moreover, although it is desirable to adopt a position compatible with current theorizing, previously developed theoretical concepts should only be abandoned if the more recent model offers sufficiently elaborated alternatives by which they can be substituted. This is, admittedly, a conservative approach, but I have come to the conclusion that it is the most viable procedure for the present purpose. It offers the double advantage of avoiding non-committing eclecticism on the one hand, and it protects us from the temptation to adopt a new hypothesis merely because it is the most recent one, on the other. More specifically, this means that although the discussion in this volume is inspired by the Minimalist Program (MP), it will draw heavily on the theory of Principles and Parameters. This solution is not only a compromise suggested by the more practical considerations just mentioned, it represents a theoretically justifiable position in view of the fact that Minimalism is not a theory but a research program (as Chomsky has stated repeatedly). Moreover, PPT is 'embedded in the Minimalist Program of the 1990s' (Smith 2000: xi).

2.2 Milestones of first language development

The goal of this volume is to reveal some of the essential similarities and differences between first and second language acquisition. I refer primarily to the nature of the knowledge which constitutes the grammatical competence of speakers of a language and to the principles and mechanisms which determine the course of their linguistic development. We cannot limit our attention to the surface forms and constructions encountered in language use, although they represent the directly observable primary linguistic data (PLD) from which we construe knowledge acquired by learners and also acquisition processes. However, specific surface phenomena do not unambiguously reflect the underlying grammatical mechanisms; rather, surface forms can be described and explained by several different grammatical analyses. Taking this into consideration, we inevitably need to go beyond the observable facts in our attempt to understand the nature of the knowledge which enables learners to use the attested constructions.

If, then, we are on the right track in assuming that first language development is guided in important ways by the LAD and that UG is the centrepiece of LAD, shaping the form of developing grammars at each moment in the acquisition process, the possible role of UG in second language acquisition must necessarily be a central issue to be dealt with here too. Moreover, since I have argued that the LAD cannot be equated with UG but minimally also comprises domain-specific linguistic discovery principles, we will also have to explore the role which these principles and mechanisms might play in the two types of acquisition investigated. In order to be able to do so, we need to know more about the ways in which UG influences L1 development. For obvious reasons, this topic cannot be addressed in much detail in just one chapter; I therefore have to refer for a more thorough treatment to textbooks introducing L1 acquisition research within a generative framework, for example Guasti (2002) or, more recently, Roeper (2007) or Snyder

(2007). For the present purpose, it is particularly important to ask which kind of empirical evidence might possibly reveal the influence of UG and domain-specific linguistic discovery principles in L1, for it should provide us with the necessary criteria to assess their respective roles in L2 acquisition.

The perhaps most promising research strategy in this case is to focus on invariant properties of child language. The rationale for proceeding this way is that it seems plausible to surmise that invariant aspects of child language are likely to reflect universal properties which can be accounted for in terms of biological foundations of language and cognitive mechanisms available to all learners. Following this research agenda and looking for invariant properties characterizing the course of L1 acquisition, one finds that most studies on child language agree on the following three characteristics of L1 development: (1) *Ultimate success*; that is, except for pathological cases, L1 acquisition is always successful in that all individuals develop full knowledge (I-language) of the target system, as already stated at the beginning of this chapter. (2) *Rate of acquisition*; L1 development happens relatively fast; for example, an impressively large part of the syntactic knowledge is acquired within one or two years, especially during the third year of life. (3) *Uniformity* of the course of acquisition, not only across individuals acquiring the same language, but also across languages.

Without going into more detail at this point, one can at least say that all three of these properties attributed to L1 development seem to suggest the existence of some kind of guiding force underlying the observable course of events, resulting in its fast rate, uniformity and ultimate success. Viewed from the theoretical perspective adopted here, the LAD and particularly UG and universal discovery principles are undoubtedly good candidates when looking for cognitive capacities likely to enable children to achieve this kind of success. Ultimately, we will have to decide whether these three characteristics of L1 can also be attributed to L2 acquisition, in order to see whether they point more towards fundamental similarities or towards differences between the various types of language acquisition. These are indeed issues with which we will be concerned throughout this volume, although to different degrees. Rate of acquisition is, in my view, not particularly important when contrasting first and second language acquisition. In fact, its role is not easy to assess in such a comparison, for rate needs to be correlated with the type and amount of exposure to the target language. Quite obviously, it would be misleading to simply count months or years needed before a learner produces a construction without error; instead, one needs to take into account quantity and probably also quality of interactions and of learner-directed speech. But independently of such additional complications, rate cannot really be regarded as a decisive argument in discussing the possibility of fundamental commonalities across various acquisition types, for, if it could indeed be shown that L2 learners acquire the same kind of knowledge as L1 children and perhaps even that they proceed through the same developmental sequences, a slower rate of acquisition would hardly justify the postulation of qualitative differences. Ultimate attainment, on the other hand, is a crucial or, as many may say, *the* crucial criterion to be considered in this debate, for if it can be argued that L2 learners are not able, for principled reasons, to acquire full competence in the target language, this will undoubtedly constitute a strong argument against the hypothesis that the two acquisition types are identical in relevant aspects. Whether this is indeed the case, is, however, more difficult to assess than might appear at first sight; in fact it may be impossible to decide on this issue on the basis of behavioural data. I will return to this topic in chapter 6; see especially section 6.4.

In what follows, the focus will be on the last mentioned of the three properties of L1 development: the uniformity of the course of acquisition and its possible explanation in terms of mechanisms and principles made available by the LAD. Uniformity, as I use the term, refers primarily to the fact that children follow the same (and indeed rather narrow) path towards the target native competence in the language of their social environment. This path is marked by gradually emerging linguistic abilities concerning perception, comprehension and production of linguistic expressions. The course of first language development is thus laid out as a sequence of linguistic milestones. At least this is all that matters for the purpose of identifying empirically testable criteria defining interindividually invariant properties of L1 development. Note, however, that UG is not necessarily the sole explanation for the set of milestones, either for their contents or for their particular ordering. The discovery principles alluded to above are likely to be relevant as well. In fact, the sequence of events comprising the milestones need not even be determined entirely by domain-specific principles.

Importantly, with respect to the notion of developmental sequence, it is strictly ordered in the sense that the order in which these milestones are attained by children is not reversible. In fact, this is precisely what uniformity means, namely that L1 development proceeds universally through an ordered sequence, not only in children acquiring the same language, but even cross-linguistically. The claim thus is that L1 acquisition follows a universal order, provided the features characterizing the sequence are defined in a sufficiently abstract fashion. Interestingly enough, children behave uniformly in yet another way: they exhibit striking resemblances in their linguistic behaviour, even in producing the same kinds of errors. Thus they reveal a uniformity of knowledge independently of the linguistic input they receive. They also behave uniformly in what they do *not* do; they do not make errors which, logically, they might have made. To give just one example, L1 learners typically overextend the use of regular morphology to irregular items, for example French *batté* instead of *battu* 'beaten'. Yet they do not systematically attach grammatical morphemes inappropriately across syntactic categories. Person agreement markers, for example, are not attached to nouns, not even in cases where other languages exhibit similar processes in the formation of verbs, for example German *die Blume* does not yield **es blumt*, although in English we find 'the flower – it flowers'. It is in this sense that the claim should be understood that learners follow a narrow path towards L1 knowledge, that is, they make the same kinds of errors and they avoid other types. The notion of uniformity intended here thus refers to a specific quality of the developmental process, namely the invariant order in which certain linguistic phenomena emerge. In other respects, language development exhibits considerable variation across children, even among those acquiring the same language. Children differ, for example, in how much time they need in order to advance from one milestone to the next and also in the overall length of time they take to proceed through the entire sequence of acquisition events. I interpret such variation as instances of quantitative variation within a qualitatively invariant pattern. Needless to say that the kind of uniformity under discussion here characterizes only the emergence of a selection of grammatical phenomena in the course of L1 development. Keep in mind that our research strategy requires that we examine those grammatical phenomena that are invariant, for only these phenomena might be constrained by the human language faculty or more specifically by Universal Grammar.

Let us, then, briefly look at some of the universally invariant characteristics of the course of first language development and try to identify features which qualify as milestones along the path to adult L1 knowledge. Again, I provide only a rough sketch, one that is not intended to replace a more thorough treatment of the issues as might be offered in textbook introductions to language acquisition. It should nevertheless be possible to draw a sufficiently detailed picture in order to formulate research questions for the intended comparison with second language acquisition. For this purpose, developments subsequent to the emergence of multi-word utterances are of prime importance. Invariant developmental patterns are attested much earlier, and they certainly strengthen the argument for an innate human language faculty since they speak in favour of a domain-specific linguistic capacity. But it does not follow that early invariant patterns already attest to the availability of some premature grammatical knowledge or, more specifically, to the early accessibility of UG. It is, indeed, rather difficult to determine reliably the moment when children's communicative behaviour is guided by grammatical knowledge. Contextual support, pragmatic information and so on contribute in important ways to ensure communicative success, and it is not implausible to suppose that children initially rely entirely on such means. Still, L1 research over the past twenty years has been extraordinarily successful in finding evidence for children's use of grammatical knowledge during much younger age periods than previously suspected. Judging from recent work of this type, using a variety of new computer-aided technologies and sophisticated experimental designs, it is very likely that investigations focusing on language comprehension will be able to further advance the development point at which grammatical knowledge emerges.

The onset of language acquisition can indeed be argued to be prenatal. Intra-uterine recordings have shown that speech sounds are perceived distinctly, and although not much is known about what kind of use is made of this potential input, it has been demonstrated that infants, only a few days old, recognize the voices of their mothers (Jusczyk *et al.* 1993). Therefore, it can be argued that enough phonetic detail is represented in the speech signal to distinguish their mother's speech from the speech of other female voices. Thus representation of non-linguistic aspects of the speech signal begins as soon as is developmentally possible. Moreover, such infants already distinguish between linguistic and non-linguistic sounds, and the former are processed in designated areas of the brain. Infants are also able, within the first days and weeks, to discriminate the language of their environment from foreign languages and, even more surprisingly, they can distinguish between (some) foreign languages (see Guasti 2002: chapter 2 for a summary of the research on these issues). Explaining the data, once again, requires supposing that infants are representing at least some aspects of the speech signal, possibly before birth. The least one can say, thus, is that newborns are neurologically and cognitively predisposed to language processing and that prenatal exposure to language is likely to have some learning effect. This is confirmed by research results on the perception and production of speech sounds during the first year of life, demonstrating a very early sensibility to acoustic features of human languages that will form the basic building blocks of sound systems (tone, intonation, consonants, vowels, etc.), increasingly focusing on properties of the languages to which the children are exposed. During their first months of life, infants perceive sound contrasts which have a phonological value in human languages, although not necessarily in the one the child is about to acquire. Moreover, they perceive certain contrasts as categorical distinctions, that is, continuous incremental changes in certain acoustic properties of sounds are not perceived continuously, such as the relative onset of vocal fold vibration (voicing) to oral cavity occlusion (so-called Voice Onset Time). Rather, at some point, an incremental change is perceived as a different 'sound' – e.g. [b] versus [p]. As early as at one month of age, infants perceive consonantal contrasts as in [ba] versus [pa] or [ra] versus [la], irrespective of whether these are part of the phonological system of their native languages. Although it has been argued that categorical perception is neither a domain-specific ability nor one that is specific to humans (Guasti 2002: 72), it clearly enables children to get into the linguistic systems of their native languages. This begins to happen during the second half of the first year, when infants attend increasingly to those properties which are essential for their native language systems. In other words, although this may at first appear as paradoxical, progress towards the target language implies that children become less successful in perceiving contrasts which have no functional values in their target languages. But what might be regarded as a loss really seems to be a necessary prerequisite for the development of the adult language system, and at the age of approximately ten months, children begin to comprehend words, that is, they are able to systematically relate sound sequences with meanings.

Similar milestones are observed in infants' early productions. During their first four months they produce a range of vowel-like sounds (approximately 80% of their productions) and a limited set of consonant-like ones, with the vowels changing rapidly. After approximately six months, 'babbling' begins, that is, children use what look like units with 'syllable structures', which, however, do not yet express meaning. Consonant–vowel combinations (CV) are preferred, reduplications are frequent, and one can detect sentence intonation patterns in these early productions. Moreover, one finds that, much like what has been observed with respect to their earliest perceptive capacities, the range of sounds which infants produce is initially not limited to the inventory characterizing the respective target languages, that is, to parental input. Progressively, however, the set of phonetic entities in their productions is reduced to what is encountered in their linguistic environment. This development begins probably already before the age of six months, but certainly soon afterwards, and at around twelve months they typically produce their first words.

These and similar findings about the perception and production of speech during the first year can be interpreted as indicating that infants bring to the task of language acquisition the capacity to detect and represent a specific set of features encountered in the speech stream which they ultimately will organize, during the second half of the first year, into *formal* properties of the languages they are exposed to. The acquisition events of the first year constitute a very significant feat, one which must indeed be regarded as a necessary prerequisite for language acquisition. Consequently, the discovery principles which underlie these events must be seen as forming part of the human language making capacity and thus of the LAD, even if at least some of the perceptual procedures involved may neither be unique to humans nor specifically designed for language processing. The fact that this early acquisition is rooted in perceptual abilities that are neither specific to language nor to humans does, however, speak against the possible claim that UG guides language acquisition during this early period. In accordance with what has been said in 2.1 above, UG should be understood as the centrepiece of the LAD which, nonetheless, embraces more than that. UG is said to constrain child grammars at every point of grammatical development, but infants, during the age period discussed so far, cannot, in fact, be credited with linguistic knowledge of the relevant sort; that is, they have not yet developed mental representations of the type available to adults, and certainly not of grammatical knowledge. It is important not to confound the fact that infants are sensitive to properties (phonetic, prosodic, etc.) of grammatical units (words, clauses, phrases) with the assumption that they have developed mental representations of such grammatical entities.

The question then is what kind of linguistic knowledge can be attributed to children at age 1;0. We have seen that they understand and use at least some words at this age. This presupposes that they have been successful in segmenting the chain of acoustic events in perceived speech and in isolating word forms, possibly already at the age of eight months. It should be stressed that this is a very significant achievement since words are typically not marked by pauses in continuous speech. In a further step, they have furthermore succeeded in establishing stable sound–meaning relations, thus systematically connecting specific word forms with at least certain concepts. Quite obviously, this, too, represents an important development by which the linguistic sign (Saussure 1916/1975) becomes available to these children. The early lexicon grows slowly during the first half of the second year, as new words are added to it in a piecemeal fashion. At around age 1;9, however, one can typically observe a spurt in the increase of the productive vocabulary from approximately fifty to over a hundred words within a short period of time; the receptive lexicon already contains significantly more items. For several months, the children remain in the holophrastic phase, that is, they use one-word utterances which, however, do not simply refer to individual objects but can normally denote complex events and actions; they thus serve similar functions as propositions in adult language.

Do these observations indicate, then, that children rely on grammatical knowledge and ultimately on UG, in their verbal productions during the first half of their second year of life? Any attempt to answer this question has to take into account the fact that these early words do not yet have the properties which items of the adult lexicon possess. The pronunciation of these words is still quite variable, and their meanings are certainly not yet equivalent to the semantic representations associated with the corresponding adult words, as should be obvious from what has been said about the holophrastic phase. In fact, it has been argued that words used during the one-word stage and even the ones attested in the earliest longer but presumably rote-learned phrases are 'prephonological' (Locke 1995: 299) in nature. In other words, the children have not yet developed a phonological system when they produce these utterances; rather, the existence of a first inventory of sound–meaning pairings is a precondition for the activation of grammatical knowledge, including the phonological component. The answer to our question therefore is, in concordance with the claims made above, that even during the holophrastic phase children's comprehension and production of language is not yet guided by grammatical principles, and their early words are still not lexical elements of the same type as the corresponding ones in the language of adults. To mention only one consequence following from this assumption, it is very likely that words and concatenations of words used during this period are not grammatical entities, in the proper technical sense of the term. Although it is true that first words are modelled on nouns of the adult language and that for some time there continues to be a dominance of words which correspond to nouns in adult language, it is highly implausible to attribute to these elements the status of syntactic categories. Not only do they lack phonological and semantic properties of their adult counterparts, they exhibit neither the distributional nor the morphological characteristics of nouns and verbs.

Recall that in assessing the nature of the linguistic knowledge of children during these early developmental phases, it is crucial not to confound the infants' sensitivity to physical cues to properties of grammatical units with the presence of mental representations of such entities. This reservation is particularly pertinent in considering the fact that this capacity is not restricted to the identification of words but applies to larger syntactic units as well, for example phrases and clauses. Segmentation becomes possible by attending to acoustic cues, and infants have indeed been shown to be particularly sensitive to prosodic properties of speech, already during their first days after birth. Perceptive sensitivity to prosodic entities correlating with syntactic units has indeed been claimed to be attested as early as at the age of approximately seven months. Soon after, infants seem to react differently to open and closed class elements, they show sensitivity to prosodically characterized clauses, and at about nine months to information coincidental with phrasal units. All this seems to indicate that infants are sensitive to the kind of information which will eventually enable them to identify syntactic units. Documenting this sensitivity is not sufficient, however, to show they have developed mental representations of clauses, phrases, functional versus referential elements, specific syntactic categories. It also does not show, obviously, that infants process the cues as *cues to* the relevant grammatical distinctions. This observation, as a matter of both logic and methodological rigour, urges conservatism on us in dealing with behavioural data drawn from habituation paradigms.

Summarizing what has been said so far and simplifying matters somewhat, one can say that infants during their first year show ample evidence of a predisposition to process language and of a sensitivity to formal properties of human languages, and they even begin to represent specific acoustic properties of their linguistic environment. They interact and communicate, of course, with people around them, and they are well on their way towards a linguistic capacity involving grammatical representations and operations. But their early verbal comprehension and production does not yet provide evidence for grammatical competence. Rather, the developmental milestones reported on are a reflection of the maturation of the brain and the cognitive capacities of these infants eventually leading to such a competence. As Locke (1995: 287) reminds us, the brain needs to develop after birth because of what is considered to be the 'premature birth' of humans; in fact, 'the human newborn's brain is only about 26 percent of what it will weigh in maturity'. One should therefore expect that it is during the period when the brain rapidly organizes that certain faculties, including species-specific ones like grammatical organization of language, become successively accessible to children. During the first half of the second year, access to grammatical knowledge does not yet seem to be possible although communicative means have improved significantly due to the fact that early words are available. It is only during the second half of the second year that children begin to make use of grammatical knowledge, in comprehension as well as in production, either because it is only then that neurological development makes it available to the child or because the necessary material on which UG principles operate had previously not been present. In the present context, it is neither necessary nor possible to discuss these two alternatives in more detail. It seems to me, however, that the latter option is less plausible, for it predicts, for example, more individual variation depending on lexical acquisition than is actually found in grammatical development.

Once we address our central issue of whether the same type of grammatical competence determines linguistic development in both acquisition types, contrasting first and second language acquisition, it will be the developmental phase ranging from approximately age 1;8 to 2;6 which we need to focus on. It is characterized by important and frequently rapid changes in children's language use. Previous developmental milestones, like the ones briefly summarized in this section, can be understood as resulting primarily from neural and cognitive maturation. The latter, however, does not lend itself to a comparison with mature language learners. Rather, as is pointed out by Locke (1995: 295), 'it is during this interval that the utterances of human children diverge from those of nonhuman primates trained in sign language (Bickerton 1990a)'; see also Bickerton (1990b). Only subsequently can developmental milestones be defined in grammatical terms, arguably an indication that UG has kicked in.

In terms of surface properties of the children's language, the first significant development consists in the emergence of multi-word utterances, soon after age 1;6. Initially, they may still represent sequences of holophrastic utterances, but productive combinations of lexical items within single utterances soon occur more frequently, and the claim that these are indeed multi-word utterances is corroborated by their prosodic properties. When verbs begin to be used more frequently, closed class items also begin to emerge in children's language. The distinction between 'closed classes' containing a limited number of elements, for example articles, copulas, auxiliaries, and 'open classes' comprising a large and in principle unlimited number of items, for example adjectives, nouns, verbs, is of crucial importance. Most grammatical theories make this distinction, although the terminology used to refer to the two types of elements varies considerably. Traditional grammars sometimes differentiate between 'empty words' and 'content words', and in the theoretical framework adopted here one commonly distinguishes between functional (non-referential) elements and lexical or referential elements (see also section 2.3, below). The particular importance of this distinction for language acquisition follows from the fact that during the first months during which multi-word utterances are used, the 'small words' tend to be omitted, and lexical elements are mostly used in only one invariant form, that is, they either lack inflectional markers or they are invariably used as rote-learned forms. This kind of usage has sometimes been called 'telegraphese' because, similarly to the language used for telegrams, costly 'empty' words are omitted. Interestingly, functional elements are responsible for just those properties of the adult language that are missing in early multi-word utterances of children, namely grammatical morphology or certain combinatory regularities allowing for word order flexibility. In other words, one initially finds simple utterances which appear to represent early sentence structures; they differ, however, from mature sentences in that inflectional morphology is not used productively or is lacking altogether, in that the order of elements exhibits little variability, or in that obligatory parts of the sentence are frequently omitted, for example subjects in languages where the mature grammar does not allow for lexically empty subjects.

Soon afterwards, beginning at around age 2;0 (±3 months), these phenomena emerge in children's speech, and many of them come in surprisingly fast and in an invariant order, across individual learners of the same language as well as cross-linguistically. The position of the verb with respect to its complements (OV/VO), already mentioned in 1.2, seems to be one of the earliest properties in which developing and mature languages converge, usually emerging before age 2;0. The first overt example of verb morphology, arguably the earliest productive use of grammatical morphology altogether, emerges when subject–verb agreement appears in those languages which require verb–argument agreement. In fact, subject–verb agreement develops before object agreement if both are instantiated in the target language, and subject clitics are attested before object clitics. Another very early phenomenon to appear is the placement of finite verbs in cases where they are separated from non-finite verbal elements, for example in French negative constructions where the finite element precedes and the non-finite one follows the negative expression (*pas*), or in most Germanic languages where the finite verb must occupy the second structural position (V2 phenomenon) of the sentence. During this phase, one can further observe the emergence of auxiliaries, modals and copulas, as well as first occurrences of articles and of nominal inflection, although determiners continue to be omitted in obligatory contexts for some time. Verbs now also carry markings encoding aspectual and temporal distinctions. In what may be regarded as the next developmental phase, during the second half of the second year, new achievements comprise, among other things, the acquisition of further tense distinctions, as well as case, gender and number markings. This is also when object clitics finally begin to be used and, importantly, subordinate clauses, introduced, where appropriate, by subordinating complementizers. Interrogation, which up to then used to be restricted to intonation questions, is now expressed by a number of different constructions, including subject–verb inversion and sentence-initial placement of question words.

In sum, leaving details aside, one can say that by the end of the third year children are able to use a substantial part of the inventory of grammatical devices offered by the target languages, and they reach this state by proceeding along a largely invariant developmental path. In the following chapters, notably in chapters 3 and 4, the developmental sequences of some grammatical phenomena will be discussed in more detail, contrasting them to invariant acquisition sequences in second language acquisition. The rationale for this more in-depth discussion of developmental sequences is that uniformity of linguistic development is an important, perhaps even the most crucial property characterizing first language development. It can therefore serve as a crucial criterion in assessing possible similarities and differences between L1 and L2 acquisition. Importantly, it enables us to formulate empirically testable hypotheses in this endeavour. In the following chapter 3, for example, I will demonstrate that one indeed finds developmental sequences in L2 acquisition, but these are not identical to the ones characterizing L1 development. In the two subsequent chapters, I will then try to answer the question of whether this finding provides evidence in support of the claim that there exist fundamental differences between the two types of acquisition.

Let me now finally return to the question raised above as to whether linguistic behaviour of children can be attributed to grammatical knowledge. In the preceding paragraphs, I have tried to argue that with regard to the first year of life, the answer to this question is a negative one. Children's impressive achievements during this period can be interpreted as providing them with the necessary tools required in order to 'get into' a grammatical system. As for the subsequent periods of holophrastic and early multi-word utterances, the question must still be answered negatively, although this decision is more difficult to make because the children seem to comprehend words and simple sentences, and they also produce what superficially look like adult words and basic sentence types. But although the summary of the discussion in the literature has had to be very brief, the conclusion based on neurological as well as linguistic evidence is fairly straightforward: namely that even in comprehension, in spite of the sophisticated use they can make of prosodic and other information, children do not show any evidence of having developed mental representations of syntactic categories, phrases and clauses. The crucial observation here is that their abilities, up to this point of development, can be argued to be due to computing linear properties of language, for example prosodic cues related to linear segmentation, early multi-word utterances as linear concatenations of elements, and so forth.

This is a particularly important point which needs to be taken into account when attempting to infer the underlying principles and mechanisms from surface properties of the language of learners. The linear order of elements undoubtedly constitutes part of the logic determining formal properties of utterances. In other words, precedence, succession, adjacency, initialization, finalization, and so on, are essential notions capturing ordering principles of language. But it is generally acknowledged that the constitutive property of human language, the one which distinguishes it from all other natural systems of communication, is that linguistic expressions exhibit an abstract hierarchical structure. In particular, it is critical that certain elements contain others. Moreover, grammatical principles exhibit sensitivity to structural principles in non-local contexts. An early example is the 'A-over-A' constraint which forbids the movement of a noun phrase contained within a larger noun phrase (see, for example, Chomsky 1965 or Ross 1967). It is this *structure dependency* of language which linguists try to capture by representing sentence structures as tree diagrams, thus defining hierarchical relationships between the components of sentences, in addition to the linear ones. On the assumption that such trees capture linguistic competence, it follows that language learners, too, need to go beyond the linear order exhibited by linguistic expressions and must detect the underlying structural or *hierarchical* relations which determine formal characteristics of sentences and ultimately, thus, the shape of utterances encountered in their linguistic environment.

Let me illustrate this point by means of some German examples quoted from Haider (1991: 22).

(1) (i) Er kommt.
He comes
'He is coming.'
(ii) Kommt er?
Comes he?
'Is he coming?'

Observing facts like those illustrated by the examples in (1), the child could plausibly infer that interrogatives are formed by reversing the order of elements in a sentence. Even certain more complex utterances would seemingly support such a hypothesis; see (2).

(2) (i) Marias Kommentare dazu folgten.
'Mary's comments on this followed.'
(ii) Folgten dazu Kommentare Marias?
Followed on this comments Mary's?
'Did Mary's comments on this follow?'

Although this is a cognitively simple principle and therefore arguably plausible, no natural language makes use of it as a grammatical operation. In other words, it is not only inadequate as a description of the relevant facts found in German interrogatives, but operations of this type are not instantiated in any human grammar. In fact, people encounter considerable difficulties when asked to repeat sequences of words in reversed order, if these are not presented in writing. This demonstrates that cognitively simple principles do not *eo ipso* constrain linguistic cognition.

An alternative hypothesis, apparently supported by these examples, is that interrogatives require clause-initial placement of an element which does not appear in this position in declaratives, probably the verb. But as is illustrated by examples like the ones in (3), linear order is again not a sufficient criterion for the definition of what has to be moved and of where it needs to be moved to. Note that even the apparently innocent term 'verb' refers to a structurally defined notion, and yet this is still not sufficient to identify the item which must be displaced. If two verbal elements are present in the sentence, interrogative formation requires only one to appear in initial position. Moreover, what may appear to be surprising from a communicative perspective, it is not the 'content' word (main verb) which is concerned here but the semantically 'empty' finite auxiliary, that is, the one which carries tense and person agreement markings; see (3) (ii) and (iii). In fact, the other verbal element can also be fronted, as in (3) (iv), but this does not yield an interrogative construction, and it triggers further word order changes involving the auxiliary which ends up in second position. But 'second' position is not a linear notion (arrived at by counting word forms in the string) either, as is shown by (3) (v) where the 'first' position is in fact occupied by two elements; rather, it refers to the second position in the sentence structure. In sum, when language learning children encounter facts in the primary linguistic data like the ones illustrated by these simple examples, they can only arrive at the appropriate generalizations if they 'know' that operations leading to word order rearrangements do not apply to chains of elements obtained merely by linear segmentation but to syntactic categories which, in turn, may have to be grouped into syntactic constituents. In other words, they must be dealing with entities which themselves exhibit an internal hierarchical structure, and the positions into which they are moved must be defined in hierarchical terms as well, rather than simply in linear ones.

(3) (i) Er hat sie im Park gefunden.
He has her in+the park found
'He has found her in the park.'

(ii) *Gefunden er hat sie im Park.
(iii) Hat er sie im Park gefunden?
(iv) Gefunden hat er sie im Park.
(v) Im Park hat er sie gefunden.

Leaving numerous details aside, a simplified structure for a sentence like (3) (v) might look like the one given in (4).

(4)

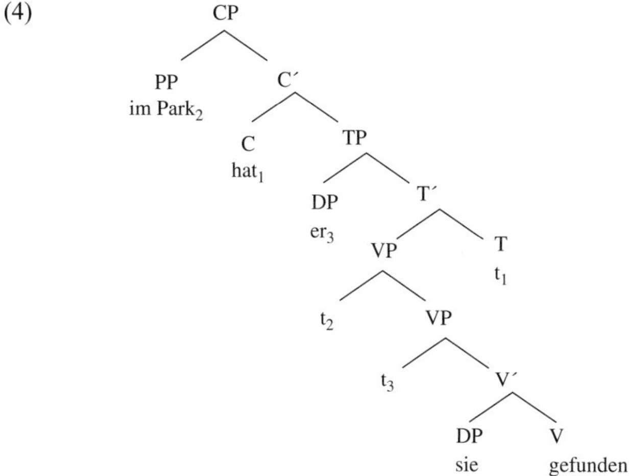

The observations on early linguistic productions reported on above amount to the claim that only after the age of 1;6 does one find evidence in the language use of children supporting the assumption that they have access to principles and operations allowing for hierarchical sentence organizations of this type. Among the phenomena which constitute evidence for structures of this sort count, for example, the use of overt verb inflection for subject–verb agreement, encoding an abstract relationship between syntactically defined elements, or structure-dependent word order rearrangements (movement), for example placement of the verb in the second position of the sentence structure (V2 effect), as opposed to simply putting an element in initial or final position (although this can, of course, also be described in structural terms), or the use of other functional elements, like auxiliaries, modals, articles and so forth. As we have seen in the brief summary of linguistic developments, all three happen during the subsequent period, ranging approximately from age 1;8 through 2;6. Consequently, we may summarize, it is during the second half or the last third of the second year that children's utterances normally contain phenomena which can be construed as evidence for the accessibility of grammatical means of organizing language.

Let us, thus, retain that some time soon after approximately age 1;6, child language exhibits properties which provide unambiguous empirical evidence supporting the assumption that child utterances are indeed instantiations of hierarchically organized sentence structures – grammatical structures, in other words, specific to human language. From a developmental perspective, the obvious question which immediately arises, then, is how and when this grammatical knowledge became available to the language learning child. This problem of the emergence of grammar is indeed one of the most controversial issues in research on first language development. But although it is of considerable theoretical interest, we cannot engage in this debate in the present context, where the focus lies on the comparison between first and second language acquisition. After all, L2 learners do have access to grammatical knowledge, even at the initial stage of L2 acquisition. It would therefore be implausible to assume that we should find similarities between the two acquisition types during very early phases, whatever the underlying logic of the emergence of L1 grammars may be. On the other hand, when it comes to explaining differences between L1 and L2 acquisition, it is precisely the accessibility of grammatical principles, plus the fact that L2 learners can, in principle, draw on previously acquired grammatical knowledge, which arguably distinguish these types of acquisition at the initial state; see section 4.2. This is why I want to give at least a brief summary of the debate on the first emergence of grammar in L1; it should also contribute to a better understanding of the issues related to the development of grammars which will be dealt with in the next section.

It seems that every logically possible approach to the problem of the emergence of grammar has indeed been advocated in the literature on L1 development. This should perhaps not surprise us too much, because the empirical basis on which this debate can draw is extremely narrow, independently of which position one holds. Linguistic productions by children during the age range concerned here are scarce, short and tightly bound to the communicative context in which they are uttered. Comprehension of grammatical structures, on the other hand, is not only difficult to test at such an early age, linguistic comprehension also relies heavily on the situative and communicative context, making it very difficult to decide to what extent an understanding of the formal properties of an utterance contributes to its comprehension. This is, perhaps, why two extreme and mutually exclusive views are both defended – the one which maintains that children always have access to grammatical knowledge, as well as the one which claims that they initially proceed through a 'pre-grammatical' phase. As for the former, it assumes that children's use of linguistic expressions is always shaped by grammatical principles, probably by UG (see Wexler 1998, among others). The problem with this hypothesis is that it is not supported by the available empirical data, as should already have become obvious in the discussion of milestones of L1 development in the first part of this section. In view of the generally scant empirical basis during the age period in question, this does not necessarily mean that this position is untenable. If, however, one wants to maintain that a particular source of knowledge has always been available, but the effects of its presence become visible only at a later moment, one is under the obligation to explain what has changed at this later point of development. Referring vaguely to maturation will not do. Thus, although this approach represents a logical possibility, it is not the most plausible one, and I will not pursue it any further here.

Concerning the alternative view, one can again distinguish two different approaches. The first one claims that early child language is shaped by non-grammatical principles which gradually turn into grammatical ones. The second one also postulates a pre-grammatical phase, but it argues that grammatical development is autonomous rather then evolving out of an earlier set of non-grammatical principles. The issue at stake here is thus the autonomy of grammar. Note that although these two approaches both assume an early pre-grammatical phase, the latter one is indeed closer in its theoretical assumptions to the above-mentioned hypothesis (grammar from the start) in that both subscribe to the idea of grammatical autonomy. In contrast, the idea of an evolution of grammatical principles out of a preceding non-grammatical system relies crucially on the belief that children can only get into a formal grammatical system by using functional properties of linguistic expression as stepping stones, relying, for example, on their semantic or pragmatic functions. As an example of this kind of functional explanation one can refer to Givón (1979: 222). He distinguishes between two communicative modalities, the pragmatic and the syntactic mode, and argues that the pragmatic mode precedes the syntactic mode ontogenetically and possibly also phylogenetically. The idea underlying this argument is that grammatical encodings replace earlier semantic-pragmatic ones in a process of grammaticalization (syntacticization, in Givón's terminology). The present context is obviously not the place to assess the advantages and disadvantages of functional explanations of the ontogenesis of grammar. I merely want to point out that they crucially depend on the idea that the emergence of grammatical devices is functionally driven. In order to support it, one must provide empirical evidence for the grammaticalization process, demonstrating, for example, that what seem to be subject–verb constructions are in fact agent–action sequences which are gradually grammaticalized as S–V. To my knowledge, this has not yet been done successfully. Moreover, the plausibility of functional explanations hinges on the well-foundedness of the claim that functional properties of linguistic expressions are indeed more transparent and thus easier to acquire for young children than formal ones. This assumption, however, has to be rejected in the light of the findings reported on, earlier in this section. There we have seen that the language making capacity directs children to cues relating to formal properties of language, well before they can grasp their semantic or pragmatic values. In other words, form precedes function, contrary to a priori functionalist beliefs.

Finally, theoretical considerations also speak in favour of the autonomy of grammar in linguistic development. I am referring here to the *continuity assumption*, first developed by Pinker (1984), who argued that it should be regarded as the null hypothesis in explanations of language development. Summarizing briefly this line of argument, one can say that it starts from the assumption that the language capacity of adults comprises mental representations of grammatical knowledge. Applying Occam's Razor leads to the conclusion that 'the fewer the mechanisms, the more parsimonious the theory and the more explanatory its accounts' (Pinker 1984: 6). As for grammatical development, this entails that the child has access to the same kind of linguistic knowledge as the adult, that is, making use of the same grammatical entities and relations. Clearly, postulating an early phase during which non-grammatical principles and mechanisms shape the children's language and, moreover, a specific process (grammaticalization) by which these are transformed into adult-like grammatical ones, is the less parsimonious account. Consequently, the continuity assumption indeed represents the null hypothesis. Note that this does not necessarily imply that it is correct. But unless compelling evidence to the contrary is found, it should be regarded as well motivated.

Does this suggest that we should abandon the idea of an initial pre-grammatical phase and adopt the above-mentioned claim according to which children have access to grammatical principles 'from the start', that is, possibly since birth? Remember that the summary of language development during the first year and a half did not provide any empirical evidence supporting this conclusion, whereas during the second half of the second year grammatical devices do appear, and they seem to develop fast, from then on. This strongly suggests a qualitative change in development which happens rather abruptly. Note that once children enter the one-word stage, it takes several months, more than half a year, in fact, before they start using grammatical forms. But once grammatical devices have emerged, children proceed rapidly through subsequent developmental phases, and in little more than one year they succeed in acquiring most of the grammar of their target language. This is why Bickerton (1990b), who discusses this discontinuous pattern of development at some length, refers to child language during what I have called the pre-grammatical phase as 'protolanguage', conveying by this term the idea that language use is not yet shaped by grammatical principles. The qualitative change can then be explained by assuming that Universal Grammar has become accessible; in other words, the hypothesis is that UG becomes available as a result of neural and cognitive maturation. Quite obviously, further evidence is needed in order to support this claim, preferably independent evidence, including insights from neurophysiological research. In the present context it must suffice to refer to the observed discontinuity of linguistic development – a fact which neither the functional approach nor the one postulating grammatical processing from the start can explain.

Returning briefly to the claim that the continuity assumption constitutes the null hypothesis for the explanation of grammatical development, one may wonder whether the line of argument sketched out here is compatible with this idea. Note that, contrary to a functional approach, it does not postulate the emergence of grammar out of a previous non-grammatical system. Rather, it assumes autonomy of grammar in that it claims that when UG becomes accessible, this does not depend in any respect on the underlying system shaping earlier linguistic expressions. In fact, even if one adopts Givón's (1979) distinction between a pragmatic and a syntactic mode, and even if one wants to argue that the pragmatic mode is operative during the pre-grammatical phase, there is no reason to assume that grammar evolves out of pragmatic principles. After all, the latter continue to be operative in adult language use, parallel to and independently of grammatical principles. In other words, what the approach advocated here objects to is the process of grammaticalization, independently of whether or not the pragmatic mode precedes grammar ontogenetically. The crucial point is that once grammatical principles become accessible, they are indeed the same in nature as the ones in mature grammars, as argued by Pinker (1984). This view is frequently referred to in the literature on L1 development as the *weak continuity* hypothesis, as opposed to the *strong continuity* hypothesis which holds that children have access to grammar during every moment of linguistic development. Whatever terminology one chooses, what matters is that as soon as children's language use is guided by grammatical principles, developing grammars are constrained by principles of UG and are thus of the same nature as mature ones.

2.3 Functional categories in early child grammar

My brief summary of linguistic development during the first two years in the life of children has led to the conclusion that it is indeed guided by the human Language Making Capacity. This can explain the uniformity of the course of development, its ultimate success, and possibly also the fast rate of acquisition. More specifically, I have argued that the nature and the particular sequence of milestones characterizing children's development can be explained by the fact that the LMC provides the children with discovery principles, many of which are domain-specific in nature, allowing them to discover formal properties of linguistic systems. At the same time, however, I have insisted on the claim that grammatical principles only become accessible to children when Universal Grammar kicks in as a result of maturational processes, some time after age 1;6. It is this subsequent development, now constrained by principles of UG, which deserves further attention for at least two reasons. The first one concerns the properties of developing grammars, the second one the question of how to explain the observed developmental sequence. In other words, we need to be concerned with property as well as with transition theory; cf. section 2.1.

As for the first point, a potential problem arises as a consequence of the continuity assumption. It concerns the question of how to account for differences between child and adult grammars if we want to maintain that both are of the same nature and that they cannot violate principles of UG. It goes without saying that child utterances differ from adult utterances, certainly during the early age period under consideration here. Does this suggest that developing grammars differ from mature ones, after all, and if this is the case, how is this compatible with the continuity assumption? Alternatively one might want to explore the possibility that the observed differences could perhaps be accounted for in terms of mechanisms of language use, rather than as reflecting different kinds of grammatical knowledge. The issue, in other words, is that of linguistic variation, in this particular case variation during the course of development. In my understanding, it should be treated as an instance of grammatical variation, rather than shoving it off into the domain of language use where it might then be ignored. The solution to the problem which I will present in the remainder of this section is that developing and mature grammars do indeed differ, but these differences fall within the variation space defined by UG. Put differently, children acquiring a language should be expected to explore all options offered by UG – and only these – independently of whether they deviate from the target system, provided these options are not in conflict with the evidence contained in the PLD.

Concerning the second point, it should be remembered that developmental sequences are, first of all, descriptive tools. This is to say that by observing that a number of grammatical phenomena emerge in a fixed and invariant order, we have not yet made a statement about the underlying logic which causes the phenomena in question to appear in just this order. We therefore cannot content ourselves with this observation without abandoning all pretensions to explanatory adequacy. If, on the other hand, we succeed in explaining developmental sequences, we will have made a contribution to transition theory and thus provided a partial solution, at least, to the developmental problem. Here again, one can search for answers in the grammatical domain as well as in the area of language use. At this point, however, I will focus exclusively on grammatical aspects, emphasizing that it should be possible to propose an explanation relying on grammatical factors if we want to maintain that UG is the centrepiece of the LAD. The approach pursued in this section attempts to account for the above-mentioned problem of variation across grammars, that is, for the properties in which child grammars differ from adult grammars and from each other at various points of development. It also seeks to explain the specific course of development, that is, it tries to account for the developmental problem as well.

One observation briefly discussed in the preceding section can serve as our starting point. Recall that the most prominent feature of child language providing evidence for the instantiation of grammatical principles is the emergence of closed class items – functional elements in our terminology. A brief glance at sentence structures like (4) in section 2.2 reveals immediately that they consist of layers of lexical (or substantive) and functional categories (FC); the former including nouns, verbs, adjectives, and prepositions (N, V, A, P), the latter comprising D(ET), T(ENSE) and C(OMP), among others. Importantly, functional elements are realized as grammatical morphemes, and a major role of functional projections is to provide 'landing sites' for moved elements, thus establishing a close connection between grammatical morphemes and word-order regularities. In other words, morphosyntactic properties of sentences are encoded by the functional layers of sentence structures. From a developmental perspective this means that the acquisition of grammar will be closely related to the availability of functional elements. Consequently, we should focus our attention on these grammatical devices when searching for an explanation of developmental sequences in the acquisition of grammar.

Our starting point thus is the observation that children initially tend to omit certain elements which are obligatory in the corresponding mature language and that many of these represent overt expressions of functional categories in adult language. Observations of this sort have led a number of researchers to suggest that early grammars lack FCs altogether; cf. the Small Clause Hypothesis (SCH) of Radford (1986, 1990) or the Structure Building Hypothesis (SBH) of Guilfoyle and Noonan (1992). An opposing view is formulated as the Full Competence Hypothesis (FCH) according to which 'the child has the adult grammar' (Poeppel and Wexler 1993: 3), in particular the functional categories of the adult grammar. In other words, the FCH claims that functional categories are instantiated in the child's grammar right from the very beginning of language acquisition onwards, even if the data from child production suggest otherwise.

This is not the occasion to recapitulate the arguments presented in favour of or against these two approaches. In fact, such a debate would probably be of only limited interest since much of it reflects mere terminological disagreement, as may become apparent in what follows. What is, however, of interest is the more principled issue of whether language acquisition involves restructuring of grammatical systems. Under the FCH, this is explicitly claimed *not* to be the case. Poeppel and Wexler (1993: 18) assert that the FCH 'has no developmental question associated with it'. This is a remarkable statement, for it amounts to saying that linguistic analyses renounce accounting for grammatical development, limiting their ambition to describing a number of successive states of grammatical knowledge, thereby eliminating the developmental problem from the agenda of language acquisition research. Rather than abandoning developmental concerns, I claim that we should attempt to define explicitly the kind of variability to be expected in the course of acquisition. In accordance with what has been alluded to above, one can predict that the variation space will be constrained by the kind of variability related to FCs across mature grammars. The parameters defining the nature and the degree of variability, however, are not yet spelled out explicitly. In fact, they are not generally agreed upon in grammatical theory. This leads to problems of argumentation, but not of substance. In what follows, I will present a number of arguments which lead to the conclusion that we must necessarily assume some kind of 'structure building', that is, some version of the Structure Building Hypothesis.

In making my case, let me begin by asking four questions. As we will see, positive answers to my questions inevitably lead to the conclusion that in developing grammars functional layers of sentence structures differ from those of mature grammars.

1. Can a given FC exhibit different intrinsic properties in different languages?
2. Can languages differ in the set of FCs instantiated in their grammars?
3. Can sentence structures lack functional layers altogether?
4. Can the structural position of a specific FC vary across languages?

As a matter of logic, a positive response to any one of these questions is sufficient to motivate my conclusion. In my exposition I will be concerned mainly with the first question. It has not received sufficient attention in the controversy about grammatical development which focused to a large extent on whether a functional category is present in the child's grammar or not. Such a monolithic conception of grammatical categories ignores what is common wisdom in the generative tradition of grammatical theorizing, based on ideas developed by linguistic structuralism, namely that grammatical categories are not syntactic primitives but are rather defined in terms of their grammatical properties, for example morphological and distributional properties in the case of syntactic categories. These properties are commonly represented by grammatical features attributed to the category in question. Thus, although we refer to a specific category by its label, for example T, C, D – or N, V, etc., for that matter – a category is a complex entity which is best represented as a feature bundle. Conceptualizing it in this fashion enables us to capture the fact that some categories share properties. It also enables us to account for cases where subcategories share most but not all properties of the main category. All this applies to lexical as well as to functional categories, although I am only concerned here with formal features of functional categories.

As for functional categories, it is obvious, I contend, that they cannot be specified by exactly the same set of features in all languages. A well-known example is that FCs vary across languages in that they contain different features attracting elements which are moved to this head. Whereas finite elements are raised to TENSE in Romance languages, they move to COMP in Germanic V2 languages. Whatever the correct featural specification may be causing this type of movement, it should be obvious that, strictly speaking, Germanic TENSE and COMP differ from their Romance counterparts. In other words, such featural variability must be tolerated across languages and probably also within languages.

Once we commit to these hypotheses about grammatical competence, it necessarily follows for language development that the child needs to figure out the featural content of each category implemented in the developing grammar. This task becomes considerably more complicated if we assume that the number of FCs and their hierarchical order are not universally predefined, either; see questions 2–4 above. Adopting this scenario, we may ask what the initial hypothesis is that the child may be expected to entertain if UG provides a set of features that will ultimately define the target grammatical categories but specifies only for a subset of them how they combine. Moreover, we must also ask how the Language Making Capacity determines to which FC a particular feature should be allocated, especially if it does not specify the number of functional heads to be implemented in the target grammar. In principle, one could imagine two radical solutions: the maximal one would allow for each feature to project an independent FC; the minimal one would require all features to be assembled within a single FC. Neither of these options is particularly plausible. What may plausibly be expected to happen when the child explores the range of options tolerated by UG would have to be deduced from a comprehensive theory of functional categories. Minimally, such a theory must (1) list the features provided by UG which can be attributed to FCs; (2) determine the set of features necessarily required for the specification of a particular functional head, for example the ones which need to be present in order for a functional head to be labelled COMP; and (3) define co-occurrence restrictions of features for particular functional heads (identifying impossible combinations as well as required combinations). Although much of this work still remains to be done and will certainly give rise to controversy, there can be no doubt that the featural composition of FCs is constrained along these lines. I predict that the range of options to be explored by the language learning child is limited accordingly.

Irrespective of the details of a theory of functional categories, a plausible assumption with respect to children's initial hypotheses about the functional layering of sentence structures is that they will first adopt a conservative approach, attributing as little structure as possible and a limited set of formal features to the target system. Proceeding in this fashion minimizes the risk of excessive structure building which would later on require 'de-learning' of some formal properties – a notoriously difficult problem for any theory of acquisition. The most parsimonious option is to postulate a single FC which, furthermore, would not be fully specified, when compared to the mature system. Such proposals have been suggested by a number of L1 researchers, for example Clahsen (1991), Déprez and Pierce (1993) and Rothweiler (1993). Clahsen (1991), in fact, proposed a single, radically underspecified functional category, FP, which later turns into CP, as more features are added, selected from the pool of features offered by UG.

In sum, grammatical categories are theoretical constructs defined in terms of their grammatical properties. The set of properties assigned to a given functional category need not be identical across languages, in spite of the fact that this category bears the same label, for example TENSE. From these and similar considerations it follows necessarily that early child grammars cannot be fully identical to their mature counterparts. In other words, even if one finds reasons to assume that a grammar at a very early point of development contains a TP projection, the featural composition of the head of this projection is likely to differ from the head of TP in the adult target grammar. More specifically, based on the hypothesis according to which initial grammars are structurally conservative, it can be assumed that early functional heads are underspecified. Some kind of 'structure building' is thus an inevitable necessity in language acquisition. The claim here is that functional categories develop incrementally, guided and constrained by UG and triggered by the learner's analysis of the PLD.

To conclude this part of the discussion, let me add a remark referring to grammatical theorizing. At the end of section 2.1, I explained that I intend to work within the theoretical framework of generative grammar but largely independent of a particular model of Universal Grammar. As will have become apparent, the ideas developed here are inspired by work in the framework of the Principles and Parameters Theory, for example the Finiteness Parameter proposed by Platzack and Holmberg (1989). It should be equally apparent that by focusing on the featural composition of categories, the suggestions outlined here are congruent with proposals of the Minimalist Program (see Chomsky 1995, 2000b). According to Chomsky, formal grammatical categories like nouns, verbs, adjectives and so on do not exist; traditional category labels are replaced by formal features. Intrinsic formal features are listed in the lexical entry, and optional features are added when the linguistic expression enters the numeration. The theory makes an essential distinction between 'interpretable' and 'uninterpretable' features. A number of authors provide theoretical as well as empirical evidence suggesting that the former are acquired before the latter; cf. Say (2001) and Tsimpli (2004, 2005), among others. Uninterpretable features, however, are the ones responsible for parametric variation; I will return to this in the following section. Incremental development of functional categories can thus be conceptualized within the MP model, assuming an initial phase during which at least some uninterpretable features are lacking, and subsequent phases during which they are successively implemented.

To sum up, it seems that the answer to the first question, 'Can a given FC exhibit different intrinsic properties in different languages?', can only be positive, and this fact alone suffices to conclude that the acquisition of functional categories necessarily entails incremental development of grammatical structures. I will therefore treat the other three questions together and only very briefly. In fact, questions 2–4 address closely related issues, and the logic of the argument is identical in all cases, basically the same as in the discussion of the first question. If, namely, it can be shown that a given functional projection is required in the grammar of one language but not in another, and/or if the hierarchical position of a given FC differs across languages, we must conclude that children in the course of L1 acquisition need to discover which FCs are implemented in their respective target grammar and which hierarchical positions these FCs occupy in the grammars to be acquired. Consequently, early child grammars cannot contain, from the earliest phases onwards, the full set of functional elements required by the mature system. Rather we should expect, here too, to find a sequence of phases during which the target structure is implemented incrementally.

However, answers to the other questions are more difficult to find. In all cases opposite views on the issues at stake have been defended in the literature. The first states that sentence structures of all languages are represented by the same base phrase marker (Chomsky 2001), containing the same set of FCs, always in the same hierarchical order (Cinque 1999, 2006). The opposite view contends that grammars of individual languages may contain only a subset of the full set of FCs made available by UG, and possibly also that their hierarchical order is variable (see, for example, Iatridou 1990, Ouhalla 1991 or Speas 1991). This is to say that such differences are interpreted as instances of *language-specific* variation, representing particularities of individual languages (cf. Bobaljik and Thráinsson

1998). As for the structural layering of functional elements, Ouhalla (1991) provides perhaps the most detailed argument suggesting that a particular functional category may subcategorize different categories in different languages. If this is correct, the hierarchical order of FCs is also subject to parametric variation; see section 2.4.

For obvious reasons, it is not possible for language acquisition research to propose definitive solutions for problems for which grammatical theory does not provide widely accepted criteria to decide on the well-foundedness of the various claims. I will therefore refrain from a more detailed discussion of these issues that could only be inconclusive in these circumstances. Let me nevertheless emphasize that these problems become even more acute for research on language development if one agrees with analyses suggesting that the originally postulated FCs INFL and COMP should be split (cf. Pollock 1989, Rizzi 1997 and contributions in Rizzi 2004), thus resulting in a larger set of functional heads. For each of them we face the question of whether they are part of every grammar, and we also need to decide on their hierarchical position in sentence structures. If we conclude that languages vary with respect to these options, it follows that the language-specific choices must be learnable, that is, the PLD must contain information allowing the child to detect the option chosen by the target grammar. A smaller set of universal FCs would obviously make this learnability problem more manageable. Unfortunately, current grammatical theorizing again offers two diametrically opposed approaches to this issue. Whereas recent developments in the MP framework aim to reduce drastically the number of functional layers in sentence structure (Chomsky 1995, 2000b) – ultimately leaving us with only the FCs *v*, T and C – the 'cartographic' school (cf. Cinque 2002, 2006, Belletti 2004 and Rizzi 2004) advocates finely grained structures containing a considerable number of functional heads. Both approaches agree, however, in postulating a universal sentence structure where the hierarchical order of functional elements is invariant. The same is true for Kayne's (1994) antisymmetry theory. If the set of functional heads is indeed strictly limited, a universal hierarchy can hardly be disputed since the claim that C subcategorizes T, and T subcategorizes *v* is supported by an abundance of empirical and theoretical findings. If, however, one has to deal with a large number of FCs, such a conclusion is much more problematic, especially if 'the presence or absence of overt expressions of a certain functional element in a language' need not 'imply the actual presence or absence of the corresponding functional projection in that language' (Cinque 2006: 6). In this case, one indeed faces a serious learnability problem which can perhaps only be overcome by postulating a universal underlying hierarchy, because it is not obvious how language learning children could possibly detect the necessary information in the primary linguistic data enabling them to determine which FCs need to be implemented in the target grammar, let alone which hierarchical order is required.

Let us thus return to the questions formulated at the beginning of this discussion and to the problem concerning the kind of variation permitted by UG and thus to be explored in the course of language development. In view of the state-of-the-art in syntactic theorizing, it is only possible to give tentative answers to questions 2–4. The strongest case can be made if one agrees to the proposed splitting of the traditional functional heads. I have argued that even for the traditional set of FCs it is virtually inevitable that we conclude that specific features are allocated to distinct categories in various languages. Under the scenario of splitting of FCs, this becomes a necessity. In other words, in view of the fact that specific features can be allocated to a variety of heads in different languages, it is inevitable that we conclude that the set of FCs instantiated in human languages cannot be identical. By insisting on labelling these categories identically across languages, the problem can perhaps be concealed, but it is not solved. The hierarchical order, on the other hand, may well be universally invariant. My tentative answer to the second question, 'Can languages differ in the set of FCs instantiated in their grammars?', is thus a positive one, whereas I believe that the fourth question, 'Can the structural position of a specific FC vary across languages?', needs to be answered negatively.

Finally, I want to add a remark concerning question 3, whether developing grammars might initially allow for bare lexical structures, lacking functional layers altogether. Note that one could infer such an option from the claim above, according to which child learners initially adopt a conservative approach, avoiding as much structure as possible. This is to say that children might, during the earliest phase of grammatical development and in the absence of unambiguous empirical evidence in favour of specific functional heads, opt for a structure corresponding to a VP or to a Small Clause. This is, indeed, what Guilfoyle and Noonan (1992) and Radford (1986, 1990) had suggested. But it appears to be in conflict with the spirit of the continuity assumption, since human grammars totally lacking functional layers do not seem to exist. This is to say that one can find specific constructions of this type, like Small Clauses, but not grammars lacking functional layers altogether.

The conclusion to be drawn from the preceding reflections on functional categories is that the featural composition of a given FC can vary across languages. Variation with respect to the selection of a specific set of FCs is also a plausible hypothesis which, however, needs to be explored further. Whether, in addition, the structural layering of functional elements is subject to cross-linguistic variation is questionable. Consequently, the only possible conclusion with respect to first language development is that the language learning child needs a certain amount of exposure to the primary linguistic data of the target language in order to implement functional categories as required by the target grammar. Stipulating a Full Competence supposedly characterizing the earliest developmental phase can at best mean that the child is a fully competent language learner. This is tantamount to saying that UG is a theory about the initial state of language development, a claim never disputed in the debate on structure development.

I thus pursue ideas developed by, among others, Radford (1990) or Guilfoyle and Noonan (1992). The claim is that the logic determining the order of phases within the invariant developmental sequences observed is guided by UG and is grammatical in nature. It does not result from processing mechanisms or inductive learning. Yet instead of postulating an initial phase totally lacking FCs and subsequent implementation of target-conforming functional heads, I propose that the child incrementally develops initially underspecified FCs.

As for the initial phase, given the arguments above, it can be characterized by the presence of either a single FC or v, T and C, if one wants to maintain that a fixed set or subset of the FCs licensed by UG is instantiated in the grammars of all human languages. My claim is that in both cases the initial FCs will be underspecified, containing only those features which universally characterize the respective category. Features which cross-linguistically may be attributed to different functional heads, on the other hand, need to be implemented where appropriate. Moreover, since feature strength varies across languages, at least some of the uninterpretable features will initially be inert and require subsequent specification of strength. In fact, if Platzack (1996) is right in arguing that *all* features are initially weak, they will all have to be modified according to the requirements of the target grammars. These processes, distribution of features over the array of functional heads and specification of feature strength, thus define what I refer to as incremental development of functional categories. It amounts to saying that early child grammars differ from mature grammars in just those properties which reflect non-activation of specific features in FCs.

The question which still needs to be addressed is whether feature specification can explain not only the differences between developing and mature grammars but also developmental sequences, that is, whether we can contribute to a solution to the developmental problem. I am optimistic that we will succeed, for the available empirical evidence clearly shows that functional layers or, more specifically, particular morphosyntactic properties related to functional features emerge in a fixed order. The emergence of some aspects of the morphosyntax of verbs can illustrate my claim in more detail. There exists abundant evidence from the literature on the acquisition of various languages indicating that children as early as during the second half of their second year of life demonstrate by their spontaneous language use that their grammars resemble the respective target systems in distinguishing between OV and VO order, and in raising finite verbs to T, and almost simultaneously to C in V2 languages. Assuming that these are properties reflecting parameterized options depending on the feature specification of functional heads, we must conclude that children specify them for the corresponding features at early points of development. Importantly, the relationship between finiteness and verb movement is both motivated by grammatical theory and corroborated by developmental observations (cf. Clahsen 1986). In generative studies, finiteness has been represented as a feature [±F] located in the verb and in either T or C. Traditionally, however, finiteness is understood as a composite grammatical notion, defined in terms of (person, number and, in some languages, gender) agreement and tense markings. This is reflected by its treatment in more recent minimalist approaches which is corroborated by findings from grammatical development: the corresponding grammatical notions emerge successively with agreement preceding tense. More precisely, it is person agreement between subject and verb which comes in first, is acquired fast, virtually without errors, and seems to be sufficient to trigger verb raising (see Meisel 1990, 1994a). If this is correct, we can conclude that the [person] feature is activated before [tense]. In fact, in languages exhibiting subject–verb as well as object–verb agreement, subject agreement always precedes object agreement (see Meisel and Ezeizabarrena 1996). The property [tense], on the other hand, is preceded by [aspect] (see Meisel 1985 or Schlyter 1990, among others). Although one can find disagreement with respect to a number of details, the fact that developmental sequences of this type characterize first language acquisition is widely acknowledged. This fact constitutes corroborating evidence for the claim that the phases of these sequences can be defined in terms of features which are successively activated and attributed to specific functional categories. This, in turn, is an encouraging finding supporting the idea that not only the defining properties of the sequences and their individual phases are grammatical in nature, but also the underlying logic of their development.

Recall that the arguments presented above led to the conclusion that the initial state of the development of sentence structures is characterized by minimal functional layering. Whether it consists of a single functional category or a limited set of FCs depends on choices imposed by syntactic theory which cannot be scrutinized here. What matters for our present purpose is that the functional head(s) do not yet contain the full array of features required by the target grammar. The basic idea is that only those properties of functional heads which are necessarily and invariantly attributed to them by UG will be specified at the initial state. In other words, similar to the distinction between intrinsic and optional features postulated for lexical categories, it is argued that functional categories are partially specified from the start, whereas the presence or the strength of other features needs to be determined in the course of acquisition.

The challenge now is to uncover the underlying logic determining the order of emergence of feature specifications. In part, the answer can be found in the interpretability of features as suggested by Roeper (1996), who claimed that interpretable features are recognized first by the child. That this approach indeed allows one to account for at least some of the empirical facts is demonstrated by Tsimpli and her associates (cf. Tsimpli 2004, 2005 or Tsimpli and Mastropavlou 2007). She argues, for example, that the 'acquisition of functional structure proceeds on the basis of the interpretability distinction of features at LF, interpretable features being acquired earlier than uninterpretable ones' (Tsimpli 2005: 180), and she provides evidence from Greek, showing that focus, negation and modality, all involving interpretable features, emerge earlier than tense, mood and agreement, which involve uninterpretable features.

Determining the nature of the initial functional elements would require a more detailed discussion. Let me merely mention that it is not obvious whether the initial, radically underspecified elements contain syntactic category information other than being specified as functional items. Following Roeper (1992), this need not be the case. He emphasizes the independence of syntactic and semantic information in lexical items and suggests that particular semantic features are associated to functional projections in adult grammar as well and proposes the following correspondences, where IP (Inflection Phrase) is equivalent to what I have labelled TP:

CP = illocutionary force (question, focus, imperative)
IP = time, modality (truth, irrealis, tense, aspect)
DP = reference (thematic roles, definite reference)

Roeper (1996: 415) further states that the 'child projects Unique Maximal Projections (UMPs) not (necessarily) found in the adult grammar'. In a similar vein, Powers (1999, 2001) refers to these items at the initial phase as 'pseudo-functional' elements, precisely because they are radically underspecified and lack syntactic category information. According to her theory, they are all heads carrying semantic features. Irrespective of whether one adopts her view on the syntactic status of these elements at the initial state, her approach does offer a possible solution to the transition problem. She demonstrates that the development of the initially 'pseudo-functional' elements is data-driven and that the sequence characterizing early phrase structure development can be accounted for in terms of functional features and the operation Merge. In minimalist syntax, Merge is the basic operation creating hierarchical structures by combining smaller structures and building larger ones out of these (cf. Chomsky 1995: 243 or Adger 2003: 69). As a result of Merge, these elements project, and features are added to them, defining and refining them. Hierarchical structures thus develop incrementally, and in this process they gradually acquire the feature specification of the target grammar.

(5)

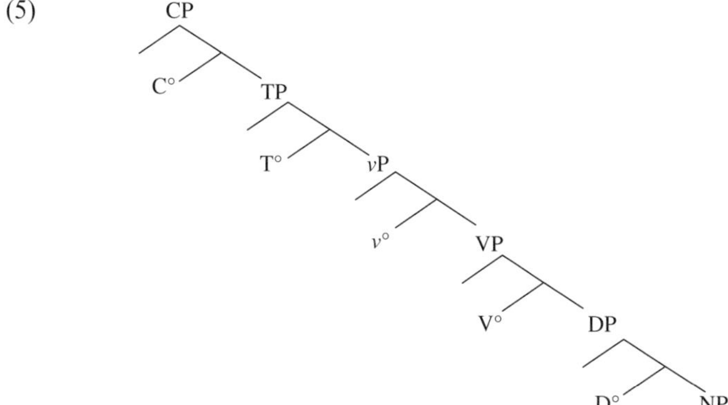

Under the assumption that the hierarchical layering of functional categories does not vary across languages and that it universally layers as in (5), we can assume that the developmental logic follows the hierarchical layering of FCs. This is indeed the implicit assumption in many or most studies which adopt the idea of structure building. If, on the other hand, additional FCs can be instantiated in some languages – as implied by the second question, above (Can languages differ in the set of FCs instantiated in their grammars?) – it is not at all obvious how their hierarchical position can be determined in the course of language acquisition. Note, however, that this problem arises independently of whether one subscribes to some version of the Structure Building Hypothesis. Moreover, the scenario outlined above and the phrase marker presented in (5) should not let us forget what we discussed in relation to our first question, namely that the featural composition of the functional heads is not identical across languages. Rather, a feature like [+F] must be attributed to C in some languages like the Germanic V2 languages, and to T in others like English or most Romance languages. Similarly, the strength of some features varies across languages. Neither of these facts seems to lead to unsolvable empirical problems since the relevant information about the distribution of features and their strength should be detectable in the primary linguistic data, given that they trigger movement operations which frequently result in different surface orderings. Whether the acquisition of these phenomena proceeds according to strictly ordered developmental sequences and whether they can then be accounted for in grammatical terms is, however, still an open question.

To conclude this section, I believe that we have seen solid empirical evidence supporting the claim that soon after age 1;6 children's utterances not only grow increasingly longer, they also become more complex, exhibiting properties which attest to the fact that they are expressions of sentence structures. Since production may very well lag behind the development of knowledge, it is plausible to assume that UG may have kicked in earlier than that, but as Jill de Villiers (1992: 425) remarks, 'the maturation is apparently sudden and all embracing: a mini puberty at 20 months with functional categories popping out all over'. The observation that child utterances now contain functional elements indicates that they reflect underlying grammatical knowledge because functional categories can justly be interpreted as constituting the skeleton of sentence structure. As for the developmental problem, I believe that the foregoing discussion has shown that syntactic theory can contribute to its solution to a significant extent, even if it is unlikely to account fully for all of it. The incremental emergence of functional elements is thus hypothesized to explain crucial aspects of early grammatical development. Relying on the set of features provided by UG for functional heads and on the operation Merge, hierarchical structures are generated. Their further development involves the addition of features to particular functional heads, the specification of feature strength, and possibly the splitting of functional heads into more specific ones, for example CP into ForceP, TopicP, FocusP, and FinP (cf. Rizzi 1997). These developments respond to language-specific variation in grammar, itself constrained by UG. In what follows, I will outline some aspects of Parameter Theory, designed to explain this interaction between universal and particular in grammar.

2.4 Parameters in first language development

In our quest for the LAD, the summaries and discussions of this chapter focused on invariant aspects of language development. Epistemological as well as methodological reasons justify this emphasis. This focus helps us to discover principles and mechanisms shared by all language learning children, thus enabling us to account for what can be seen as the constitutive properties of first language development: ultimate success and uniformity, and possibly also its rate. Uniformity, however, is not to be confounded with invariance. Invariant systems are fossilized and cannot change, because change necessarily leads to variation, certainly across time, but typically also within systems, where variability attests either remnants of the earlier states or emergence of new ones. Unlimited variability, on the other hand, would speak against the assumption of an underlying developmental logic guided by a specific language making capacity. But this is not what one finds in first language acquisition. The fact that all children are able to attain full grammatical competence in the languages they are exposed to, by interacting with caretakers and peers, supports the idea of an underlying logic, as does the observation that the course of development is uniform. Yet since this is the case for all human languages, irrespective of their structural particularities, the guiding force – our hypothesized LAD – needs to be able to cope with this (limited) amount of variation characterizing the target systems. It is in this sense that the LAD necessarily has to be conceptualized in such a way that it will be able to explain universal as well as particular aspects of language acquisition. Our review of some of the milestones of linguistic development in section 2.2 indicates that the discovery principles enabling children to get into the linguistic system, many of them domain-specific in nature, leave little room for variability, although they do interact with the properties detected in the ambient language(s) from very early on and increasingly so. Grammatical development guided by UG, however, clearly does involve cross-linguistic variation, as should be apparent from the discussion in section 2.3, demonstrating that functional elements exhibit universal as well as language-specific properties. As argued in 2.1, developing grammars must conform to principles of UG in the same way as mature ones, but children can explore the variation space offered by UG. We should find cross-linguistic variation reflected in the development of individuals.

The preceding remarks do not apply exclusively to the theory of Universal Grammar. Rather, any theory of grammar faces the challenge of explaining how universal and particular properties shape individual grammars. Theories of acquisition must account for the way in which universal and particular interact in the course of development. Not surprisingly, grammatical theories are not equally successful in dealing with both challenges. Depending on their epistemological preferences, they fare better with either universals or particulars. As is to be expected, UG excels in its treatment of the former. However, as it moved away from formulating language-specific rules towards construction-independent principles of grammars, the problem of explaining cross-linguistic variation in a systematic fashion became an ever more urgent necessity. The solution to this problem has been to propose a model incorporating both universal principles and parameters allowing language-specific properties (cf. Chomsky 1981a, 1981b for a first outline of Principles and Parameters Theory). The basic idea underlying the notion of grammatical parameter is that some of the principles of UG do not fully specify the properties to which they refer but offer more than one option, probably two (binary choice); see 2.1. Parameters must therefore be set to one of the given values. Importantly, the principles and their potential values are given by UG which thus defines universal as well as particular properties of grammars and thereby restricts the variation space accordingly.

As will be immediately apparent from these remarks, Parameter Theory constitutes the core component of a grammatical framework which aims to explain not only properties of developing grammars, but also the course of acquisition. Recall what was said earlier about the tasks of the language learning child, deducible from the nature of the linguistic phenomena to be acquired. On the one hand, children must learn inductively lexical items and other language-specific phenomena. In order to come to grips with this task, they can rely on general problem-solving capacities, much like in other learning situations. But since linguistic expressions are rather special, abstract entities, they also have to resort to domain-specific principles and mechanisms provided by the LAD, like the discovery principles referred to in 2.2 above. Importantly, however, the LAD has been defined as containing substantive principles as well, that is, knowledge about the structure of language available prior to experience. In other words, structural knowledge is not learned inductively; it must be triggered in order to be instantiated in the developing grammar. I will return to this distinction between learning and triggering shortly. It is this innate or a priori knowledge which is represented by the principles of UG. As for the latter, a distinction has been made between parameterized and invariant, non-parameterized universal principles. From an acquisition perspective, they can be said to define two further tasks for the language learning child, in addition to inductive learning. Non-parameterized principles apply invariably if the phenomena to which they relate occur in the target language. Note that the child's task merely consists in (unconsciously) identifying the phenomena in question, thus instantiating the previously available knowledge. This is a process rather different from what is commonly understood by 'learning' because the child is not given a choice. Remember that some theoreticians speak here of language 'growth', and referring to this as a 'task' of the child may even be misleading. With respect to parameterized principles, however, the situation is quite different – here the child indeed faces a special acquisition task. It requires the interaction of information drawn from innate knowledge and knowledge gained by experience. In order to be able to set the parameter to one of the values offered by UG, the learner needs to identify the triggering evidence in the structural properties underlying the available input data. It is for precisely this reason, namely that parameter setting happens at the interface of a priori and acquired knowledge, that it represents one of the most interesting aspects to be investigated by acquisition studies.

From considerations of this kind it follows that Parameter Theory should be of particular concern both for theories of grammar and of linguistic development, including not only acquisition, but also diachronic change. Surprisingly, however, this is actually not the case. After an impressive beginning in the 1980s when numerous important studies appeared (e.g. Borer 1984; Hyams 1986; Roeper and Williams 1987; Jaeggli and Safir 1989; Lightfoot 1991), interest in Parameter Theory slowed down considerably in the 1990s, mostly because the initially proposed 'macro-parameters' (cf. Baker 1996) seemed not to stand up to scrutiny; I will return to this issue below. Another reason seems to be that with the advent of the Minimalist Program the theoretical status of the notion of parameter appeared as somewhat uncertain (see Uriagereka 2007 for a recent contribution to this discussion). As a result, we are currently facing a more than unsatisfactory situation. On the one hand, there can be no doubt that the theory of UG – independently of whatever model one adopts – cannot do without the concept of grammatical parameter. It must recur to this or to an equivalent notion in order to account for cross-linguistic differences, language acquisition or change. On the other hand, parameters as developed in the 1980s undoubtedly need to be revised and replaced by more narrowly defined 'micro-parameters'. To put it differently, Parameter Theory indeed continues to be a core element of a UG theory, but important modifications are necessary. Yet in spite of recent efforts (e.g. the contributions in Biberauer 2008), a comprehensive and widely accepted version of such a theory is not available. Instead, researchers seem to rely on a more intuitive notion of 'parameter', especially in studies on language acquisition and diachronic change. This, however, is not only an unsatisfactory state of affairs for the theory of UG, it is also an unfortunate situation for acquisition theory, because the most crucial arguments in the debate on parallels and differences between types of acquisition refer to phenomena related to grammatical parameters. It would be overly ambitious, I am afraid, if I were to try to sketch a comprehensive parameter theory, as a sideline of the discussion of first and second language acquisition. What I can attempt, however, is to outline some fundamental aspects, based on previous summaries of earlier versions of Parameter Theory (cf. Atkinson 1992, Meisel 1995 and, more recently, Snyder 2007). The goal of this approach is to identify properties parameters must minimally comprise, irrespective of particular theoretical models, and to search for empirically testable evidence distinguishing parameter setting from other types of learning.[1]

Let me begin by repeating what has been said before, namely that the notion of parameter refers to universal principles which are, however, not fully specified by Universal Grammar. Importantly, the principles as well as the options resulting from this underspecification are given by UG. As an illustration of what this means, we can refer again to the placement of finite verbs, mentioned in the preceding section where it was argued that the feature [+F] representing finiteness may be located in either T or C. A principle of UG requires that finite verbs are moved to a functional head above VP; the parametric choice in this case states that [+F] may be instantiated in either of these functional elements. This has been called the Finiteness or the Verb Movement Parameter. What matters here is that finite verb movement, the feature [+F] and its possible locations, are provided by UG and need not be learned. The acquisition task of setting the parameter to one of its possible values exclusively refers to the activation of one of the given options.

The reason why I recapitulate this is to emphasize that parameters are part of the a priori knowledge and that parameter setting crucially implies a developmental process which does not involve learning in the usual sense of the term. No new information about grammar needs to be incorporated into the knowledge system because the relevant information is part of the knowledge prior to experience. Parameter setting should therefore be understood as a cognitive process which involves experience-driven *triggering* of previously available knowledge. This distinction between learning and triggering of knowledge is a defining characteristic of parameter setting. In fact, if it can be shown that parameter setting is largely independent of inductive learning, this constitutes an indirect but particularly strong piece of evidence supporting the claim that children have access to a priori knowledge – in other words that they are guided by the LAD.

It is therefore all the more important to demonstrate that the distinction between learning and triggering of knowledge is not merely a theoretically motivated stipulation, but that it refers to distinct mental activities resulting in empirically discernable acquisition processes. This is indeed possible, as is argued by Carroll (1989). Since learning involves extraction of previously unavailable structural information from the primary linguistic data, it requires frequent exposure to the input, possibly over an extended period of time, and it probably needs salient and unambiguous input data; but it will nevertheless exhibit intra- and interindividual variation due to trial and error procedures. Triggering, on the other hand, differs from learning in each of these points: it involves extracting from the PLD information about which of the given structural options correspond to the target grammar. Consequently, we predict that it will happen fast given exposure to relevant input, requires less frequent and simple input data, and the developmental pattern is expected to be much more uniform across individuals. Quite obviously, this statement describes only superficially what characterizes triggering data. In fact, in order for the child to be able to extract the relevant information, a number of quantitative[2] as well as qualitative[3] prerequisites must be met (see Meisel 1995). In the present context I have to limit my discussion to those points which are likely to shed light on similarities and differences between L1 and L2 acquisition and refrain from a more thorough treatment of the, by no means trivial, triggering problem. Let me merely make one point explicit, even if it should be obvious from what has just been said about triggering: parameter settings are triggered not by primary data, but as a result of grammatical analysis. In other words, triggers consist of structural information. Learners must therefore be able to parse utterances and to assign to them structural representations. If the structural analysis of an utterance contains a triggering element, the parameter is set to the corresponding value.[4]

In order to substantiate the claim that the distinction between learning and triggering refers to distinct mental activities resulting in empirically discernable acquisition processes, we must ask how this difference translates into empirically testable facts. From what has just been said, it follows that learning in the usual sense of the term involves inductive procedures, scrutinizing the PLD over an extended period of time in an attempt to discover regular patterns, and applying trial and error procedures on the way to the target construction. One may therefore expect that the acquisition process will exhibit ups and downs, reflecting this kind of learning process. Moreover, since distinct learner types are likely to take different approaches to the respective learning tasks, one can predict that we shall find considerable variation across individuals in how they proceed. Triggering, however, should result in uniform acquisition patterns across learners since it is based on knowledge available prior to experience. Most importantly, it should happen faster, and it may be expected to result in abrupt changes in language behaviour because, as claimed above, a limited exposure to the PLD should suffice to identify the triggering information, and once this is achieved, the target structure should be attained almost instantaneously since learners need not proceed by trial and error in order to discover the correct solution. In sum, acquisition processes are predicted to exhibit rather different patterns of development, depending on which type of acquisition is involved. Consequently, the course of acquisition provides us with empirical evidence enabling us to distinguish between learning and triggering.

An example from a study of bilingual (French and German) first language acquisition can serve as an illustration of this point (see Meisel 1989 for a more detailed discussion). The bilingual child C. begins using verbs at age 1;9, and as is shown by figure 2.1, quoted from Meisel 1988, the first inflected finite forms emerge at age 1;10. Only two months later, at age 2;0, finite forms are provided in

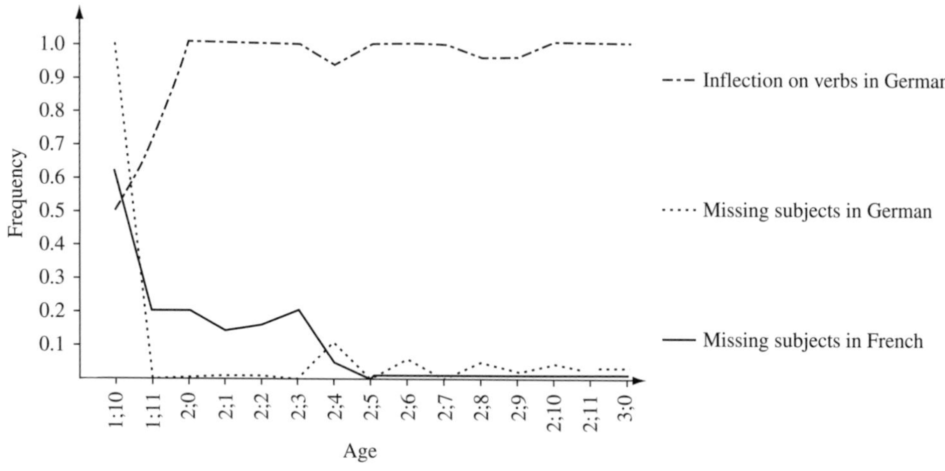

Figure 2.1: *Subject–verb agreement in 2L1 acquisition: German–French*

virtually all cases where they are required by the adult grammar. This rapid emergence of verb inflection coincides with the emergence of grammatical subjects, and within one month, from 1;10 to 1;11, the frequency of subject omission drops from 100% to 0%. This suggests that the child has acquired the grammatical notion of subject–verb agreement. Note that this presupposes not only the mental representation of abstract syntactic categories but also implicit knowledge about a long-distance relationship between a hierarchically defined property (subject) and the verb which is c-commanded. What matters in the present context is the nature of the acquisition patterns for finite verb forms and for subjects. As predicted, they both exhibit abrupt changes and lead to complete success in the acquisition of the target constructions.

Another important characteristic of parameter setting which will allow us to distinguish empirically between learning and triggering of knowledge emanates from the theoretical notion of parameter, as first suggested by Chomsky (1981a: 6). Since parameters and their possible values are defined at an abstract level of grammatical structure rather than in terms of surface properties of the target language, setting a parameter to a specific value typically causes a *cluster* of superficially unrelated grammatical properties to appear in the language. How this clustering of surface phenomena relates to a particular parametric choice crucially depends on how the theory of grammar conceives of parameters. Conceptions of parameters have changed considerably; as a result of recent grammatical theorizing, in the framework of the Minimalist Program, parameters are defined more narrowly than in the original Principle and Parameter Theory of the 1980s and 1990s. I will return to this issue later in this section. What is of prime importance for our present discussion is that, irrespective of the theoretical model, the clustering effect (i.e. the fact that a number of surface phenomena depend on the setting of a single parameter) is a crucial and defining property of grammatical parameters, thus lending this concept considerable explanatory force, as pointed out by Chomsky (1981a). This does not exclude the possibility that some parameters may not entail clustering (see Meisel 1995). If, however, parameters each determined individual grammatical properties, the concept would lose its theoretical attractiveness, and parameters would merely be descriptive devices.

The clustering effect of parameter setting can be illustrated by means of the Null-Subject (or pro-drop) Parameter (NSP), probably the most extensively studied parameter. Whereas some languages allow empty subjects in tensed clauses (e.g. Spanish), others normally require this position to be filled lexically (e.g. English). The NSP specifies the grammatical conditions which must be met for this empty category *pro* to be allowed to occur. These conditions have changed considerably over time, but they do relate to the featural composition of the functional head T (see Hyams 1986, 1989, or Goldbach 1999: 25 for a summary of various approaches to the NSP). Importantly, for the current topic of clustering, it has been suggested that this parameter relates not only to (a) empty subject positions, but to a number of other syntactic properties, as well. Null-subject languages should, for example, (b) not exhibit expletive elements, such as English *it* and *there* in *it seems* or *there is*. On the other hand, they allow (c) free inversion of subjects in simple sentences. Other properties which have been claimed to be related to the NSP are: (d) long wh-movement of subjects, (e) empty resumptive pronouns in embedded clauses, and (f) apparent violations of the so-called *[that-trace] filter (Chomsky 1981a: 240). It is of secondary importance whether these six properties are indeed all related to the NSP. In fact, virtually all of them have been questioned at some point in the syntactic literature (see, e.g., Haider 1994). Research on L1 acquisition, on the other hand, suggests that at least the first three (empty subjects, no expletives, subject–verb inversion) are indeed related to the setting of the NSP to one of its values (see Hinzelin 2003).

Another example, more in tune with the Minimalist Program, is the above-mentioned Verb Movement Parameter (VMP). In French, for example, movement of the finite verb to T results in a number of word order changes in the surface linearization of elements, for example the finite verb precedes the negator *pas* (6i) and certain adverbs (6iii), whereas the non-finite verb follows these elements, as is shown by (6) (ii) and (iv). Similar effects can be observed in constructions with quantification at a distance and with floating quantifiers (see Ayoun 1999).

(6) (i) Pierre n'aime pas ce film.
'Pierre does not like this film.'
(ii) Pierre ne veut pas voir ce film.
Pierre NEG wants not to see this film
'Pierre does not want to see this film.'
(iii) Jean voit souvent Marie.
Jean sees often Marie
'Jean often sees Marie.'
(iv) Jean a souvent vu Marie.
'Jean has often seen Marie.'

The important implication of the clustering effect of PPT as well as MP style parameters for the theory of language acquisition is that it entails that learners need to discover only one of the surface properties indicating the correct setting of the parameter for the particular language. The presence of one property ought to have deductive consequences for the emergence of the others. Thus, we might predict that all others should then emerge simultaneously. The interesting consequence of the clustering effect is therefore that it makes an empirically testable claim which allows us to distinguish parameter setting from learning of construction-specific features. In the latter case, the empirical prediction is that the various surface phenomena need to be acquired individually, that is, they will not necessarily emerge simultaneously. No obvious predictions follow for the time course of induction. As a result of triggering, however, the various phenomena related to a specific value of a parameter will appear within the same developmental phase, that is, within a short period of time.

Having dealt with a couple of properties of parameter setting and with some empirically discernible evidence that ought to result from these two types of acquisition processes, we need to consider briefly the consequences of the setting of parameters to one of their values, in other words the question of whether *resetting* of parameters is at all possible. This issue will be of exceptional importance for the study of second language acquisition (see chapter 5, especially 5.2). But why should this be relevant for L1 development? There exist, in fact, two reasons why it might be an issue for L1 studies, too. The first one is that some authors (e.g. Hyams 1986) have argued that parameters, at the initial state of L1 development, should come pre-set to a default value, for example the NSP would initially be set to the [+NS] default. If this were correct, it would be necessary to change the initial setting during subsequent acquisition phases in those cases where the value required by the target grammar differs from the default setting. I will not pursue this discussion because the idea of an initial default setting does not seem to stand up to scrutiny (see Meisel 1995 for a summary of this debate). But even if this suggestion were to be maintained, changing a default setting has been argued to be substantially different from *re*setting of a parameter fixed on one of its values subsequent to exposure to the PLD (see Lebeaux 1988).

The second scenario may offer more serious reasons for considering the possibility of parameter resetting. If L1 children happened to set a parameter incorrectly, how could they retreat from this erroneous choice? Surprisingly, this question is hardly ever discussed in the acquisition literature, but I think that the possibility of setting parameters incorrectly should not be excluded in an a priori fashion. An interesting finding is presented by Müller (1994b), discussing the case of a bilingual (German–French) boy who seems to have set the Verb-Second Parameter to the wrong value in his acquisition of German. What this means is, leaving details aside, that the finite verb is not raised to Comp but to a functional head below CP and the subject to the specifier position of the same functional projection. In this way he succeeds in producing correct surface orders in main clauses. Once he starts using subordinate clauses, however, this results in target deviant verb-second and verb-third patterns. Interestingly, he eventually learns the correct ordering, but he does so for each complementizer separately, in an item-by-item process extending over a period of approximately two years. Using the distinctions discussed above between triggering and induction, Müller's case study provides exactly the features to suggest inductive learning of the properties of the target grammar. The pattern of data observed in this case study contrasts markedly with the rapid developmental changes by the correct parameter setting.

This case already suggests that parameter resetting may not be possible in L1 development. In fact, several authors have offered theoretical as well as empirical arguments indicating that this option should be ruled out for principled reasons (see Clahsen 1991 or Müller 1994b). A first argument which I will not explain in more detail has been presented by Clahsen (1991), who shows that potentially problematic facts can be handled without recurring to resetting. A more constrained theory of language acquisition excluding resetting is thus descriptively adequate, constituting a more parsimonious solution to the developmental problem. More importantly, allowing for parameter resetting inevitably leads to the so-called pendulum problem (Randall 1990). This refers to the possibility of multiple resetting due to ambiguous or conflicting evidence encountered in the data. It is well known that primary data exhibit this kind of ambiguity, and this includes constructions which are analysable as potential triggers (see Valian 1990a, 1990b). Crucially, it is not possible to determine in a principled fashion how and at what point multiple resetting would have to stop. Yet there is no evidence whatsoever suggesting that children constantly reset parameters, not even during a limited time period, and this constitutes, in my opinion, the strongest argument against the possibility of resetting. Not surprisingly, then, we find broad consensus in L1 research that parameter resetting should be excluded as a potential mechanism in L1 development. Initially, both (or all) values of a parameter are available to the child, but once a parameter has been set to a specific value as a result of experience with primary data, this setting cannot be changed any more. In the apparently rare cases where a wrong option has been chosen, target-like constructions emerge in a piecemeal fashion.

Before concluding this brief summary of some central issues of Parameter Theory, I want to add a few comments on the issue relating to the fact that the notion of 'parameter' has undergone significant changes since it was developed in the 1980s. In the preceding section 2.3, I argued that functional elements develop incrementally and that parametric options refer to feature specifications of functional heads. This is in line with the assumption that formal features replace traditional syntactic categories and, in fact, with the spirit of the Minimalist Program, in general. More specifically, we can now state that syntactic parameters relate to uninterpretable features of functional heads, as envisaged in our discussion of the role of functional categories in child grammars. In other words, this concept of parameterized variation refers either to the distribution of these features across functional heads or to the specification of the strength of these features. This implies three possible types of parameterizations:[5]

1. A feature or even a particular functional head need not be instantiated in every grammar.
2. The location of a feature may vary across languages, i.e. a given feature need not be instantiated consistently in the same functional head across grammars.
3. The strength of a feature in a functional head can vary across grammars; this includes the possibility that all formal features are initially weak.

Following this approach, parameter theory retains all the essential characteristics of parameters mentioned above, adopting however a more narrow definition of the notion of parameter than in the Principles and Parameters Theory of the 1980s. Parameterized variation refers to

1. functional heads;
2. a priori grammatical knowledge which can be triggered;
3. a course of acquisition exhibiting
   a. fast and complete acquisition and abrupt changes in language use;
   b. clustering effects, resulting in the simultaneous emergence of superficially unrelated linguistic phenomena during the same developmental phase.

Importantly, these characteristics are all reflected in the data and can therefore be scrutinized by means of empirical analyses. This is not only true of the varying strength of features or the language-specific distribution of features across different functional heads, that is, for points b and c listed above, but also for the temporary non-instantiation of a specific feature or head. To illustrate this by just one example, let us assume that developing grammars initially lack features which ordinarily define crucial properties of Comp. The prediction then is that child language, at this point of development, will not only lack embedded clauses, but also all those main clause word order patterns which depend on movement to CP, for example clause-initial wh-elements, subject–verb inversion and so on. In a study investigating the L1 acquisition of Basque, Barreña (1994) not only confirmed this prediction, he further demonstrated that the various constructions depending on movement to CP emerge simultaneously during a later phase of development, thus providing evidence for a clustering effect in the incremental development of functional layers as well.

Early versions of parameter theory already shared characteristics 2 and 3 with this feature-based approach, but parameters used to be defined much less narrowly. The most crucial change in PPT came about as early as in the 1980s, following the suggestion by Borer (1984) to move the burden of parametric choice from the computational component to the lexicon. Chomsky (1989) picked up on this idea and proposed that 'If substantive elements (verbs, nouns, etc.) are drawn from an invariant universal vocabulary, then only functional elements will be parameterized.' Yet although, to my knowledge, Borer's suggestion did not meet with principled objections, researchers tended to deal with this issue in a somewhat cavalier way and continued to propose parameters not restricted to properties of functional heads. In other words, parameters developed in the PPT model constitute a rather heterogeneous mix as should become obvious by looking at the sample which Atkinson (1992) discussed, for example the Head-Direction Parameter, the Specifier Parameter, the Move-alpha Parameter, the Bounding Node Parameter, the Direction of Case-Marking Parameter and the Direction of Theta-Marking Parameter. A more detailed review would reveal that some of the PPT-style parameters already conform to requirements of more recent theorizing; others can easily be reinterpreted in terms of properties of functional heads, for example the Finiteness (Verb Movement) or the Null-Subject Parameter. But some clearly do not conform to the requirements of a more restrictive parameter theory, for example the Bounding Node Parameter or those referring to directionality. There are good reasons, I believe, to opt for a more strictly defined theory of parameters, and this crucially implies that they should refer exclusively to functional categories (see Meisel 1995). Whether this indeed entails that parameterization does not affect the computational component of the human language faculty but only the lexicon, as proposed by Borer and Chomsky, is still an open question, depending largely on one's interpretation of the term 'lexicon', as is pointed out by Snyder (2007: 160). Snyder (2007: 13) also observes, 'the tendency in the Minimalist literature on comparative syntax . . . to propose PandP-style parameters where needed, albeit with a certain degree of discomfort'. What matters for the ensuing discussion is that not only for PPT-style parameters, but for all parameters it will be necessary to critically scrutinize the cluster of surface properties which allegedly depend on the setting of a parameter to a particular value, even in cases where a reinterpretation of a traditional parameter in terms of properties of functional categories is possible. In some instances, like in the case of the Null-Subject Parameter, the proposed clusters do not seem to be based fully on theoretical deduction but on stipulated prototypicality. Italian, for example, appears to be regarded as a prototypical null-subject language, and this has led to the prediction that all null-subject languages share the six properties listed above, although this does not even seem to be correct for closely related languages like Portuguese or Spanish. It remains to be seen which of these properties can indeed be explained in terms of the feature composition of a functional head, that is, as resulting from the very property which licenses phonetically empty subject positions.

The motivation for these comments on PPT-style parameters is the fact that arguments pro or contra parallels between first and second language acquisition are frequently based on evidence for parameter setting in L2 acquisition. The discussion in the following chapters relies on research carried out over more than thirty years and can therefore not ignore this kind of evidence. It would not be fair and probably not even possible to restrict this debate to MP style parameters. Rather, I intend to consider evidence referring to both types of parameters, focusing however on those which refer to functional categories or which can be reinterpreted in this way.

To conclude this *tour d'horizon* of principles and mechanisms guiding first language development, let me remind you that it is all about grammatical knowledge and about how it is acquired. A description, as comprehensive as possible, of the linguistic objects which children can produce and comprehend marks an important first step in our quest for the LAD, but the ultimate goal is to understand the nature of the knowledge underlying language use and the mechanisms by which it is acquired. As for the latter, research on L1 development suggests that the LAD minimally comprises the following principles and mechanisms which, importantly, can be distinguished by means of empirical analyses:

1. Discovery principles directing learners towards formal properties of linguistic expressions.
2. Inductive learning mechanisms, partly domain-specific in nature.
3. Invariant principles of UG.
4. Parameter setting, as defined above.

The properties identified in this survey as characterizing L1 development will serve as the basis for comparison with L2 acquisition, and since invariant developmental sequences provided us with insights into how the LAD determines language acquisition, chapter 3 will deal with the role of developmental sequences in second language acquisition.

2.5 Suggested readings and topics for discussion

Suggested readings

On milestones of language development and on how to explain them:

Guasti, M. T. 2002. *Language acquisition: The growth of grammar*. Cambridge MA: The MIT Press, pp. 23–53.

Locke, J. L. 1995. 'Development of the capacity for spoken language' in P. Fletcher and B. MacWhinney (eds.), *The handbook of child language*, pp. 278–302. Oxford: Blackwell.

Further aspects of Parameter Theory are discussed by

Meisel, J. M. 1995. 'Parameters in acquisition' in P. Fletcher and B. MacWhinney (eds.), *The handbook of child language*, pp. 10–35. Oxford: Blackwell.

Snyder, W. 2007. *Child language: The parametric approach*. Oxford: Oxford University Press.

Topics for discussion

- In section 2.2 we saw that children focus from very early on on formal characteristics of their ambient languages; this focus enables them to discover properties of the grammars of their languages. The presumably innate mechanism guiding them consists of a set of 'discovery principles', understood as a bootstrapping system rather than a part of UG proper. Gather information on these principles and bootstrapping, referring to textbooks on language acquisition or psycholinguistics. Is it possible to distinguish between different types of such principles? Are these specific to language acquisition?
- In the generative literature, UG is frequently equated with the LAD. In section 2.1 it was argued that such an approach represents too narrow a view of language acquisition and that UG is better seen as the centrepiece of the LAD which, in addition, minimally comprises a set of *discovery principles* bootstrapping the child into the grammatical system (see the preceding paragraph) and *learning mechanisms*

enabling the child to acquire language-specific constructions not constrained by principles of UG. Arguably, the principles and mechanisms of these components of the LAD are all domain-specific in nature, relating to formal properties of human languages. However, language acquisition must draw on broader knowledge sources; the Language Making Capacity must therefore comprise more than the LAD, including domain-general learning principles. What other mechanisms can be attributed to the LMC? (Consult textbooks on language acquisition or psycholinguistics to answer this question.) How do processing mechanisms fit into the picture? What would speak in favour of or against a model according to which the LMC comprises domain-general as well as domain-specific components?

- Functional categories play a crucial role when it comes to explaining the underlying logic of language acquisition, not only in this chapter but throughout the entire volume and, in fact, in much of the literature on language acquisition. As mentioned above, generative studies distinguish between functional (non-denotative) elements and lexical or denotative elements. Similar distinctions were already introduced by traditional grammars, although the defining criteria vary considerably and consequently also the classification of particular categories. Scrutinize a non-generative grammar of your choice for such defining criteria for syntactic categories and contrast them to those given in an introductory textbook to generative syntax. Which categories are classified inconsistently across grammars? Look, for example, at conjunctions, prepositions or postpositions, and inflectional affixes. It has been suggested that some prepositions (postpositions) are functional elements but others are not. Can you provide arguments supporting this claim?
- Many studies of first language development discuss at some length the *continuity assumption*. Frequently, a distinction is made between a 'strong' and a 'weak' version of this assumption, depending on whether all or only some of the grammatical properties of mature grammars are attributed to developing grammars. In section 2.2, I intimated that this is not in line with Pinker's (1984: 6) original proposal, which was that child and adult grammars may be assumed to be identical in nature. This does not necessarily entail that the same set of functional elements are instantiated in each. Try to explicate the notion of continuity as developed in section 2.2 and contrast it with what you find in an introduction (of your choice) to first language acquisition research. Do you consider the different notions to be notational variants of one another or do they reflect distinct epistemological approaches?

3 Obvious (observable) similarities and differences between first and second language acquisition: Developmental sequences

3.1 Observable phenomena

The *tour d'horizon* undertaken in the previous chapter, surveying some core aspects of the human Language Making Capacity, was designed to provide us with the necessary means for formulating the kinds of questions which, when answered adequately, should reveal essential properties of the learners' (transitional) grammatical competence. Although my goal is to discover similarities and differences in first and second language learners' *underlying* knowledge systems, I will begin by examining phenomena which are directly accessible by observation. In a second step, questions will be asked which aim at deeper insights, inquiring whether the observed commonalities reflect common underlying knowledge and whether differences should indeed be explained as reflecting distinct knowledge bases or different mechanisms of language use.

Uniformity has been argued to be a crucial property of L1 development. As far as the developmental chronology of grammatical items and structures is concerned, we see remarkably little variation across individuals. Moreover, children tend to make the same types of 'errors', avoiding other types of deviations from the adult norm which, in principle, might have been expected to occur. Findings of this sort suggest that L1 development is guided by an underlying mechanism shared by all learners, possibly the LAD we are searching for. It is therefore a reasonable research strategy to inquire whether similarly invariant acquisition sequences can be found in L2 acquisition. If learners with different L1 backgrounds proceed through identical sequences when acquiring the same L2, it is plausible to conclude that they too have access to a common underlying acquisition device and that transfer from L1 plays a significantly less important role in second language acquisition than assumed by the Contrastive Analysis approach to L2. The principal issue of our discussion, however, concerns the question of whether first and second language acquisition are guided by identical principles and mechanisms – and these might still be different, even if we concluded that they are the same across different types of L2 learners in a variety of settings. It is therefore necessary to take a further step and compare L1 and L2 acquisition sequences and to ask subsequently whether or not these findings support the hypothesis of a common acquisition device. The goal of the present chapter, in other words, is to examine in some detail acquisition sequences proposed for second language acquisition and to compare them across different L2 learners and with those found in studies investigating first language development.

3.2 Acquisition orders: Grammatical morphemes

The beginning of L2 interlanguage studies, soon after Corder's (1967) programmatic paper claiming at least partial identity of first and second language acquisition, was marked by an extraordinarily successful research paradigm confirming the predicted similarity between these two types of acquisition, the so-called Morpheme Order Studies. These studies, most prominently represented by H. Dulay and M. Burt, were inspired by the research of Roger Brown and his students on first language acquisition.[1]

Brown (1973) found in a longitudinal study with three children (known under the aliases Adam, Eve and Sarah) that grammatical morphemes which are generally omitted in early child utterances emerge in a specific order, leading him to suggest a fixed order of acquisition. A morpheme is considered to be acquired when it is used in an adult-like fashion. In order to decide when this was achieved, a criterion was applied which was first suggested by Cazden (1968). According to this acquisition criterion, a form has been acquired at the time of 'the first speech sample of three, such that in all three the inflection is supplied in at least 90 percent of the contexts in which it is clearly required' (Cazden 1968: 435). Note that the 90% criterion is not motivated by theoretical considerations but rather by empirical findings, because Cazden and Brown observed that once children comply with it, the frequency of use of target-like forms does not drop significantly any more. Based on the findings from each of the children studied by Brown, rank-order correlations among the three orderings were calculated which exhibited a surprising degree of invariance. Brown's ordered list contained fourteen items, including bound as well as free morphemes; see (1).

(1) L1 morpheme acquisition order according to Brown 1973: 274

1. present progressive	*-ing*	8. articles	*a, the*
2. preposition	*in*	9. past regular	*-ed*
3. preposition	*on*	10. 3rd person regular	*-s*
4. plural	*-s*	11. 3rd p. irregular, e.g.	*has*
5. past irregular, e.g.	*went*	12. uncontractible aux	*be*
6. possessive	*-'s*	13. contractible copula	*be*
7. uncontractible copula	*be*	14. contractible aux	*be*

This pattern of acquisition was corroborated in a cross-sectional study by de Villiers and de Villiers (1973) with twenty-one English-speaking children. Two different procedures for ordering the morphemes resulted in high rank order correlations. Similarly high rank order correlations were found when the data of these children were compared to those of Adam, Eve and Sarah. The only major discrepancy was that Brown had found that contracted forms of the copula and of the auxiliary *be* were acquired after the uncontracted ones, whereas de Villiers and de Villiers found the reverse ordering. In spite of the fact that none of these authors could come up with a satisfactory explanation for this divergence and although they also found some variation across individual children in their studies, the commonalities are so overwhelming that we would be missing generalizations if we attributed them to mere chance. There is a consensus that this research has uncovered a crucial property of first language development, namely that the acquisition of a number of grammatical features follows an order which is largely the same across individuals. A plausible inference from this insight is that the underlying mechanisms determining this developmental order are identical across individuals and largely unaffected by external influences. What exactly its nature is remains to be seen. Before examining Brown's ideas concerning this issue, let us first look at second language acquisition.

The L2 Morpheme Order Studies resumed the ideas propagated by Corder (1967), suggesting that second language learners' errors might be essentially similar to those committed by children learning their first language. Looking at these studies, it should, nevertheless, be borne in mind that they were carried out at a time when Contrastive Analysis was still the predominant L2 research paradigm. Consequently, many of the arguments put forth were directed against CA, most importantly against the allegedly overwhelming role of transfer from L1 as *the* crucial explanatory factor in L2 acquisition. As an alternative, Dulay and Burt advocated the L2 = L1 hypothesis according to which an innate 'active mental organization' (Dulay and Burt 1972: 236) of the knowledge about the L2 leads to specific processing strategies resulting in linguistic 'rules' which are then gradually adjusted to those characterizing the target system. The proponents of this approach argued that L2 acquisition is better characterized as resulting from 'creative construction' rather than as habit formation (interference). Dulay and Burt (1972) claimed furthermore that an analysis of learner errors will enable acquisition researchers to arrive at an empirically founded decision on this issue, for the creative construction hypothesis predicts that L2 learners use non-target structures which occur in the speech of children acquiring this language as their mother tongue ('developmental errors'). Habit formation, on the other hand, predicts interference errors, that is, structures not found in L1 acquisition of the target language but reflecting properties of the learner's first language. Dulay and Burt (1973) then scrutinized errors in the speech of 145 Spanish-speaking children between five and eight years of age learning English in the USA. The data had been collected using the 'Bilingual Syntax Measure' (Burt, Dulay and Hernández 1973), designed to elicit natural speech from children. Distinguishing between developmental, interference and so-called 'unique' errors, the latter being those which do not fit into one of the two other categories, they found 85% developmental, 3% interference and 12% unique errors. They concluded that creative construction plays a significantly more important role in L2 acquisition than habit formation (interference).

Perhaps even more importantly, based on data from approximately 250 Spanish- and Chinese-speaking children aged five to eight years, Dulay and Burt (1973, 1974) found a common acquisition order. It included eleven morphemes or 'functors', among which were nine of those studied by Brown (1973), plus 'pronoun case' (*he/him*, *they/them*, *she/her*) and 'long plural' (*houses*). The two authors developed a rather sophisticated methodology allowing them to determine the order of acquisition for the Spanish and the Chinese group of learners as well as for the combined group. As in the work by Brown and his associates, an essential criterion was whether or not a morpheme appeared in the required context. Different scores were assigned, depending on whether no functor (0), the wrong one (1) or the correct one (2) was supplied. In order to level out individual variation, the order of acquisition was computed for learner groups rather than for individuals using various methods of computation (see Dulay, Burt and Krashen 1982: 216 for a detailed discussion of methodological issues). Dulay and Burt (1974) concluded that the order of acquisition was almost identical for Spanish and Chinese children; see (2).

(2) Child L2 morpheme acquisition order according to Dulay and Burt 1974

1. pronoun case	7. past regular
2. articles	8. past irregular
3. present progressive	9. long plural
4. copula	10. possessive
5. plural	11. 3rd person regular
6. auxiliary	

In spite of the fact that the Morpheme Order Studies of the 1970s paid much attention to methodological concerns and adhered to standards more stringent than what was common practice at the time, some of the most serious objections raised against their results focused on methodological issues, for example Rosansky (1976), Andersen (1978a) and Wode *et al.* (1978) (see Long and Sato (1984) for a review of this debate and Dulay, Burt and Krashen (1982) for a reply to some of these criticisms). Ignoring the details of this discussion, the crucial question with respect to our current interests is whether the proposed acquisition orders must be regarded as an artefact of the specific methods of collecting, analysing and interpreting the data. I believe that Larsen-Freeman and Long (1991: 92) are right in concluding:

> In sum, despite admitted limitations in some areas, the morpheme studies provide strong evidence that ILs exhibit common accuracy/acquisition orders.

This is not to say that all objections can safely be discarded. One problem is that the ordering is not equally well motivated for each possible pair of elements within the sequence. Although studies based on different groups of learners, using varying research methodologies, yielded statistically significantly related orders, some orderings turned out to be more robust than others. In addition, assuming that frequency of forms correctly supplied in the required contexts (accuracy order) indeed reflects order of acquisition, the individual items are not equidistant on the assumed chronological hierarchy, that is, some are clustering around almost identical values whereas others exhibit clearly different rankings. In order to capture this fact, Dulay and Burt (1975) and Krashen (1977) grouped several morphemes together proposing what Krashen called a 'natural order' of second language acquisition; see (3). The idea is that all items in an earlier box are acquired before all of those in a later one and, conversely, the acquisition of an element in a later box implies the acquisition of all those displayed in all earlier ones. No claim, however, is made with respect to the order of acquisition of morphemes contained in one and the same box.

(3) Natural order for L2 acquisition; based on Krashen (1977)

present progressive plural copula auxiliary article

past irregular

past regular 3rd person possessive

This order is based on analyses of more data than the one given in (2), above, including studies with adult second language learners of English. The first adult L2 study confirming the order proposed by Dulay and Burt was the one by Bailey, Madden and Krashen (1974), analysing the speech of seventy-three Spanish-speaking and non-Spanish-speaking instructed learners. Larsen-Freeman (1975) examined twenty-four adults from four different L1 backgrounds (Arabic, Spanish, Japanese and Persian); she tested them twice over a six-month period, using different elicitation procedures, both oral and written. Again this revealed similar orders across L1 groups, and although there were differences between reading and writing and some effect for L1, transfer from the first languages could not explain the orders obtained.

As impressive as these results are, even a cursory glance at the orders summarized in (1), (2) and (3) immediately shows that the L2 orders are not the same as those established for L1 learners. Remember that the reason we examined the morpheme studies in some detail was that their authors claimed to have found invariant patterns in the chronology of L2 acquisition, reminding us of invariant developmental patterns in L1 acquisition. The L1 patterns suggested that underlying mechanisms common to all children are guiding first language development. In view of the observed differences between L1 and L2 orders, we are now facing the problem of deciding whether these should be interpreted as indicating that substantially distinct mechanisms underlie first and second language acquisition, or whether one can maintain the claim that an identical Language Making Capacity is accessible in both cases and that these differences should be attributed to additional factors intervening in various types of acquisition. In a more general fashion, this problem was formulated in chapter 1 (see section 1.3); it now emerges with respect to differences in acquisition orders, and it will occupy us again and again throughout the entire volume. It can, in fact, be regarded as the core issue of our discussion.

In formulating this problem, we have returned to the question concerning the mechanisms *underlying* language acquisition, raised at the beginning of this chapter. Note that nothing has been said so far as to what might cause learners to acquire grammatical morphemes in an invariant order, let alone what might determine the specific orders proposed by Brown (1973), Dulay and Burt (1973, 1974), Krashen (1977) and others. As for the L1 order presented in (1), Brown (1973) considered three possible explanatory factors: frequency of use of these forms in the parents' speech, semantic complexity and grammatical complexity. Brown ruled out frequency as a determining factor because he did not find a significant correlation between the rank ordering of frequency averaged across parental pairs and the mean order of acquisition by the children. Brown (1973: 368) as well as de Villiers and de Villiers (1973: 277) agreed, on the other hand, that semantic and grammatical complexity, when combined, do make the correct predictions. However, no adequate theories were available to these authors which explained semantic and grammatical complexity in a satisfactory way. They deplored that no 'general theory of semantic complexity' (Brown 1973: 369) existed; instead, they had to rely on a somewhat ad hoc approach. As for grammatical complexity, it was mainly defined in terms of syntactic transformations, their number and their internal complexity. Again, this was perceived, even at the time, as not satisfactory (Brown 1973: 379); it has indeed proven since to be an unreliable measure, and the transformations invoked have disappeared altogether from grammatical theory. Yet this is not to say that the correlation found between grammatical complexity and the order of acquisition was purely accidental.

At any rate, the differences between first and second language orders cannot be explained adequately in terms of the explanatory factors considered by Brown (1973). Dulay and Burt speculated that because of cognitive maturation, semantic complexity does not represent the same kind of problem for children aged five to eight as it does for younger children. This argument should apply to adult learners as well (see, for example, Bailey, Madden and Krashen 1974: 237). If, according to Brown, only a combination of grammatical and semantic complexity may be expected to determine L1 acquisition, cognitive maturation could perhaps account for the similarities across L2 learners and for the differences between L1 and L2. But this hypothesis remains rather vague, and although Dulay and Burt repeatedly refer to 'universal language processing strategies' as an explanation for the L2 orders, they do not elaborate on the nature of these strategies nor on what exactly their effect might be, other than resulting in omission and overgeneralization of morphemes. Note that *processing* strategies are normally understood as part of a system of language *use* rather than pertaining to the underlying knowledge base or to grammatical competence. All this confirms that the creative construction approach did not succeed in explaining why the morphemes included in these studies appeared in just that order, neither for first nor for second language acquisition. Dulay, Burt and Krashen (1982: 202) arrive, in fact, at a very similar conclusion:

> The L2 acquisition order is somewhat different from the L1 order . . . although not enough work has been done yet to determine the specific reasons underlying the differences. Such a determination would comprise a major contribution to cognitive developmental psychology.

I believe that this is a correct assessment of the situation. In spite of a number of weaknesses in detail, the accuracy/acquisition orders have found enough empirical support to justify further efforts searching to explain them. We should not be content with a description of facts. In chapter 2 we saw that the underlying system guiding L1 language development can be adequately described in grammatical terms. A reasonable approach in our quest for principles and mechanisms determining the underlying logic of these L2 sequences is to explore as well a grammatical explanation of L2 orders. More recent linguistic and psycholinguistic theories offer new and better tools for this job. However, simply relying on new theoretical concepts will not suffice; the acquisition orders themselves need to be re-examined. In the shape in which they appear in (1)–(3), they lump together grammatically and probably also psycholinguistically unrelated features. The first step in any attempt to find a grammatical explanation must be to tease these orders apart, to break them up into grammatically coherent bundles. It remains to be seen whether the thus redefined sequences and a more sophisticated grammatical theory are indeed able to yield more satisfying results.

The idea that sequences should be grammatically motivated has also been advocated by Gregg (1984) and has, in fact, been explored in a number of studies. Following suggestions by Krashen, Madden and Bailey (1975) and by Krashen (1977), Andersen (1978b) distinguished between verbal versus nominal morphemes, on the one hand, and between bound versus free morphemes, on the other, thus arriving at what he called 'natural groupings'. He studied eighty-nine adult learners of English (seventeen to nineteen years of age) in Puerto Rico. His analysis referred to thirteen morphemes, most of them familiar from the sequences given in (1) to (3) above, that is, the copula *be*, auxiliary *be*, progressive *-ing*, past regular and irregular, 3rd person regular *-s*, plural *-s*, possessive *-'s*, and the articles *a* and *the*, here counted separately since they appear in different obligatory contexts. In addition, two contexts for a 'zero article' were counted, that is, cases where Spanish requires the use of an article whereas English leaves the determiner position lexically empty (*Then she goes to_school*) and instances where Spanish also requires a zero form (*He is giving_ food to the animals*). Finally, Andersen added to this list the past participle and the auxiliary *have* which only appeared as '3rd person irregular' in Brown 1973.

In his extremely thorough and detailed analysis, contrasting the results from various methods of calculating rank orderings, Andersen (1978b) was able to show that variation across learner groups as well as across individuals can be reduced to an insignificant minimum if distinct sequences are established, defined in terms of the categorial status (nominal–verbal) and the combinatorial type (bound–free) of the morphemes. This is true for orderings along one dimension, that is nominal–verbal *or* bound–free, as well as for combinations of both, that is verbal-bound, verbal-free, nominal-bound, nominal-free. These results are displayed in (4) and (5); random variation only exists between elements appearing on the same line, for example between past irregular and past regular forms. Moreover, broken down in this fashion, the results of this study also correlate significantly with Krashen's (1977) 'natural order', see (3), and with the results obtained by other studies, for example Bailey, Madden and Krashen (1974) and Larsen-Freeman (1975).[2] Interestingly enough, however, Andersen (1978b) found that these orders differ in important ways from those for first language learners, as becomes evident if one compares them with (1).

(4) Implicational orders of verbal morphemes in L2 acquisition; Andersen (1978b)

free	bound
copula	
auxiliary *be*	progressive
past irregular	past regular
auxiliary *have*	3rd person
	past participle

(5) Implicational orders of nominal morphemes in L2 acquisition; Andersen (1978b)

free	bound
definite article *the*	
indefinite article *a*	plural
zero article	possessive

We may now ask whether we have indeed come closer to a plausible grammatical explanation of accuracy/acquisition orders in L2. Andersen (1978b) stated that these orders do seem to capture acquisition sequences rather than merely reflecting accuracy of use, and he presented further evidence that they do *not* parallel L1 orders. As for the grammatical explanation we are looking for, the bound–free morpheme distinction is not entirely satisfactory. Note that these findings do not show that free morphemes generally precede bound morphemes or that bound morphemes precede free ones in acquisition – a result which might have been explained in terms of perceptual saliency, ease of processing, or some other properties of language use. Instead, what has been demonstrated is that there is an internal order within the two sets of free and bound morphemes, respectively. What determines this order remains a mystery. Differentiating between verbal and nominal functors, however, may get us closer to our goal. It refers to a genuine grammatical classification, and it succeeds at least in disentangling those strings of elements for which neither grammar nor language processing can plausibly establish any relationships, for example between verb suffixes for past tense and possessive constructions of the *N's N* type. But as with the bound–free distinction, it does not establish a logic accounting for the internal orders in the two groups, nor does it make any claims concerning the chronological ordering of the two groups with respect to each other.

An attempt to find such an underlying developmental logic is made by VanPatten (1984). In his analysis, he further differentiates between verbal morphemes and auxiliaries. Although he deals with rank orderings in a more superficial way[3] than Andersen (1978b), he arrives at similar conclusions. He hypothesizes that those morphemes which bear more 'semantic information' or which have the strongest 'communicative impact' will be learned first. Unfortunately, his claims are highly speculative since he provides no theoretical analysis of the semantics of the forms in question, and they rely on *post-hoc* assessments of the morphemes in terms of semantic and communicative importance. This is not to say that an approach of this type could not contribute to a better understanding of the acquisition process. It does not, however, go beyond what Brown (1973) or Dulay and Burt (1974) suggested, concerning semantic complexity, even if communicative aspects are invoked.

Let us return, then, to the search for grammatical explanations, keeping in mind the differentiation of various orderings according to grammatical categories. An obvious way to approach the problem is to reinterpret the role of grammatical morphemes in the light of more recent theoretical developments concerning functional categories. As shown in chapter 2, parameterized principles of UG aim at explaining interlinguistic as well as intralinguistic variation in terms of functional categories. According to the Structure Building Hypothesis, grammatical development in first language acquisition is determined primarily by the accessibility of functional categories and by their internal feature specifications. Aspect, tense, modality, definiteness and number are crucial grammatical concepts related to functional categories, auxiliaries, the copula, tense and aspect affixes, as well as determiners and nominal inflection for case, number and gender count among the morphological means expressing them. In other words, with the possible exception of the prepositions *in* and *on* from Brown's (1973) study, all the morphemes listed in tables (1)–(5) are lexical realizations of functional elements. The obvious question thus is whether their order of acquisition can be explained referring to the functional layers of sentence structure.

This hypothesis is examined by Zobl and Liceras (1994) using these tools supplied by more recent developments in the theory of grammar. Discussing morpheme orders in L1 development, they adopt the Structure Building Hypothesis (see section 2.3 in the preceding chapter). Assuming structures like (6) and (7) leads them to predict 'category-specific development' and, more specifically, that elements related to DP should appear before those related to IP (or TP).

(6)

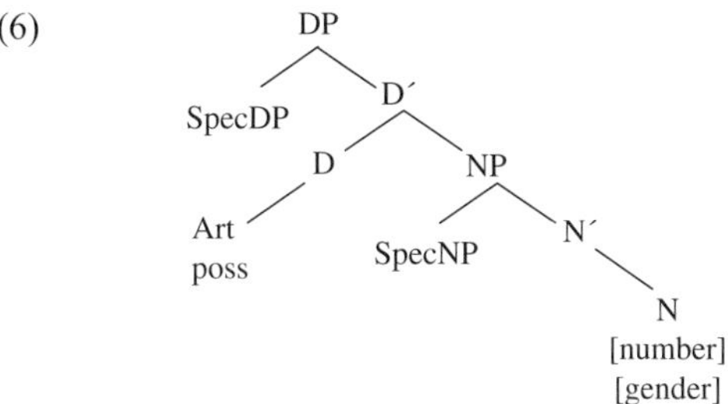

(7)

IP
SpecIP
I′
I
[tense]
[agr]
VP
DP
V′
V
DP

They believe this to be confirmed by the fact that articles and the possessive *'s*, under their analysis both instantiations of the head of DP, cluster together in the orders given by Brown (1973) and de Villiers and de Villiers (1973). Unfortunately, they do not elaborate on the role of the plural *-s*, the other nominal element. It can be argued, however, that [number] is an inherent feature of nouns (Müller 1994a). To be precise, it is a value on the feature [count]; as such it can be considered to be an interpretable feature in terms of more recent theorizing. Note that an uninterpretable feature [number] exists too, that is, when number is marked on the determiner, as for example in French *le*, *les*. In other words, distinguishing between interpretable and uninterpretable features, the plural *-s* under discussion may be said to encode overtly the former type and should be expected to appear in children's speech before the emergence of uninterpretable ones. Concerning verbal elements, the analysis adopted by Zobl and Liceras (1994) claims that auxiliaries as well as the copula are generated in V and raise to INFL where tense and agreement features are base-generated, whereas in English these features are said to be lowered with main verbs which do not raise to INFL. The use of all these elements thus depends on the accessibility of INFL and, consequently, they should be developmentally related. Zobl and Liceras find that this is indeed the case – with the exception of irregular forms (e.g. *has*) which they treat as instances of 'lexical learning'. The one clearly problematic fact is the early emergence of progressive *-ing*, chronologically preceding the nominal elements and separated from all other verbal elements. Zobl and Liceras (1994) surmise that, similarly to the plural marker on nouns, *-ing* is attached in the lexicon, as opposed to being the result of a syntactic process like, for example, 3rd person agreement. They further speculate about explanations for the internal order of INFL-related morphemes, suggesting, for instance, that if an element needs to be moved to a functional position, this might contribute to later acquisition, particularly affix-lowering in English, a grammatically and typologically marked option requiring 'greater representational strength' (1994: 66) which is furthermore believed to cause accessibility difficulty in language processing. I do not want to dwell any further on this issue for it involves a complex argument which would have to be re-examined in the light of more recent grammatical theorizing. Moreover, I believe that it is neither totally convincing nor entirely successful. It cannot, for example, account for the fact that the copula and the auxiliary *be* are developmentally separated.

In my view the most important result of this study, and certainly the one for which the strongest evidence is given, concerns the differences between first and second language acquisition, thus confirming the analysis performed by Andersen (1978b). The main point is that the 'category-specific development' observed in L1 does not hold for L2 acquisition. Instead, the authors find 'cross-categorical development of both the functional categories and their affixal exponents' (Zobl and Liceras 1994: 62). This, they contend, results from the fact that, in L2, functional projections are available from the beginning. In other words, they support the hypothesis according to which grammatical knowledge about sentence structure is transferred from the first language, thus making functional projections accessible to the L2 learner from the start. I will deal with this issue in some detail in section 4.2 of the following chapter. The empirical consequences of this assumption, in the present context, are that morphemes dependent on different functional categories appear more or less simultaneously whereas others related to the same functional domain are scattered over the acquisition sequence; compare Krashen's order given in (3), above. Articles, for example, cluster with auxiliaries, but the possessive *'s* comes in much later, together with 3rd person regular and regular past morphemes. The auxiliary *be*, on the other hand, is quite distant from the latter two, as opposed to the order in L1 where the three cluster together.

If L2 orders cannot be explained in terms of the development of functional projections, how are they to be accounted for? Zobl and Liceras (1994) suggested that the free–bound morpheme distinction can do this job. This may come as a surprise, given that in Andersen's (1978b) study this distinction could not explain the internal order of verbal or nominal morphemes. The difference is due to the fact that Zobl and Liceras distinguish in their analysis between syntactic inflections like 3rd person *-s* and lexical ones like plural *-s* or progressive *-ing*, and their explanation is not intended to extend to the latter. That just these appear at the very top of the L2 order is remarkable in itself and appears to indicate that the functional–lexical distinction does play a role in determining the course of L2 acquisition even if functional categories are indeed accessible to L2 learners from very early on.[4] Zobl and Liceras (1994: 73) specify that it is not the free–bound distinction alone which explains the L2 order. When it comes to bound morphemes, movement is again seen as contributing to acquisition difficulty. Consequently, bound verbal and nominal affixes requiring movement are ordered last, that is, possessive *-s*, 3rd person *-s* and past regular *-ed*.

To sum up, the various types of Morpheme Order Studies have been successful in uncovering significant commonalities across individual learners as well as across learner groups. However, in order to be able to interpret the common acquisition order, it has been necessary to split it up into several ordered sequences. This revealed important differences between first language acquisition, on the one hand, and child and adult second language acquisition on the other. In L1 acquisition, the order of acquisition of morphemes can be explained by distinguishing between elements learned as lexical items as opposed to those dependent on the accessibility of functional categories. The order of acquisition of the latter can then be accounted for in terms of incremental development of functional elements. As for second language acquisition, the lexical–functional distinction again appears to be relevant. But here the order of acquisition of elements related to functional categories does not seem to follow an underlying logic determined by internal properties of functional heads or by their layering in sentence structures – possibly because they are already available at the beginning of L2 acquisition rather than becoming accessible successively as in L1 development. The bound–free distinction, on the other hand, is apparently relevant in second but not in first language acquisition, an observation also made by Wode (1978).

One important finding of the various Morpheme Order Studies which should not be underestimated in spite of the difficulties in uncovering the causal factors of the acquisition sequences is the fact that transfer from the learners' first language clearly plays a minimal role in all of this. It has been demonstrated beyond any reasonable doubt that child as well as adult learners of a particular L2 proceed through identical sequences, irrespective of their different L1 backgrounds. The proponents of the Morpheme Order Studies justly concluded that the important role attributed to L1 transfer by studies carried out in the framework of Contrastive Analysis was clearly not corroborated by empirical facts. I will return to this issue in section 4.3.

3.3 Developmental sequences: The syntax of negation

The discovery of ordered sequences in first and second language acquisition is beyond any doubt a particularly significant contribution to the theory of language development. Yet in order to be able to assess its relevance for the nature of the underlying grammatical knowledge base of learners, it would be useful to define the notion of 'sequence' more precisely and to test it against a broader range of evidence, that is, other than the emergence of particular morphemes and from target languages other than English.

Let us begin by reconsidering the notion 'sequence' which was introduced informally in section 2.2, and let me start with some methodological considerations. In the preceding section I mentioned that the Morpheme Order Studies have been criticized on methodological grounds. Most of these criticisms proved not to undermine the overall pattern of the orders but were directed rather at the position of individual items in an order. Serious doubts were also raised against interpreting 'accuracy order' as 'order of acquisition'. It is to this criticism that I briefly want to return.

One issue on which many researchers appear to agree is that, at least for second language acquisition, the criterion of 'correctly supplied in obligatory contexts' is fallacious. If, for example, learners use a form systematically, including contexts where it is not acceptable in the target language, or if they consistently omit forms, including contexts where the target norm requires omission, applying this criterion would result in crediting them with a kind of grammatical knowledge which they do not actually possess. In other words, overuse as well as avoidance strategies would be misinterpreted (see Long and Sato 1984: 259 for a discussion of these and related issues). A similar point is made by Wode, Bahns, Bedey and Frank (1978) who argue that this kind of analysis leads to a misinterpretation of rote-learned forms, counting them as evidence for rule-governed knowledge although they are in fact instances of lexical learning. Phrasing it in a more principled fashion, one can say that it is of essential importance to distinguish between the acquisition of grammatical concepts and the learning of the inventory of forms required to express these. To mention one example, it is one thing to know that the finite verb agrees with its subject, but it is an entirely different matter to learn the entire set of verbal suffixes encoding subject–verb agreement in a language with a rich inflectional system. Brown (1973: 372) already touched upon this issue, but he did not draw consequences concerning the 90% criterion in L1 studies. There are, in fact, a number of reasons to believe that the omission of elements which are obligatory in the target language does not necessarily indicate a lack of knowledge on behalf of the learner. Omissions may, instead, result from processing limitations if, for example, a given construction has been acquired but is still difficult to use (see Meisel, Clahsen and Pienemann 1981). Considerations of this type led, later on, to the formulation of the Missing Surface Inflection Hypothesis (MSIH) (see Haznedar and Schwartz 1997, Lardiere and Schwartz 1997, Lardiere 1998a or Prévost and White 2000a, 2000b).

All this really only confirms the well-known fact that performance does not simply mirror competence. Although this represents by no means a new insight, it must lead to a reconsideration of how we want to understand 'correctly supplied'. Note that neither Cazden (1968) nor Brown (1973) required a form to be used correctly in 100% of contexts, and recall that the 90% criterion was motivated empirically, not theoretically. Dulay and Burt adopted this criterion, but it soon became apparent that learners who have clearly acquired L2 grammatical knowledge frequently fail to reach this level of accuracy in their L2 speech production. As a consequence, some authors (e.g. Cazden, Cancino, Rosansky and Schumann 1975: 42 and Andersen 1978b) suggested an 80% criterion for L2 acquisition – a modification which may be intuitively plausible but which lacks not only theoretical justification but also the kind of empirical support which had been adduced for the 90% level in L1 studies. Manipulating the criterion in this way actually leads to significantly different interpretations of one's empirical findings. J. D. Brown (1983: 32), for example, showed that at a 60% level the entire list of morphemes (twelve in his case) proves to be valid. He also demonstrates that accuracy varies over time, and he argues convincingly that there is no reason to assume that the acquisition rate should be the same for each morpheme. Consequently, cross-sectional studies at various points of development will result in different accuracy orders. The same point was made by Meisel *et al.* (1981: 113) who showed that structures which appear early in learners' speech may continue to be used for an extended period of time at a low level of accuracy whereas others emerge late but are used correctly from the first occurrence onwards.

Problems like the ones just mentioned have led researchers to display their findings in such a way as to give the percentages of usage in the contexts required by the target language, rather than as a binary option *acquired: yes/no*. The advantage of this procedure is that it reveals the variability of use and is thus more likely to capture the process of acquisition rather than merely focusing on its result, a point strongly advocated by Wode *et al.* (1978). These authors further suggest not limiting one's attention to 'correct' usage. If, for example, learners supply a plural form /s/ where English requires /z/, they nevertheless give evidence of having acquired plural markings. Note, however, that by proceeding in this fashion we have not yet solved our problem, for the question remains as to what percentage of usage indicates successful learning. The difficulty is best illustrated by asking how to interpret low percentages of usage, for example at a 20% to 30% level. If one eliminates rote-learned forms, one may plausibly argue that even such low levels of accuracy must be understood as indicating that the learners have acquired grammatical knowledge, for otherwise it would remain mysterious how they could have succeeded in using the structure in question at all. Rather than ignoring these 20% to 30% of uses, one must ask why the learners do not do better in putting their acquired knowledge to use. This question is pursued in some detail in Meisel *et al.* 1981, who argue that low levels of accuracy indeed reflect difficulty of use rather than lack of knowledge. Nevertheless, the issue of when an item or a structure may be considered to have been acquired remains controversial, and a generally accepted solution has not yet been found. Perhaps the most critical aspect of the procedure just outlined is that by abandoning the 90% criterion, a non-arbitrary quantitative criterion is not available any more, and accepting low frequencies of use carries the risk of crediting learners with more knowledge than they actually possess. But we do have a powerful and, it seems, reliable instrument which can safeguard against such risks, namely implicational scales (see Hyltenstam 1977, Andersen 1978b, Meisel *et al.* 1981, among others).

The idea is that forms and structures which are claimed to have been acquired and which are part of a developmental sequence can be plotted on an implicational scale of the form A ⊃ B ⊃ C ⊃ D ⊃ E ⊃ F ⊃ . . . Z. That is, if learners have acquired C, they have also acquired D, E, F and so forth, but not A or B. In other words, if a developmental sequence is defined in terms of implicationally ordered grammatical phenomena and if the implicational relationship holds in spite of low frequency of use of some of these phenomena, this constitutes strong empirical evidence in support of the claim that these forms or structures are indeed acquired in a strictly ordered fashion.

In what follows, the term 'developmental sequences' will thus be understood as referring to a sequence of grammatically related and chronologically strictly ordered phases or stages (see Felix 1982). Each of these steps is defined in terms of (one or more) grammatical properties which have been acquired during the period in question. A feature can be said to be acquired when it is used productively, that is, if it appears more regularly than by chance, provided it is not restricted to specific linguistic or situational contexts and so on. I will dispense with any sort of precise quantitative criterion of acquisition since this would have to be an arbitrary choice anyway. There has also been some debate concerning the terms 'stage' and 'phase', but I believe that this is a terminological quarrel which we do not have to engage in. Both terms seem to be acceptable, but since linguistic properties characterizing one specific step do not necessarily disappear when a learner proceeds to the next, I prefer the term 'phase', which seems to convey this gradual transition. Finally, concerning the strict ordering of the phases of a sequence, learners are predicted not to violate the ordering established by the sequence, but a particular phenomenon may not appear at all in the speech of some learners. This interpretation of strict ordering is claimed to be the psycholinguistic correlate of implicational scales.

In short, having summarized the discussion on the emergence in a fixed but apparently unmotivated order of grammatical morphemes correctly supplied in obligatory contexts and having presented strictly ordered acquisition sequences of grammatically related phenomena, it is perhaps time to move on from the by now all too familiar set of morphemes to another grammatical domain. This might allow us to gain further insights concerning the problem of which parallels and differences between first and second language acquisition one is likely to discover. The syntax of negation is an obvious candidate. Not only is this a grammatically coherent and adequately limited structural problem space, it also represents a reasonably well-studied phenomenon for first and second language acquisition and for a number of target languages. Before discussing problems relating to the acquisition of the grammatical knowledge required for the production of such constructions, we should have a brief look at how the syntax of negation is handled by grammatical theory and how it is instantiated in the grammars of French, German and Spanish, the languages for which I will then present some acquisition data.

Focusing on clausal negation, we are mainly concerned with the syntactic status and structural position of the negative element (NEG). Dahl (1979), in a typological survey of 240 languages from forty different families, found that NEG can be (a) an independent syntactic element, frequently an adverbial, (b) a verbal affix or (c) an auxiliary. Some languages require the use of double negation, for example Standard French[5] *ne – pas*; the clitic *ne* may be regarded as belonging to the b-type. With respect to the position of NEG, the crucial observation is that there is a strong tendency to place it next to the finite verb. In French the positions of both negative elements are strictly fixed, *ne* preceding the finite verb to which it is cliticized and *pas* following the finite element, usually appearing adjacent to it.

(8) Il (N') *a* PAS servi le millésime à son amie.
'He has not served the vintage (champagne) to his friend.'

German is an SOV language (see sections 1.2 and 2.2), but only the non-finite verb in main clauses occupies the final position. The finite verb appears in the second position of the main clause. In subordinate clauses, all verbal elements are placed clause-finally, the finite part following the non-finite one ($V_{inf}V_{fin}$).

(9) (i) In diesem Jahr *muss* die Oktobersonne den Riesling retten.
'This year the October sun must rescue the Riesling.'
(ii) Man weiß, dass der junge Wein im November kommen *wird*.
'It is known that the young wine will arrive in November.'

In main clauses, the negative expression *nicht* follows the finite verb and precedes the non-finite verbal element. Its unmarked position is indicated by 2 in examples (10) and (11), immediately before the non-finite verb; it can also precede the direct object, as indicated by 1, but the preferred reading for this construction is to interpret as an instance of constituent negation. In subordinate clauses NEG precedes both verbal elements, as in (11). What is remarkable is that in all these cases NEG is normally not adjacent to the finite verbal element.

1 2
(10) Er *hat* seinem Freund (NICHT) den Champagner (NICHT) angeboten.
'He has not offered the champagne to his friend.'

1 2
(11) ... dass er seinem Freund (NICHT) den Champagner (NICHT) angeboten *hat*
'... that he has not offered the champagne to his friend'

Let us now see how these facts can be captured in structural descriptions. Following Pollock (1989), NEG is interpreted as a functional category projecting to NEGP. The structural position of this phrase is controversial, but we may assume that, in Romance and Germanic languages, it immediately dominates VP, as proposed by Ouhalla (1991) and Déprez and Pierce (1993).

(12) Standard French

```
CP
├─ SpecCP
└─ C′
   ├─ C [+WH]
   └─ TP
      ├─ SpecTP
      └─ T′
         ├─ T [+F]
         └─ NEGP
            ├─ SpecNEGP
            └─ NEG′
               ├─ NEG
               │  └─ ne
               └─ VP
                  ├─ pas
                  └─ VP
                     ├─ DP
                     └─ V′
                        ├─ V
                        └─ DP
```

(12) is a simplified version of a negative structure in French. The subject is generated in SpecVP position and has to move to SpecTP; the finite verb first raises to NEG and [NEG +V] subsequently to T, that is, *ne* raises together with the finite verb.

In languages like Spanish the negator *no* occupies the same position as French *ne*, and the same analysis applies, that is, the negator is cliticized to the finite verb and moves to T. These languages differ from Standard French in that they do not require an element corresponding to French *pas*. The syntactic status of *pas* is, in fact, also a controversial issue. (12) follows Zanuttini (1989) treating it as an adverbial expression adjoined to the phrase dominated by NEGP. What matters for the present purposes is that *pas* does not move whereas [*ne*+Vfin] is raised to T, and all authors seem to agree on this point, thus accounting for the fact that the finite verb always precedes *pas* in surface order, and the non-finite verb as well as the object follow *pas*. Colloquial French differs from Standard French in that the head of NEGP can be lexically empty.

One of the major structural differences between German and the Romance languages is that most categories in German are head-final. What further differentiates them is the fact that the German finite verb is raised to COMP where it occupies the second position (V2 effect) since a maximal projection (the subject, an object or an adverbial) must raise to SpecCP. Both properties are shown in (13); the operator [+F] in (12) and (13) marks the position where the finite verb is moved to. Note that *nicht* shares important properties with French *pas* and may also be analysed as being adjoined to VP. Let us now see how one can define the acquisition tasks of the child acquiring the syntax of negative constructions. The crucial problem appears to be the option of analysing NEG as the head of a NEGP as opposed to NEG as a maximal projection. All other tasks are not, in fact, directly related to negation but to the implementation of several layers of functional categories above VP and to their head-first/head-last directionality.

(13) German

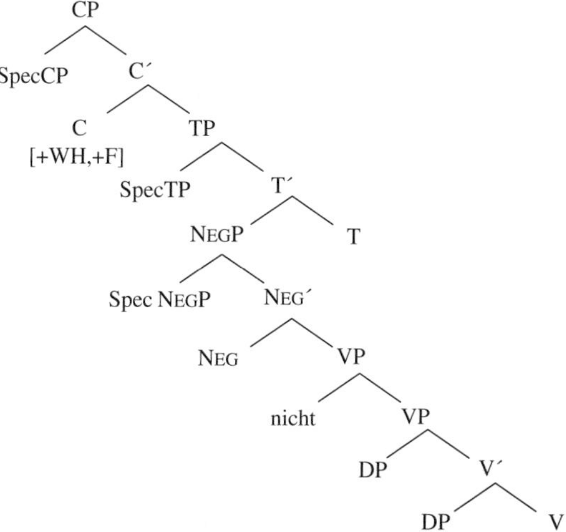

Using the approach advocated in chapter 2 (2.3), our assumption is that children's initial sentence structures either lack some of the functional categories of the target grammar, or functional heads lack part of their features, or the strength of these features is not yet specified. The initial structure might thus consist of a VP dominated by an underspecified functional projection, FP. Consequently, only once the target functional layers are established will the German finite verb rise to COMP, going through the head of NEGP. If NEG is a head, it forms a unit with the finite element, and both are moved together. If NEG is a maximal projection and the head of NEGP is empty, the negator stays behind and appears in postverbal position in surface sequencing. We thus expect to find that, initially, NEG is adjoined to VP. As soon as the verb is raised out of VP, the option between NEG as a head or as a non-head becomes relevant. It is unlikely, however, that this will constitute a major problem, for the data providing the necessary evidence are salient and are frequently encountered in the input. In other words, once the [±finite] distinction is available, triggering verb movement, the syntax of negative constructions should not cause acquisition problems. A brief look at some empirical findings will show to what extent these expectations are met.

At least for English and some other Indo-European languages, the relevant facts have been known since the classic studies by Klima and Bellugi (1966) and McNeill and McNeill (1968). Based on these and some further investigations, Wode (1977: 100) suggested three universal stages in the development of negative structures which can be summarized as in (14). Since our focus lies on syntactic problems, one word negation, anaphoric negation and the choice of the adequate lexical item are less relevant for the present discussion. The crucial point is that at stage II, when negative multi-word utterances emerge, the negator appears in external position.

(14) Developmental sequence of negation in L1

I. One word negation	*no, nein, non*, etc.
II. Multi-word negation	NEG placed in external position
IIa. Anaphoric negation	NEG in utterance-initial position
IIb. Non-anaphoric negation	NEG usually in utterance-initial, occasionally in final position
III. Clause-internal negation	

Subsequent research dealing with these and other languages confirmed this developmental pattern. The acquisition of negation in French has been studied by Pierce (1992), Déprez and Pierce (1993) and Meisel (1997a), among others. As expected, NEG first appears in external position. Note that this is almost exclusively *pas*, mostly in final position; *ne* is never attested during the period examined here, and anaphoric *non* appears only in some isolated examples, also in final position. In addition, Déprez and Pierce (1993) find some utterances with *pas* in initial position, and, as was to be expected, it precedes the subject in such cases, and the verb is always non-finite. This is good evidence in support of the claim that during this developmental phase, NEG is adjoined to the VP containing the subject which is not yet raised to SpecTP. With respect to subsequent clause-internal placement of NEG, all authors agree that French children almost never place finite verbs incorrectly after *pas* or non-finite verbs before *pas*. In other words, as soon as there is evidence that child grammars distinguish between finite and non-finite elements, the finite verb rises to TENSE and precedes *pas* which, in turn, precedes the non-finite verb. The development of the syntax of negation in German has been studied by, among others, Wode (1977), Park (1979), Clahsen (1983, 1988a), Mills (1985) and Meisel (1997a). Once again, one finds that NEG is first placed externally. *Nein*, the element reserved for anaphoric use in the adult language, occasionally appears in non-anaphoric function, in first as well as in last position. When preposed, it precedes the subject, thus confirming the hypothesis which claims that NEG is adjoined to the VP containing the subject. *Nicht*, on the other hand, is placed almost exclusively in final position. As in the other languages reported on, the emergence of clause-internal negation coincides with that of the [±finite] distinction and verb movement. *Nicht* now always follows the finite and precedes the non-finite verb. The same results are obtained in studies of Spanish (see, e.g., Pierce 1992 and Meisel 1994b) and Basque, a non-Indo-European language (Meisel 1994b), to mention just these two examples.

In sum, then, child language data from different languages confirm the hypothesis that NEG is initially placed externally. Structural analyses support the claim that it is adjoined to the VP containing the subject. It may appear to the left or to the right of the VP, but one can observe a strong preference for the position favoured by the adult target language. As soon as one finds evidence for a productive use of finite forms, NEG is placed clause-internally. This indicates that subjects as well as finite verbs have been raised to their appropriate positions in a functional projection. In those languages where NEG is generated in the head of NEGP, it is raised together with the verb. In other words, the option of analysing NEG as a functional head or as a maximal projection adjoined to VP does not appear to represent a problem for the child. One can, indeed, argue that, besides the fact that NEG may have to be cliticized to the finite verb, the syntax of negation merely consists in the implementation of NEGP into the phrase structure. This explains why the acquisition of sentence negation happens fast and virtually without errors in the languages studied so far, in spite of the fact that the surface properties of negative constructions in these languages differ significantly.

The question to be asked now is whether second language learners succeed equally well in acquiring negative constructions. At the beginning of the 1980s, negation was perhaps the most frequently studied feature of second language learners' interlanguage. The overwhelming majority of these studies, however, focused on English as a target language (e.g. Ravem 1968; Milon 1974; Cazden *et al.* 1975; Cancino, Rosansky and Schumann 1978; Stauble 1978; Schumann 1979). In spite of disagreement in detail, there was consensus in assuming that learners follow an invariant acquisition sequence. Most authors also agreed that the same sequence holds for child and adult L2 learners (for summaries of the research of this period, see Schumann 1979 and Wode 1976, 1981). The sequence suggested by these studies can be summarized as in (15).

(15) Acquisition sequence of negation in L2 English

I. Anaphoric negation	*no*
II. Non-anaphoric external negation	NEG+Adj/V(P)/N(P)
III. Internal negation	
IIIa. NEG preposed with main verbs	X+*no/not/don't*+V(P)
IIIb. NEG postposed with auxiliaries	X+copula/aux+*no*+Y
IV. Target-like negation	restructuring of unanalysed forms, *do* auxiliary

All authors seem to agree that NEG is initially placed preverbally and that target-like constructions are first used with auxiliaries and the copula. The question, however, is how to explain this sequence. As for the preposing of NEG, one might suspect that it is the result of transfer from L1, since Spanish, the first language of many of the learners studied, requires this order. Transfer, however, becomes less plausible in view of the fact that Milon (1974) and Stauble (1984) obtained similar results with Japanese learners of English, although in Japanese NEG follows the verb. The same observation holds for the Norwegian child learning English, studied by Ravem (1968), since in Norwegian, too, NEG follows the verb. Wode (1976), however, did find some examples at stage III where German children acquiring L2 English placed NEG in postverbal position as in (16), suggesting that the L1 might play a limited role, after all. But he concluded that transfer was not the only and probably not the best explanation, and that these constructions could not be interpreted as evidence against the sequence given in (15). Hyltenstam (1977, 1978), furthermore, postulated roughly the same acquisition sequence, having analysed the speech of learners of Swedish with thirty-five different first languages. Given that NEG in Swedish, much like in Norwegian or German, is placed after the finite verb, this suggests that preposing of NEG cannot be explained satisfactorily as transfer from the learners' L1.

(16) John go not to the school.

Alternatively, one could hypothesize that L2 learners proceed similarly as L1 children in that verbs are initially not raised out of VP (see Tomaselli and Schwartz 1990). Although this does not explain why NEG preposing should be preferred over postposing, it might account for the post-auxiliary position of NEG, assuming that auxiliaries and the copula are base generated in TENSE, and NEG remains in its position adjoined to VP. But such an approach, too, runs into serious problems given that learners who seem to have acquired tensed forms continue to use *no*+V (see, e.g., Milon 1974). Clearly, the strong connection between finiteness and verb movement, amply documented for first language development, does not hold for second language acquisition.

We are, in other words, again left without a satisfactory explanation for the observed sequences. Hoping to shed some more light on this problem, let us now look at the L2 acquisition of two other languages, French and German, both placing NEG after the finite verb in surface sequencing, as opposed to the learners' first languages, Spanish, Italian and Portuguese, which require preposing of NEG to the finite element.

The L2 acquisition of negation in French by adult Spanish-speaking learners has been studied by Noyau (1982), Trévise and Noyau (1984) and Meisel (1997b), among others. Based on their use of negators, the learners studied by Noyau and Trévise can be grouped as in (17). The expression listed first for each group is the one used most frequently, the items put in brackets only occur in a few isolated examples.

(17) Learner groups according to French L2 negation

Group	Negation
I	ne_pas, ne_, (_pas)
II	ne_pas, _pas, (ne_)
III	_pas, ne_pas

Preposed *ne_* in the speech of learners of groups I and II is certainly the most surprising finding here, given that it is used infrequently in Colloquial French. One would have expected *pas* to appear in its place, but *pas* in preverbal position is actually attested only once in this corpus. The question then is whether *ne_* exemplifies the early phase of L2 acquisition during which NEG appears in initial position. This, however, is rather unlikely, for the group I learners studied by Trévise and Noyau (1984) are, in fact, not beginners. The most plausible hypothesis seems to be that their use of *ne_* is induced by language teaching and is then further stimulated by perceived similarities between the L1 and the L2. In fact, all learners of groups II and III had received French language instruction (see Meisel 1997b for a discussion of this problem).

In order to be able to decide on the question of whether there is a phase during which NEG is placed preverbally or in a position preceding the VP, we need evidence from the period of first contact with the target language, preferably based on longitudinal data. For L2 French, such data are indeed available (see Perdue 1993a, 1993b). Surprisingly, an analysis of two of the learners in this corpus (Meisel 1997b) does not find evidence to support an early phase of NEG preposing. Only *non* is placed sentence-initially, but in the overwhelming majority of cases these are instances of anaphoric negation. *Pas* is placed postverbally, from the first occurrence onwards, but it initially only appears in formulaic expressions like *je ne sais pas* 'I don't know'. By the time *(ne)_pas* is used with a number of different verbs, its usage corresponds to that of Colloquial French. Notice that one learner never reaches this phase, and it takes the other one twenty-three months to get there. One might add that *pas* IS preposed when negating a constituent, as required by the target norm. Note also that no occurrence of preverbal *ne_* is attested here.

In sum, longitudinal French L2 data do not support the claim that second language learners invariantly go through an early phase of L2 acquisition during which NEG appears in initial position in clausal negation. This is all the more surprising in the case of Spanish-speaking learners, because transfer from L1 should enhance the use of this hypothesized interlanguage construction. As for the relation between verb movement and NEG placement, neither of the two learners, over the entire period of observation, uses finiteness productively. As a consequence, the position of the finite verb before *pas* can hardly be explained as the result of movement of finite elements. This confirms the observation based on English L2 data that the correlation between finiteness and NEG placement found in L1 does not hold for second language learners.

The acquisition of negation in German, in a setting similar to that of the learners of French discussed here, has been studied in the ZISA[6] research project, combining a cross-sectional and a longitudinal study. The results of the cross-sectional part are summarized by Clahsen, Meisel and Pienemann (1983). The interpretation of the findings of this study was guided by the multi-dimensional model of second language acquisition developed by Meisel, Clahsen and Pienemann (1981). According to this model, one needs to distinguish between a developmental dimension defining the invariant sequence through which all learners of a specific L2 proceed as they approach the target system, and a dimension of variability characterizing the variation space explored by different types of learners using the L2 knowledge available at a given point of development. From this it follows that not every linguistic feature in which learners' interlanguages differ can automatically be interpreted as characterizing a phase of L2 acquisition; it might rather indicate a difference in use between learner types, possibly even during one and the same acquisition phase.

As for the syntax of negation, the question thus is whether an acquisition sequence like the one given in (15) indeed captures a developmental pattern rather than learner type-specific language use. A first answer is proposed in the ZISA cross-sectional study where it is shown that, at any given point of development, learners do not consistently use the same kind of negative construction, that is, they place NEG before the verb or in standard-like postverbal position, and some even use both constructions. Clahsen, Meisel and Pienemann (1983: 148) argue therefore that the use of preverbal negation characterizes a specific type of learner rather than a phase of L2 acquisition. Learners of this type commonly resort to a strategy of language use which consists in placing the negator immediately before the element to be negated, in constituent as well as in phrasal negation (see Meisel 1983a). The answer to our question about the nature of the sequence (15) thus is that it conflates properties of the developmental and of the learner-specific dimension of L2 acquisition. Preverbal negation is indeed used most frequently during early phases when L2 knowledge is limited and successful communication may depend on the availability of simple linguistic patterns. But the fact that some learners never resort to such means and others continue to do so during late acquisition phases suggests that preverbal negation is not properly defined in terms of grammatical development alone and, conversely, it does not define a 'universal' phase of L2 acquisition.

A brief look at longitudinal data, in this case from three of the learners of the ZISA study (Italian, Portuguese and Spanish, respectively), should again help us to evaluate the claims based on cross-sectional data (for details, see Meisel 1997b). It reveals considerable variation among the learners and speaks against an initial universal phase of preverbal NEG placement. The Spanish learner, for example, strongly favours postverbal negation right from the beginning and during the entire sixteen-month period of her stay in Germany. One merely finds a few isolated examples where NEG precedes non-finite verb forms and a single one where she places NEG before a modal. The Italian learner, on the other hand, places NEG pre- and postverbally, but preverbal placement is the clearly dominant pattern, especially during the first months of his stay in Germany; note that this usage includes preposing of NEG to finite verbs and to modals. Later on, NEG is sometimes postposed after modals and finite verb forms. The Portuguese learner initially also both preposes and postposes the negative element, with non-finite as well as with finite verb forms, but finite forms undoubtedly do not express finiteness yet. Soon, however, postposition becomes more frequent, but this is again true for non-finite verb forms as well as for finite ones. It appears, thus, that postverbal placement of NEG is acquired independently of finiteness.

To conclude, one can say that the L2 developmental sequence proposed for the syntax of negation essentially predicts that NEG is initially placed preverbally and that postverbal placement, if required by the target system, is first acquired with auxiliaries and the copula. Satisfactory explanations for why NEG should first appear preverbally, however, are difficult to find. The solution proposed by some authors is to postulate some universal mechanism (e.g. Schumann 1978 and Wode 1981), allowing learners to resort to 'simplified' structures. An examination of data from longitudinal studies and from languages other than English revealed, however, that learners do not invariantly go through an initial phase of NEG preposing – in spite of the fact that the negator does precede auxiliaries as well as main verbs in the first languages of these learners. The explanation suggested here is that the use of preverbal negation characterizes a specific type of learner, rather than an early phase of L2 acquisition. A further finding of crucial importance for our research interests is that the acquisition of NEG placement is independent of the acquisition of finiteness. Some learners, at least, use French and German postverbal negation well before they begin to acquire target-like tense and agreement markings on verbs. Occasionally, the negator even precedes modals and the copula. This, in turn, shows that although the target-like postposition of negators may first emerge with the copula and with auxiliaries, as observed by Hyltenstam (1977) and others, it does not indicate that finiteness and the placement of the negator are developmentally related as in L1 acquisition.[7]

In sum, then, we have seen that the acquisition of the syntax of negation by second language learners proceeds through sequences which clearly differ from those found in L1 development. 'External' position in L1 refers to clause-external placement, that is, preposed NEG precedes the subject – in L2 acquisition this is a rare or 'ephemeral' construction (Larsen-Freeman and Long 1991: 94), for NEG normally follows the subject and is thus placed externally to a VP which does not contain the subject. This can be interpreted as indicating that sentence structures underlying early L2 utterances already contain functional projections, possibly transferred from L1 (see chapter 4, section 4.2 for a discussion of the initial state of L2 grammars). The second and most important difference between the two types of acquisition concerns the developmental relationship, in L1 acquisition, relating the emergence of the [±finite] distinction and verb placement and consequently also target-like placement of the finite verb with respect to the negative element. This generalization clearly does not hold for L2 acquisition. In fact, NEG is even placed after non-finite verb forms, in L2, a position allowed by neither the L1 nor the target grammar and not encountered in L1 acquisition either. Not only do the sequences differ in the two types of acquisition, but the L2 sequences are not explained satisfactorily, neither by the Structure Building Hypothesis nor by some version of the transfer hypothesis. This holds for the sequence proposed for L2 negative constructions as well as for the ordered L2 sequences of morphemes and stands in clear contrast to findings from L1 development.

3.4 A preliminary balance

The discovery that second language learners, at least in naturalistic acquisition without formal instruction, proceed through invariant acquisition sequences defined in terms of the grammatical properties emerging in their speech, is perhaps the most important reason for researchers to hypothesize that first and second language acquisition share more similarities than had previously been suspected. This assumption gained further plausibility when some researchers began to suspect that developmental sequences might be identical, at least in important parts, in first and second language acquisition. Moreover, rather than merely being a mixture of L1 and L2 structures, L2 learners' interlanguage was found to be characterized by 'creative constructions' suggesting that for L2, too, there is a specific kind of language acquisition capacity. But as intriguing as such similarities may be, the crucial question remained unanswered, that is, whether the two types of language acquisition are guided by the same underlying mechanisms.

The Morpheme Order Studies turned out not to be very enlightening, in this respect, since they were largely descriptive and did not really try to answer the obvious question as to *why* these morphemes should be acquired in the observed order. In fact, due to the heterogeneity of the morphemes studied, neither linguistic nor psycholinguistic attempts at explanations were successful. These studies did, nevertheless, reveal differences between first and second language learners, whereas child and adult L2 learners exhibited significantly similar orders. These findings were confirmed when researchers reinterpreted morpheme orders in terms of grammatically more coherent sequences, based on the assumption that the accessibility of functional categories is guiding language acquisition – a hypothesis only confirmed for L1 development.

The same conclusion could be drawn after an examination of developmental sequences for negative constructions. In first language development, the emergence of clause-internal placement of NEG coincides, in all languages studied, with the acquisition of the [±finite] distinction. The crucial point is that the developmental pattern, that is, both the initial placement in external position and the virtually error-free acquisition of NEG relative to the finite verb, follows naturally from grammatical accounts of the relevant facts. More precisely, the fact that the syntax of negation, in languages with rather different surface word orders, is acquired rapidly and apparently without much effort parallels the grammatical analysis which explains these structures in terms of finite verb movement – an unproblematic acquisition task in L1 development, as has been shown for several languages. This situation is by no means the same in second language acquisition. The fact, for example, that German *nicht* may precede finite verbal elements and follow non-finite ones suggests that this is not the result of movement of finite elements as in L1 development and in adult grammars. A possible explanation would be that the negator itself is moved, an option not offered by UG for elements like *pas* or *nicht* (see Meisel 1997b). If this is indeed the case, we can hypothesize that second language learners, in this particular case, resort to linear sequencing strategies which apply to surface strings rather than using structure-dependent operations constrained by UG. This is to say that a learner of French or German, who discovers that NEG is placed postverbally in the target language, is able to use a corresponding construction without taking the [±finite] distinction into account. Note that the NEG+X strategy which some learners seem to rely on is also linear in nature. In this fashion, one can furthermore account for the marked differences between various L2 learners, as opposed to the uniformity in L1 development, not only with respect to the rate of acquisition and the ultimate success, but also with regard to the preference for pre- or postposition of NEG. I will discuss these learning strategies in more detail in section 5.3 of chapter 5.

Our preliminary balance, thus, speaks in favour of the hypothesis postulating substantial differences between first and second language acquisition. But whereas the differences are indisputable as far as the observable phenomena are concerned, it is by no means obvious that the underlying acquisition mechanisms will also be different. The invariant and perhaps even universal patterns found in L2 acquisition sequences are too robust to be ignored, and the fact that grammatical explanations have not been very successful does not mean that they cannot work for principled reason. In other words, the core issue of the discussion, as I called it above, has still not been addressed directly, namely whether differences in the underlying knowledge systems and acquisition mechanisms are responsible for the observed differences or whether additional factors related to language use play causal roles – or perhaps even both. In order to be able to address this issue, let us first see what we know about the underlying grammatical knowledge, in first and especially in second language acquisition. Understand this as an invitation to read chapters 4 and 5!

3.5 Suggested readings and topics for discussion

Suggested readings

In view of the seminal influence which Roger Brown has had and continues to have on first and second language acquisition research, I strongly recommend reading at least part of his 1973 book. A representative example of the Morpheme Order Studies is the paper by Heidi Dulay and Marina Burt (1974). Roger Andersen's (1978b) paper is an excellent example of an empirically sound and methodologically careful work on L2 acquisition. The paper by Meisel, Clahsen and Pienemann (1981) may be useful for a better understanding of the notion of developmental sequence. Wode 1976, reprinted 1978, gives a good idea of the problems related to the acquisition of negative constructions.

Andersen, R. W. 1978. 'An implicational model for second language research', *Language Learning* 28: 221–82.

Brown, R. 1973. *A first language*. Cambridge, MA: Harvard University Press, pp. 247–82.

Dulay, H. C. and M. K. Burt 1974. 'Natural sequences in child second language acquisition', *Language Learning* 24: 37–54.

Meisel, J. M., H. Clahsen and M. Pienemann 1981. 'On determining developmental stages in natural second language acquisition', *Studies in Second Language Acquisition* 3: 109–35.

Wode, H. 1976. 'Developmental sequences in naturalistic L2 acquisition', *Working Papers in Bilingualism* 11: 1–31; reprinted in E. M. Hatch (ed.) 1978. *Second Language Acquisition: A Book of Readings*. Rowley, MA: Newbury House, pp. 101–17.

Topics for discussion

- In this chapter and throughout this volume, acquisition order plays a decisive role as a crucial piece of empirical evidence when contrasting first and second language acquisition. It presupposes a conceptually satisfying and empirically corroborated treatment of what can count as 'acquired'. Yet a non-contentious and generally accepted notion of 'acquired' does not seem to exist. In L2 research in particular, a variety of defining criteria are applied. Starting from the discussion in sections 3.2 and 3.3, draw up a list of criteria which must minimally be met in order for a linguistic form or construction to be considered as 'acquired'. Note that this may differ in first and second language acquisition. Compare your own definition with what you find in at least two introductions to language acquisition (L1 and L2).
- The notion of 'developmental sequence' is of particular importance because it serves as the major criterion defining invariant aspects of grammatical development. As defined in section 3.3, it implies a strictly ordered sequence of 'stages' or 'phases' in the course of acquisition. As has become evident from this discussion and that of the Morpheme Order Studies in 3.2, the question of what exactly characterizes a 'stage' or 'phase' is a matter of much controversy. Ingram (1989: chapter 3) discusses the notion of 'stage' at considerable length. Keeping Ingram's discussion in mind, do you think that the definition of 'developmental sequence' suggested in this chapter is adequate or do you believe it needs to be modified? State the ways it would have to be refined or broadened!
- Not all properties of grammars emerge in an interindividually or even cross-linguistically strictly ordered sequence. This does not mean, however, that they appear in a random fashion. In L2 acquisition, for example, the order and the frequency of use of some properties have been argued to reflect different approaches to the tasks of L2 acquisition and are therefore characteristic of various learner types; see the

multi-dimensional model of L2 acquisition by Meisel, Clahsen and Pienemann (1981). Based on this outline of the multi-dimensional model and on the discussion of the acquisition of the syntax of negation in 3.3, try to find reasons for why the emergence of some grammatical phenomena characterizes types of learners rather than reflecting a grammar-internal developmental logic. You may want to return to this issue after having read the next three chapters of this volume and compare your suggestions with those presented there.

- Acquisition orders and developmental sequences make claims concerning the chronology of language acquisition. In order to scrutinize the validity of these claims, longitudinal studies – documenting the course of acquisition for some individuals – appear to be the optimal methodological choice. In 3.3, however, it was argued that cross-sectional studies can also provide insights into the course of acquisition over time. Can you give arguments supporting or contradicting this second claim? What about experimental studies – can they inform us about the chronology of acquisition? Consult language acquisition textbooks on this issue and draw some preliminary conclusions.

4 The initial state and beyond

4.1 Transitional interlanguage grammars?

Investigating parallels and differences between first and second language acquisition from a cognitive perspective inevitably directs one's attention to the role of the LAD as a guiding force of grammatical development. This is the basic idea which I follow in contrasting these two acquisition types, and this is why I presented the quest for the LAD as the principal goal of the current enterprise (cf. chapter 1). The review of some central characteristics of first language development in chapter 2 then led to the conclusion that it is indeed determined in essential ways by the human Language Making Capacity (LMC) of which Universal Grammar is the centrepiece. Following the continuity assumption, this means that the child's implicit knowledge of language contains the same kinds of categories and relations as adult grammars and, importantly, that no component of the child's grammar, at any point of development, violates principles of UG. If this conclusion is correct, it justifies the claim that the LAD determines the developmental logic in L1 acquisition, and it immediately raises the question of whether the same is also true for second language acquisition. Recall from chapter 1 (section 1.2) that interlanguage studies attributed 'transitional competences' to L2 learners. Assuming that this is an adequate description of the learners' knowledge, it follows that second language acquisition can also be conceived of as a sequence of approximative systems. But this does not yet answer the question of whether some or even all of these systems are constrained by UG in essentially the same fashion as L1 developing grammars.

In chapter 3, we saw that L2 acquisition proceeds through invariant developmental sequences which seem to be largely independent of grammatical properties of the respective first languages but which are not identical to the sequences attested in L1 development. Both these findings are potentially of crucial significance for the issue at stake here, but they appear to be pointing in different, and perhaps even in opposing, directions. If, on the one hand, L2 learners with different L1 backgrounds proceed through similar or identical acquisition sequences, this finding would constitute a serious challenge to claims attributing a major role to L1 transfer in L2 acquisition, and would support the idea of 'creative constructions'. Unfortunately, the nature of the latter was never explained in any detail, but invoking creativity was clearly intended to suggest operations similar to those in L1 acquisition, possibly reflecting guidance by the LAD. On the other hand, the fact that L1 and L2 sequences are not identical seems to indicate that the underlying logic is not the same in the two cases, and it casts doubt on the assumption that the LAD is determining L2 acquisition in essentially the same way as L1 development. Quite obviously, however, both these possible conclusions require further consideration, and it is the goal of this chapter to provide it.

The issue is to determine whether L2 developmental sequences exhibit the properties commonly attributed to grammars of natural languages, including developing grammars in L1 acquisition. Put differently, the central task of this and the following chapter is to ask whether a second language learner's competence can justifiably be described, at each point of the acquisition process, as a transitional grammar conforming to the constraints imposed by UG on grammars of natural languages. This focus on UG[1] is inevitable if one adopts the view according to which UG is defined as the core component of the LAD, but it does not prevent us from taking other principles and mechanisms into account, nor does it commit us to an all-or-nothing alternative. Note that the question about UG-conforming transitional grammars in L2 refers to early as well as to later acquisition phases. In fact, the initial state of the L2 learner's linguistic knowledge is of particular importance, for many subsequent acquisition tasks depend on the nature of the linguistic knowledge at the onset of the acquisition process. If, for example, it is initially determined by grammatical properties of the previously acquired language, this in itself might account for the fact that developmental sequences in the two acquisition types are not identical, since the starting points of the two trajectories would thus be substantially different. As should already become apparent by this remark, the two issues of L1 transfer and UG conformity of grammatical knowledge in L2 are intertwined. This is why they will both be addressed in this chapter.

4.2 The initial state of L2 grammatical knowledge

Let us begin at the beginning of the process of L2 acquisition – not a trivial logic in second language research where, for quite some time, the kind of linguistic knowledge available to L2 learners during very early phases of the process of L2 acquisition received little attention. Only during the second half of the 1990s did this change, and a number of researchers began to address this issue explicitly, as is evidenced, for example, by publications such as Perdue 1996 or by contributions to Eubank and Schwartz 1996, investigating what sort of knowledge determines the shape of the earliest L2 utterances. However, the interest in this question does not seem to have lasted for a sufficiently long period, since we are still far from having reached a broad consensus on this issue.

One source of knowledge for learners is their linguistic environment, that is, the primary data in the L2 input. These, however, are meaningless for the acquisition process unless learners can assign grammatical analyses to them (cf. Carroll 1996, 2001, forthcoming). How and to what extent this becomes possible is a problem which deserves to be studied in some detail, a task which cannot, however, be tackled in this textbook. I will, nevertheless, address these issues at least briefly in the following chapters (see 5.3 and 6.3). What can already be stated at this point is that the linguistic input can only provide learners with information about structural properties of the target language if they have available mechanisms allowing them to assign grammatical interpretations to utterances encountered in the PLD. In other words, even at the onset and during very early phases of the subsequent process of L2 acquisition learners must resort to grammatical knowledge, that is, simultaneously and even prior to extracting from the input information about grammatical properties of the target language. What may at first sound paradoxical can, in fact, be achieved by resorting to a priori knowledge provided by UG, as is obviously the case in L1 development, or by relying on grammatical knowledge acquired previously, most importantly in the first language. This amounts to saying that accessibility to UG principles and transfer from L1 grammars are not only prime candidates to consider when we attempt to determine the kinds of knowledge which shape L2 utterances, they indeed seem to represent necessary knowledge sources for the learner even at the initial state of the acquisition of L2 grammars. Alternatively, one might consider the possibility that early phases of L2 acquisition are not primarily shaped by grammatical but by pragmatic principles or by semantic properties, as implied by the concept of a so-called *Basic Variety* (cf. Klein and Perdue 1997). At this point, I will not pursue this idea; for some critical remarks, see Meisel 1997c. Assuming that both UG and transfer shape early L2 utterances does not tell us, however, whether learners necessarily resort to both kinds of knowledge and, if yes, to what degree, or whether they are likely to play a more or less important role at different moments in the course of acquisition. Let us therefore first take a look at the initial state and ask what we can learn about the respective role played by UG principles and L1 transfer during the earliest phases of L2 acquisition.

Leaving aside, for the time being, the specific role of the input, we thus face several logically possible hypotheses about the nature of the initial linguistic knowledge of L2 learners, depending, on the one hand, on the role attributed to L1 transfer and, on the other hand, on whether L2 learners can be shown to be able to access principles and parameters of UG. Note that, in both cases, this is not merely a binary choice, since it seems plausible to assume for either of the two sources of knowledge that they might only be partially available. With respect to transfer, this means that learners may approach the task of learning a second language without any reference to previous linguistic experience, or that they do rely on knowledge from their L1 grammar. But in the latter case, transfer can happen in a wholesale fashion, or it may apply selectively to only parts of the grammatical system. This gives us the three options: full transfer, partial transfer and no transfer. A similar differentiation is possible with respect to the accessibility of UG, that is, full UG access, partial UG access and no access to UG. Full access implies that UG remains directly accessible to the L2 learner, possibly during the entire acquisition process. If this hypothesis is confirmed, we may undoubtedly answer the question formulated above (4.1) positively and conclude that L2 approximative systems conform to the principles of UG at each point of the acquisition process. The third option refers to the radically opposed view according to which knowledge about the second language is in no way determined by UG. This amounts to saying that it is fundamentally different in nature from the native competence and that it is likely to comprise different types of categories and relations. In other words, if this hypothesis is correct, an L2 competence is not a transitional grammar, properly speaking; instead, it should be conceived of as a cognitive system mimicking mental representations and processes of native grammars. Note that if one was to conclude that L2 learners only have 'indirect access' to UG via the L1 grammar, as is frequently claimed in studies on L2 acquisition, this is tantamount to saying that they have *no* UG access, and the term 'indirect' access is actually a misnomer. If, namely, UG principles and parameters are only operative in L2 learners' linguistic knowledge systems to the extent that they can be derived from previously acquired grammatical systems, this implies that UG cannot be accessed by the learners, even though their L2 system is partially constrained by UG principles. The term 'indirect access' thus confounds conformity to UG principles with accessibility of UG and should therefore be abandoned. The remaining option, partial access to UG, finally, comprises elements of the other two in that it assumes that a subset of the UG principles remains accessible to UG learners. Consequently, L2 approximative systems are predicted to conform in part, at least, to UG principles. Whether this is also the case in those instances where learners cannot rely on UG principles and need to compensate this lack of knowledge by other means remains to be seen. I will return to this issue in section 4.4 and in the following chapter 5.

Summarizing what has been said so far, we find that the following six options are likely to characterize the initial state of L2 acquisition. The question, however, is whether all logically possible combinations are equally plausible.

(1) Full transfer	(A) Full access to UG
(2) Partial transfer	(B) Partial access to UG
(3) No transfer	(C) No access to UG

Let us, then, look at some imaginable scenarios for the initial state of L2 knowledge, focusing on the role of these two knowledge sources.[2] The first observation is that the 'no transfer' option seems to play hardly any role in current thinking about L2 acquisition. Presumably, this reflects the fact that, in all likelihood, it would lead to implausible scenarios, no matter which hypothesis about access to UG it is combined with. If, for example, both negative options are chosen (3-C), the prediction is that L2 learners should find themselves in a situation similar to that of 'wild children' who did not acquire a first language before puberty (see Curtiss 1977). Such a view is counterintuitive and seems not to be defended in current L2 research. If, however, a negative answer is only given to the first question (no use of L1 knowledge) combining it with option (A) (full access to UG) it is predicted that L2 acquisition parallels monolingual L1 development to an extent blatantly in conflict with the empirical facts (see White 1989a: 121). As far as I can see, this position is not defended either. Combining the 'no transfer' view with the hypothesis that UG is partially accessible (3-B), is hardly a more plausible position, for it does not exclude the possibility of L1 influence for UG-type grammatical knowledge while at the same time rejecting L1 transfer. In sum, then, the 'no transfer' option appears to be the least suited as an explanation of the learner's initial state of knowledge about the L2.

As for the question of whether principles of UG determine the early knowledge systems of L2 learners, the negative option, 'no UG', cannot be discarded as easily. This hypothesis has indeed been entertained by some researchers, for example by Clahsen and Muysken (1986), although this does not entail the claim that L2 knowledge in its totality does not conform to UG principles. One must keep in mind the context in which these authors initiated their discussion (see 4.4); their position was developed as an alternative to the 'full access' hypothesis. The idea that UG-constrained L2 properties might also result from what has been called 'indirect access' to UG (see above) was not yet entertained explicitly. In other words, if L2 learners can tap their L1 grammars, using them as a source of knowledge guiding L2 acquisition, the L2 system will partly conform to UG principles in spite of the inaccessibility of UG principles in L2 acquisition. Once they took this possibility into account, Clahsen and Muysken (1989) indeed supported the idea that L1 grammars can determine the shape of L2 grammatical systems. It thus follows that the 'no UG' option cannot yet be dispensed with since it is compatible with the idea of 'indirect access to UG', which, however, does not imply access to UG, contrary to what this infelicitous term seems to convey. Yet it also follows from this consideration that the 'no access to UG' view predicts that whenever acquisition tasks are not covered or backed by L1 knowledge, L2 learners should be expected to resort to learning mechanisms which are not specific to language, and they might thus come up with solutions which are not grammatical ones, in the technical sense of the term. Although I certainly do not want to exclude this possibility, that is, that learners might opt for non-domain-specific alternatives, the 'no access to UG' perspective on L2 acquisition may well be too strong a hypothesis. I will return to this issue.

Before engaging in a discussion of the scenarios for the L2 initial state of L2 grammars, it should be useful to consider a critical remark which concerns a methodological problem but which also reflects a theoretical weakness that is potentially damaging for all hypotheses to be presented, to a degree that their interest for L2 research could be severely diminished. I am referring here to the fact that it is not at all clear what the term 'initial state' is intended to mean in L2 research. It was borrowed from L1 research where it refers to the a priori knowledge which the child brings to the task of language acquisition, before exposure to the PLD (see the discussion in chapter 2). Quite obviously, it must mean something very different in L2 acquisition where all learners, by definition, have had extensive experience with language acquisition. In fact, this is precisely the reason why I decided to focus here on the two major potential knowledge sources, UG and the L1 grammar. If, however, the term refers to a point before any exposure to L2 data, I do not see how its investigation could possibly reveal anything about L2 acquisition, let alone enable us to determine the respective role of UG and L1 grammars. Minimally, learners at the 'initial state' must have acquired some vocabulary in order for us to be able to investigate which grammatical knowledge source they draw on at this point. It is, however, highly implausible to assume that learners should be able to acquire a set of lexical items without at the same time learning any of their morphosyntactic properties – except perhaps in a specially designed classroom context, but certainly not in naturalistic settings like the ones on which the studies investigating the L2 'initial state' are based. In fact, even if lexical learning without acquisition of grammar was possible, the term 'initial state' cannot plausibly refer to the state previous to experience. In other words, it can at best be meant to refer to a 'very early' phase of acquisition. Unfortunately, however, nowhere in the literature dealing with this issue have I been able to find an explicit statement explaining the meaning of either 'initial' or 'very early' – does the second month or the second half of the first year still qualify as such? Let me emphasize that this is not simply a pedantic criticism insisting unduly on meticulous definitions. If we lack a theoretically adequate understanding of such a crucial term, it will be difficult if not impossible to scrutinize it empirically.

To make things worse, many or rather most of the researchers investigating the 'initial state' of L2 acquisition are not even concerned with very early phases of L2 acquisition in their empirical studies. Rather than analysing data from the first weeks or months of exposure to the L2, they focus on later periods, hoping to be able to make inferences about the initial state by studying subsequent changes. This, of course, further complicates the already difficult task of assessing the respective roles of UG and L1 knowledge in early L2 acquisition. Epstein, Flynn and Martohardjono (1996), for example, do not use longitudinal data at all but present an experimental study intended to provide evidence against the assumption of partial transfer. At the time of testing, the child learners in their study had spent an average of three years in an English-speaking country, the adult learners an average of one year, and they had had an average of three and seven years of formal English instruction, respectively. How we can possibly gain insights into what constitutes these learners' initial state of knowledge remains mysterious. Grondin and White (1996), on the other hand, do use longitudinal data. They report on two English-speaking children learning French who, at the age of 4;9 and 4;5, respectively, attended a bilingual nursery programme. The data examined, however, were collected during the subsequent kindergarten programme or during first and second grade years, because the children's spontaneous speech production in French, at the end of the nursery programme, was still too limited.

This means that 'the earliest utterances' referred to in this study were collected after one year of exposure to French. Schwartz and Sprouse (1994, 1996), finally, discuss the language use of one Turkish learner of German who had spent nine months in Germany at the onset of the recording period. But they do not even focus on the earliest productions in this corpus, because he does not yet use full sentences in German, although he apparently could understand some German at this point. One might therefore have expected them to investigate the learner's comprehension of syntax. If studies of, say, relative clause processing done before relative clauses emerge in learner speech show reliance on L1 dependencies or processing strategies, this would suggest that the initial state is simply never observable in L2 acquisition. But since Schwartz and Sprouse merely analyse linguistic productions and are primarily interested in grammatical constructions which are typically not used by early learners, that is, finiteness, verb placement and case marking, their 'Stage 1' begins exactly one year after the learner's arrival in Germany. In my opinion, one year or more of exposure is not what can plausibly qualify as the 'initial' state of L2 acquisition, not even as a very early phase. It is, perhaps, not necessarily impossible to gain insights into the kind of knowledge available during the earliest phase of acquisition, basing one's analyses on data collected during later phases. But one might expect to be informed about how such insights can be attained. I am, however, not aware of such a discussion in the literature on the 'initial state' of L2 acquisition.

Let us, nonetheless, now turn to a brief review of scenarios suggested for the initial state of L2 grammars, despite these theoretical and methodological concerns. By examining them in more detail, we may hope to understand what kind of knowledge they attribute to the learner at this point of acquisition and what the assumptions are which they make concerning the process of approximation towards the target systems.

The most radical position advocated is the Full Transfer/Full Access to UG (FTFA) hypothesis proposed by Schwartz and Sprouse (1994, 1996).[3] The claim of this hypothesis is that

> the initial state of L2 acquisition is the final state of L1 acquisition . . . excluding the phonetic matrices of lexical/morphological items.
>
> (Schwartz and Sprouse 1996: 40)

This is to say that the starting point of L2 acquisition and the initial state of L1 development should be radically different. In other words, L1 transfer is regarded as a major source of knowledge shaping the initial state of learners' grammars. Principles of UG are claimed to be of equal importance, but the proponents of this hypothesis do not state explicitly what constitutes evidence for the claim that L2 learners have 'full' access to UG during the earliest phases. Let me thus first focus on the issue of L1 transfer at the initial state.

If we take the 'full transfer' claim literally as an answer to the question of what characterizes the onset of L2 acquisition, we should expect to find relexification of entire L1 sentence structures. In other words, no later than when a critical mass of lexical items has been learned, L2 learners should use complex syntactic constructions transferred from L1 and filled with L2 lexical material. This, of course, is only true if lexical learning does not affect the syntactic structures into which the lexical material is inserted. Schwartz and Sprouse (1996) seem to believe that this is indeed possible and suggest that learners merely tag L2 'phonetic matrices' to L1 'lexical/morphological items'. If, however, lexical learning has similar effects in L2 acquisition as in L1 development, it will trigger syntactic changes; see, for example, the approach advocated by Clahsen and Penke (1992) following ideas developed by Pinker (1984). In other words, if 'lexical learning' also implies learning of grammatical properties of the L2 lexical items and not just mapping of L2 phonetic strings onto an L1 entry, the lexical learning hypothesis predicts that the linguistic knowledge at the initial state will be altered in the process of lexical acquisition. Lexical learning, in the relevant sense, will mean learning of abstract grammatical properties, for example that adjectives follow nouns in French (*un soulier noir*) rather than preceding them as in English (*a black shoe*). This amounts to saying that structures underlying even very early L2 utterances are most probably not identical to L1 structures. Consequently, we should not expect constructions of the sort predicted by FTFA to ever occur in L2 production. This, of course, renders this hypothesis immune against empirical counterevidence.

Let us, nevertheless, set aside these objections and try to spell out some of the empirical predictions of the Full Transfer/Full UG Access Hypothesis. The ones discussed explicitly by Schwartz and Sprouse relate mainly to verb placement and to the use of null subjects, wh-words and determiners. With respect to verb placement, a distinction needs to be made between finite and non-finite verbs, a by now familiar fact mentioned repeatedly in the preceding chapters. The standard analysis of word-order phenomena of this type assumes that verbs are generated in the head of VP and are then raised to functional projections, for example TP or CP. As we have seen in 3.3, some languages differ in that particular projections may be either head-final or head-initial and also in that finite verbs are raised to different functional heads. Consequently, full transfer implies that L2 grammars at the initial state will exhibit L1 type characteristics for both these properties. It thus predicts that learners transfer head-final order to an SVO grammar if their L1 is an OV language and left-headedness of the VP to an SOV language if their L1 is of the VO type. The surface position of non-finite verbs is expected to reveal this internal order of the VP. Finite verbs, on the other hand, should be raised to the position required by the L1, a category possibly different from the one where these verbs appear in the target system, and perhaps also different in its headedness. Take the example of learners of German whose L1 is a Romance language. The prediction in this case is that early L2 German should be an SVO language lacking the V2 effect, that is, the finite verb is raised to the head of TP rather than to CP; compare structures (1) and (2).

(1) Romance languages

```
CP
├── SpecCP
└── C´
    ├── C [+WH]
    └── TP
        ├── SpecTP
        └── T´
            ├── T [+F]
            └── NEGP
                ├── Spec NEGP
                └── NEG´
                    ├── NEG
                    └── VP
                        ├── DP
                        └── V´
                            ├── V
                            └── DP
```

(2) German

```
CP
├── SpecCP
└── C´
    ├── C [+WH,+F]
    └── TP
        ├── SpecTP
        └── T´
            ├── NEGP
            │   ├── Spec NEGP
            │   └── NEG´
            │       ├── (empty)
            │       └── VP
            │           ├── nicht
            │           └── VP
            │               ├── DP
            │               └── V´
            │                   ├── DP
            │                   └── V
            └── T
```

This appears to be empirically correct, as is evidenced by the acquisition sequence suggested by Meisel, Clahsen and Pienemann (1981) to which I will return in section 4.4; that is, SVO order dominates initially, and verbs appear in third rather than in second position if a constituent is fronted and precedes the subject (XSVO). Looking at other language pairs, however, the facts are not as clear and the findings are more ambiguous, for example if German is the target and Turkish the native language, as in the case of the learner studied by Schwartz and Sprouse. Since Turkish is a head-final but not a V2 language, both finite and non-finite verbs should appear in final position, and early Turkish-L2 German should lack the V2 effect. Schwartz and Sprouse indeed report that non-finite verbs are always placed in clause-final position, but they acknowledge that they do not find any finite verbs in clause-final position (1996: 44) – clearly in contradiction to the Full Transfer hypothesis. Their solution is to postulate a 'Stage 0', not attested in their corpus. In other words, the empirical findings by Schwartz and Sprouse (1996) do not corroborate the predictions of the Full Transfer/Full Access to UG hypothesis for the initial state of L2 acquisition, and postulating an unattested preceding stage is hardly a satisfactory solution. After all, it is precisely this very early phase which is at stake here, and one would have expected a study designed to explore the initial state of L2 acquisition to be based on the appropriate kind of empirical evidence. As it stands, the Stage 0 is merely a stipulation, and this means that the FTFA hypothesis does not rest on solid foundations. We thus need more information on this hypothesized earliest acquisition phase. In fact, this is not only a request for empirical evidence in support of the full transfer claim. We also need to be informed about how full transfer constrains the opportunities offered by full access to UG – and vice versa. Note that if one accepts that full UG access is possible in L2 acquisition, the question immediately arises of why learners do not simply rely entirely on this source of knowledge, which should allow them to proceed much like L1 children, if only they could ignore their previously acquired L1 knowledge. Remember that one of the core issues here consists in determining the respective role of the two types of knowledge which, according to the FTFA hypothesis, are fully operative at the initial state. In rejecting the logically possible 'no transfer' option, above, I implicitly stated that simply ignoring the L1 knowledge does not seem to be possible. But if we want to maintain that UG is fully accessible, we are under an obligation to offer an explanation for why transfer appears to be inevitable. Merely postulating full transfer will not suffice. Quite to the contrary: a scenario like the one alluded to in the quote from Schwartz and Sprouse (1996) de facto implies that the initial state is characterized exclusively by this one source of knowledge, relegating the possibility of access to UG to subsequent phases in acquisition where its function is to allow learners to retreat from the consequences of the initial full transfer. This is certainly a logically possible scenario, but without further theoretical motivation, it is hardly a very plausible one, and its empirical justification rests largely on the stipulated Stage 0.

By defining the initial state of L2 acquisition in terms of the L1 grammar of learners, we encounter a serious problem concerning subsequent learning processes. In order for learners to be able to learn the L2, they must be able to at least partially parse and process the input data. More precisely, what constitutes potential input for learners is mere noise (or sound waves), until learners are able to assign mental representations to sound waves. 'Only these mental representations can be the starting point for language learning' (Carroll 2001: 4). But since the parser is fed and depends on one's grammatical knowledge, learners relying entirely on their L1 grammar should not be able to parse and comprehend even the simplest L2 utterances whenever the L1 and the L2 grammars differ. If, for example, the first language only allows OV order, they should not be able to parse a German main clause with the finite verb in second position. Consequently, 'full transfer' predicts in some cases that learners do not have access to processable input, a crucial prerequisite for language learning (see Carroll 1996). At this point, I cannot follow up on this issue, but I will return to it in section 4.3 when discussing the role of transfer in more detail and in 5.3, dedicated to inductive learning. I do want to emphasize, however, that referring to the final state of L1 acquisition as the initial state of L2 acquisition seems to create more problems than it solves for a theory of L2 acquisition. Schwartz and Sprouse (1994: 349) acknowledge that '[p]art of the machinery of the L1 grammar has to be relinquished'. But when and how this is achieved remains unclear. Let me add that pointing to 'full access to UG' will not solve these problems. As for the latter, what is needed is a principled account of how learners can successfully resort to UG knowledge in order to alter the final state of the L1 grammar at 'Stage 0'. Appealing to UG access whenever L1 transfer does not account for the observed facts – and vice versa – may allow one to cover all potentially problematic cases, but such ad hoc solutions will ultimately not be satisfactory.

To conclude this part of the discussion, I believe I have shown that the Full Transfer/Full Access to UG hypothesis suffers from a number of serious empirical and theoretical weaknesses, at least as far as the 'total transfer' claim is concerned. The at first sight attractive formula according to which the final state of L1 acquisition is the initial state of L2 acquisition not only entails important conceptual problems, it is also not able to account for the known empirical facts. Note that it revives ideas propagated by Contrastive Analysis (cf. chapter 1), modified primarily in that transfer now refers to more abstract entities, that is, to underlying structures, parameters and so forth, rather than to surface properties. It is therefore subject to many of the criticisms mustered against CA. It is in fact surprising that the proponents of the Full Transfer hypothesis do not attempt to account for the findings of interlanguage studies of the 1970s and 1980s, demonstrating that L2 learners, independently of their first languages, go through identical acquisition sequences, at least in some areas of grammatical development (see 3.2). It is conceivable that the FTFA hypothesis might be able to account for the results of this body of L2 research – but this would have to be demonstrated.

Recall that when outlining possible scenarios of what might determine learners' initial hypotheses about the L2 grammar, I concluded that it seems implausible to exclude L1 transfer altogether, and I therefore discarded the 'no transfer' option (3). The preceding discussion suggests that option (1) 'full transfer' does not lead to satisfactory results either, even if more empirical evidence needs to be considered. The next step will now be to explore possible intermediate approaches. A number of authors supporting the Full Access to UG hypothesis have, in fact, attempted to define the role of transfer more restrictively. When adopting this scenario of 'partial transfer' (i.e. option (2)), the crucial problem is to identify possible instances of transfer in a principled, non-ad hoc fashion. The Minimal Trees Hypothesis (MTH) and the Valueless Features Hypothesis (VFH) propose two closely related but nevertheless different solutions to this problem.

The Minimal Trees Hypothesis proposed by Vainikka and Young-Scholten (1994, 1996a, 1996b)[4] represents an attempt to make use of insights from first language development in second language acquisition research. It is inspired by the Structure Building Hypothesis (Guilfoyle and Noonan 1992) presented in chapter 2 (2.3), according to which functional categories are not accessible during early phases of L1 grammatical development. Early sentence structures would thus resemble VPs, and subsequent developmental stages are characterized by the grammatical properties of functional projections which gradually become available in learners' grammars. The MTH states that in L2 acquisition too, initial sentence structures contain only lexical categories (e.g. V, N) and their projections. Vainikka and Young-Scholten claim that L2 learners transfer these from the L1 grammars, together with the directionality of their heads, but not the L1 functional categories. Subsequently, a head-initial underspecified functional projection (FP) is said to emerge in the L2 grammatical system which develops into a head-initial AGRP as agreement features are acquired. The parameter values related to these functional projections are not transferred from L1, however; rather, 'functional projections develop through interaction of X'-Theory with the input' (Vainikka and Young-Scholten 1996a: 13).

In their analysis of L2 German by learners with different L1s (Korean, Turkish, Romance languages), Vainikka and Young-Scholten (1994, 1996a, 1996b) review empirical evidence which they believe corroborates their claims. Korean and Turkish learners, for example, are observed to initially prefer verb-final constructions, whereas Italian and Spanish learners tend to use left-headed VPs. The L2 linguistic behaviour of both groups thus appears to reflect properties of the respective L1 grammars. Yet these findings do not unambiguously support the MTH. In fact, other word order patterns are encountered in these data which prove to be more problematic for this analysis. One of the facts to be explained is that learners whose L1 grammars generate left-headed VPs place verbs in two different positions, preceding objects, adverbials and so on as well as following them clause-finally. Vainikka and Young-Scholten propose to account for this observation by assuming that these learners switch from left-headed to head-final VPs during the VP-only phase, thus yielding two VP stages, Ia and Ib, characterized by two distinct grammars. Note, however, that the Romance-speaking learners of German already use head-final VPs at stage Ia and that they continue to use at stage Ib what Vainikka and Young-Scholten (1996b: 161) call 'residual head-initial VPs'. In other words, they appear to resort to two grammars at both VP stages.

As for the subsequent development of functional projections, the crucial claim is that these functional elements are not transferred from the L1 grammar. Rather, their emergence is triggered by lexical learning and guided by UG. The main argument intended to justify this claim relies on the fact that Vainikka and Young-Scholten find no evidence for L1 properties of these projections, for example in the directionality of functional heads. Quite surprisingly, the underspecified functional projection FP which is argued to emerge first is invariantly analysed as head-initial, even in L2 German of Korean and Turkish learners, although the corresponding functional projections in both L1s and in the target language are head-final. In other words, the head-initial property of FP is stipulated independently of the learners' experience with the target language.

As should have become apparent from this short description, the MTH makes partly the same empirical predictions for the initial state of L2 acquisition as the Full Transfer hypothesis, at least with respect to verb placement. At the VP stage as well as at Stage 0, postulated by Schwartz and Sprouse (1996), transfer of L1 order is expected to happen. This appears to be confirmed by the differences in word-order patterns between Romance learners of German, on the one hand, and Turkish and Korean learners, on the other. Vainikka and Young-Scholten (1996a: 15) indeed find that 98% of the utterances in their Korean and Turkish corpus exhibit verb-final order. To the extent that this finding can be confirmed, it does support the claim that the linear orientation of syntactic heads is transferred from the L1. I will return to this issue immediately.

Although the MTH agrees with the Full Transfer hypothesis in predicting transfer of L1 word order for lexical categories, the two approaches differ in how these surface patterns are explained. The MTH but not the FTFA hypothesis postulates early sentence structures containing only a VP. This, however, leads to a number of theoretical problems. The first one concerns the total absence of functional layers, which arguably violates UG principles, as argued in 2.3 (see also Clahsen, Penke and Parodi 1994). But since this is a point which could probably be remedied and in which the MTH follows the original suggestion by Guilfyole and Noonan (1992), I will not pursue this here. The second point is potentially more damaging. Recall that the idea of structural development in first language acquisition is based on a version of the parameter theory according to which parameters refer exclusively to functional categories (see 2.3). The question thus is how transfer of head directionality of lexical categories can be explained in this framework. If linear orientation of grammatical heads is a parameterized option, it should not be a property of lexical but of functional categories, as is argued by Ouhalla (1991). In other words, in the absence of functional categories, transfer of the position of the verb cannot be accounted for within this theoretical framework. An equally serious problem is the alleged switch between stage Ia and Ib from left-headed to head-final VP. How this could be accomplished, following current parameter theory, remains mysterious. In fact, the empirical evidence adduced by the proponents of the MTH weakens their argument rather than strengthening it, for it suggests that phenomena characteristic of a specific acquisition stage, for example 'residual head-initial VPs', continue to be used during subsequent stages. Although this possibility cannot be rejected in an a priori fashion, it does cast doubts on the claim that clause-final placement of verbs at stage Ib is the result of parametric change in the grammar of L2 learners of German.

In sum, then, this hypothesis is flawed by a number of conceptual shortcomings, and, as we will see below, it also encounters serious empirical problems. Whereas the Full Transfer hypothesis overemphasizes the role of initial transfer from the L1 grammar, the MTH has not fully succeeded in explaining partial transfer in a principled and non-ad hoc fashion.

Let us finally look at the Valueless Features Hypothesis (VFH), developed by Eubank (1993/94, 1994, 1996), and ask whether it fares better in this respect. He argues that both lexical and functional categories are transferred from the L1. Crucially, however, it is claimed that the parameterized values of features in functional heads are not transferred because they depend on overt inflectional morphology which is never transferred. This is to say that this approach maintains, contrary to the MTH, that the L2 grammar, at the initial state, may contain functional projections. But as opposed to the Full Transfer hypothesis, the featural properties of these projections are said to differ significantly from both the L1 and the L2 grammar in that features are 'inert'. Learners must discover the L2 values and thus also the strength of these features when acquiring morphological properties of the target language.

In order to see what kinds of developments are predicted to occur under this hypothesis in early L2 acquisition, let us look at one example. Verb placement can serve this purpose again, this time in relation to the negator in L2 English of child L2 learners whose first languages are German or French. In 3.3, we saw how negative constructions are analysed in the latter two languages, and the respective structural descriptions are reproduced in this chapter as (1) and (2), above.

(3) (i) Jean ne prend pas le métro
Jean NEG takes not the subway
'Jean doesn't take the subway'
(ii) *Ne prendre pas le métro est dangereux
NEG take+inf not the subway is dangerous
(iii) Ne pas prendre le métro est dangereux
'Not to ride the subway is dangerous'
(iv) Ne pas être en ville est bien
NEG not to be in town is nice
(v) N'être pas en ville est bien
'Not to be in town is nice'

Remember that French finite thematic verbs precede the negator *pas* whereas non-finite verbs may only precede *pas* if they are non-thematic (see (3)). In German main clauses, all finite verbs are placed in clause-second position (V2 effect) where they precede the negator *nicht*, whereas non-finite elements appear in clause-final position, after complements and negation; in subordinate clauses, both the non-finite and the finite verb follow the negator (NEG+V-f+V+f). As for English, the crucial facts can be summarized by stating that thematic verbs cannot raise from V to T, but non-thematic verbs do appear in this position. In non-finite clauses, however, this is different. Thus, in finite clauses thematic verbs always follow *not*, and a non-thematic verb, for example dummy *do*, is obligatorily placed to the left of the negator; in non-finite clauses, non-thematic verbs may be placed either to the left of the negator or to its right. The standard explanation of these facts refers to the strength of features in functional heads (see Eubank 1994: 373 for a concise summary). In French and German, <strong> features result in finite verb movement to left-headed T or C, respectively; non-finite verbal elements remain in V, left-headed in French, head-final in German. If features are negatively specified, raising of thematic verbs is always prohibited. In English, where thematic verbs never raise, the relevant feature is noted as <weak>. The VFH adds to this the idea that inert features, that is, those neither specified as <strong> nor as <weak>, result in optional effects of V-movement.

The French–English interlanguage data show that non-thematic verbs occur mostly to the left of the negator, occasionally to the right of *not*; thematic verbs, however, are placed uniformly to the right of *not*, that is, one never finds constructions like (4), corresponding to (3) (i), as the Full Transfer hypothesis predicts.

(4) *Jean takes not the subway.

This is strong evidence supporting the claims that the L2 grammar distinguishes between thematic and non-thematic verbs and that feature strength indeed plays a role in L2 acquisition. The suggested explanation argues that during a period when agreement morphology is present but not obligatory, 'Agr [T in our diagrams, JMM] is optionally either non-finite or finite, the latter indicating weak inflection' (Eubank 1993/94: 197); from this it follows that thematic verbs cannot raise past NEGP, but non-thematic verbs can, since weakness of agreement only affects thematic verbs.

As for German–English interlanguage, we have seen in chapter 3, section 3.3 that at the proposed first stage of non-anaphoric negation, the negator precedes a lexical category or projection; at the subsequent stage II, the negator follows non-thematic *is*, and at stage III, thematic verbs are negated, with NEG appearing pre- as well as postverbally. The problem of verb placement arises at stage II.[5] In order to account for the constructions characteristic of this stage, Eubank has to make the additional, though not implausible assumption, that *is* does not yet encode finiteness; rather, it is a suppletive form which is not raised to T (or AGR) but remains in V. At stage III what needs to be explained is the optionality of verb raising as well as the causes for why uninflected verbs raise. This is where the claim that feature values do not transfer comes into play. Importantly, one finds differences between various interlanguages due to specific properties of the L1 grammars. In the French–English data no thematic verb ever precedes the negator, and in German–English interlanguage the verb does raise past NEG. Remember that German finite verbs move to C^0 – in this approach caused by the presence of TENSE in C^0. The claim, then, is that the value of the AGR feature is either <non-finite> or <weak>, at this stage, whereas an <inert> value appears under TENSE. Following this argument, finite non-thematic verbs may raise to AGR^0 (or T in our structure) but no further; finite thematic verbs, on the other hand, must proceed to C^0. Non-finite verbs are also allowed under C^0 because of the <inert> value of TENSE. Moreover, 'non-finite varieties of both thematic and non-thematic verbs may remain *in situ* in VP' (Eubank 1996: 99). All this leads Eubank (1996: 101) to predict that 'if verbs are not raised, then no inflection should appear, but if they are raised past negation, then inflection will appear optionally'. Leaving technical details of this analysis aside, what matters is that feature values seem to be relevant in distinguishing early learner grammars from later ones or from the target systems.

At this point, having briefly reviewed three approaches trying to explain the initial state of second language acquisition, it should be useful to attempt a preliminary summary of the results of this discussion. One conclusion must be, I believe, that no convincing case has been made for the Full Transfer hypothesis. Although it is perhaps too early to dismiss it definitively, the currently available evidence does not support it but suggests rather that the idea of partial transfer accounts more adequately for what we know about the initial state. As pointed out above, the plausibility of such a solution depends essentially on whether it is possible to determine in a principled fashion which parts of the L1 knowledge are likely to be activated by learners at the initial state and, in fact, during the entire process of L2 acquisition. If we were to choose between the two competing hypotheses dealing with this issue, our brief review suggests that the idea of an initial grammar lacking all or even most functional elements is conceptually less plausible in L2 acquisition than in first language development. This conclusion speaks against the Minimal Trees Hypothesis, at least as an explanation of partial transfer. The notion of featural underspecification of functional categories seems to fare better in this respect. The Valueless Features Hypothesis thus seems to be the most promising of the three competing approaches. The fact that it is also easily compatible with the explanation of L1 grammatical development advocated in section 2.3 of chapter 2 contributes, of course, to its attractiveness, although this concerns the availability of UG principles, rather than the role of L1 transfer.

But although such theoretical considerations are of crucial importance, given that our goal is to gain insights into the underlying logic shaping the two types of language acquisition, a first test and, in fact, a sine qua non criterion on which to base the evaluation of the various hypotheses is their observational and descriptive adequacy. In other words, the problem is also an empirical one, and we may therefore hope to get a clearer picture by checking the explicit and implicit predictions of all three approaches against the available empirical evidence. Since most of these predictions refer to changes subsequent to the initial state, thus also relying on the availability of UG principles, I will deal with them again in sections 4.3 and 4.4 and also in chapter 5, where the role of UG in L2 acquisition will be discussed in more detail.

The choice between VO and OV order, however, characterizes the initial state or at least the earliest phases of the process of L2 acquisition, and all three hypotheses refer explicitly to word-order phenomena. They, in fact, coincide in postulating that, due to transfer of head directionality in the VP, the position of verbs is initially determined by the L1 grammar. But although this appears to make correct predictions for learners whose L1 exhibits VO order, the empirical facts are at least ambiguous when OV order is expected to be transferred to the L2, as became apparent in the study by Schwartz and Sprouse (1996). The claim that head directionality is transferred from the L1 to the L2 grammar becomes even less convincing if we take other studies into account. Wode (1981), for example, analysing the acquisition of English by German children, found hardly any examples of OV order, and Pfaff and Portz (1979), comparing the use of SVO and SOV patterns by Greek and Turkish children acquiring German, observed that the Turkish children use verb-final utterances less frequently than the Greek. Klein and Perdue (1997: 314) report similar findings studying L2 English of Punjabi and L2 German and Dutch of Turkish learners, Punjabi and Turkish being OV languages. They conclude that 'While this pattern [SOV, JMM] thus clearly reflects source language influence, such influence is rare overall'. The latter case is particularly significant since the source language, Turkish, as well as the target languages, German and Dutch, exhibit OV order. This confirms findings by Jansen, Lalleman and Muysken (1981) and Clahsen and Muysken (1986) who report that OV order, although it is used by some learners, is clearly not the dominant pattern in the speech of Turkish learners of German and Dutch.

These findings suggest a preference for SVO order, but they call into question the claim that this can be explained as a result of L1 transfer, since alleged transfer appears to operate only in one direction, that is, from VO to OV, whereas the same kind of cross-linguistic influence does not seem to affect VO order if the L1 is an OV language. The dominance of SVO order in interlanguages is also observed in other settings. Note, first of all, that although the majority of the world's languages exhibit SOV order (one estimate is that they make up 52%, as opposed to 32% SVO languages), creoles as well as other contact-induced languages are overwhelmingly or possibly even in their totality of the SVO type.[6] This is certainly true in all cases where at least one of the contact languages is SVO, but even in situations where neither of them has this underlying order, for example Berbice Dutch Creole which exhibits SVO order although both its Dutch superstrate and its major substrate Eastern-Ijo are SOV (see Kouwenberg 1992). Yet whereas these observations show quite unambiguously that the preference for SVO order cannot be the result of transfer of underlying word order, they do not reveal in a straightforward fashion what other cause might explain this pattern to emerge.[7] One possibility is that L2 learners rely on surface order regularities. Observe that Dutch as well as German both use surface SVO order, for example in simple main clauses if the verb is moved to second position. Kouwenberg (1992: 293) indeed suggests that the SVO order of Berbice Dutch Creole is the 'result of perceived similarities between surface orderings' in Dutch and Eastern-Ijo, the latter apparently also allowing for SVO order in certain contexts. One might add that while this accounts for the fact that VO order is indeed an option in this setting, it does not explain why it is the preferred one. In the present context, I cannot pursue this issue, but I would like to mention that psycholinguistic research suggests that SVO sequences may be easier to parse than SOV chains (cf. Krems 1984, Hemforth 1993, or Weyerts, Penke, Münte, Heinze and Clahsen 2002). In other words, preference for SVO order may very well result from processing preferences rather than from the transfer of L1 grammatical knowledge.

Since our goal is to test some of the empirical predictions made by the three hypotheses about the L2 initial state, we should not limit our attention to the phenomenon of verb placement but take other grammatical areas into account, too. One of the advantages of the Minimal Trees Hypothesis is that it makes strong empirical predictions when it postulates the absence of functional elements at the initial state of L2 acquisition. One should thus expect elements normally located in functional projections to be absent in early L2 speech, for example determiners (DP), modals and auxiliaries (TP), and wh-words (CP). Both the Valueless Features and the Full Transfer hypotheses contest this claim. Contrary to the prediction of the MTH, Grondin and White (1996) state explicitly that they find determiners and question words in early utterances. These observations are pertinent because they differ from findings from L1 acquisition of French, and because few changes occur in the further course of L2 acquisition in these cases. In other words, they seem to indicate that L2 learners possess a kind of knowledge which L1 learners lack at this point of development, and which appears to be close if not identical to that of the target system. But since these findings are not based on data from the earliest phase of L2 acquisition the issue cannot be considered as settled. The kind of data needed in order to arrive at firm conclusions in this debate must capture very early phases of L2 acquisition and should preferably be longitudinal in nature.[8]

The study by Parodi (1998) does analyse data of this sort, including speech samples by six of the learners recorded as part of the ZISA longitudinal study and two Turkish learners recorded by the ESF research group, all acquiring German as a second language. She not only confirms the findings of Grondin and White (1996) concerning the presence of determiners (definite and indefinite articles, demonstratives, possessives) and question words in early L2 speech, she also presents evidence showing that modals, auxiliaries and complementizers are used from early on. The data, in fact, leave no doubt with respect to these findings, although Parodi observes some variation across learners (i.e. it is not the case that each of the items mentioned appears in the first recording of every learner) and across the various items studied (some are used more frequently than others). What matters is that all these elements are attested at the learners' first stage of L2 acquisition, and this refers, in the case of most of the Romance learners, to a period as early as the first or second month of contact with German. Consequently, functional projections must be accessible to L2 learners even at the initial state, since the use of determiners, modals, auxiliaries and wh-words depends on the availability of DP, TP and CP. Parodi (1998) in fact further strengthens her argument by comparing the L2 learners to bilingual children acquiring French and German simultaneously, demonstrating that all the elements under discussion are initially absent and emerge successively in bilingual first language acquisition. This confirms our conclusion, above, that structural development is less plausible as an explanation of second language than of first language development, and it leads to the further conclusion that the Minimal Trees Hypothesis fails at the level of observational adequacy. In fact, this result should not come as a surprise, for we saw in the previous chapter (section 3.2) that Zobl and Liceras (1994), who also explored the idea of carrying the Structure Building Hypothesis over to L2 research, had to conclude that functional projections are available from early on in second language acquisition.

In conclusion, we may now ask what we have learned about the initial state of L2 acquisition. Remember that we identified three possible knowledge sources likely to shape L2 learners' initial linguistic systems: input made available by the L2 environment, transfer from the L1 grammar, and principles of UG. Since UG influence is easier to detect by studying how the initial state is changed when early systems are brought closer to the target grammar, the discussion of this problem has been postponed to chapter 5. Similarly, the role played by the linguistic input cannot be assessed without reference to mechanisms of language processing, and the discussion of this issue therefore has to wait until chapters 5 (5.3) and 6 (6.3). As for L1 transfer, the results are not yet conclusive, but based on our current knowledge, 'no transfer' can be ruled out, and full transfer turned out not to be a plausible hypothesis either, leaving 'partial transfer' as the most promising solution. The question of how 'partial' is best defined in a theoretically satisfactory and empirically adequate fashion cannot be answered definitively in the present context, but the Valueless Features Hypothesis emerged as a plausible and viable approach, compatible with theories about L1 acquisition.

On the positive side, two points can be made on which most L2 researchers seem to agree. First, the linguistic knowledge of second language learners can be explained in grammatical terms, for example referring to the presence or absence of grammatical elements, the distinction between finite and non-finite verbs, verb placement and so forth. This supports the idea that L2 speech is organized according to abstract grammatical principles rather than representing concatenations of semantically or pragmatically defined elements (but see Klein and Perdue 1993 for an opposing view). In other words, the cognitive principles organizing L2 speech are domain-specific in that they refer to linguistic objects and relations. Whether this grammatical knowledge is constrained by UG principles and whether L2 learners have direct access to Universal Grammar still remains to be seen, however. But assuming that L2 knowledge can indeed be characterized in terms of domain-specific principles and mechanisms, this finding already represents an important insight into the nature of L2 acquisition, supporting the claim that parallels between these types of acquisition do exist. The second point on which there seems to be consensus, on the other hand, points towards differences between L1 and L2 acquisition, since it concerns the fact that the initial state of L2 acquisition is markedly different from that of L1 development. Irrespective of what the causes for these differences are, it necessarily follows that the points of departure for the acquisition processes are not the same, and it could be for this reason alone that they proceed through distinct acquisition sequences. In order to be able to determine whether L1–L2 differences indeed result from the fact that the starting points are distinct whereas the same means are employed in order to reach a possibly identical goal (native competence), it is necessary to examine the sequence of steps and the transition processes more closely. This will be done in section 4.4 and in chapter 5, and I will try to show that these differences are not simply due to differences at the initial state but that they are more fundamental in nature.

4.3 Transfer of knowledge or knowledgeable transfer?

Before turning to a discussion of the developmental processes leading from the initial state to the ultimately attainable knowledge of the L2 target system, I want to dwell some more on the transfer issue. After all, the results obtained in the previous section are rather modest. My claim has been that transfer from the L1 definitely happens, although 'full transfer' appears to overstate the case, leaving us with a not very stringently defined version of the 'partial transfer' hypothesis. In view of the fact that 'transfer' or 'interference' is arguably the most frequently studied topic in the area of second or foreign language learning, this is admittedly a meagre result. On the other hand, in a textbook exploring parallels and differences between first and second language acquisition, it might suffice to observe that transfer effects do exist in L2, thus contributing to the observed L1–L2 differences. Moreover, it is precisely the sheer amount of publications on this issue which should discourage me from attempting to present even a rough outline of the major aspects of this debate. The reason why I nevertheless want to return once more to this issue is that it is closely intertwined with the problem of identifying the principles and mechanisms shaping the acquisition process. If we assume, at least for the sake of argument, that L2 learners are in principle able to attain native-like or at least near-native grammatical knowledge of the target language and that their L2 knowledge previously contained L1 properties, it inevitably follows that L2 acquisition essentially involves grammatical reanalyses and restructuring processes. As we will see in the remainder of this volume, restructuring is not impossible but difficult from the perspective of developmental linguistics, and costly from the point of view of psycholinguistics and learning theory. Pienemann (1998a, 1998b) therefore argues that choosing a wrong starting point may make it very difficult or even impossible for learners to attain native-like knowledge of the target grammar. Before discussing possible restructuring processes, it should thus be useful to gain a somewhat better understanding of the nature of grammatical transfer.

Unfortunately, the various models trying to account for transfer at the initial state have not been very useful in this respect. In fact, the nature of transfer remained opaque. I believe that this is largely due to the fact that all the approaches dealt with in the previous section deduced their claims about transfer from considerations based on grammatical theory without taking learning or processing mechanisms into account. This led to three implicit assumptions which all need to be questioned:

1. Transfer is understood as a property of mental grammars.
2. Transfer effects are strongest during early phases of L2 acquisition.
3. Transfer affects a wide range of grammatical phenomena.

In what follows, I will briefly address these three points, taking into account research results obtained previously to the studies on the initial state in the mid-1990s, because they are not biased in favour of or against the hypotheses defended here, and some of them draw on extensive empirical bases and do not have to resort to unattested facts suspected to occur at points of acquisition preceding or following the periods investigated.

In my view, the first point is indeed the crucial and decisive one. All the above-mentioned hypotheses trying to explain second language learners' initial phases of L2 acquisition fail to distinguish between the mental representation of grammatical knowledge about the L2 and mechanisms of language use, most importantly the structure and working of the parser and the formulator. Without even considering the latter, *all* phenomena encountered in L2 speech are treated as properties of the grammars of learners. I believe this to be a major shortcoming of many acquisition studies carried out in the theoretical framework of the theory of UG, and although this is particularly obvious when it comes to explaining grammatical transfer, it is equally damaging when trying to explain other aspects of L2 acquisition as will become apparent later on; see, for example, section 5.3 of the following chapter or chapter 7. When dealing with cross-linguistic influence (Sharwood-Smith and Kellerman 1986), it has long been known that it is essentially necessary to distinguish between *fusion* of grammatical systems, that is, instances where properties of grammar G_a are integrated into G_b, as opposed to cross-linguistic influence in language *use*, resulting, for example, from the activation of G_a when producing or comprehending G_b.

As we saw in chapter 1, studies carried out in the Contrastive Analysis framework tended to equate learners' linguistic competence with a set of habits in language use, thus postulating 'mind-less' behaviour. The anti-mentalistic theory of language and of learning underlying CA did not allow for a psycholinguistically plausible interpretation of the notion of 'habit' in terms of parsing, processing and production mechanisms. But subsequently, based on an early version of UG theory, L2 researchers suggested as an alternative explanation that an innate 'active mental organization' of L2 knowledge (Dulay and Burt 1972: 236) leads to processing strategies resulting in learner-specific linguistic rules. This prepared the way for a definition of 'transfer' taking grammatical knowledge into account as well as mechanisms of use. It is therefore difficult to understand why scenarios attempting to characterize the initial state of L2 acquisition should rely on knowledge alone, without further discussion of this issue. They offer, as an unfortunate alternative to the earlier notion of transfer as a kind of linguistic behaviour without (mentally represented) knowledge, a view of transfer as grammatical knowledge largely or totally independent of linguistic experience. In my opinion, both options fall short of what is needed in order to explain the known empirical facts in a theoretically insightful fashion. Transfer should instead be understood as a process of language use relying on previously acquired grammatical knowledge.

This is by no means a novel proposal; it rather adopts early suggestions and empirical findings according to which the notion of 'transfer' should be understood as referring to a process of language learning and use (cf. Kellerman 1977, 1979, 1987, among others). This means, on the one hand, that, as opposed to CA studies, we adopt a cognitive perspective from which it follows that possible objects of transfer processes are only those categories and relations which can plausibly be assumed to be part of mental representations of linguistic structures. Quite obviously, this refers not only to elements at surface structure but also to properties defined at abstract levels of grammar, for example underlying word order phenomena dependent on head-directionality (Meisel 1983b). The latter claim comes close to the idea of transfer of L1 parameter settings in studies adopting the Principles and Parameters Theory and also to what is suggested by the hypotheses discussed in our previous section. On the other hand, and contrary to these suggestions, this view does not imply transfer of mental representations of grammatical knowledge as implied by the scenarios developed for the L2 initial state, most strongly by the Full Transfer hypothesis. The claim rather is that cross-linguistic influence operates indirectly via processes of language processing, learning and use. It is trivially true that at the initial state and during very early L2 acquisition phases, learners have little or no knowledge of the target language. One may therefore plausibly assume that they make use of all available resources in their efforts to get access to processable input, as explained by Carroll (2001). Exposed to naturalistic input, they may have no other option than to use the L1 parser (fed by the L1 grammar) in their attempt to parse and process parts of L2 speech. This is not the same, however, as saying that their L2 grammar is initially identical to the L1 grammar. Rather, learners apply a number of strategies of language use and of learning which allow them to communicate as successfully as possible while at the same time building up a body of knowledge about the L2. The grammatical knowledge thus acquired may be assumed to then feed into the parser and the formulator, gradually adapting these performance systems to the L2 requirements.

At first sight, it may appear as if these two notions of 'transfer' differ in only subtle ways. In fact, however, the conceptual differences are substantive, and the empirical consequences are far reaching. As for the former, let me mention the fact that conceiving of transfer as a process rather than as the result of a fusion of mental representations of grammatical knowledge avoids a number of problems alluded to before. For one, it does not encounter the restructuring problem noted at the beginning of this section which emerges if an explanation of grammatical development requires frequent reanalyses and subsequent restructuring of core properties of 'entrenched' (Pienemann 1998b) grammatical knowledge. Moreover, it avoids the paradoxical conclusion presented in the preceding section 4.2 according to which L2 constructions reflecting instances where the source and the target grammars differ would not be assigned structural descriptions and, consequently, learning should not be possible because learners cannot detect the grammatical particularities of the target language. The apparent paradox is avoided by attributing the necessary flexibility to the systems of language use. In case of parsing failure, for example, alternative solutions can be tested by scanning surface chains and by allowing the parser to interact with other modules, for example semantic knowledge (see Carroll 2001).

What also speaks strongly against the idea of transfer of knowledge is the well-established fact that cross-linguistic influence not only affects the L2, but that, conversely, an L2, particularly if it is strongly dominant in the linguistic environment, can also affect a person's first language (see Sorace 2000 for one such example). This suggests that we are not looking at transfer of mental representations of grammatical knowledge, unless it could be demonstrated that the L1 grammar was permanently damaged. Similarly, it has been observed that children growing up bilingually, with two 'first languages', and who easily succeed in differentiating from very early onwards the two grammatical systems of their ambient languages, do sometimes show effects of cross-linguistic interaction in the later course of linguistic development (see Meisel 2001, 2007b for state-of-the-art discussions of related issues). There is no indication of fusion of grammars in these cases. In fact, bilingual children show very little evidence of transfer, and virtually none in syntax or morphology. We can therefore infer that the various instances of cross-linguistic interaction are the result of online activation of the other language. We know indeed that both languages are always activated (see Grosjean 2001). What happens in the cases studied here is apparently that the respective other language is accessed. This may be a relief strategy enabling the bilingual to retrieve knowledge which is not or not readily available in the other language. It may also happen involuntarily, if the activation of the other language is not successfully inhibited (see Hulk 2000). This explanation also accounts for the fact that the observed effects appear in only some children and only temporarily.

The latter remark leads us to turn to a consideration of the empirical consequences of the two competing explanations of transfer. A surprising and particularly unsatisfying finding of the discussion in section 4.2 is that the empirical results of the studies mentioned present an extremely blurred and fragmented picture. In some cases no L1 influence whatsoever could be detected, and in others the L1 pattern is only one of several options. Wode (1981), for example, analysing the acquisition of English by German children, Klein and Perdue (1997) studying L2 English of Punjabi and L2 German and Dutch of Turkish learners, or Jansen *et al.* (1981) found that OV emerges in the speech of only some learners and never as the dominant pattern in their use of the L2, contrary to what is predicted by the various hypotheses about the L2 initial state. Vainikka and Young-Scholten (1996a), on the other hand, report that 98% of the utterances in their Korean and Turkish corpus exhibit verb-final order. How are we to interpret such contradictory and heterogeneous results? Importantly, if we were dealing with transfer of knowledge, variation in the frequency of use of a particular phenomenon by L2 speakers should correspond roughly to the variability in the respective L1. Thus, if a (parameterized) principle of the L1 grammar was integrated into the early L2 knowledge system, we would expect to find that the L1 pattern is used predominantly or exclusively, at least until the L2 grammar is restructured as a consequence of sustained exposure to data from the target language. Occasional or low frequency usage does not support the hypothesized transfer of grammatical knowledge. The question then is why proponents of this hypothesis can only occasionally report the predicted predominant use of L1 pattern like Vainikka and Young-Scholten (1996a) or Haznedar (1997) who found almost categorical use of OV order in the early L2 English of one Turkish boy.

The commonly offered answer to this question is that those who fail to detect massive L1 influence in L2 speech must have missed the earliest phase, the Stage 0. But it is precisely in some of the studies which capture very early phases of L2 acquisition that the predicted L1 influence is not attested (e.g. Wode 1981 or Clahsen, Meisel and Pienemann (1983), who both analysed longitudinal data of learners, children and adults, in a naturalistic setting). Interestingly, similar results are obtained in a study of tutored learners by Håkansson (1997, 2001). This is all the more surprising since, in this case, learners do not transfer VO order into an OV language, and they fail to transfer the V2 effect where it would have yielded the correct target property. Håkansson (1997) analysed the speech of Swedish and Danish learners, thirteen to fifteen years of age, who acquired German in a classroom setting. Both source languages are of the VO type, as opposed to the German target, but they share with German the property of V2. Out of 202 word-order errors of the Swedish learners, only 3 are due to the use of VO where German requires OV, and this includes the data from forty-eight seventh-graders who had studied German for only two months, two hours per week. The case against an explanation in terms of transfer of grammatical knowledge from the L1 is further strengthened by the fact that 37% of these learners (42% among the early learners in the seventh grade) failed to use the V2 construction (187 of the 202 errors, amounting to 93% of the target-deviant word order pattern), although the same construction is required by the Swedish L1. These findings demonstrate that it is not warranted to simply interpret every surface similarity between learners' interlanguages and their L1's as resulting from transfer, a point emphasized by the results obtained by Eubank, Bischof, Huffstutler, Leek and West (1997) who looked at Chinese-speaking learners of English, both non-raising languages. That study showed that the L1 Mandarin and Cantonese learners readily gave verb-raised interpretations of sentences. Eubank *et al.* (1997) explained this result in terms of unspecified, inert features, still persisting in their grammars. Irrespective of whether one adopts this explanation, had these been learners whose L1s allowed for verb raising, how could we have demonstrated that their behaviour was not determined by their L1 grammars?

My claim is that the findings according to which cross-linguistic interaction does not lead to a predominance of L1-type patterns in L2 speech but to a more moderate effect are not an artefact of data collection methods but reflect, instead, the nature of L1 transfer as a process of language use. As argued above, learners make use of all available resources in their efforts to process input, including the L1 parser fed by the L1 grammar. Importantly, this is not their only resource, but they can apply a number of strategies of language use and of learning which enable them to build a body of knowledge about the L2. Under this view, it is to be expected that L1 effects can but need not occur in all instances where the grammatical phenomenon in question appears in L2 utterances. In other words, depending on the linguistic context and on communicative situations, learners may sometimes rely on their L1 knowledge, but not at other times. In situations, for example, where communicative demands exceed the possibilities offered by the currently available approximative L2 system, learners may resort, consciously or unconsciously, to the L1. Moreover, some learners are expected to avoid L1 transfer whereas others use this option freely. This kind of intrapersonal and interpersonal variation with respect to effects of grammatical transfer has indeed been observed by Clahsen *et al.* (1983). In fact, if transfer from L1 is understood as one of several options available to learners, it is possible to identify types of L2 learners according to the preferred kind of resource. One such option is to rely on another previously acquired second language. Another one consists of inductive learning strategies, for example generalizations based on perceived surface properties, as suggested by Kouwenberg (1992) as an explanation of SVO order in a Dutch-based creole. As a last example I want to mention 'simplification' strategies, studied extensively in L2 research (see Andersen 1983b or Meisel 1977, 1983a, among others). Transfer can thus be defined as a strategy of L2 acquisition (see Jordens and Kellerman 1981, Vincent 1982 or Meisel 1983c, among others).

These and similar observations speak strongly in favour of a notion of transfer as a knowledge-based process rather than as transfer of knowledge. Let me add that this interpretation of transfer also accounts for the fact that effects of cross-linguistic influences sometimes emerge, disappear and emerge again over time in the speech of the same learner (see Meisel 2007a). Transfer of grammatical knowledge would have to explain how the phenomenon in question is implemented in the transitional grammar, then eliminated, and finally implemented again – a highly implausible scenario.

Let me now turn to the second point. The three scenarios discussed in 4.2, trying to capture the initial stage of L2 acquisition, all predict that transfer effects should be strongest during early phases of L2 acquisition. Following from the assumption that learners initially rely on mental representations of L1 grammatical knowledge, transfer effects are expected to be attenuated during subsequent phases as a result of grammatical restructuring supported by UG principles and triggered by increasing exposure to the target language. This view, however, is in conflict with empirical facts discovered by earlier studies. At least in some linguistic domains the frequency of use of constructions which can be argued to be due to L1 transfer increases during later phases (cf. Jordens 1977 or Kellerman 1977, 1979).

Claims to the effect that learners rely most heavily on L1 knowledge at the onset of acquisition seem to be based on the tacit but only apparently trivial assumption that its main cause is lack of knowledge about structural properties of the target language. It may therefore be useful to recall that Zobl (1980) already presented strong arguments against this 'Ignorance Hypothesis' and that he demonstrated that learners must attain a certain level of grammatical development before transfer is activated. More specifically, he suggested that what induces transfer is the perception by the learner of a well-motivated structural similarity between the two languages (Zobl 1979a). The notion of 'perceived similarity' is crucial here and is also argued for by Kellerman (1977, 1979) and Jordens (1980). Only once they have acquired sufficient knowledge about the L2, do learners begin to make (implicit) guesses about the structural relatedness of the two languages in question and, consequently, about large-scale transferability of L1 elements or structures (see Kellerman 1979). Note that this 'similarity' need not correspond to what linguistic descriptions of the two languages might yield. What matters is what learners are able to detect. This idea is, in fact, corroborated by the repeatedly mentioned observation according to which learners tend to rely on surface properties in perceiving similarities in form or in meaning. In sum, contrary to the claims about massive transfer at the initial state of L2 acquisition, these and similar studies suggest that grammatical transfer from the L1 is most likely to happen once learners have acquired not only a set of vocabulary items, but also a basic knowledge of the structural properties of the target language. Let me add, nevertheless, that this does not exclude the possibility of transfer during early phases by some types of learners, if transfer is indeed a strategy to which different learner types resort to different degrees and in different ways, as suggested above (see also Meisel 1983c).

The idea that lack of knowledge may in fact inhibit transfer has been explored more recently by Håkansson, Pienemann and Sayehli (2002) and Pienemann, Di Biase, Kawaguchi and Håkansson (2005) who proposed a partial transfer approach, the Developmentally Moderated Transfer Hypothesis (DMTH) based on Processability Theory (PT) developed by Pienemann (1998a, 1998b). Following up on the above-mentioned findings by Håkansson (1997, 2001) that Swedish learners of German do not initially transfer V2 although this would yield the correct German word order, Swedish and German both being V2 languages, they argue that V2 is not transferred at the initial state because it can only be transferred when the interlanguage system can process the construction in question.[9] The results obtained by researchers adopting the DMTH not only contradict the prediction of 'full transfer' at the initial state, they also demonstrate that processing requirements guide the incremental acquisition of L2 approximative systems and that the possibility of transfer is constrained by the acquired grammatical knowledge at every given point in the course of acquisition.

Table 4.1: *Subjects: Grammaticality judgement task*

	Learner group	Number of learners
I	Learners after 15–25 hours of French instruction	16
II	Learners after 25–50 hours of French instruction	17
III	Learners after 50–75 hours of French instruction	15
IV	Advanced learners after several years of French instruction	11
V	Native speakers	8
Total		**67**

To conclude this point, let us have another look at some empirical facts, focusing again on the OV/VO distinction discussed above. My purpose is to see whether OV order is indeed preferred at the initial state, as expected under all three scenarios discussed in the preceding section for learners whose L1 is of this type and who acquire a VO language. In other words, since it is not used categorically as transfer of knowledge predicts, does OV at least emerge as a frequently used pattern during very early phases of L2 acquisition?

In a study with adult German learners of L2 French,[10] we scrutinized various types of data searching for massive and possibly 'full' transfer of word order during early phases (see Möhring 2005). The data consisted of grammaticality judgements and of elicited productions. The former were collected by replicating in part the study by Hulk (1991) who investigated the acquisition of French by adult L1 speakers of Dutch, an OV language just like German; see Table 4.1.

French requires vVO (modal or auxiliary – main verb – object) order as in (5) in root as well as in subordinate clauses whereas German exhibits vOV order in root and OVv in embedded clauses (see (6)). Initial transfer of OV order thus predicts that beginners should judge French sentences with vOV order in main and OVv order in embedded clauses as grammatical and sentences with vVO-order as ungrammatical. In the elicited productions, one should expect to find SvOV in root and SOVv in embedded clauses.

(5) (i) Le serpent a avalé sa proie.
'The snake has swallowed its prey.'
(ii) Le serpent veut avaler sa proie.
'The snake wants to swallow its prey.'
(iii) Il pense que le serpent a avalé sa proie.
(iv) Il pense que le serpent veut avaler sa proie.

(6) (i) Der Kleine Prinz hat die Rosen gegossen.
The Little Prince has the roses watered
'The Little Prince watered the roses.'
(ii) Der Kleine Prinz will die Rosen gießen.
'The Little Prince wants to water the roses.'

(iii) Er glaubt, dass der Kleine Prinz die Rosen gegossen hat.
He believes that the Little Prince the roses watered has
'He believes that the Little Prince watered the roses.'

(iv) Er glaubt, dass der Kleine Prinz die Rosen gießen will.

Hulk (1991) found grammaticality judgements of this sort in her Dutch–French data. Since the frequency of incorrect judgements decreased with increasing length of exposure to the target language, she suggested that the Dutch learners initially transferred OV order into French before resetting the parameter to the VO value.

Our German–French study, however, does not support this finding, possibly because of methodological differences, as suggested by Möhring (2005). In the present context, the details of this debate are perhaps not relevant, except for the fact that the Dutch study did not include a control group of French native speakers, and some of the test sentences used by Hulk (1991) were not accepted by the native French control group in our study. More importantly, the two studies differed in how they analysed the data. Whereas Hulk (1991) only considered group results, Möhring (2005) assessed the judgements given by individual learners. This revealed that most L2 learners behaved inconsistently, rating sentences with the same structure as acceptable in one instance and as unacceptable in another. More specifically, SvVO sequences were sometimes rejected as incorrect and SvOV sequences were accepted as grammatical, but not all judgements of the respective learners are compatible with an underlying OV order, because several learners who rated SvVO order as 'impossible' in French consistently rejected SvOV sequences as equally 'impossible'. These results reveal that learners are uncertain about the grammaticality of these constructions and tend to 'overcorrect' even target conforming sentences. This is confirmed by a further task of this study where we asked subjects to correct sentences which they had rejected as ungrammatical. It turned out that in many cases the corrections did not in fact address word order violations. Subjects indeed never changed SvVO to SvOV order, but they frequently did change SvOV to SvVO. We therefore concluded that transfer effects detected in the grammaticality judgement test cannot be interpreted as corroborating the idea of transfer of grammatical knowledge. If anything, they confirm the hypothesis according to which some learners resort to transfer as to a strategy of L2 use.

The results of the productive elicitation test are even more revealing. The subjects were again adult learners of French with German as their native language. A native French interviewer presented pictures, encouraging the subjects to describe the activities depicted, designed to trigger the production of transitive constructions, for example a man reading a book; see Table 4.2.

The fact that all learners except Tim consistently produced utterances containing SvVO sequences in all contexts represents, in my view, convincing evidence against the claim that the head-final order of the VP is transferred from the L1 grammar, and certainly against the Full Transfer hypothesis. Since Tim uses a

Table 4.2: *Subjects: Elicited production task*

Learner group	Number of learners	Name of learners
Learners with 15–25 hours of French instruction	7	Karl, Gauschi, Tim, Matthias, Dorit, Jens, Gwendolin
Learners with 50–75 hours of French instruction	7	Petra, Carola, Hyma, Yada, Peter, Norbert, Christian
Native speakers	5	Jérôme, Cécile, Dédé, Sandra, Valérie

variety of word-order patterns, his occasional use of OV sequences does not suffice to support the Full Transfer hypothesis either.

In sum, the analysis of grammatical judgements and of elicited production data of adult German learners of French very clearly shows that these L2 learners do not transfer the underlying OV order of German to French. Most of the learners participating in this study, even the very beginners, rate SvVO sequences in French as correct and SvOV sequences as incorrect. This finding speaks strongly against the assumption that transfer exerts the strongest influence at the initial state of the L2 grammatical knowledge.

The third point, finally, which I only want to address briefly, is primarily directed against the Full Transfer hypothesis. As remarked in section 4.2, Full Transfer predicts that L2 learners' earliest utterance structures contain all grammatical properties of the L1 structure, and only these. In order to support this claim, it will not suffice to demonstrate that a given phenomenon like the extensively discussed head-directionality of the VP categorically or predominantly characterizes early L2 structures – although not even this proof has as yet been provided. Rather, it must be shown that all relevant L1 properties are present simultaneously in L2 learners' knowledge about a given sentence structure. No such evidence has ever been presented. More disappointingly, no one to my knowledge has ever attempted to substantiate such a claim. Not only do we not possess evidence of early L2 utterances as relexified L1 structures, certain possible transfer effects have never been documented, as far as I know, for example amalgamating the article with the noun if the L1 grammar analyses the definite article as a nominal suffix as in Romanian or Swedish. To mention another example, one hardly finds an example of Romance N+Adj order in the longitudinal German L2 data of the ZISA corpus (see footnote 8), let alone systematic use of this order of elements.

To put it differently, the Full Transfer hypothesis is in conflict with the frequently discussed claim that transfer is selective (Zobl 1980) and does not affect all grammatical phenomena, across the board. According to Zobl (1980), selectivity refers to formal properties that make L2 structures immune or receptive to

L1 influence. It could also be determined by processing constraints as suggested by the proponents of the DMTH. In fact, the idea of selectivity of cross-linguistic effects is also discussed extensively in the research literature on the simultaneous acquisition of two or more languages, referring to the 'vulnerability' (Meisel 2001) of some but not other structures to cross-linguistic interaction (see Meisel 2007b for a state-of-the-art discussion of this issue).

At any rate, there exists very broad consensus that transfer is more likely to happen with certain linguistic features than with others, phonological and lexical transfer being the most common and morphological transfer the least probable to be encountered. Most researchers also agree that transfer plays a significant role in language use. It has been shown, for example, that it typically affects principles of discourse organization (Rutherford 1983). In other words, learners use pragmatically motivated word-order patterns, for example topicalization, in contexts where this is appropriate in their L1 but not in the L2. Finally, a number of researchers have suggested that cross-linguistic influence is limited to the interface where morphosyntactic and semantic-pragmatic phenomena interact (cf. Hulk and Müller 2000, Allen 2001 or Serratrice, Sorace and Paoli 2004, among others).

To finally conclude this debate of the role of transfer as a knowledge source of L2 learners, we can state that transfer should be understood as a mental activity, as a process rather than as a structural property, and that it does not necessarily play a decisive role at the initial state of L2 acquisition. Thus, rather than transfer of knowledge, we may expect to find knowledgeable transfer. If this is correct, it follows that although grammatical transfer from the L1 is undoubtedly one of the phenomena which distinguish these two acquisition types, it is unlikely to cause substantial differences in the nature of the linguistic knowledge of L1 and L2 learners. We will have ample opportunity to return to this issue, in the remainder of this chapter as well as in the following one.

4.4 Beyond the initial state: Approximative systems

man muß was tun
muß man was tun
was muß man tun
tun muß man was
        man hätte was getan
        hätte man was getan
        was hätte man getan
        getan hätte man was
tun was man muß
was man tun muß
tun muß man was
was muß man tun

(Franz Mon[11])

Word order and specifically verb placement is undoubtedly one of the best-studied grammatical phenomena in language acquisition research, and it therefore provides an ideal testing ground for hypotheses about principles and mechanisms underlying the various types of language acquisition. This is why I suggest examining it in a little more detail, the question now being what the sequence of approximative systems may look like, once learners move away from the initial state towards the target system. We are, in other words, concerned again with developmental sequences and with the kind of knowledge underlying them. Remember that we saw in chapter 3 that second language acquisition, much like first language development, is characterized by invariant acquisition sequences, although the L2 sequences differ from those found in L1. Considering what has been said about the initial state of L2 acquisition, that is, that transfer from L1 may exert some influence and that the starting point is certainly not the same in L1 and in L2 acquisition, could it then be that the differences between the acquisition sequences in the two types of acquisition are due to this difference in where acquisition starts off?

The example to be discussed here is verb placement in German. As has been mentioned repeatedly in the previous chapters and earlier in the current one, German exhibits a variety of word order patterns, depending on pragmatic as well as on grammatical factors. The poem by Franz Mon above attests to this, although it does not, of course, explore all the possibilities of the language. German word order in general and verb placement in particular thus represents a complex acquisition task, and this is probably the reason why there exists an abundant literature dealing with this problem in both first and second language acquisition. The crucial facts to be discovered by the learner have already been mentioned in chapter 1. In order to facilitate the following discussion, I will summarize them again here, and in (7) I reproduce some of the examples given earlier together with a few others added for the present purpose. They illustrate that, although surface SVO order does occur in simple main clauses (i), the finite verb is, in fact, placed in second position (V2 effect), see (iv)–(v), preceding the subject and following the first constituent (topicalized object or adverbial); the non-finite verb, on the other hand, appears normally in final position in (ii)–(iv). Adverbial expressions occur clause-finally (i) as well as clause-initially (v) and internally (iii). In subordinate clauses the finite verbal element also appears at the end of the clause (vi), now following the non-finite one (vii).

(7) (i) Sie probiert den Wein (morgen).
She tastes the wine (tomorrow)
'She is (will be) tasting the wine (tomorrow).'

(ii) Sie will den Wein probieren.
She wants the wine to taste
'She wants to taste the wine.'

(iii) Sie hat (gestern) den Wein probiert.
She has (yesterday) the wine tasted
'She tasted the wine (yesterday).'

(iv) Einen Chardonnay will sie probieren.
A Chardonnay wants she to taste
'A Chardonnay she wants to taste.'

(v) Morgen probiert sie den Chardonnay.
Tomorrow tastes she the Chardonnay
'Tomorrow she will taste the Chardonnay.'

(vi) . . . dass sie den Wein probiert
that she the wine tastes
'. . . that she tastes the wine'

(vii) . . . dass sie den Wein probieren will
that she the wine to taste wants
'. . . that she wants to taste the wine'

Recall from chapter 3 (section 3.3) and section 4.2 that the standard analysis of verb placement assumes that German grammar makes use of head-final order for lexical as well as for functional categories, for example VP and TP. Verb raising depends on the featural composition of functional categories, and although the precise nature of these features is still a matter of discussion, the general assumption is that feature strength determines whether the verb is raised and where verbal elements are moved to. In a verb-second language like German, a maximal projection, that is, the subject, an object or an adverb, is moved to the specifier position of CP, and the finite verb has to go to the head of CP, for this is where the relevant 'strong' feature attracting the moved element is generated (cf. (2) in section 4.2). If the earlier IP is split into AGROP-TP-AGRSP and possibly more functional projections, the verb moves through all the respective heads on its way to C. The non-finite verb either remains in V or is raised to the lowest verbal functional head, depending on one's analysis. For the present purpose, the intricacies of the analysis are of little importance. One important point, however, is that in subordinate clauses the finite verb is stranded in a verbal functional projection below the head of CP if the latter position is already occupied by some lexical item, that is, a subordinating complementizer.

In order to be able to place verbs in the position required by the target grammar, learners thus have to find out about the head order of syntactic categories, distinguish between finite and non-finite verbal elements as well as between main and subordinate clauses, and they have to be able to place the finite verb in second position in main clauses. In first language acquisition, the necessary knowledge appears to become accessible successively, thus determining the course of grammatical development. In a number of publications, Clahsen (1982, 1986, 1988c) has laid out this developmental sequence for monolingual German children, and it has proven to be valid also for the acquisition of German by bilinguals; see, for example, Meisel 1986, 1990 or Müller 1993 for children acquiring German and French simultaneously. Table 4.3 displays this sequence, omitting the initial one-word stage.

A number of observations are important here. First of all, V-final order is preferred from the outset, suggesting that the head-final directionality of the VP

Table 4.3: *Developmental sequence of word order in L1 German*

I. Variable word order (SV, OV, VO), but predominantly V-final.
II. Non-finite verbs appear exclusively in final position; finite verbs in final or in second position.
III. Finite verbs appear exclusively in second position
IV. Embedded clauses with subordinating conjunctions emerge; finite verbs are placed in final position.

is discovered early. Secondly, as soon as the children distinguish between finite and non-finite verbal elements, the latter are never raised erroneously; finite verbs may occasionally fail to be moved out of final position, but if they are raised, verb-second position appears to be attained easily. Finally, final position of finite verbs in subordinate clauses does not seem to be a difficult learning task, either. This ease of acquisition was, in fact, to be expected under the analysis of the mature system, outlined above; since the landing site of the verb, the head of CP, is occupied by the complementizer, the finite verb simply remains in the head of the verbal functional projection below CP, that is, no specific subordinate clause word order needs to be 'learned'. Still, the relative ease with which the children go through this sequence of grammatical development is noteworthy.

A developmental sequence of word order regularities has also been established for second language learners acquiring German in a non-tutored setting (see Meisel *et al.* 1981). Although it was initially based on the ZISA cross-sectional study (see footnote 8) with adult learners speaking a Romance language as their L1, it has subsequently been corroborated, with only minor modifications, by the results of the ZISA longitudinal study (see, for example, Clahsen 1984 and Meisel 1987a, 1991). Other studies confirmed these findings and came to the conclusion that the same sequence also emerges when one examines the learning process of learners with other first languages or when one compares it to L2 acquisition by children (Pienemann, 1981, 1998a, 1998b) and by instructed learners (Pienemann 1984; Ellis 1989). Meisel *et al.* (1981) argue that this sequence reliably defines acquisition phases for German as a second language, and subsequent research has indeed established it as probably the most robust evidence for L2 acquisitional sequences. It is shown here as Table 4.4, illustrated in (8) by one learner utterance for each stage.

(8) (i) faule deutsche drink kakao (Rosa I)
Die faulen Deutschen trinken Kakao.[12]
'Lazy Germans drink cocoa.'

(ii) mittag frau mann komme essen salon (Pepita S)
Mittags kommen die Frau und ihr Mann zum Essen in das Wohnzimmer.
'At noon, wife (and) husband come eat (in) the dining room.'

(iii) die schwere worten so hab' ich auf die hand geschrieben (Eduardo P)
Die schwierigen Wörter habe ich so auf die Hand geschrieben.
'The difficult words I have written (so) on my hand.'

Table 4.4: *Developmental sequence of word order in L2 German*

1. SVO/ADV	invariant order: subject–verb–object/adverbial
2. ADV–PRE	adverbials appear in initial position
3. PART	non-finite verbal elements (including particles) are placed in final position
4. INV	subject–verb inversion, e.g. after preposed adverbials
5. ADV–VP	adverbials are inserted between the verb and its complement
6. V–END	finite verbs in subordinate clauses appear in final position

(iv) und dann zwei jahre zu späte komm ich mit mein kinder (Estefânia P)
Und dann, zwei Jahre später, bin ich mit meinen Kindern gekommen.
'And then, two years later, I arrived with my children.'

(v) da is immer schwierigkeit (Giovanni I)
Da gibt es immer Schwierigkeiten.
'There is always (a) problem.'

(vi) es ist nicht einfach (Janni I)
Es ist nicht einfach
'It is not easy
weil ich den ganzen tag so schwere arbeit habe
weil ich den ganzen Tag so schwere Arbeit (zu tun) habe.
'because I have such hard work (to do) all day.'

Since the observational adequacy of this sequence is not questioned, we can now examine how learners proceed step-by-step through this sequence of acquisition phases. The crucial questions to ask here are whether the L2 learners succeed in acquiring the kind of knowledge which, according to the syntactic analysis outlined above, underlies the mature native German system, and to what extent the L2 approximative systems parallel or differ from the respective L1 intermediate grammars. The fact that differences do exist is obvious and can easily be seen by comparing the two sequences in Tables 4.3 and 4.4. But if this is merely the consequence of choosing a different starting point, as is suggested by the question raised at the beginning of this section, it might be possible to revise this initial hypothesis and thus develop a system qualitatively not distinct from native grammars, even if this revision should require an extended learning process.

The first acquisition task identified by the syntactic analysis of the German target grammar requires determining the head directionality of syntactic phrases. Examining the VP, to begin with, brings us back once again to the transfer issue. The exact nature of the first phase defined by invariant word order is indeed the only controversial point concerning the observational adequacy of the L2 sequence in so far as it has been claimed that the initial SVX phase (X referring to objects and/or adverbial expressions) is not found with learners whose L1 exhibits OV order. In other words, what is controversial about this phase is whether it is characteristic of all learners or only of those with a VO language as L1 (see section 4.1, above). As far as factual correctness is concerned, the resolution of this controversy is an empirical matter which should eventually be solved on the basis of more adequate data. At this point, we are concerned with the consequences for further developments. Let us, therefore, for the sake of argument, consider both possibilities, initial VO and OV order. Recall that the earlier discussion of this issue in 4.3 revealed that transfer, if it is indeed a driving force of early L2 acquisition, cannot alone be held responsible for the use of certain word order patterns by L2 learners, since one finds unambiguous cases of dominant VO order in situations where both the source and the target language are of the OV type. A possible explanation of this fact is that if the target language allows for surface SVO order in some syntactic contexts, learners may be induced to formulate a wrong hypothesis. Note that an explanation of this kind is not necessarily in conflict with the one relying on transfer, for this may well be a case of convergence (Silverstein 1972) where L2 properties appear to confirm, wrongly in this instance, a notion familiar from the L1. But transfer here refers to surface phenomena, that is, it results from 'perceived similarities' (Kouwenberg 1992: 293) due to convergent surface structures.

It appears, thus, that second language learners rely strongly on surface properties of languages, and this may lead them astray when it comes to discovering more abstract features of the target language. Focus on surface phenomena is, of course, a familiar idea in L2 research, and it is also explored by Clahsen and Muysken (1986) in their analysis of early VO order in L2 German. They suggest that L2 learners refer to canonical sentence schemas, as defined by Slobin and Bever (1982) who claim that these schemas, based on the order in simple active declarative sentences, exhibit the dominant order of languages, that is, VO for German and Dutch. According to more recent psycholinguistic findings, this preference may be better accounted for in terms of parsing preferences, as mentioned in section 4.1, assuming that SVO sequences are easier to parse than SOV chains (cf. Weyerts *et al.* 2002 and others). If an explanation along these lines captures this aspect of second language acquisition adequately, the question of why children acquiring German as a first language do not rely on this dominant order too must appear as all the more intriguing. The solution to this puzzle offered by Clahsen and Muysken (1986: 111) is that children possess 'the capacity to postulate an abstract underlying order', in other words that they are guided by UG. The UG knowledge on which L1 learners draw consists primarily of the principles determining phrase structure, that is, the X-bar principle in the theory of UG adopted by Clahsen and Muysken,[13] the theory of predication according to which a syntactic predicate must have a subject, and the principles constraining head movement. The primary data contain sufficient evidence indicating that the specifier positions where the subject may appear are to the left of the respective projections. Since it can further be deduced from linear sequencing in surface strings that the verb may either follow or precede the subject, the only analysis accounting for these facts and conforming to the principles of UG requires leftward movement (raising) of the verb; rightward movement of the subject, on the other hand, is excluded by the ECP (Empty Category Principle; cf. Chomsky 1981a, 1986), an invariant universal principle requiring, simply stated, that the empty trace must be governed by the element moved out of this position. Once leftward movement is established as the correct solution for head movement, the 'optimal grammar', according to Clahsen and Muysken (1996: 112), for a language tolerating VO as well as OV surface patterns is obviously one which assumes OV as the underlying order. It is not necessary, I believe, to go further into the details of their analysis in order to understand that the argument presented by Clahsen and Muysken (1986) basically says that UG principles favour one and probably only one solution, and this explains the uniformity and relative ease of acquisition mentioned above (see Table 4.3). Note that if guidance by UG principles leads to the 'optimal solution', the fact that L2 learners are not able to find this solution must cast doubts on the Full Access to UG hypothesis for L2 acquisition.

Independently of whether one accepts the claim that access to UG enables the learner to discover the optimal grammatical analysis of the data, it is generally agreed that L1 learners analyse German from early on as an OV language, and that at least some L2 learners initially treat German as an SVO language. Let us examine then what the consequences are of the initial VO hypothesis. In order to be able to produce utterances with discontinuous verbal constructions as in (7) (ii), non-finite parts of verbs, including separable verbal particles as in *ansehen* 'to look at' – *sie sieht ihn an* 'she is looking at him' – have to be moved into clause-final position (see phase 3 in Table 4.4). Furthermore, if an adverbial expression or an object is fronted, as seems to be the case in phase 2 in Table 4.4, the subject and the finite verb have to be inverted (phase 4 in Table 4.4) in order to avoid verb placement in third position (*V3). In non-generative grammars, the traditional assumption is that it is the subject which moves in this case, again to the right. Thus, whereas with underlying OV order only one movement operation (V2) is required, that is, head movement of the verb to C (phase III in Table 4.3), two operations are needed with underlying VO order, PART and INV in Table 4.4, in order to generate structures of the type illustrated in (7) (i) to (v). Most importantly, both movements go towards the right. I should add that under both analyses one also needs, of course, operations placing maximal projections in initial position, for example ADV–PRE in Table 4.4, or topicalization (of the subject or of an adverbial, for example) in Table 4.3. A similar situation arises in subordinate clauses where underlying VO order requires two rightward movements, placing the non-finite (PART) *and* the finite verb (V–END, in Table 4.4) at the end of the clause, whereas under the OV hypothesis one type of head movement is sufficient, the same one which is also required in main clauses, except that the finite verb cannot proceed to CP and is stranded in the head of TP. Phase IV of L1 acquisition is thus not characterized by new developments with respect to verb movement; it merely indicates that the children now use subordinate clauses. With L2 learners, on the other hand, the course of acquisition of subordinate clause word order is particularly interesting, for the VO order re-emerges in this context. This may not be surprising as far as the placement of finite verbs is concerned since V–END has been identified as the last phase of the developmental sequence, and most naturalistic L2 learners never reach this phase (Clahsen *et al.* 1983). Interestingly, however, VO patterns reappear in subordinate clauses with non-finite verbs as well, that is, with learners who are capable of placing non-finite verbs in final position in main clauses. The use of these constructions by Romance learners of German (see Müller 1998) constitutes strong evidence suggesting that they have not changed the directionality of the VP to head-final order.

In view of the persistence of VO order with learners whose L1 is of the SVO type, one might wonder whether Turkish and Korean learners of German fare better, in this respect, since they have been claimed to transfer head directionality from their L1, treating German as an OV language. As we have seen in 4.2, Vainikka and Young-Scholten (1996a: 15) indeed report that OV order is strongly dominant at the early stage captured by their Korean and Turkish corpus, and Schwartz and Sprouse (1996: 44) still find clause-final position of non-finite verbs in the utterances of their Turkish learner, at a later stage. In the light of the contrary findings presented in section 4.3, however, this does not necessarily have to be interpreted as a case of transfer of underlying head directionality but may very well result from strategies of language use or from perceived similarities of surface orders. The latter interpretation has the advantage of being better suited to explain intra- and interindividual variation. The fact that L2 learners tend not to use a single word order pattern categorically has been observed frequently, and it is hardly plausible to assume that only some but not other underlying orders are transferred, irrespective of surface similarities. At any rate, it may be the case that learners whose first language exhibits OV order detect this property easily and have no need for an additional operation like PART, placing non-finite verbs in clause-final position.

Learners, however, who perceive an OV language with mixed OV and VO surface orderings, like German, as predominantly VO do have to make adjustments of this kind in order to be able to produce the target patterns, and this definitely complicates their acquisition tasks, as we saw. But the crucial point about the differences between L1 and L2 acquisition observed above is not so much that L2 learners of German having adopted VO order need to acquire more syntactic operations than children working with the OV hypothesis in L1 development. Rather, the more serious problem is that it may not be possible to formulate these operations as grammatical processes conforming to the principles of UG. This, at least, is the argument made by Clahsen and Muysken (1986), a claim which triggered an extensive discussion among L2 researchers. Since some of the more technical aspects of this discussion have become obsolete by subsequent changes of the theory of Universal Grammar, we need not recapitulate all its details. The most important point is that verb movement has to be a structure-preserving operation (Emonds 1976), but under the head-initial assumption there is no position at the end of the clause into which the verb could be moved; consequently, both PART and V–END violate UG constraints. This is, no doubt, an important argument which is not affected by changes in grammatical theory. On the contrary, it is strengthened by later formulations of constraints on head movement. Trace theory, for example, requires that the moved head c-command its trace. As already pointed out above, rightward movement is therefore ruled out to the extent that it implies lowering rather than raising.[14] Clahsen and Muysken (1986: 115) further observe that PART moves a non-homogeneous set of elements (verbal particles, infinitival and participial verbs) out of different positions; it can thus hardly be considered as one type of operation. In the case of INV, their arguments are less plausible and need not be repeated here. Note that, surprisingly, they interpret 'inversion' as verb movement over the subject, a suggestion which is in accordance with assumptions made by generative syntax but which is not supported by empirical observations based on the data on which their analysis is based. If, thus, we are right in assuming that learners move the subject to the right over the verb, similar objections can be raised against this operation as against the rightward movement of non-finite verbs.

Thus although some of the arguments are less convincing than others and some have to be restated in contemporary theoretical terms, the thrust of the argumentation still appears to be correct. Clahsen and Muysken (1986: 95) conclude that 'children have access to the LAD while adults in L2 acquisition do not'; adults rather use, they claim, 'general learning strategies'. While the conclusion that UG is not accessible to L2 learners may be somewhat premature (see section 4.2), and although it is not really clear what they mean by 'general learning strategies', their results strongly suggest that the linguistic knowledge of L2 learners about the target language contains at least some mechanisms which are not grammatical devices conforming to the principles of UG. It is therefore not surprising that this approach soon came under attack by proponents of the Full Access to UG hypothesis, duPlessis, Solin, Travis and White (1987) being the first ones to publish a rejoinder. The common aim of the various opposing analyses has been to demonstrate that the conclusions suggested by Clahsen and Muysken can be avoided if one changes some theoretical assumptions and performs different syntactic analyses. The proposed modifications are of two types: they make a number of additional or different assumptions about grammatical theory and about the grammar of German, and they assume that L2 learners restructure their initial grammar in the course of further developments.

Most of the suggested revisions of the grammatical analysis can be ignored here, I believe, not only because many of the technical arguments have become obsolete in the meantime, just like some of those presented by Clahsen and Muysken (1986), but also because they were less than convincing right from the start. For example, duPlessis *et al.* (1987) had to postulate a number of additional parameters, some of which were never heard of again in the more than twenty years which have passed since the publication of their reply. As a result, the alternative analysis they propose has a strong taint of an ad hoc solution which, in important parts at least, lacks independent motivation and seems to be primarily or exclusively motivated by the case to be made against Clahsen and Muysken (1986). One point of the analysis, however, should be retained, namely the assumption, based on Travis 1984, that the directionality of the IP (TP in our terms) in German is head-initial. I will return to this point shortly.

The alleged restructuring of initial grammars by L2 learners primarily refers to the head directionality of the VP, that is, it has been suggested that L2 learners reanalyse the VP as head-final. According to duPlessis *et al.* (1987) and Schwartz and Tomaselli (1990), this happens at stage 3 (PART). The question of when this might occur is of secondary importance, but the idea of restructuring is indeed a crucial one. Note that it is generally acknowledged that the initial VO hypothesis causes major problems for later grammatical developments in L2 acquisition, and also that the assumption of word order 'rules' violating the principles of UG can only be avoided if the head directionality of the VP and possibly also of the IP (TP), according to Tomaselli and Schwartz (1990), is indeed possible. Consequently, the subsequent debate focused on the issue of whether L2 learners can change parameter settings. This issue will be at the core of our discussion in the following chapter. Here, it should be noted that Clahsen and Muysken (1986, 1989) object, justly, I believe, that neither duPlessis *et al.* (1987) nor Schwartz and Tomaselli (1990) presented empirical support for their claims. Rather, they showed that one can develop an analysis which is not in conflict with the data if one introduces a number of additional mechanisms. This is not to say, however, that it is empirically adequate. Remember that in the ZISA developmental sequence on which the arguments of Clahsen and Muysken (1986, 1989) are based (see Table 4.4), each phase is defined in terms of a set of data emerging for the first time during just this period of acquisition in the speech of learners. Yet the approaches which compete with Clahsen and Muysken do not give any direct empirical evidence for the acquisition steps through which they assume the learners to proceed; instead, they have to postulate concurrent acquisitions, one effacing the empirical effects of the other. To mention just one example, one should expect to find a significant increase in the number of verbs occurring in final position as a result of the reanalysis of the VP as head-final. Yet this is clearly not the case, and duPlessis *et al.* (1987) attempt to account for the lack of empirical repercussions of their proposal by postulating that the 'reanalysis to SOV is concurrent with a verb movement rule'. In other words, they have to assume that simultaneously with the change of head directionality in VP, head movement of the finite verb to (left-headed) IP is supposed to come in. As a result, the surface pattern will be identical to the one encountered before these two alleged changes happened. There is, of course, no a priori reason why two properties of the target grammar should not be acquired simultaneously, but unless one can explicate the theoretical reasons why this happens simultaneously and provide empirical evidence for the claim that it actually does, this can only be qualified as an ad hoc solution. Worse, it is further weakened by the fact that it requires additional mechanisms, which are not independently motivated, in order to explain why SVO order is again found, at later stages, in embedded clauses, and why learners continue to place verbs in third position after preposed constituents like adverbials (*V3). Finally, the analysis by duPlessis *et al.* (1987) is not even adequate at the observational level. As they point out themselves (p. 67), the one kind of structure incompatible with their proposal consists of an SVfinVnon-finO sequence with the finite verb raised and the non-finite verb preceding the object. This type of pattern is indeed attested frequently in the ZISA longitudinal data. Müller (1998), for example, reports that she identified a period lasting from week 22 (length of stay in Germany) until week 56 in the recorded speech of one Italian learner, Bruno, during which VO and OV patterns co-occur, as in (9), from week 26 of the recordings with Bruno.

(9) aber ich habe gehort viele problematische diskussion von Alfio
'but I have heard many problematic discussion by Alfio'

To sum up, head directionality of the German VP which is discovered early and easily by L1 children is undoubtedly a serious problem for L2 learners. Many if not all learners treat German as a VO language. This appears to be primarily motivated by surface properties of German word order. The VX hypothesis, however, whatever the causes for its emergence may be, leads to considerable complications when learners attempt to generate structures required by other verb order options offered by German. Assuming that L2 learners' increasing knowledge about the target variety consists of approximative grammatical systems which are restructured in such a way as to reflect the acquisition sequence summarized in Table 4.4, at least parts of these systems inevitably violate principles of UG. This consequence could perhaps be avoided if the VX hypothesis was abandoned early on, certainly no later than during phase 3. But the evidence presented so far does not corroborate the claim that L2 learners restructure their initial grammars by setting the directionality of the VP to head-final.

Let us therefore briefly look at head directionality of other syntactic categories, that is, the functional categories serving as landing sites of moved verbal elements. This brings us to the second acquisition task, verb movement, which, in fact, consists of two problems which learners have to solve: one concerning the functional head the verb is moved to and the other one relating to what causes movement. I will begin with the first and assume, as I have done throughout this chapter, that there are at least two functional elements above VP, namely TP (or IP, especially in earlier publications) and CP (see (2), above). Head directionality is unproblematic in the case of CP, in German, since all elements which are commonly assumed to be placed there appear in clause-initial position. But with respect to TP, the issue is more controversial, for it has been suggested repeatedly that IP might be left-headed in L2 German. The reasons motivating this proposal are obvious: assuming that the VP exhibits head-final order, an analysis of this kind offers two verbal positions, one clause-finally, one preceding the complement and following the subject. In other words, based on this assumption one can account for two frequently encountered surface positions of German verbs, yielding SXV and SVX. What this analysis does not readily account for is the V2 pattern XVS. But this is at least temporarily a welcome consequence, for as long as learners have not reached phase 4 in Table 4.4, they do in fact use *V3 patterns. As should be apparent, a left-headed TP is an attractive solution only if the VP is head-final. Otherwise, either the VP or the TP must eventually be restructured. As it turns out, these options define, in fact, the main parameters along which the various published proposals vary. They further disagree on what makes the learner choose a particular head directionality and on how to account for the V2 effect in L2 German.

As mentioned above, duPlessis *et al.* (1987) postulate head-initial ordering of the IP even for native German. If this is correct, German sentence structure combines properties of both structures given in section 4.2, a VP as in the standard grammatical analysis of German (2) and a TP as in Romance (1). This is certainly a possible analysis of German, although it is not widely adopted for reasons I do not want to go into. Let me only mention that it is not obvious under this analysis which structural position the finite verb occupies in subordinate clauses requiring clause-final placement of all verbal elements. Recall that, according to these authors, L2 learners initially assume that the IP as well as the VP are left-headed; consequently, only the VP must be restructured. Schwartz and Tomaselli (1990), on the other hand, do not adopt the left-headed IP hypothesis for mature German. They therefore have to argue that the IP too needs to be restructured in the course of L2 acquisition, namely at stage 6 in Table 4.4, that is, at the point when verbal elements appear in the final position of subordinate clauses. Looking at the proposals discussed in the previous sections, we find that the Full Transfer as well as the Valueless Features hypothesis predict that functional projections are transferred from the L1 grammar. Consequently, Turkish and Korean learners should assume that the IP of the target grammar is head-final, placing finite verbs systematically in a position following their complements, whereas Romance-speaking learners are expected to place finite verbs predominantly in a position preceding their complements. But this is not what one finds in the data. Instead, all learners of German strongly prefer the VfinO order, a rather surprising finding given that for Korean and Turkish learners, both the source and the target language are generally assumed to have head-final IPs. The Minimal Trees Hypothesis captures this fact by claiming that the first functional projection above VP is left-headed. Vainikka and Young-Scholten (1996a) do not, however, provide an explanation for why this should be the case; they merely state that it results from an interaction of X-bar theory with the input. This really only says that the evidence can be found in the primary data. In other words, L2 learners rely on surface properties of the target language, as noted repeatedly here.

To sum up, it is widely assumed that the TP in L2 German is at least temporarily left-headed. Transfer of head directionality is hardly a satisfactory explanation for this claim, even less so than for the directionality of the VP. Rather, this observation confirms our earlier hypothesis that L2 learners draw primarily on information available in L2 surface strings. At any rate, the repeatedly proposed left-headedness of TP in L2 German leads me to the same conclusion at which I arrived discussing the VP: unless the head directionality of the TP is eventually changed to head-final, L2 learners will have to resort to operations which do not conform to principles of UG, as claimed by Clahsen and Muysken (1986). It is therefore not surprising that all authors favouring the Full Access to UG hypothesis, including duPlessis *et al.* (1987), argue that L2 learners do change IP directionality. This, they claim, is another instance of resetting parameter values. They do not, however, provide empirical evidence for this, other than pointing to the fact that finite verbs are placed in final position of subordinate clauses as of stage 6 in Table 4.4. Whether parameter resetting is a more plausible solution than postulating an operation like V–END remains to be seen. The discussion in chapter 5, especially section 5.2, will hopefully shed some light on this issue.

I think, however, that an argument from first language acquisition research should already be mentioned here, for it might be relevant for second language acquisition as well. Although head directionality seems to be acquired easily and rapidly in L1 German, as I have argued above, it has nevertheless been suggested that a functional category other than Comp might be left-headed in German child grammars (see Clahsen 1991; Meisel and Müller 1992). The reason for this is that children at this point of development use apparent V2 constructions but not any other element or structure related to the CP, for example either embedded clauses or wh-elements. This has led to the conclusion that the respective child grammar lacks a CP and that the finite verb is raised to a left-headed functional projection (FP) allowing arguments (subjects, objects) as well as non-arguments (adverbials) in its specifier position (see section 2.3). Although the head of FP hosts the finite verb, it is not identical to TP; rather, it is defined as an underspecified category which might turn into a CP once it is specified for the full set of features required by the mature grammar (cf. Clahsen 1991). Thus although FP is motivated by distributional properties of finite and non-finite verbs, just like the left-headed IP (TP) in L2 research, it reflects a very different kind of linguistic knowledge and has therefore quite different syntactic properties. Note also that this hypothesis does not entail resetting parameter values.

One of the essential differences characterizing the course of first and second language acquisition respectively concerns the so-called V2 effect. For L1 learners, placement of finite verbs in second position of the sentence structure is unproblematic. During phase II in Table 4.3 some children fail to raise all finite verbs, leaving them in clause-final position (see also section 4.2); this is, however, a rare phenomenon which appears only briefly in the course of L1 development.[15] The crucial point is that as soon as finite verbs are moved out of the final position, they appear regularly in V2 position, that is, preceding the subject if an adverbial is preposed. Although some *V3 patterns do occur in this context, they are very rare and disappear rapidly (see Clahsen 1982). Whether the verb is raised to the head of CP at this point or to FP, as suggested in the preceding paragraph, is of secondary importance in the present context. Looking at L2 acquisition, the differences become immediately apparent, for *V3 order represents a particularly persistent pattern in the speech of L2 learners of German. A syntactic analysis of this construction would have to state that the adverbial is adjoined to the sentence, a common phenomenon in Romance languages, rather than being moved to the specifier position of FP/CP. Consequently, preposing of this element does not trigger verb raising out of TP. The adjunction option for a fronted element could result from cross-linguistic influence by the L1 when Romance-speaking learners are concerned. But it is unlikely that this is the correct explanation because *V3 patterns are used by other learners as well, whereas I know of no evidence suggesting that German learners of a Romance language prefer V2 order. At any rate, the issue here is not so much what causes these constructions to appear in the speech of L2 learners but what enables learners of German to eventually place the verb in post-subject position. Recall that the ZISA acquisition sequence displayed in Table 4.4 suggests that it is subject–verb inversion (INV) which makes V2 sequences possible. If this was to be understood as an instance of subject movement to the right of the verb, it would be ruled out as a grammatical operation conforming to UG, as has been shown by Clahsen and Muysken (1986). However, if this is to suggest that verbs move to the left, that is, to the head of CP, it implies that the preposed element is not adjoined but is placed in the specifier position of CP, for syntactic theory links these two kinds of movement to one another. From this again it follows that L2 learners need to restructure their intermediate grammar in one more respect, and this is indeed what duPlessis *et al.* (1987: 68) propose. They argue that learners reset the 'adjunction parameter' (Travis 1991: 356) which gives a yes/no option for adjunction of fronted elements.

Thus once again, in trying to gain insights into the underlying knowledge guiding the course of language acquisition as it manifests itself in the developmental sequences represented in Tables 4.3 and 4.4, we find that L1 development can be accounted for quite successfully in syntactic terms, whereas in L2 acquisition we face the alternative between parameter resetting or allowing for the possibility that learners use an operation not conforming to the principles of UG. In other words, much of what we have learned so far suggests that the answer to our most crucial question, asking whether the same kind of mechanisms underlie first and second language acquisition, depends essentially on the theoretical plausibility and empirical well-foundedness of the idea of parameter resetting in L2 acquisition. It appears to be time, then, to move on to chapter 5, where this issue will be examined more carefully. But a couple of points still need to be mentioned before the new chapter can be opened. One of them concerns the possibility of deciding empirically between the two alternative explanations. In the cases examined so far, this was not really possible, for the approaches advocating parameter resetting are largely based on the same data as the ones postulating non-UG conforming operations. Here, however, an empirical test is indeed feasible since the predictions are not identical if inversion is understood as rightward movement of the subject rather than as head movement, a raising operation, moving the verb leftward. We do, in fact, have some evidence supporting the rightward movement hypothesis, for in cases where the utterance contains more than one object or adverb, learners tend to place the subject at the very end of the clause rather than immediately after the verb (see Clahsen 1984).

(10) (i) wie heiss' in deutsch Nederland? (José SL)
how named in German Nederland?
'What is "Nederland" called in German?'
(ii) jetzt liest ein buch Susanne (Ana SL)
now reads a book Susanne
'Now, Susanne reads a book.'

The type of construction illustrated by (10) is obviously not used frequently by learners who are not very advanced, just entering phase 4 of the L2 sequence in Table 4.4, but instances of subject insertion in between the verb and a complement, that is, YVfinSX, are even less frequent. Scrutinizing the ZISA longitudinal data, for example, reveals that they are virtually non-existent during phase 4 in the speech of the five learners who advanced as far as this phase or beyond, that is, Giovanni IL, Ana SL, Zita PL, Bruno IL, and José SL.[16] Only those who proceed further in the acquisition of German appear to be able to replace this kind of subject movement to the right of the clause by true subject–verb inversion. Note that, if this observation is correct, the emergence of 'inversion' patterns cannot be interpreted as an unambiguous indication of the acquisition of target-like head movement resulting from parameter resetting, not even as evidence for the implementation in the L2 grammar of a local permutation rule of subject–auxiliary inversion (Baltin 1982), but rather as a kind of subject extraposition of uncertain grammatical status which might, in fact, be a case of finalization in the surface string. For the time being, the case must remain open. I will return to this issue in chapter 5, section 5.3.

The last point, now, concerns the question of what causes the verb to move. Remember that it depends on the strength of the features in functional heads whether a verb raises to this position. The precise nature of the mechanisms involved need not concern us here, although they play an increasingly important role in recent versions of the theory of Universal Grammar, particularly in the Minimalist Program, as observed by Radford (1997: chapters 5 and 6). Simply keep in mind that verb raising is closely related to the [±finiteness] distinction on verbs. The logical connection between the two phenomena is evidenced by the chronology of L1 development and needs to be explained by grammatical theory. One way to achieve this in the framework of the Principles and Parameters Theory was to postulate an operator [+F] attracting the finite verb. Since the position to which the verb is moved varies across languages, Platzack and Holmberg (1989) suggested a 'finiteness parameter' determining the functional head which can host the finite verb; see (1) and (2) where this is indicated as one of the properties distinguishing Romance languages and German. In the Minimalist Program, it is the strength of uninterpretable features which causes the finite verb to raise to the respective functional head (see chapter 2, section 2.3).

One aspect of this issue which remains somewhat opaque is the problem of what determines feature strength. After all, some languages like English lack features strong enough to cause raising of thematic verbs altogether. Rich overt morphology encoding finiteness on verbs obviously plays an important role, but it is apparently neither a necessary nor a sufficient condition for attributing <strong> features to a grammar. For the time being, we have to content ourselves with the descriptive generalization according to which a grammar contains <strong> features if a language exhibits overt movement of finite verbs, and the absence of such movement indicates that no <strong> feature is available. The absence of an independently motivated defining criterion for feature strength makes it more difficult, of course, to decide on the strength of a particular feature in the linguistic knowledge of learners.

Let us nevertheless have a brief look at the hypotheses discussed in section 4.2, asking what they predict with respect to verb movement. Beck (1998) offers, in fact, a fairly detailed comparison of these three approaches, using the example of a source language without raising (English) and a target language with raising (German). For this scenario, the Full Transfer hypothesis predicts that, in accordance with the L1 grammar, verbs should initially not be moved but will later be raised obligatorily as L2 feature strength is discovered. The Minimal Trees Hypothesis predicts no raising at the initial VP-only stage, optional raising at the FP stage when the projection is still underspecified with respect to the features which might trigger verb raising, and obligatory raising once the head of IP (TP) has been fully specified. The Valueless Features Hypothesis, finally, predicts optional raising during an early phase when functional categories are underspecified, and obligatory raising once they are fully specified. Interestingly enough, Beck's (1998) results from a reaction-time experiment with early and late English-speaking learners of German confirm none of the three hypotheses. She finds instead that both learner groups exhibit optional raising and that there is no developmental relation between the acquisition of inflectional morphology on verbs and verb placement.

It is this latter point which is particularly relevant in the present context, for if the connection between finiteness and verb raising can indeed be explained as the result of one and the same parametric choice, the developmental dissociation of the two phenomena argues strongly against an account of word order acquisition in terms of parameter (re)setting. This is precisely the argument made by Clahsen (1988b) who points out that the expected developmental connection is found in L1 but not in L2 German. The dissociation he observed in L2 acquisition has since been confirmed in a number of studies (e.g. Meisel 1991 and Parodi 1998). Recall that it also became apparent in our discussion of the acquisition of the syntax of negation in chapter 3. These results are particularly damaging for the Valueless Features Hypothesis, which relies on the acquisition of L2 inflectional morphology in order to trigger the target-like setting of featural values.

One way to save a parameter setting approach to L2 acquisition in spite of such findings might be to distinguish between the acquisition of grammatical concepts and the learning of the inventory of forms required to express these, as discussed in section 3.3. In other words, the learners' knowledge about finiteness and L2 feature strength might be argued to be independent of their success in learning the respective forms of L2 inflectional morphology. This type of argument is indeed made by Schwartz and Sprouse (1996: 57). Although this certainly represents a theoretically legitimate possibility, it is hardly convincing unless the empirical facts are identified which might count as corroborating or falsifying evidence. Currently, such evidence is not available. Feature strength is empirically indicated by verb placement alone, and verb raising, in turn, is the only possible indication of feature strength. This scenario seems to suggest that the acquisition of verb morphology is in fact irrelevant for the issue of feature strength, and neither verb raising in the absence of L2 morphology nor lack of raising in spite of successful morphological learning – both attested in the above mentioned studies – are recognized as constituting valid evidence under this approach. Many will find this situation less than satisfactory. Although there can be no doubt that abstract grammatical analyses are needed in language acquisition research, this does not mean that empirical evidence can be dispensed with. At any rate, even if the dissociation of syntax and morphology seems to be evident in these cases, this does not warrant the claim that the representation of grammatical knowledge – feature strength, in this case – is not deficient, as argued by the Missing Surface Inflection Hypothesis (MSIH) mentioned in section 3.3. Rather, it may well be that the L2 learners' grammatical knowledge is indeed deficient and that this is permanent damage, as implied by Beck (1998). The dissociation of verb raising and verbal inflectional morphology certainly has to be considered as possible evidence against a parameter setting explanation of L2 acquisition. I will return to this issue in chapters 5 (especially sections 5.2 and 5.3) and 7.

To conclude this section, we can now ask what has been learned about the changes subsequent to the initial state and whether the findings obtained here speak in favour of similarities or of differences between first and second language acquisition. Examining how learners succeed in performing the tasks they face when acquiring German verb placement, we observe indeed a number of significant differences between types of acquisition. The preceding sections revealed that L1 and L2 learners make different assumptions about basic word order, and a plausible explanation for this fact seems to be that ambiguous surface evidence leads L2 learners to analyse German as an SVO language whereas L1 learners succeed in discovering the correct underlying OV order. Since children's ability to access UG is commonly thought to make this achievement possible, adult L2 learners' failure to perform similarly suggests that they do not have direct access to UG any more. Moreover, assuming that they treat German as an SVO language entails the conclusion that they develop word order procedures which are not grammatical operations as defined by UG. In order to avoid this conclusion we would have to hypothesize that they restructure their L2 grammar, replacing a left-headed by a head-final VP. Empirical evidence for this type of restructuring, however, has not been offered. The same situation arises with respect to

IP-headedness. If one wants to avoid the conclusion that L2 grammars violate UG principles, one has to claim that an initially left-headed IP is changed to head-final by parameter resetting, but empirical support for this claim is lacking too. Finally, we have found reasons to believe that the verb-second effect, achieved without apparent difficulty by L1 learners raising the finite verb into the head of CP, is mimicked by L2 learners by placing the subject after the verb, possibly even in clause-final position. Once again, L2 acquisition would look more like L1 development if it could be argued that V2 phenomena depend on the value to which an adjunction parameter is set. But what might cause verb raising in L2 grammars remains mysterious given that in L2 acquisition one does not find the developmental relation well attested in L1 development between the emergence of the [±finiteness] distinction and verb raising.

Let me finally try to summarize briefly how the results obtained in this chapter might help to answer the question raised at the beginning, concerning the possible role of the LAD in L2 acquisition. The crucial point here is to determine whether the L2 acquisition process can be characterized as a sequence of approximative systems and whether the L2 learner's knowledge, at each point of development, can be qualified as a transitional competence constrained by principles of Universal Grammar. The answer is positive only in so far as we do find a sequence of approximative systems which, at least in part, make use of the same categories and relations as in L1 development. L2 acquisition is thus defined in terms of domain-specific cognitive operations applying to language-specific mental objects. On the negative side, there exists strong evidence indicating that L2 learners' linguistic knowledge systems also contain operations which cannot, it seems, be formulated in such a way as to represent operations conforming to UG principles. L2 learners seem to rely very strongly on properties displayed by surface strings of the target language rather than applying UG principles in order to discover abstract underlying structures. In fact, not even transfer of underlying properties of the L1 appears to be as plausible as a cursory examination might suggest. L1 influence operates by directing learners' perception towards L2 properties rather than via transfer of knowledge representations. Note that claims to the effect that L1 influence is more limited than might have been expected should be welcome to those who find more similarities than differences between L1 and L2 acquisition, because L1 transfer necessarily adds to L1–L2 differences. Yet it now seems that grammatical transfer is neither the only source of differences nor is it the one entailing the most serious consequences. In fact, the discussion of German verb placement has shown that differences in the initial hypothesis are decisive, irrespective of whether or not they are caused by L1 influence. The most crucial issue and perhaps the most controversial one, however, concerns the possibility of revising initial knowledge representations. Proponents of the Full Access to UG hypothesis claim that L2 learners restructure their transitional grammars by (re)setting parameters to the values required by the target grammar. Their opponents deny this and argue, instead, that approximative systems of L2 learners contain properties violating UG principles. In sum, there can be no doubt that the question of whether parameters can be set to values distinct from the ones instantiated in the L1 grammars is decisive in determining whether the underlying knowledge of L2 learners is fundamentally different from the grammatical competence of children and whether both learner types have access to identical knowledge sources. The following chapter is therefore dedicated to the issue of parameter setting in second language acquisition, but it will also consider alternative possibilities like inductive learning.

4.5 Suggested readings and topics for discussion

Suggested readings

Since sections 4.2 and 4.4 present detailed summaries of and comments on a number of publications, it is important to become familiar with at least some of these papers. I therefore recommend reading the following:

Clahsen, H. and P. Muysken 1986. 'The availability of universal grammar to adult and child learners: A study of the acquisition of German word order', *Second Language Research* 2: 93–119.

duPlessis, J., D. Solin, L. Travis and L. White 1987. 'UG or not UG, that is the question: A reply to Clahsen and Muysken', *Second Language Research* 3: 56–75.

Eubank, L. 1993/94. 'On the transfer of parametric values in L2 development', *Language Acquisition* 3: 183–208.

Schwartz, B. D. and R. A. Sprouse 1996. 'L2 cognitive states and the Full Transfer/Full Access model', *Second Language Research* 12: 40–77.

Vainikka, A. and M. Young-Scholten 1996b. 'The early stages in adult L2 syntax: Additional evidence from Romance speakers', *Second Language Research* 12: 140–76.

To supplement the discussion of transfer in section 4.3, the following paper will be useful:

Håkansson, G., M. Pienemann and S. Sayehli 2002. 'Transfer and typological proximity in the context of second language processing', *Second Language Research* 18: 250–73.

Topics for discussion

- In section 2.2 of chapter 2, we discussed the *continuity assumption* in research on first language development. Summarize the main idea expressed by this assumption, including the so-called 'strong' and 'weak' versions of it. Examine it in the light of what has been said in this chapter about the initial state and subsequent developments in L2 and consider how it could be applied to second language acquisition. Compare your conclusions to what is argued in introductions (of your choice) to L2 acquisition research. Where do you see parallels and differences between L1 and L2 acquisition?
- The various attempts to account for L2 learners' knowledge at the initial state of acquisition, discussed in section 4.2, make different

claims about the role of L1 grammars as well as about the degree to which early L2 knowledge resembles that of children during early phases of L1 development. Concerning the latter, compare the Basic Variety (cf. Klein and Perdue 1997) to the Minimal Trees Hypothesis or its more recent variant, Organic Grammar (cf. Vainikka and Young-Scholten 2006).

- Approaches to L2 acquisition which postulate full access to UG rely crucially on learners' ability to alter the strength of features contained in functional heads. Explain the notion of 'strength' in this context, referring to an introduction to generative syntax (of your choice) and state explicitly what kinds of empirical evidence would reveal feature strength in mature and in developing grammars. What has the theory of syntax to say about feature strength and (obligatory, impossible or optional) syntactic movement?
- The Missing Surface Inflection Hypothesis could be accused of postulating acquisition achievement which cannot be verified empirically in that it claims that non-finite verb *forms* really encode finiteness. Summarize what kind of empirical evidence is in fact offered by proponents of the MSIH, and add further types of such evidence, if possible.

5 Developing grammatical knowledge: Parameter setting and inductive learning

5.1 Access to UG principles in L2 acquisition

Our quest for the LAD, the principles and mechanisms of the human mind enabling the child to acquire language, and the exploration of its fate in the course of subsequent developments, has so far revealed a number of substantial parallels as well as pointed differences between first and second language acquisition. As such, this is hardly a surprising result. Rather, this summary of the state of affairs corresponds to what could be expected and to what was actually suspected at the starting point of our discussion in chapter 1. I nevertheless believe that we have made some headway since we are now able to substantiate such expectations in terms of specific characteristics of linguistic development. We saw in chapters 2 and 3 that learners of both acquisition types proceed through invariant sequences in their acquisition of syntactic and morphological properties of the target languages. Yet these sequences are not identical in L1 and in L2 acquisition. Moreover, the two types of acquisition differ substantially even at the initial state and during very early developmental phases, as discussed in chapter 4. These findings result from descriptive generalizations based on a wide array of empirical observations. Whereas some of these refer to phenomena which, although attested in both acquisition types, differ with respect to their order of emergence or in that they appear in different structural contexts, others distinguish L1 and L2 in that they occur in the speech of only one type of learner, for example certain positions of the negative element reported on in section 3.3, differences in the acquisition of bound versus free morphemes (3.2), or the placement of non-finite verbs in verb-second contexts (4.4), all characteristics of L2 speech.

Accumulating descriptions of differences between types of acquisition will not, however, suffice if we want to come closer to an explanation of the acquisition processes, even if most of these differences concern observations which are not controversial. As mentioned in the research agenda outlined in the first chapter and as pointed out repeatedly since, this can only be achieved by means of insights into the nature of the underlying principles and mechanisms of acquisition. If, for example, it turned out that the finding of distinct developmental sequences could be accounted for satisfactorily by the fact that the starting points of development are not identical, this would speak against the assumption of fundamental differences in the acquisition mechanisms. Yet in view of the evidence reviewed in the previous chapters, this appears to be an increasingly unlikely solution. Instead, the differences seem to be of a more profound nature. This suspicion is nurtured by the finding that linguistic development in the first language can be accounted for in terms of grammatical principles (cf. 2.3 and 2.4) whereas this is only partially possible in L2 acquisition, as has become obvious in chapter 3. If, moreover, proceeding through the phases characterizing the L2 acquisition sequence of word order regularities discussed in section 4.4 indeed involves operations not conforming to UG principles, this strongly supports the idea of fundamental differences between L1 and L2 acquisition. Similarly, if placement of the negative element depends on adjacency relationships rather than on finite verb raising, or if postverbal position of subjects results from rightward movement of the nominal element, this suggests that L2 learners rely in at least some instances on learning and/or production mechanisms which are not part of the acquisition device subserving L1 development. In other words, some domains of the linguistic knowledge of L2 learners cannot be explained in terms of principles of Universal Grammar, whereas equivalent aspects of L1 utterances can in fact be accounted for by UG principles.

Remember that a crucial argument supporting this conclusion refers to the fact that L2 learners at the initial state of acquisition typically make implicit (or explicit) assumptions about structural properties of the target language which are markedly distinct from those assigned to corresponding structures by developing as well as mature native grammars of these languages. Consequently, only by revising the initial hypotheses might L2 learners be able to develop grammatical knowledge qualitatively similar or identical to that of native learners. In chapter 4, I argued that the necessary changes for this type of revision imply restructuring of the transitional grammars which, in the framework of Principles and Parameters Theory (PPT), crucially involves parameter 'resetting', that is, fixing parameters on values different from their initial or previous settings. In fact, as should have become obvious by the discussion in the previous chapter, the question of whether parameter (re)setting is indeed a cognitive mechanism available to L2 learners arises inevitably if one assumes that transfer can play some role at the initial state of L2 learners' grammatical competence. To the extent that transfer involves L1 values of parameters, one must address the question of whether these settings can be changed subsequently if they differ from the target value. But this is by no means the only scenario in which parameter resetting becomes a crucial issue. As pointed out in section 4.2, a similar situation arises in cases where a particular parameterized option is not instantiated at all in the L1 grammar but is part of the L2 grammar. If the claim is that, in this case, the inert parameter is initially set to a default value (see section 2.2), exactly the same consequences follow, that is, it has to be set to a different value. If, on the other hand, one wants to claim that the parameter value is initially open, it will subsequently have to be set to a specific value, as required by the target system. In both cases, all parameterized options offered by UG need to be accessible to the L2 learner – unless inductive learning enables learners to make the necessary changes in their interlanguages.

At this point, it is perhaps useful to proceed as at the beginning of the preceding chapter, reviewing the logical possibilities with respect to access to UG and summarizing the most likely interpretations of the claim that access to UG is possible in L2 acquisition. Although this goes beyond the question concerning the role of parameters and the possibility of parameter (re)setting, it might help us to attain a better understanding of these issues and to relate them to the broader issue of whether UG principles, parameterized or not, determine the content and the development of L2 grammatical knowledge. As mentioned in chapter 4 (see also Meisel 2000a), one can distinguish between three proposals, namely (A) Full access to UG, (B) Partial access to UG and (C) No access to UG. As with transfer, the intermediate position (B) needs to be specified in a theoretically satisfactory way with respect to what kind of knowledge is accessible and what is not, in order to be able to make principled predictions rather than contenting ourselves with ad hoc claims. The distinction made by the Principles and Parameters Theory between parameterized and non-parameterized principles indeed allows us to phrase the question about access to UG in a more subtle way since the answer may well depend on the kind of principle one refers to. Moreover, UG access may or may not be mediated by previously acquired languages, most likely by the grammatical knowledge about the L1. In fact, once one considers the possibility that solutions for the 'access to UG' problem could depend on the importance attributed to these distinctions, that is, parameterized versus non-parameterized principles and direct versus indirect accessibility, it immediately becomes obvious that this is not only the case for option (B), partial access. As a consequence, a number of different scenarios should be considered, rather than merely the initial 'UG or not UG' option or the only slightly more sophisticated threefold distinction 'full/partial/no access to UG'.

(A) Full access necessarily implies that learners have access to all principles and parameterized options, at every point of acquisition. Although it formulates a categorical statement, the Full Access hypothesis still leaves room for variation, depending on what role is attributed to previously acquired knowledge. Learners may be expected either (a) to draw on the knowledge provided by UG unless specific reasons induce them to first explore the possibilities offered by the L1 grammar, or (b) to rely initially on previously acquired knowledge and to resort to UG knowledge only if the former fails to provide the desired results.

(C) No access obviously means that L2 learners do not have direct access to the wealth of implicit knowledge provided by UG. But here too, different conclusions can be drawn concerning the knowledge sources available in L2 acquisition. (a) One possibility is to maintain that L2 learners have to rely entirely on non-linguistic, that is, non-domain-specific cognitive operations. (b) Another option is to argue that principles instantiated in the L1 grammar can be used in L2 acquisition, although parameter values cannot be changed since the alternative parametric options are not available any more. Principles not activated in the L1 grammar (non-parameterized and parameterized ones) are, of course, lost. In other words, under this scenario 'no access' means that UG principles are only

Table 5.1: *Scenarios involving partial access to UG knowledge in L2 acquisition*

UG principles	not activated in L1	activated in L1
(a) parameterized	+	–
non-parameterized	+	–
(b) parameterized	–	+
non-parameterized	–	+
(c) parameterized	–	–
non-parameterized	+	+

indirectly available via the L1 grammar, much like in version (b) of the Partial Access hypothesis presented below. Consequently, the learners' knowledge about grammatical properties of the L2 target language may be expected to conform in part to constraints imposed by UG on natural grammars. 'No access' thus does not necessarily entail that L2 knowledge should violate all the constraints imposed by UG on natural languages and that L2 learners will develop 'wild grammars'. Rather, such violations are predicted to occur only in those domains in which L1 and L2 grammars differ.

(B) Partial access can refer to the parameterized/non-parameterized distinction as well as to the alternative between previously activated or not activated principles. This allows for a number of logical possibilities, though not all are of equal plausibility. Table 5.1 presents a schematic overview of the more likely ones.

(a) One imaginable scenario implies that only principles not activated in the L1 grammar can be accessed in L2 acquisition. The idea behind this assumption is that UG principles turn into target grammar principles, becoming part of the native grammar as the L1 is acquired. This amounts to saying that UG gradually self-destructs in the course of L1 development. Parameterized principles *not* activated in L1 would thus be accessible as in L1 and could be set to the appropriate target value. As for the UG principles activated in L1, on the other hand, they are not directly accessible for L2 learners, but they are assumed to be available via the L1 grammar. Parameter values which are not identical in L1 and L2, however, cannot be reset since the kind of knowledge enabling the learner to do this has been lost with the pristine state of UG. At any rate, this would not count as an instance of access to UG, given that it involves access to UG-related knowledge via the L1 grammar.

(b) The second option means that only principles activated in the course of L1 development can be accessed in L2 acquisition. The rationale behind this idea is that knowledge not activated during the appropriate period of language acquisition degenerates, possibly as a result of neural maturation. Only UG knowledge activated in L1 remains available. In the case of parameterized principles this may lead to problems when the L2 target setting differs from the one in the L1. Setting parameters to values not implemented in the L1 grammar amounts to saying that UG knowledge *not* activated in the course of L1 development continues to be available in L2 acquisition, contrary to the basic line of argument of this second option according to which UG knowledge needs to be activated early on in order to remain accessible. Only if it can be argued that all possible values are activated in the process of setting a parameter to a specific value will the option(s) not chosen by the L1 grammar remain available to L2 learners. Although it is difficult to see what kind of psycholinguistic mechanisms might allow for the latter possibility, it cannot be excluded out of hand, and this approach (b) thus remains ambiguous with respect to the 'resetting' issue.

(c) The third option is that only non-parameterized principles continue to be accessible in L2 acquisition. This hypothesis is based on the assumption that parameterized principles – and only these – are subject to maturational changes (see Smith and Tsimpli 1995). From this it follows that open parameters, that is, parameterized grammatical options not instantiated in the L1 grammar, cannot be fixed anymore and L1 settings of parameter values cannot be altered in L2 acquisition. In my opinion, this is the most plausible of the three options of proposal (B) (partial access to UG) considered here. I will therefore deal with it in more detail below, and this brief characterization must suffice for the time being.

This schematic review of some possible scenarios confirms our suspicion that the broader question of whether or not L2 learners can access UG knowledge can only be answered if a number of more specific issues are settled. The extent to which learners rely on L1 knowledge in order to be able to develop an L2 competence, however, is not one of them, in spite of the fact that this issue is frequently referred to under the label of 'indirect access' to UG. In reality, the idea of 'indirect access' via the L1 grammar is compatible with all three types of approach (A, B, C) and is thus not dependent on one's position with respect to the access problem. The various scenarios demonstrate, instead, that the question of whether parameters can be set to different values is indeed the crucial one. As opposed to the claim of the Full Access hypothesis, the No Access (C) as well as the various versions of the Partial Access (B) hypothesis mentioned here all predict, though in different ways, that setting a parameter to a value different from that in the L1 grammar ('resetting') should not be possible. As for principles or parameter values *not activated* in L1, (C) as well as (B) (b) envisage problems for all types of principles, whereas (B) (c) maintains that only parameterized principles cannot be set any more. In fact, to the extent that changing the settings of parameters requires the continued availability of information provided by UG but not instantiated in the L1 grammar, the two questions are closely related, focusing on different aspects of the problem. To sum up, the two issues highlighted here are the following:

i. The *restructuring* issue, whether parameters can be (re)set to different values once they have been fixed in the L1 grammar.

ii. The *inertia* issue, whether UG knowledge not activated during L1 development can be accessed in the course of L2 acquisition.

Note that not all logically possible positions offered by these scenarios are defended in published research on L2 acquisition. It is, in fact, frequently difficult to allocate individuals or publications to a specific scenario. I will, nevertheless, try to summarize how these two issues are treated by currently debated hypotheses on L2 acquisition. The Full Access hypothesis in its various forms relies on both assumptions addressed in (i) and (ii), although proponents of the (A) (a) version like Flynn (1996) emphasize (ii), whereas those favouring (A) (b) stress (i), for example Schwartz and Sprouse (1996). Proponents of the No Access hypothesis, on the other hand, necessarily have to reject both (i) and (ii). Note that the (C) (b) scenario to which I would assign Bley-Vroman (1989, 1990) or Clahsen and Muysken (1989), among others, actually represents the so-called 'Indirect Access' hypothesis, postulating the availability of UG knowledge via the L1 grammar, although critics of the No Access hypothesis tend not to acknowledge this possibility (e.g. Flynn 1996). As for the various versions of the Partial Access hypothesis, (B) (a) strongly relies on (ii), allowing for the setting of unset parameters while rejecting (i), that is, resetting of fixed parameters. Surprisingly, neither (B) (a) nor (B) (b) seem to be explored in published work on L2 acquisition, although they are not implausible hypotheses, provided one accepts parameter resetting as a possibility at least for L1 development. (B) (c), finally, rejects (i), but it accepts (ii) in part, that is, for non-parameterized principles (see Tsimpli and Roussou (1991), Hawkins (1994), Hawkins and Chan (1997) and, for a more recent proposal in line with developments of the Minimalist Program, Tsimpli and Dimitrakopoulou (2007)).

In sum, this brief review shows that most of the above-mentioned scenarios can or rather must be discarded if the questions implied in (i) and (ii) are answered negatively. If it can be shown that parameter resetting is not possible, Full Access, that is, (A) (a) as well as (A) (b), and Partial Access in one of the (B) (b) versions are out. If, on the other hand, setting of inert parameters (not activated in L1) is not possible in L2 acquisition, (A) (a) and (b) and (B) (a) are out. Given that (C) (a) seems to be implausible for principled reasons and is not defended in current research, this leaves us with (B) (c) and (C) (b). In fact, (B) (c) is not entirely independent of the inertness issue either since it maintains that non-parameterized principles remain available to child and adult L2 learners. In other words, if we can draw firm conclusions with respect to these two problems, the restructuring and the inertia issue, we will be much closer to an answer to the central question of our discussion, concerning the role of the LAD in first and second language acquisition. This is why these two issues need to be discussed in some detail in this chapter.

5.2 Parameter (re)setting

At this point in our quest for the LAD, the *restructuring issue* has emerged as the single most important problem which, if solved adequately, should enable us to gain significant insights concerning the fate of the Language Making Capacity beyond the earliest years of child language development. The crucial importance of restructuring emphasized by the schematic overview presented in the preceding section should not, in fact, come as a surprise in view of the many widely acknowledged differences between first and second language acquisition, some of which were mentioned in the preceding chapters. To the extent that they are due to differences in the underlying grammatical knowledge, and under the commonly held view that approximative systems, in the course of L2 acquisition, increasingly resemble the target system, it follows that early learner grammars must necessarily be restructured. Although there is considerable disagreement on which of the observable differences reflect distinct grammatical representations rather than differences in usage, there can be no doubt that at least some of these phenomena can only be accounted for in terms of grammar. If, for example, an OV language is (initially) analysed as a VO language as discussed in section 4.3, independently of whether or not this is caused by transfer from the L1, this must be interpreted as a fact of grammar. In fact, if transfer is understood as an import of grammatical knowledge from another language, the restructuring issue becomes even more crucial, and ever more so if one adopts a view according to which transfer plays a central role, as does the Full Transfer hypothesis.

The fact that restructuring is a crucial issue to be dealt with in L2 research is not so surprising. What is perhaps more surprising is that parameter setting plays such a central role in this context. Acquisition implies much more than the ability to reproduce adequate surface strings. If, then, parameter values can be transferred from the L1 grammar, the question of whether it is possible to set them to a new value in acquiring the second language is indeed of special importance for a characterization of the linguistic knowledge of the L2 learner.[1]

This issue needs to be stated explicitly at this point in the discussion. The main concern of the type of second language acquisition research advocated here is to gain insights into the underlying principles and mechanisms enabling the L2 learner to learn. It is thus part of a more broadly conceived research programme investigating the nature of the human Language Making Capacity. This is also what motivates and justifies the comparison of various acquisition types, like the similarities and differences between first and second language acquisition. From this perspective, we must address the question of whether the principles determining first language development continue to be operative in the course of L2 acquisition. Since we adopted the view discussed in chapter 2 and elsewhere in this book that UG constitutes an essential part of the LMC, the fate of UG principles is necessarily of prime importance. The exact nature of these principles depends, of course, on the state of grammatical theorizing, and our understanding of the human endowment for language necessarily changes as theories of grammar and of development change. Parameter theory has undergone significant modifications since its early version put forth by Chomsky (1981a, 1981b) and others. As argued in chapter 2, parameterized principles of UG can still be considered to be the most adequate theoretical tool when it comes to accounting for universals as well as particulars of grammatical development in children's first languages.

This is why the setting/resetting issue must also be a major concern for L2 research – and it has, in fact, been one of the major issues in generative work on L2 acquisition since the mid-1980s. In recent years, however, the interest in this problem seems to be fading, and one finds remarks to the effect that it is time to address new questions. This attitude is perhaps due to the unsatisfactory state-of-the-art of Parameter Theory, commented on in chapter 2, and also to a feeling that the debate on the possibility of access to UG has led to a situation of stalemate. Although it goes without saying that new issues need to be put on the agenda of L2 acquisition research, others cannot be abandoned merely for the sake of innovation. Trying to answer questions concerning the extent to which the child's endowment for language remains available in successive language acquisition – and more specifically how parameterized principles of UG fare – represents, in my view, the most important challenge for language acquisition research. It promises to lead to insights not only into the nature of language acquisition but into the human language faculty more generally. It would reflect rather negatively on this sub-discipline of the language sciences if L2 acquisition research gave up on this issue without having reached a satisfactory result. It should, furthermore, not be forgotten that progress has been made in this debate, as has been pointed out by White (2003: chapter 1). The discussion of the 'access issue' has moved beyond the fundamentalist 'UG or not UG' alternative towards more subtle inquiries of the possibility of partial access, as mentioned in section 5.1 and in the preceding chapter.

Further progress in this debate is possible, I believe, but we can only gain deeper insights into the problems at stake here if we are explicit about and, if at all possible, agree on what the issues are and how the respective claims and hypotheses can be tested empirically. These may seem to be rather obvious requirements, but a large body of published work dealing with the issue of access to UG does not meet them, due to a focus on surface manifestations of language acquisition. Remember that what is at stake is knowledge about the target language(s) and ultimately the cognitive capacities enabling learners to develop this knowledge. Assuming that UG is a centrepiece of the LAD and of the more broadly defined Language Making Capacity, it follows that the question of whether UG or rather which parts of UG can still be accessed when languages are acquired successively becomes a crucial one. The reason why I mention this once again is that it must be absolutely clear that the object of our investigations is the acquired knowledge, not merely the utterances produced when this knowledge is put to use. It really should not be necessary to insist on the well-known fact that it is possible to produce (and comprehend) target-conforming strings without having acquired the grammatical knowledge underlying native usage of these utterances. Even an essentially unnatural principle like the one alluded to in chapter 2 (section 2.2), postulating reversal of the order of elements in interrogative utterances, can result in the production of correct surface patterns. In other words, demonstrating that (some) learners successfully produce and/or comprehend specific target-conforming constructions is not tantamount to demonstrating that L1-like grammatical knowledge has been acquired, let alone that this has been achieved by recurring to UG principles. This debate where one side refers to alleged differences in underlying knowledge and the other side points to similarities encountered in the data is reminiscent of a *dialogue des sourds* as in Molière's comedies, where interlocutors apparently engaged in a conversation about a given topic really talk about different things.

As entertaining as this may be, it is preferable, in the interest of a fruitful discussion, to attempt to attain common ground by identifying issues which seem relevant from the perspectives of the various approaches pursued in L2 research. This should actually not be all that difficult in the particular case under discussion here, since defendants of the Full Access, No Access and Partial Access hypotheses all agree that their claims refer to the transitional knowledge systems of learners, and they would probably not disagree with the claim that the restructuring issue, as it is outlined in section 5.1, raises a central problem of second language acquisition.

What is much more controversial is the question of what constitutes conceptual or empirical evidence in support of or against the claims made by the different hypotheses. As for the former, the answer depends on which hypotheses are contrasted. In order to limit the scope of this discussion, I will not engage in a debate of all logically possible options. The brief characterization of a number of scenarios presented in section 4.2 of the preceding chapter and in section 5.1, above, can serve as a starting point. Even a superficial comparison of these options reveals that the crucial choice is between full or partial access/transfer. The No Transfer hypothesis was dismissed (4.2), and although the case is by far not as clear with respect to the No Access hypothesis, a number of considerations (5.1) speak in favour of partial access. If the claim that L2 learners have only partial access to UG could be refuted, it would necessarily follow that the no access option, too, has to be abandoned. Only if partial access can be shown to be a more plausible claim than the one postulating full access, might the No Access hypothesis have to be put back on the research agenda. I might add that, to my knowledge, this hypothesis is currently not entertained in L2 acquisition research. Focusing then on the full/partial access alternative, we need to keep in mind that the review of possible scenarios has shown that the possibility to set parameters to values different from that in the L1 grammar (resetting) is of crucial importance since all versions of the Full Access hypothesis and, in fact, the (B) (a) version of the Partial Access hypothesis are untenable if resetting turns out to be impossible. 'Partial' access can, of course, be defined in other terms, as well, but at this point we are only concerned with the claim that parameterized principles are responsible for fundamental differences between L1 and L2 acquisition (cf. Tsimpli and Roussou 1991, Towell and Hawkins 1994, Smith and Tsimpli 1995, Eubank and Gregg 1999, and others). Just to be clear with respect to the above formulated requirement of defining the relevant issues, let me state explicitly what should really be obvious: Evidence adduced in order to decide between full versus partial access to UG must refer to parameterized principles of UG. It is therefore necessary to agree on which aspects of grammar reflect parameterized options. Needless to say that evidence relating to non-parameterized principles might be of interest for the full versus no access alternative, but it is irrelevant for the present debate on partial access.

The most controversial point concerns the question of which facts can arguably be interpreted as empirical evidence for parameter (re)setting. Not only must they obviously relate to parameterized principles, they must provide empirically testable evidence demonstrating that the acquisition process under investigation is indeed an instance of parameter setting. Although the conceptual distinction between this and other types of acquisition processes is well established (cf. Carroll 1989), it is only rarely taken into account in studies discussing the access issue. As should be evident, the crucial point is that parameter (re)setting refers to the activation of knowledge which, in principle, is already available to the learner, prior to experience with the target language (see section 2.4). In fact, this is what the entire debate about the role of UG in language acquisition is all about. To state this once again: It is not about the question of whether a given grammatical phenomenon is learnable but rather whether it is implemented in the learner grammar via activation of innate knowledge, this innate knowledge being triggered by experience rather than resulting from learning by experience alone. The demonstration that learners are able to use target forms related to the grammatical phenomenon in question constitutes a significant observation on the study of L2 acquisition, but it has little to say about whether L2 learners continue to be able to access UG knowledge in the process of acquiring these forms.

The challenge is thus to identify a set of empirically testable criteria which will allow us to discriminate underlying acquisition mechanisms. That this is possible, in principle, has been shown for first language development in chapter 2 (section 2.4). Parameterized variation has been argued to relate to functional heads, at least in syntax, and since it refers to a priori grammatical knowledge, it is triggered and does not have to be learned in the traditional sense of the term. From this it follows, among other things, that acquisition should happen fast and exhibit discontinuity in acquisition patterns, for example abrupt changes in target-conforming usage. Moreover, one should be able to detect clustering effects, resulting in the simultaneous emergence of superficially unrelated linguistic phenomena during a given developmental phase (see Bley-Vroman 1990 or Meisel 1991).

Under the assumption that partial access to UG implies that parameterized UG principles are no longer directly accessible in L2 acquisition, resetting of parameters should not be possible (cf. Tsimpli and Roussou 1991). In accordance with recent theorizing about functional categories (see section 2.3 above), we can therefore expect to find that L2 learners will encounter major problems when acquiring grammatical phenomena dependent on properties of uninterpretable features[2] of functional categories (cf. Tsimpli and Dimitrakopoulou 2007, among others), more specifically, if the grammars of the L1 and the L2 differ with respect to distribution or strength of such features. The Full Access hypothesis, on the other hand, predicts for this case that L2 learners will set parameters to the L2 target value. The question then is whether proponents of this hypothesis provide empirical evidence of the kind just alluded to when attempting to demonstrate that L2 acquisition is indeed characterized by parameter 'resetting' in these cases. Needless to say that other types of empirical evidence which could help to distinguish parameter setting from other kinds of learning processes are equally welcome.

Let us first scrutinize some of the available reports on alleged cases of parameter resetting for evidence of *clustering* effects. Recall that since parameters and their possible values are defined at an abstract level of grammatical structure rather than in terms of surface properties of the target language, setting a parameter to a specific value typically should result in the emergence of a *cluster* of superficially unrelated grammatical properties during the same phase of grammatical development.

It is not possible to attempt to present an exhaustive review of the large body of research on this issue. Instead, I will limit this discussion to some representative publications dealing with three parameters which have been introduced in previous chapters and which are likely to be compatible with more recent views developed in the framework of the Minimalist Program (see section 2.4). The focus will thus be on parameters meeting the criterion that parameters refer to functional heads, the Null-Subject (Rizzi 1982) and the Verb Movement (Raising) Parameter. I will also look at the OV/VO Parameter which can arguably be formulated in such a way as to meet this criterion.

Interestingly enough, most of the L2 literature on parameter resetting does not even address the issue of a clustering effect or other types of empirical evidence in support of the claim that one is indeed dealing with instances of parameter setting. This is all the more surprising since some of the earliest studies investigating the access issue did, in fact, take this into account. White (1989a: 82), for example, explicitly states that clustering of syntactic properties should be expected to be found in resetting as well as in setting of parameters, since in many cases grammatical theory links such clusters of properties to specific settings. Chomsky (1981a: 240) indeed states that 'the most interesting topic ... is the clustering of properties related to the pro-drop parameter, whatever this turns out to be'. He then lists five such properties of the *Null-Subject* (or pro-drop) *Parameter*:

(1) (i) missing subjects
(ii) free inversion in simple sentences
(iii) long *wh*-movement of subject
(iv) empty resumptive pronouns in embedded clauses
(v) apparent violations of the *[that-t] filter

Unfortunately, it does not become clear why these and just these properties are attributed to the Null-Subject Parameter. We are merely told that Italian exhibits these characteristics, that is, Italian is treated as a prototypical null-subject language, and other languages are implicitly assumed to share the same properties. In the meantime, it has become clear that this is not necessarily the case (see the discussion in 2.4). On the one hand, there is one important feature of null-subject languages missing in this list, see (vi); on the other hand, not all of them appear in all languages of this type.

(vi) no expletive subjects

What matters in the present context, however, is not whether we can agree on an exhaustive list of properties. It is likely to change as a result of grammatical theorizing anyway, and it may well be that not all null-subject languages exhibit the full set of properties. Recent research results suggest that a distinction should be made between consistent and partial pro-drop languages (see the contributions in Holmberg 2009 and especially Barbosa 2009). Moreover, L1 as well as L2 learners, at the relevant point of development, may not yet use the types of constructions providing the contexts where the properties in question are predicted to surface, at least not in spontaneous production. If, for example, learners only use main clauses, it is not possible to decide whether they have access to the kind of grammatical knowledge necessary in order to process more complex constructions. Yet if they do not use the required linguistic contexts, grammaticality judgements on these construction types may not be reliable. At any rate, in order to demonstrate that acquisition happens via parameter (re)setting, it suffices to show that some of the core properties (see section 2.4), for example (1) (i), (ii) and (v) or (vi), emerge simultaneously in the language of L2 learners.

White (1985) was probably the first to address the question of whether syntactic phenomena related to the Null-Subject Parameter clustered in the speech of L2 learners who are claimed to have transferred the value of this parameter from their respective first languages and to subsequently have reset it according to the requirements of the target grammars. She studied fifty-four adult Spanish learners of English and a control group of nineteen French L2 learners of English – French is analysed as a non-null-subject (NNS) language and Spanish as a null-subject (NS) language. The cluster of surface phenomena investigated include properties (i), (ii) and (v), listed above, and the learners were asked to give grammaticality judgements on a list of written sentences containing grammatical as well as ungrammatical constructions and to correct those sentences which they judged as ungrammatical.

Spanish learners accepted ungrammatical English sentences where the subject was missing more often than members of the French control group, although this difference was not statistically significant in half of the test items. White (1985: 53) finds that Spanish 'beginners were more inclined to accept missing subjects in English and that there was a gradual improvement . . .' Unfortunately, this interesting study does not address the question of why French learners should have any problems at all if the setting of the NSP is responsible for these findings. With respect to English sentences with incorrect subject–verb inversion, some of the learners of both groups again accepted them as correct, though less frequently than the examples with null subjects. In four out of the five cases the French learners did worse than the Spanish. Finally, concerning ungrammatical constructions due to 'that-trace' violations, no significant differences between the two groups were found. Although these findings are not entirely unambiguous in this respect, they are interpreted as indicating that Spanish learners transfer the [+null-subject] setting of the parameter from the L1 into the L2 grammar. A comparison of learners at different levels of proficiency is interpreted as support for the claim that this group of learners increasingly behaves as required by the L2 norm in their judgements of English sentences.

Interestingly, White (1985) also asks whether any individual among the fifty-four Spanish learners of English succeeds in making the correct judgements for all three properties attributed to the parameter. She finds that only five of them correctly rejected both sentences with 'that-trace' violations, and although they also rejected VS patterns, only three of them judged sentences with null-subjects correctly as well. Sixteen Spanish learners of L2 English rejected at least one of the two 'that-trace' sentences, and although all but one of them realized that VS declaratives are not possible in English, only ten of them also judged null-subject sentences as unacceptable, though not categorically. Finally, the eighteen who judged VS as unacceptable in English failed to reject English sentences without overt subjects.

These findings led White (1985: 58) to conclude that only some properties of the parameter are transferred to English – contrary to what the concept of 'parameter' predicts and in spite of the fact that her own hypothesis had been that all properties should be carried over into the L2. More importantly for the present discussion, she finds 'less support' for the hypothesis that all properties of the parameter will be 'lost' together. In other words, neither the group results nor the analysis of the performance of individual learners support the claim of a clustering effect in this alleged case of parameter resetting. Consequently, if we assume that this effect is a decisive criterion which must be met if one wants to maintain that the observed approximation of L2 learners' linguistic behaviour to the requirements of the target norm is indeed due to the restructuring of their transitional grammatical systems by means of parameter resetting from an L1 to an L2 value, we must conclude that this study does not support the idea of parameter resetting. Quite to the contrary, it provides strong evidence against this hypothesis.

Other studies dealing with the Null-Subject Parameter do not fare any better in this respect, although this is probably the parameter which is most frequently investigated in L2 research; see, among others, Hilles (1986, 1991), Phinney (1987), Liceras (1989), Tsimpli and Roussou (1991), Lakshmanan (1991, 1994, 1995), Platt (1993), Al-Kasey and Pérez-Leroux (1998), Liceras, Díaz and Maxwell (1999), or the overviews and summarizing discussions by White (1989a, 1996, 2003), Flynn (1996), Gass (1996), or Kaltenbacher (2001). These studies demonstrate, at best, that only some of the properties associated with the NSP cluster developmentally in the speech of only some of the learners investigated. In fact, several of them find that merely the (im-)possibility to omit subjects is acquired easily and successfully. It is important to interpret these insights in the light of recent approaches to syntactic theory. Following the version of parameter theory outlined in chapter 2 (sections 2.3 and 2.4) for first language development, the original version of the NSP cannot be maintained, and this means that not all the properties attributed to the NS-cluster can actually be motivated by the specific syntactic properties characterizing the NS languages. If, however, parameters are defined in terms of properties of uninterpretable features of functional categories, as suggested in chapter 2, the NSP relies primarily on the feature composition of T (cf. Holmberg 2009). As mentioned before, at least three (empty subjects, no expletives, subject–verb inversion) or perhaps four (including apparent violations of the * [that-t] filter) of the traditionally assumed properties can probably still be attributed to the NS cluster. These should be expected to cluster developmentally in L2 acquisition. However, currently available evidence does not confirm this prediction and has not provided empirical evidence for the claim that parameter setting indeed happens in the course of L2 acquisition.

More importantly, some studies present findings which explicitly contradict the claim that parameters can be reset, for example Clahsen and Hong 1995, Hong 1995 and Kaltenbacher 2001. Clahsen and Hong, for example, investigated German L2 acquisition by Korean learners, focusing on subject–verb agreement and null subjects. Note that Korean does not have subject–verb agreement and allows null subjects and objects in main and embedded clauses. The two languages thus differ in both respects, and transfer from the L1 can therefore be ruled out in both cases as an explanation of successful acquisition. In L1 German, the acquisition of agreement covaries with the systematic use of overt subjects, as predicted by grammatical theory (see Clahsen and Hong 1995: 64). The particular interest of this study stems from the fact that it does not rely on grammaticality judgements but is based on reaction time experiments, which arguably allow for a more reliable assessment of the grammatical knowledge of L2 learners. They were given sentence-matching tasks in which they had to decide whether two sentences are identical or not. Since grammatical sentences typically require less processing time than ungrammatical ones, these experiments seem to successfully tap the learners' grammatical knowledge without obliging them to judge the grammaticality of the stimuli.

The results of this study suggest that no developmental clustering exists between subject–verb agreement and the NS property in L2 acquisition.[3] Note that this investigation was not, in fact, concerned with the NS cluster as defined above. It focused instead on only one property (empty subjects) of the NSP and related it to another one which reveals, however, a crucial property of the functional category in question (T in our current theoretical framework), required for the identification (cf. Rizzi 1986) of lexically empty subjects in NS languages. This is to say that the use of lexically empty or realized subjects can only be interpreted as resulting from a setting of the NSP to the target value if these two surface phenomena emerge simultaneously in the language of L2 learners. The mean scores for the twenty native German speakers of the control group showed that the response time for the ungrammatical stimuli was indeed longer than for the grammatical ones, as predicted by the design of the experiment. This was true of nineteen of the twenty natives but not of the majority of the thirty-three adult Korean learners of L2 German. Two of them had not acquired either of the constructions investigated, and eighteen L2 learners had acquired only one of the two. Only thirteen subjects patterned like the native speakers; but even in their case we do not know whether they acquired the two phenomena simultaneously or successively. Moreover, the difference in reaction time between grammatical and ungrammatical sentences was not statistically significant for these learners. Clahsen and Hong (1995: 77) therefore concluded that 'subject–verb agreement and the correct properties of null subjects are developmentally dissociated in L2 acquisition'. It is worth noting that many more of the L2 learners had acquired the correct properties of null subjects (but not agreement) than vice versa. Clahsen and Hong (1995: 77) remark that this indicates that 'the distribution of null subjects is easier to learn than subject–verb agreement'. More importantly, this finding clearly indicates that the correct use of null subjects by L2 learners in their case cannot be the result of parameter setting since the latter is grammatically a prerequisite for the former. A plausible guess might be that they rely instead on discourse or context information and probably on distributional learning.

To sum up our discussion of the Null-Subject Parameter, the incontestable result is that we have not found empirical support for the predicted developmental clustering effect in second language acquisition. Rather, the various properties of the NS cluster emerge successively whereas in L1 development they appear within one developmental phase, that is, simultaneously or within a very short period of time (see chapter 2 (section 2.4)). This strongly suggests that L2 learners do not set the parameter to the L2 value in cases where its setting differs from that of the L1 grammar. In view of this finding, one might wonder why the parameter resetting issue is so intensely debated. One reason may be the fact that it is extremely difficult, if not impossible, to provide positive evidence for a negative claim – in this case for the impossibility of setting parameters to a new value. In many or most cases it is possible to analyse grammatical constructions encountered in L2 speech or results of experiments in more than one way. In the discussion in chapter 4 (4.4) of the analysis of L2 word order acquisition by Clahsen and Muysken (1986) we saw an illustration of this dilemma. The same situation arises again when White (2003: 106) comments – quite correctly – that the findings by Clahsen and Hong (1995) could lead to conclusions other than these authors suggest. She argues, for example (White 2003: 107), that the failure of Korean learners to acquire subject–verb agreement in German might not reflect a lack of syntactic knowledge but a failure to fully acquire German verb morphology. Unfortunately, this amounts to saying that the acquisition of this knowledge cannot be tested empirically. Yet for our present purposes, it is not necessary to engage further in this discussion. What matters is that even if we follow White's line of argument, it is still the case that no evidence has been provided which would support the claim of developmental clusters of the type predicted to emerge if parameter resetting happens in the acquisition of the phenomena under discussion. To put it differently, although the research results reported here may not unambiguously demonstrate that L2 learners cannot access UG, we have definitely not been offered evidence demonstrating that they can reset parameters. Since White (2003: 113) concedes that it is a 'reasonable premise' to expect developmental clustering effects to happen if parameters of UG are unimpaired, the lack of this kind of evidence can justifiably be interpreted as a strong argument against the alleged full access to UG in L2 acquisition.

In order to strengthen this argument, we must, however, show that the lack of developmental clusters is not a problem related to this particular parameter (NSP), possibly because it is not satisfactorily defined by syntactic theory. Let us therefore look briefly at two other parameters which have been studied fairly extensively in both first and second language acquisition.

The Verb Movement Parameter can serve as another test of parameter resetting in L2 acquisition. Lydia White was again one of the first L2 researchers who published on this issue (e.g. White 1991a, 1991b, 1992, 1996). Here, too, she points out that parameters account for clusters of properties which superficially seem to be unrelated. White (1996: 88) mentions that clustering effects are attested in L1 development and explains the clustering properties of this parameter by citing the differences between English and French (Emonds 1978; Pollock 1989), resulting from different settings of this parameter; see (2) adapted from White 1996: 88.

(2) (i) *John likes not Mary
Jean n'aime pas Marie.
(ii) *John watches often television
Jean regarde souvent la télévision.
(iii) *My friends like all Mary
Mes amis aiment tous Marie.
(iv) *Likes she John?
Aime-t-elle Jean?

As we saw before (cf. chapter 4.2), finite verbs raise to the head of TP in French, thus placing them in a surface position preceding the negator *pas* as in (i), certain adverbs as in (ii), as well as quantifiers as in (iii) which occupy the same position as these adverbs, that is, below TP. Since French finite verbs raise further to CP in interrogatives, they also precede subjects, as in (iv). The four constructions can thus be accounted for by the fact that finite verbs are moved in French whereas in English, which does not allow for verb raising, the corresponding constructions are all ungrammatical.

Given this contrast between English and French, English L1 learners of L2 French, and conversely French L1 learners of L2 English, represent particularly valuable sources of information if we want to determine whether parameters can be (re)set in L2 acquisition. Studies investigating this language pair show that only some properties tend to cluster in the course of L2 acquisition, but not all four of them. Unless one can offer principled reasons why the specific subset observed in a given study – and why only a subset of the phenomena in question – emerge within one acquisitional phase, this finding must be interpreted as solid empirical evidence against the alleged process of parameter setting in L2 acquisition. Proponents of the access to UG hypothesis, however, seem not to be irritated by this finding, although it runs against what they predict.

White (1992), for example, reports that Francophone learners of English never use **John likes not Mary* or **Likes she John?*, and she concludes in her discussion in White 1996: 96 'that the parameter has been reset, in this aspect at least (*sic*)'. In other words, the other properties of the parameter, finite verb placement with respect to adverbs and quantifiers, are not acquired simultaneously. Consequently, the result of this study does not, in fact, support the claim that resetting of parameters is a learning mechanism characterizing L2 acquisition since neither the predicted clustering effect nor other empirical reflections genuine to parameter resetting are attested in the data. The same conclusion can be drawn from the findings by White (1991a, 1991b) who investigated Francophone learners of English in a classroom setting. They accepted and produced constructions like (2) (ii) (**John watches often television*) where the finite verb precedes adverbs. Once they had undergone instruction focusing on adverb placement in English, their use of this pattern declined, but this improvement did not extend to interrogative contexts. Interestingly, when Trahey and White (1993) tested whether the acquisition of adverbial constructions could be enhanced by providing massive positive evidence for target-conforming word order like *Mary often watches television*, they observed a dramatic increase of target-conforming usage but no decrease of ungrammatical ones. This suggests that exposure to the relevant primary linguistic data is not sufficient to trigger parameter setting in second language acquisition.

Subsequent research investigating the acquisition of verb movement by L2 learners has not been successful either, I contend, in its attempts to provide evidence for parameter resetting. Most studies do not even address the issue of how to distinguish empirically between parameter setting and other types of linguistic learning. One of the few authors who, like Lydia White, acknowledges the relevance of the clustering effect as a central piece of evidence for parameter setting is Ayoun (1999). She studied the same language pair as White (1991a, 1991b, 1992), English and French, focusing however on L2 French as acquired by Anglophone learners. A review of previous work on the Verb Movement Parameter in L2 acquisition leads her to the conclusion that it 'yielded mixed results with only partial support for parameter resetting'. She then sets out to demonstrate that parameter resetting is nevertheless a possible learning mechanism in L2 acquisition, arguing, however, that 'partial clustering of parametric syntactic properties may be taken as initial evidence of successful parameter resetting' (Ayoun 1999: 104). This is indeed what she concludes, based on a study of L2 learners (second, third and fourth year of instruction) of English as well as of French native speakers.[4] The L2 learners showed no improvement in their grammaticality judgements over time with respect to negative constructions. As for adverbial constructions, only the highest proficiency group (fourth year) performed better, and with quantifiers the results were mixed, although their performance tended to improve over time. Ayoun (1999: 118) interpreted these findings as suggesting that resetting had taken place in only some of the contexts and with only some of the lexical elements tested. On the production task, the learners achieved higher scores, and Ayoun (1999: 120) summarizes that 'the effects of parameter resetting are progressively taking place in these learners' grammars', but only partially since adverbial constructions do not exhibit these effects. Note, however, that if parameter setting can occur incrementally and partially, it becomes behaviourally indistinguishable from inductive learning. Moreover, learners across all proficiency levels attain high scores on the properties which are claimed to cluster, for example higher than 80% even for the lowest proficiency group. Such data thus do not reveal how these learners have acquired knowledge of the Verb Movement Parameter.

The idea of partial clustering comes as a surprise, especially since Ayoun explicitly mentions that the four properties subsumed under this parameter depend on the same syntactic operation of finite verb movement. In order to motivate the assumption of only partial resetting, she refers to a suggestion by Flynn and O'Neil (1988: 16). These authors, however, do not offer theoretically motivated justifications for this radical revision of the notion of parameter. They refer rather to Lust (1988) whose contribution to the same edited volume they introduce in their paper. Lust views the L1 knowledge as a handicap for L2 learners who therefore have to 'learn' the cluster of surface property related to a particular setting of a parameter (I will return to this argument below in discussing the gradual acquisition of surface properties depending on a given parameter). This view is echoed in Ayoun's (1999: 110) assumption according to which 'the mismatch or overlap in parameter settings slows down L2 acquisition'. L2 learners therefore 'need to be exposed to (an undetermined amount of) evidence over a sufficient period of time for full parameter setting to occur'.

This line of argument is truly astonishing; it maintains the terminology but effectively abandons the notion of 'parameter' as it is conceptualized by the theory of grammar. More seriously, no attempt is made to construe a theoretically motivated justification for this revision. Quite on the contrary, by acknowledging that we are dealing here with a single syntactic mechanism, movement of finite verbal elements triggered by an uninterpretable feature located in a functional head, the developmental prediction is confirmed. It states that the various surface patterns should emerge within the same developmental phase. From a grammatical perspective, it simply does not matter whether the verb is raised over an adverb, a negative element or whatever other constituent located above VP but below the functional head to which the verb moves – once the trigger is identified, the verb must be raised. In fact, there is no obvious acquisitional reason either why movement over an adverb should cause more or fewer problems for the learner than movement across a negative element. If, however, learners do not use a given construction, for example if they do not use clause-internal adverbs, subject–verb–adverb patterns can of course not be attested during the developmental phase in question. But as soon as adverbs of the relevant type occur, finite verbs should precede them. The proponents of a 'partial clustering' in L2 acquisition do not argue against these claims, as far as I can see. When they observe that the expected 'full' clustering effect is not confirmed by the data, they merely state a fact which disconfirms a prediction which necessarily follows from their claim of parameter resetting. Stating that the various surface properties must be learned and pointing to a slowed down process requiring a 'sufficiently' long period of exposure to the target language amounts to nothing less than acknowledging that L2 acquisition – at least in these instances – requires inductive learning and cannot in fact rely on parameter setting. It is difficult to come up with a more convincing argument against the idea of parameter resetting as a crucial learning mechanism in L2 acquisition.

A third and last parameter should be dealt with here at least briefly, namely the *OV/VO* (or *Head Direction*) *Parameter* for which it has been claimed that resetting of its original L1 value is possible. As mentioned above, our discussion focuses on parameters defined in terms of uninterpretable features of functional heads, an approach motivated by the hypothesis that accessibility to uninterpretable features is subject to maturational changes and can therefore be predicted to be the most probable cause for fundamental differences between first and second language acquisition. These considerations seem to speak against the Head Direction Parameter as a candidate for resetting because it is commonly defined in terms of adjunction direction, that is, whether the head of a syntactic projection is adjoined to the left or to the right of its complement (see Chomsky 1981a; Stowell 1981). Conceptualized in this way, it does not seem to refer to the featural composition of syntactic heads, and it includes functional as well as substantive (or lexical) elements. Importantly for the present purpose, this version of the parameter is also unsatisfactory in that it offers only a binary choice rather than relating to a cluster of surface properties. Consequently, it does not enable us to make empirically testable predictions for language development. It is one of the mysteries of the history of syntactic theory how the Head Direction Parameter could have continued to be accepted in its traditional form and why it was exempt from constraints developed in parameter theory, although it had long been acknowledged that parameters should refer exclusively to functional heads. Only more recently do we find a serious discussion of this issue; see Svenonius 2000, where different accounts of OV/VO or headedness are presented. In what follows, I will refer to a proposal by Neeleman and Weerman (1997, 1999). Although it does not conform to the constraint according to which parameterization depends on the featural composition of functional categories, it does define a cluster of seemingly unrelated surface properties, thus enabling us to make predictions about the course of language acquisition, and it relies partially on properties of functional categories. Whether this means that it can be reformulated in such a way as to meet all requirements of current parameter theory remains to be seen, however. It certainly fares better than previous versions of the parameter on which much of the L2 literature dealing with this issue is based.

This becomes apparent when one compares it with the state-of-the-art summary presented by Flynn (1996) in her survey article on parameter setting in L2 acquisition. Rather surprisingly, she does not define the notion of parameter, nor does she address the question of what kind of empirical evidence might help to determine whether L2 acquisition indeed involves parameter setting. Flynn (1996: 123) merely states that 'parameters specify dimensions of structural variation across all languages', and she proceeds by presenting the Head Direction Parameter as an illustrative example. A clustering effect in the sense that a set of superficially unrelated grammatical properties emerge if the parameter is set to one of the values offered by UG is not observed in L2 acquisition. However, a similar effect is said to be attained by postulating a 'correlation' between head-direction and adjunction direction. I am not sure how this is to be interpreted, since we are not informed about how the two are linked by a single grammatical principle,[5] nor that grammars across languages are not consistent with respect to these two phenomena. At any rate, the postulated 'correlation' is not sufficient to qualify as an instantiation of the clustering effect predicted by parameter theory.

In this respect, at least, the OV/VO Parameter, as proposed by Neeleman and Weerman (1997, 1999), fares much better. According to these authors, different settings of the parameter lead to differences with respect to basic word order, verb-adverb-object sequences, particle constructions and so forth. Leaving technical details aside, their claim is that Case theory plays a crucial role in explaining these facts. In line with Chomsky (1995), they argue that linear order is not stipulated in syntax but by conditions imposed at PF, dependent on Case theory and the licensing of empty categories. OV/VO variation depends on the direction of head government which, in turn, depends on two variables: domain and direction. Neeleman and Weerman (1999) propose that a particular setting of the directionality parameter entails a specific setting of the domain parameter, and they argue that the domain can be defined syntactically or phonologically. Assuming a strong inclination to shift to phonological information as soon as possible, Neeleman and Weerman (1999: 25) predict that in VO languages head government is defined in prosodic terms, whereas in OV languages the object and the verb are not contained in the same phonological domain, and in order to establish a head government relation between these elements, syntactic information must be accessed. These ideas are illustrated by a Contrastive Analysis of Dutch and English, and Neeleman and Weerman (1997) demonstrate that the cluster of surface properties associated with the two settings of the parameter indeed emerge during the same developmental phase in L1 acquisition of these languages, whereas an experimental study with L2 learners of the same languages showed that only two of the phenomena studied had been acquired successfully. It should be added, however, that not all the properties related to the parameter are attested in child speech at the point of development when the parameter is set, because this happens during an

Table 5.2: *Surface clusters linked to the OV/VO parameter in German and French*[a]

	German	French
Verb–complement order in main clauses	vO Ich sehe den Mann 'I see the man'	vO *Je vois l'homme* 'I see the man'
	vOV *Ich habe den Mann gesehen* I have the man seen 'I have seen the man'	vVO *J'ai vu l'homme* 'I have seen the man'
Verb–complement order in embedded clauses	OVv . . . *dass er den Mann gesehen hat* . . . that he the man seen has '. . . that he has seen the man'	vVO . . . *qu'il a vu l'homme* '. . . that he has seen the man'
Adverb placement	Adv DP Vv . . . *dass er gestern den Mann gesehen hat* . . . that he yesterday the man seen has '. . . that he has seen the man yesterday'	vV DP Adv *Il a vu l'homme hier* 'He has seen the man yesterday'
	DP Adv Vv . . . *dass er den Mann gestern gesehen hat* . . . that he the man yesterday seen has '. . . that he has seen the man yesterday'	(*)vV Adv DP **Il a vu hier l'homme* 'He has seen yesterday the man' *Il m'a raconté aussitôt la nouvelle* He me has told immediately the news 'He immediately told me the news'
Particle constructions	PP Prt Vv . . . *dass sie vom Flugzeug abgesprungen ist* . . . that she from the plane off jumped is '. . . that she has jumped off the plane'	–
	*Prt PP Vv * . . . *dass sie ab vom Flugzeug gesprungen ist* . . . that she off from the plane jumped is '. . . that she has jumped off the plane'	–
	DP Prt Vv . . . *dass sie das Telefon abkaufen wollen* . . . that they the telephone Prt buy want '. . . that they want to buy the telephone'	–
	*Prt DP Vv **dass sie ab das Telefon kaufen wollen* . . . that they Prt the telephone buy '. . . that they buy the telephone'	–

[a] V = non-finite verb forms; v = finite verb forms.

early developmental phase when some of the structural knowledge required in adult language has not yet been acquired, for example embedded clauses.

Möhring and Meisel (2003) put this version of the OV/VO Parameter to a test, analysing the acquisition of German (OV) and French (VO) in a study comparing the simultaneous L1 acquisition of these languages by bilingual children (2L1) and comparing the results for 2L1 German with adult L2 German by L1 Spanish and Portuguese (Romance VO languages like French) learners. Table 5.2, adapted from Möhring and Meisel 2003: 300, lists the surface properties in which mature German and French differ and which depend on the setting of the OV/VO Parameter as proposed by Neeleman and Weerman (1999), that is, verb–complement order in main and embedded clauses, adverb placement (between the object and the verb in OV languages – Neeleman and Weerman refer to this operation as 'scrambling') and particle constructions (in OV languages the particle occurs adjacent to the verb). Since the latter do not exist in French, German offers more possibilities to test predictions concerning the clustering effect. What further complicates the search for empirical evidence in French is the fact that, as a result of verb movement, finite verbs can precede certain adverbs (see 2 (ii) above). V–Adv–O order as a result of 'scrambling', however, is not possible in VO languages, but it may not always be easy to distinguish these two types of constructions in spontaneous speech. In German, on the other hand, embedded clauses introduced by complementizers like *dass* 'that' reliably indicate the underlying order since the finite verb is not raised to T or C in these constructions. German thus seems to be the better test case, but the emergence of French word order is nevertheless quite revealing when contrasted with the acquisition of an OV language like German because this comparison can rely not only on the differences with respect to the construction types attested in early L1 development – the fact that surface patterns *not* tolerated by a particular setting of the parameter (e.g. OV) are *absent* in the (French) speech of the children, is revealing as well.

The study of the grammatical development of two children, Pascal and Annika,[6] acquiring French and German since birth, that is, as two 'first' languages, confirms indeed the predictions derived from the OV/VO Parameter. Möhring and Meisel (2003) found that around age 1;10 (Pascal) and 2;2 (Annika), respectively, the parameter had been set to the target-conforming value in both languages. One can in fact surmise that this happened even earlier but that the children were not yet able to use the necessary linguistic sequences which would have revealed it. This suspicion is corroborated by comprehension studies (see, for example, Guasti *et al.* 2001). Regardless, the analysis of the speech production of these two children shows that the cluster of phenomena related to the OV/VO parameter are all used as soon as the required contexts appear in the data. The children thus exhibit distinct developmental patterns in their two languages and the same ones as the respective monolinguals in each of their languages (cf. Clahsen 1982 and Ferdinand 1996, 1997). Importantly, this applies to main as well as subordinate clauses, although German requires different orderings in these cases.

This development contrasts strongly with the course of L2 acquisition. Möhring and Meisel (2003) compared these children's acquisition of German with the emergence of word order in the speech of two adult L2 learners, Zita (L1 Portuguese) and Ana (L1 Spanish), two of the most successful learners investigated by the ZISA research project, introduced in chapters 3 (section 3.3) and 4 (section 4.2). Zita was first recorded during week 13 of her exposure to German, and the recordings continued until week 132. The recordings with Ana lasted from week 16 to week 65 of her contact with German. Subsequently, she was recorded repeatedly in Spain where she spent several weeks and again twice after she had returned to Germany, that is until the seventy-eighth week after her first arrival in the country. Over a period of about one year or longer, the two learners produced exclusively VO sequences in main clauses. Only during week 67 (Zita) and week 50 (Ana) of their exposure did they begin to use OV patterns, mostly with infinitival verb forms. As for OV in embedded clauses, Zita produced only one example which can possibly be analysed as an OV sequence, and this happened in week 132, the last week of recording. In Ana's data this pattern emerges in week 59, but she continued to use VO order during the entire period investigated. The fact that VO is used predominantly or exclusively in embedded clauses at a point of acquisition when OV seems to have been acquired in main clauses constitutes strong evidence against the claim that this surface pattern results from setting the parameter to the OV value. I should add that a similar developmental pattern has been observed by Müller (1998) who studied the acquisition of word order in embedded clauses by Bruno (L1 Italian), another L2 learner of German from the ZISA corpus.[7] During an extended period of time he used only VO in embedded clauses, and the first OV sequence appeared in the sixtieth week of exposure to German. Müller argues that Bruno learned the word order of German embedded clauses in an item-by-item fashion, depending on the complementizer introducing the embedded clause, rather than generalizing over the structural context as would have been the case if the parameter had been set to the OV value. As for constructions containing an adverb, Zita and Ana inserted adverbs between verbs and objects only when the object followed the verb; that is to say, one finds V–Adv–O and Adv–O–V but never O–Adv–V sequences. Particles, finally, are extremely rare in the speech of these two learners – there are five examples in Zita's data and a single one in the recordings with Ana. Although some of them are adjoined to the left of infinitives, the database is too small to determine whether they have acquired target placement of these elements.

In sum, we find that the L2 learners use some of the surface patterns related to the OV/VO Parameter in a more or less target-like fashion whereas with others they deviate considerably from the target norm. Importantly, they use these patterns inconsistently, that is, when they produce OV and vOV order in main clauses, they continue to use VO and vVO in embedded clauses. The results of this study show quite unambiguously that Ana and Zita, unlike the bilingual L1 learners Annika and Pascal, learn each of the phenomena associated with the OV/VO Parameter separately. In fact, target-conforming word order in embedded clauses or with constructions containing adverbs was not acquired at all during the period investigated. The conclusion which one can draw from these findings is that L2 learners only acquire some of the phenomena linked to the parameter. Moreover, they learn them individually, over an extended period of time and relying on distributional analysis based on specific words. This is definitely not the kind of evidence required to support parameter resetting. Whereas the predicted clustering effect is indeed detectable in monolingual and bilingual L1 development, no such evidence has been found in analyses of L2 acquisition.

In fact, summing up our discussion of the first, and arguably most important, type of empirically testable evidence, the clustering effect, one can conclude with considerable confidence for the three parameters dealt with here that this effect does not appear in the course of L2 acquisition, although it has been detected in L1 development. Even if one wants to question the validity of some of the evidence presented in support of the latter claim, as does, for example, White (2003: 112) in her review of Neeleman and Weerman (1997), the fact remains that none of the extensive efforts designed to lend support to the idea of parameter (re)setting in L2 acquisition has been successful so far. As we saw in the foregoing discussion, proponents of this hypothesis have either ignored the absence of cluster effects or else resorted to a modified proposal arguing for 'partial' clustering without, however, being able to offer a theoretically motivated justification for this concept. Weakening the notion of parameter so that parameter setting is indistinguishable from induction is obviously not a credible solution supporting the alleged role of UG in L2 acquisition. Simply ignoring the possibility of a clustering effect is not a satisfactory solution either, unless one replaces it by some other empirically testable criterion for (re)setting.

Admittedly, it is possible that the clustering effect will surface when other areas of grammar are investigated. Albeit this is merely a remote possibility at this point in time, considering the amount of work which has already been dedicated to this issue, it cannot be excluded a priori. As mentioned repeatedly before, it is notoriously difficult to prove the non-existence of a particular phenomenon. For the time being, we can only wait to see whether future research will indeed produce the kind of evidence required.

Let me emphasize that the minimum requirement which must be met in order to support the idea of parameter resetting in syntax is that the parameters in question should refer to functional categories, as has been argued in section 5.1 and at the beginning of this section 5.2. Moreover, the Partial Access to UG hypothesis adopted here further claims that parameters are restricted to properties of functional heads, arguably referring exclusively to the distribution and strength of uninterpretable features. If one aims to refute this hypothesis, it will be necessary to demonstrate that (re)setting is possible for parameters which meet these requirements. As suggested above, the Null-Subject Parameter can undoubtedly be interpreted in this way, and in the case of the Verb Movement Parameter, this is uncontroversial anyway. As for the Head Direction Parameter, this is much less obvious, but it should at least be possible to formulate it in such a way that it refers to functional heads, even if it is not obvious whether its properties depend on uninterpretable features. At any rate, in its traditional form, it merely refers to a type of cross-linguistic variation, but this does not qualify as parametric variation in the sense alluded to. Consequently, a large body of L2 research relying on what used to be conceived as a 'parameter' referring to head directionality of lexical categories becomes irrelevant for the debate on the resetting issue. Remember, for example, our discussion of the Minimal Trees Hypothesis in chapter 4 (section 4.2). It makes strong claims concerning the head directionality of the VP. Yet if parameters are constrained in such a way as to refer to properties of functional heads only, alleged transfer of VP headedness and subsequent changes to the directionality required by the target grammar cannot be explained in terms of parameter setting any more. In fact, since functional categories are claimed to be lacking initially, the MTH will have to do entirely without parametric options when attempting to explain the initial state of L2 acquisition. The Valueless Features Hypothesis, on the other hand, fares much better in this respect since it is based on the assumption that parameterized values of functional heads are not transferred, and L2 learners must therefore determine the strength of features of functional heads. This is clearly more in line with recent developments in parameter theory.

Under the assumption that parameters refer exclusively to functional heads, other parameters mentioned in the L2 literature will also have to be discarded. They capture merely generalizations concerning 'dimensions of structural variation across all languages', as becomes apparent by the quote from Flynn (1996: 123) cited above. Parameters, however, are intended to capture more abstract properties of grammars and not simply cross-linguistic or interindividual variation. Consequently, studies referring to the acquisition of properties reflecting this kind of variation have nothing to contribute to the debate on (re)setting. They are simply irrelevant, in this respect. Although we are losing a body of potential empirical evidence by imposing these constraints on what counts as a grammatical parameter, a more constrained theory of parameters should not only be welcome, but it is a necessity for a theoretically sophisticated and empirically accountable approach to the problem of fundamental differences between first and second language acquisition. The summary of the debate in section 4.4 on whether L2 grammars conform to principles of UG has shown very clearly that an insufficiently constrained parameter theory allows too many options, thus making it virtually impossible to develop a theoretical argument of this kind.

Let us finally move on and examine very briefly one more type of empirical evidence which can shed light on the problem of whether parameter (re)setting indeed happens in the course of L2 acquisition. If, for the sake of argument, we ignore the clustering effect and focus on individual properties related to particular parameter settings, we are still able to distinguish triggering of parameter settings from other types of acquisition processes when we consider developmental patterns. Remember that the discussion in chapter 2 of the role of parameters in L1 development revealed that triggering which relies on knowledge available prior to experience not only results in uniform acquisition patterns across learners, it also happens fast and produces abrupt changes in language use since limited exposure to the PLD will suffice to identify the triggering information. Once this has been achieved, learners are able to use the target structure almost instantaneously because they need not proceed by trial and error in order to discover the correct solution. Learning in the usual sense of the term, on the other hand, involves inductive procedures, scrutinizing the PLD over an extended period of time during which learners attempt to discover regular patterns, applying trial and error procedures on their way to the target construction. We may therefore expect that the acquisition process will exhibit ups and downs, reflecting this kind of learning process. Moreover, since distinct learner types are likely to take different approaches to the respective learning tasks, one can predict considerable variation across individuals in how they proceed.

In chapter 2, section 2.4, a diagram displayed the developmental pattern of a bilingual child acquiring subject–verb agreement, exhibiting precisely the kind of pattern predicted in the case of triggering of grammatical knowledge. Within two months of the emergence of the first finite verb forms in German, they are used in almost all required contexts. At the same time, the frequency of subject omissions drops from 100% to 0%. If we compare this to the pattern exhibited by Zita, the L2 German learner (L1 Portuguese) introduced above when discussing the OV/VO Parameter, the contrast could hardly be greater, as is shown by figure 5.1. In the first recording, she is not yet able to use inflectional suffixes productively, but she does use finite forms and, in fact, only finite verbs which, however, must be interpreted as rote-learned forms. Subsequently, the rate of her inflected verb forms in contexts where finite verbs are required varies considerably, but it never exceeds 80% during the period investigated, that is in more than two

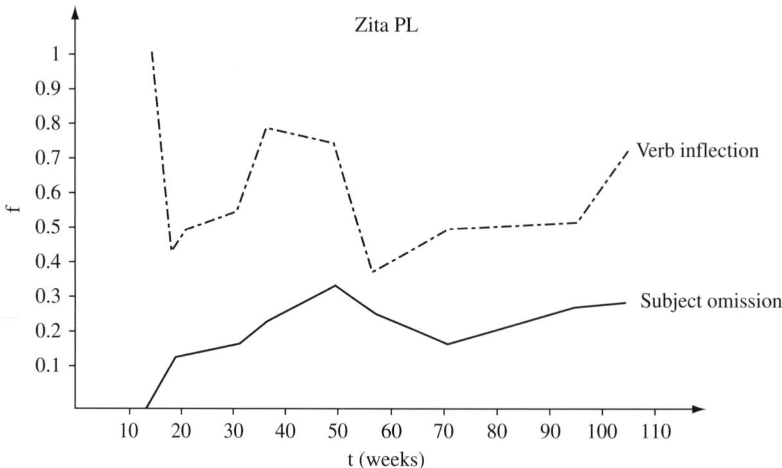

Figure 5.1: *Subject–verb agreement in L2 German (L1 Portuguese)*

years of exposure to German. Note also that subject omissions do not decrease as the use of finite verbs increases, as was the case in L1 acquisition and as is to be predicted as a consequence of the grammatical relation between these two phenomena. Thus, the L2 pattern does not exhibit the abrupt change towards the target norm. Instead, we observe the ups and downs in the acquisition process predicted to occur as a result of learning by trial and error.

In fact, to my knowledge no published research has as yet shown that surface properties related to a given parameter emerge abruptly in the speech of L2 learners in cases where the grammars of their L1 and of the target language choose different values of the parameter in question and where the learners initially used patterns corresponding to the L1 setting of the parameter. Instead, a number of authors state explicitly that this is not the case. White (1985: 59), for example, in her above mentioned study of the Null-Subject Parameter, analysing the acquisition of L2 English by L1 Spanish learners, observed a 'gradual improvement with level in ability to judge the sentences with missing subjects'. This led her to conjecture that 'these problems will not necessarily persist'. In other words, learners whose L1 is a null-subject language are said to be able to discover that the target L2 grammar does not allow for empty subjects. This, however, happens in the course of a gradual process which, moreover, proceeds independently of the process by which the surface manifestations of other properties dependent on the same parameter are acquired, that is, the ban against subject–verb inversion in declaratives and 'that-trace' violations. Another example is the study by Hilles (1986), also dedicated to the Null-Subject Parameter. She investigated the L2 acquisition of properties (i) (missing subjects) and (vi) (no expletive subjects), as well as an additional one according to which null-subject languages do not allow lexical material in Aux, an assumption which I will ignore in the present context. She observed a slow but steady increase of lexical subjects and an equally slow and steady increase in the use of expletives, and the latter are said to be the last to be acquired. In other words, the two properties are learned independently and in a slow and gradual fashion, thus failing to provide evidence in support of the idea of parameter (re)setting in L2 on both criteria, the clustering effect and abrupt changes in the developmental pattern.

Similar findings have been reported on in more recent studies investigating the Null-Subject as well as other parameters. In the foregoing discussion of the clustering effect, I mentioned several authors who observed that target-conforming usage of the constructions related to the Verb Movement Parameter or the OV/VO Parameter emerge gradually over an extended period of time. Ayoun (1999), for example, stated that L2 learners need to be exposed to the triggering data 'over a sufficient period of time' to attain target-like linguistic behaviour and that 'performance will improve with the level of proficiency'. The empirical results discussed by Flynn (1996) also demonstrate that head directionality, one of the earliest and fastest achievements in L1 development, is not learned rapidly in L2 acquisition.

More references to similar statements could be added, demonstrating that abrupt changes of the sort characterizing L1 development are not attested in the developmental patterns encountered in L2 acquisition. This speaks very strongly against the claim that L2 learners can (re)set parameters. In fact, the discussion of the notion of parameter in chapter 2 (section 2.4) and again at the beginning of this section 5.2 has shown that what distinguishes it from other types of learning is the fact that it implies the activation of knowledge available prior to experience – knowledge which needs to be triggered by structural information contained in the primary linguistic data. It necessarily follows that acquisition via parameter setting must be fast and always successful, as is indeed the case in L1 development. One should therefore expect that proponents of the resetting hypothesis in L2 acquisition would make special efforts in an attempt to demonstrate that alleged instances of parameter setting are not simply the result of learning in the more traditional sense. Yet this is not the case. On the contrary, they address this issue only rarely. Moreover, when it is discussed at all, the main purpose appears to be to blur empirically testable differences between triggering and learning. Lust (1988: 314), for example, acknowledges that parameter setting in L1 development happens fast. But she then adds: 'While the parameter value of a grammar may be instantaneously reset, the wide set of deductive consequences instantiated in language-specific knowledge cannot be so, since each of these by necessity must involve learning.' The problem of L2 acquisition is attributed to changing 'the computational processes involved in the execution of UG's constraints on the real task of language acquisition'. The latter remark is strikingly reminiscent of the reasoning developed in the framework of Contrastive Analysis where, under the influence of behaviourist learning theory, it is claimed that L2 acquisition consists crucially of changing linguistic habits (see chapter 1, section 1.2). Although it is trivially true that the specific lexical expressions of the target language must be learned, it remains largely mysterious why the acquisition of the structural properties related to a particular parameter, 'by necessity', should have to be learned. At any rate, if this was indeed correct, the claim that the value of a parameter can be 'instantaneously reset' would be impossible to test empirically. Consequently, the issue of parameter setting and of UG accessibility in L2 acquisition more generally would at best be a theoretically motivated stipulation, hardly worth the attention it has received in L2 research over the past twenty-five years – and in this volume.

My conclusion from this review of possible empirical evidence for parameter (re)setting is that claims to the effect that L2 learners set and reset parameters in the course of their acquisition career are based on the fact that L2 learners are found to be able to acquire the necessary knowledge to produce at least individual constructions related to a grammatical parameter, in a way approximating native language use. But what does this tell us about the underlying mechanisms of language acquisition? Since no one seriously argues that specific properties of grammar are not learnable, the question is whether this represents evidence in support of parameter resetting. If this was the case, learners who have acquired one of the clustering phenomena (e.g. free inversion for the Null-Subject Parameter or the position of negative elements related to the Verb Movement Parameter), possibly after having received negative evidence as suggested by

White (1996: 101), should soon begin to use the other properties of the parameter as well. Developmental relationships of this sort are indeed attested in L1 but not in L2 acquisition. Parameter setting should also result in abrupt changes in the use of constructions depending on a particular value of the parameter. Again, no such developmental patterns are attested in L2 acquisition. Consequently, the only possible conclusion to be drawn from these research results is that the resetting hypothesis is not supported by the available empirical evidence. This is also the conclusion drawn by Bley-Vroman (2009: 184) who states that 'in 20 years of SLA research, not a single study has convincingly demonstrated the sort of triggering and clustering that might have been expected'.

Since, as discussed at the beginning of this chapter, parameter setting constitutes decisive evidence allowing us to distinguish between the Full Access to UG and the Partial Access to UG hypotheses, this conclusion also speaks strongly against the Full Access hypothesis. White (2003: 100), however, objects that 'failure to acquire L2 parameter settings does not necessarily indicate failure of UG'. This is certainly correct, but it does mean that proponents of the Full Access hypothesis have failed to provide the most crucial empirical evidence in support of their claims.

If, then, I am correct in concluding that parameters cannot be (re)set in L2 acquisition, what does this tell us about the nature of the grammatical knowledge of L2 learners? In chapter 2, section 2.3, I argued that parameters refer to uninterpretable features of functional heads. Since grammars differ with respect to the distribution of such features across functional categories as well as with respect to the strength of these features, we should expect to find that L2 learners will encounter difficulties in both these cases. Take the example of the Verb Movement Parameter which relies on both these properties. If the L1 of learners does not allow for verb raising whereas the L2 does exhibit this property, the corresponding grammars differ with respect to feature strength. If, on the other hand, both grammars do require verb movement, there may still be a problem with respect to the location of the feature in question, for example in acquiring an L2 which exhibits theV2 effect if the L1 is a non-V2 language.

Concerning feature *strength*, White (2003: 129) claims that L2 research has demonstrated that L2 learners are able to change the strength of features of functional heads to the value appropriate for the L2, contrary to the predictions of the Partial Access to UG hypothesis. Somewhat surprisingly, she refers to Yuan 2001 in order to back up this claim. Yuan (2001) studied French, German and English L2 learners of Chinese, a language which lacks grammatical verb inflection and does not permit verbs to raise to TP (or IP in Yuan's theoretical framework). The learners were asked to do an oral production as well as a grammaticality judgement task, focusing on constructions containing frequency adverbs, that is, *S-V-Adv-XP versus S-Adv-V-XP. Since English, like Chinese, does not allow thematic verb raising whereas German and French are verb-raising languages, one might expect to find that French and German, as opposed to English, learners accept and produce the ungrammatical Chinese pattern quite frequently – if one follows one of the three hypotheses on the initial state of L2 grammars discussed in 4.2 with respect to their assumptions about initial transfer of grammatical knowledge. Yuan (2001: 263), however, presents robust evidence demonstrating that this is not the case, not even for beginners. In fact, the French, German and English learners do not differ significantly.

How are these results to be interpreted? There can be no doubt that they represent problems for the three scenarios on the initial state of L2 acquisition, as Yuan (2001) correctly notes. In fact, they blatantly contradict the Full Transfer/ Full Access to UG (FTFA) hypothesis, since no traces of full transfer have been detected. They are also problematic for the Valueless Features Hypothesis (VFH) and the Minimal Trees Hypothesis (MTH) which predict optional movement at the initial or at an intermediate stage, respectively. However, Yuan's (2001) conclusion according to which his findings show that French and German learners of Chinese have set the Verb Movement Parameter to the non-raising value as early as at the initial state of the L2 acquisition of Chinese is even more problematic. It relies entirely on what L2 learners do *not* do (verb raising), and it fails to account for the fact that the German and French learners do not differ significantly from their English counterparts. Note that White (2003: 80) is ready to interpret Yuan's claim as evidence against the VFH although his findings are also in conflict with her own results from the analysis of L2 English acquisition by Francophone learners (White 1992). Her findings are, in fact, also in conflict with the claim that the parameter has been reset since, as mentioned above, the French learners behaved differently in their use of adverbial constructions as compared to negative and interrogative structures. White's (2003: 131) solution is to surmise that two different functional heads are involved here, AGR and T rather than INFL as in Yuan's analysis, and that one is therefore dealing with two distinct parameters. But as she admits herself, it is not obvious 'why feature strength of different categories should be reset at different times' (White 2003: 132) and why the Francophone learners in her study do not raise verbs consistently over adverbs as they should do if they had still set one of the two suggested parameters to the <strong> value rather than having it reset to the <weak> value of the English target grammar. Thus, contrary to the summary presented by White (2003: 132), these results are clearly not consistent with the claim that the strength of T or of some other functional category has been reset to the L2 value.

A number of other observations further weaken the claim that these findings speak in favour of sensitivity to feature strength and parameter resetting. First of all, Yuan (2001) studied only one of the phenomena related to the Verb Movement Parameter: the position of verbs with respect to adverbs. More importantly, as mentioned before, Yuan's conclusion that the parameter has been reset to the L2 value is based on the fact that movement does *not* happen. Although this is, in principle, a perfectly legitimate argument, its validity turns out to be questionable if its logic cannot be reversed. Note that it has indeed been observed repeatedly that L2 learners do not move verbs when movement should not happen, that is, in cases where the L2 (e.g. English) does not allow movement but the L1 (e.g. German) requires it. Wode (1981) reported that the German child L2 learners of English in his study did not use V2 order in English. Yet similar results have not been obtained for identical language pairs in studies examining the reverse case, that is, when movement is required by the L2 (German) but not by the L1 (English). In fact, no evidence for early resetting of the parameter from the <weak> to the <strong> value has as yet been offered (cf. our discussion in chapter 4, especially in section 4.3). I might add that this is also true for child L2 acquisition. Pierantozzi (2009), analysing German child L2 learners of French and French child L2 learners of German (age of onset between three and four years), found that the former never move the verb to the head of CP, they thus do not produce ungrammatical *V2 patterns in French. Conversely, however, French learners of German fail to produce grammatical V2 constructions in the appropriate contexts, thus using ungrammatical *V3 order even during later stages of acquisition.

In order to explain these facts in terms of features of functional heads, it will be necessary to account for this asymmetry – a challenge which has not yet been met successfully in L2 research. One way to solve this problem might be to appeal to some kind of markedness hierarchy which would capture the fact that a particular phenomenon represents an acquisition problem only if learners with L_a as their L1 acquire L_b as an L2, but not in the reverse language combination, that is, when L_b is the L1 and L_a the L2. My suspicion, however, is that all attempts to explain these facts will fail if they are restricted to grammatical considerations alone. Instead, acquisition mechanisms should also be taken into account. Rather than resetting the value of the Verb Movement Parameter, L2 learners seem to adopt a conservative approach to the acquisition task, refraining from verb movement if surface properties of the target language offer cues constituting evidence against displacement operations. Interestingly, Yuan (2001: 265) argues that this is indeed the case in Chinese. Not only does this language lack grammatical verb inflection, the surface position of thematic verbs and their complements in relation to adverbs and the negator provide sufficient positive evidence in this respect. If parameter settings had been transferred, we should find that these learners, at least initially, use predominantly the type of constructions required by their L1. This, however, is definitely not the case.

In sum, my conclusion holds that L2 learners do not have access any more to the kind of UG knowledge which would allow them to fix parameter values in the L2 grammar if the parameter in question is not instantiated in their L1 grammar, or to reset parameters to different values in cases where the L1 and the L2 grammar choose different settings. This applies to the distribution as well as to the strength of formal features in functional heads. This state-of-affairs can be accounted for by the Partial Access to UG hypothesis but not by the Full Access to UG hypothesis. The least one can say is that the latter lacks the necessary empirical support. I might add that its conceptual plausibility also dwindles if we do not limit our attention to grammar-internal assumptions but are willing to embrace more general cognitive considerations. Recall from our discussion in chapter 2, section 2.4, that L1 research has provided solid evidence supporting the claim that parameters cannot be reset in the course of L1 development. The view that parameter settings cannot be altered across the lifespan of an individual is also widely accepted in diachronic linguistics (see Meisel forthcoming). If this is correct, it would be rather implausible to surmise that such an option should be available to L2 learners. In fact, from an evolutionary perspective, it is unlikely that a cognitive mechanism which had not been accessible in the course of development should be available to the mature system.

To conclude this section, let me repeat that if parameter (re)setting is not an option available to L2 learners, this is not to say that it is impossible for them to acquire and use correctly the various constructions related to a particular parameter setting. They will, however, have to rely on other cognitive resources and on different types of learning mechanisms, including inductive learning. The implications and consequences of this conclusion will be explored in a little more detail in the following section of this chapter.

5.3 Inductive learning

In chapter 2, discussing first language development, a distinction was made between different types of acquisition mechanisms, most importantly between acquisition as triggering of genetically transmitted knowledge and acquisition as learning in the traditional sense. In this chapter, the focus has so far been on triggering, especially as it is instantiated in parameter (re)setting, and this discussion has led to the conclusion that L2 learners cannot set parameters to values not instantiated in their L1. The question which inevitably arises at this point is what happens in these cases in L2 acquisition.

To my knowledge, there is no reason to believe that particular properties of languages cannot be learned without the guidance of UG. I therefore start from the fairly uncontroversial assumption that all constructions encountered in target languages can, in principle, be acquired by second language learners. But when we say that all surface properties of natural languages are learnable, this does not necessarily mean that they will be acquired in the same fashion and with identical results as in L1 acquisition. Rather, if UG is indeed not fully available any more as a knowledge source guiding grammatical development, a plausible hypothesis is that L2 learners will resort to other knowledge sources and different types of learning mechanisms in those instances where children acquiring their L1 can rely on the triggering of grammatical knowledge via parameter setting. Probably the most obvious alternative is to further exploit the source of information which is of prime importance anyway and which is readily available, namely the primary linguistic data provided by the linguistic environment. In other words, where triggering of genetically transmitted information is no longer an option, learners can try to extract the necessary information about underlying formal characteristics of the target language by means of generalizations about observable properties of the input data, relying on inductive learning when triggering has become impossible as an acquisition mechanism.

The claim that the utterances encountered in the ambient language(s) serve as a knowledge source for L2 learners, that these data serve as 'input' to the linguistic learning process, is quite obviously neither new nor surprising. In fact, from the perspective of more traditional approaches to second language acquisition (see also section 1.2) it may appear as self-evident or even trivial. But although in some domains, for example in lexical learning, the input accessible to L2 learners undoubtedly constitutes the prime source of information, the question of how this information is extracted from the primary linguistic data and transformed into mentally represented linguistic knowledge is by no means a trivial one. In fact, when it comes to explaining the acquisition of grammatical knowledge, for example structure-dependent relationships between elements in syntax or phonology, we are still far from understanding how learners attend to the relevant information in the PLD and how they succeed in processing it in the course of language acquisition. As is argued by Carroll (2001, 2002a, 2002b), the most popular proposals in linguistics as well as in psychology fail to give satisfactory answers to these questions, and although important insights have recently been gained which may help us to better understand the problem of how L2 learners transform the 'raw material of second language acquisition' (Carroll 2001) into grammatical knowledge, the role of input in L2 acquisition is far from being well understood.

Moreover, there remain doubts concerning the central claim of this section that input-based learning, in principle, could enable L2 learners to acquire a kind of linguistic knowledge allowing them to produce and comprehend constructions which in native grammars are generated by knowledge acquired via the triggering of parameter settings. These doubts emanate from the discussion of the so-called *Logical Problem of language acquisition* termed *Plato's Problem* by Chomsky (1986), referring to the discrepancy between experience and knowledge in grammatical development, an issue at the very core of UG theory. The idea which it is meant to capture is that native grammars of natural languages comprise knowledge which is not encoded in the primary linguistic data in a way which would allow children to extract it by means of inductive learning when exposed to the data in the course of communicative interaction. If, however, this type of information is part of the mature knowledge system but cannot be gained by experience, it must have been in the system prior to experience, in other words it represents innate knowledge (see 2.4). This line of argument provides crucial support for the existence of UG. It is strengthened by a number of observations on the nature of the primary linguistic data: (1) Essential information about the grammatical structure (including phonological as well as morphosyntactic properties) of linguistic expressions is not conveyed overtly by these expressions, nor can it be deduced from the communicative context. (2) Some important grammatical properties of the target system are not attested sufficiently frequently in colloquial speech to be learned inductively within the time lap during which these properties are known to be acquired by children. (3) Enough utterances in colloquial speech are either structurally incomplete or ungrammatical, either because they are only acceptable in specific contexts, or they result from performance errors violating grammatical and/or pragmatic norms to complicate a theory of acquisition in which learners rely exclusively on exemplars or on statistical properties of input. Consequently, learners cannot rely exclusively on the positive evidence which they find in the data. (4) Children typically do not have access to negative evidence, that is, if they use a structure not encountered previously in their linguistic environment and which does not appear in the PLD soon after they first used it, they have no means of deciding whether it is indeed a possibility allowed by the target grammar or whether they should drop it again. (5) Many children receive little or no explicit feedback relating to the grammaticality of their utterances. But although this varies depending on the cultural settings, all children acquire grammatical knowledge about their L1, and neither rate nor ultimate success of grammatical development seems to depend on this.

The conceptual well-foundedness of the Logical Problem of language acquisition, its significance for theories of grammar and of L1 grammatical development, and in fact the soundness of each of the arguments put forth in its support have all been questioned over the years in particularly heated debates. Even the most cursory summary of this controversy would exceed by far the limits of the present discussion, and I will therefore not engage in such a discussion, especially since I do not think that by doing so we could gain significant insights into the issue at stake here, the role of inductive learning for the acquisition of grammatical knowledge by L2 learners. I think it is fair to say that research investigating more thoroughly the kind of input and feedback which children acquiring an L1 receive, and particularly the way in which caretakers adapt their language to what they believe children are able to process, has demonstrated quite convincingly that the primary linguistic data are in many cases less deficient than they have been claimed to be, thus reducing the impact of arguments (2) to (5). But it is also true that it has never been shown that the development of grammars must fail, remain incomplete or will be seriously delayed in settings where children cannot count on this kind of support and have to make do with less rich data. More importantly, the most crucial argument, and indeed the only one on which the idea of a discrepancy between experience and knowledge ultimately depends, is the first one, asserting that mental grammars contain information which cannot be learned inductively from properties of the stimuli available to the child in the PLD. This claim has been referred to as the *Poverty of the Stimulus Hypothesis*, and although this is often equated with the Logical Problem of language acquisition, the two are really conceptually distinct, as has been argued by Felix (1987: chapter 2) and more recently by Carroll (2001: 208), who offers a concise presentation of the arguments in favour of the relevance of the Logical Problem for an explanation of first language acquisition, highlighting the importance of the Poverty of the Stimulus Hypothesis (2001: 222).

Assuming then that the Logical Problem of language acquisition indeed captures a constitutive characteristic of L1 development, the question still is whether the same or a similar point can be made for L2 acquisition. This is not necessarily the case, if only because L2 learners have already successfully acquired the grammar of their native language on which they can arguably rely when facing such problems in the course of L2 acquisition, as argued by Bley-Vroman (1987, 1989, 1990) or Schachter (1990). Moreover, L2 learners, especially adults, possess the necessary cognitive and linguistic means which should enable them to circumvent most of the problems alluded to above. Even learners without formal language training are able to reflect on grammatical properties of the target language, they can ask metalinguistic questions providing them with feedback and negative evidence, and, at least in tutored second language learning, grammatical information not directly available in the data is supplied by instruction. Plato's problem is thus not a logical necessity for L2 acquisition whereas this seems to be the case in L1 development. In fact, more recent research suggests strongly that factors like the ones just alluded to do indeed play a role in L2 acquisition and that there is no logical problem of second language acquisition (Carroll 2001: 208).

In generative L2 research, proponents of the Full Access to UG hypothesis nevertheless rely heavily on the assumption that the Poverty of the Stimulus Hypothesis or the Logical Problem characterize not only first but also second language acquisition; see White 2003: 22 for a presentation of this view, or Schwartz 1996, 2004 who regards the claim that poverty of the stimulus effects do exist as the 'conceptual core' (Schwartz 2004: 97) of generative grammar and as a fundamental insight into the nature of both first and second language acquisition. One cannot but wonder how such blatantly contradictory claims can be maintained and pursued simultaneously in second language research. I suspect that this profoundly unsatisfactory state-of-the-art is directly related to the epistemological deduction of the Logical Problem of language acquisition. As mentioned above, the logic of the argument states that knowledge which can be argued to be part of mental grammars of mature speakers must be provided by the LAD if it cannot be extracted inductively from the PLD. Proof of the hypothesis thus depends entirely on the latter assertion, namely that the relevant information cannot be attained by induction relying exclusively on the data. This is certainly a perfectly legitimate argument, but it leaves defendants of the hypothesis in a somewhat uncomfortable position when it comes to giving empirical support to its claims, since it is difficult if not impossible to provide positive evidence for the non-existence of a fact or a process. L1 researchers have been able to make a reasonably strong case in this situation because they do not have to rely on the Poverty of the Stimulus Hypothesis alone. It can also be argued that children's immature cognitive system does not provide them with compensatory cognitive mechanisms when structure dependency cannot be detected in a straightforward fashion in the stimuli (cf. Carroll 2001: 215). In order to make a similarly strong case for L2 acquisition, it will be necessary to demonstrate that the compensatory mechanisms which L2 learners undeniably have at their disposal are not sufficient to do this job.

This is, admittedly, not an easy task, since, as stated above, we are far from understanding in sufficient detail how learners attend to the relevant information in the PLD and how they succeed in processing it in the course of language acquisition. We should nevertheless expect that researchers who claim that particular aspects of target grammars cannot be learned inductively will at least attempt to demonstrate either that learning mechanisms of this sort cannot succeed for principled reasons or that attempts to this effect have failed systematically. Yet to my knowledge, no such studies have been carried out and published. Instead, advocates of the Full Access to UG and the Poverty of the Stimulus hypotheses have limited their attention entirely to what L2 learners can achieve, without even trying to understand where the limits of their possibilities are. Over the past years, a wealth of studies have been carried out with the aim of showing that L2 learners possess grammatical knowledge, the source of which supposedly can neither be inductive learning based on the primary linguistic data nor their L1 grammars (see Bley-Vroman, Felix and Ioup 1988, White 1990, Martohardjono and Gair 1993, or Dekydtspotter, Sprouse and Anderson 1997, to mention only a few of the earlier ones). However, in my view, they have at best shown that some L2 learners are able to use certain constructions which can be argued to depend on UG-related grammatical knowledge in a fashion similar to native speakers of the target language in question. Unfortunately, these findings are of only limited significance for the question of whether there exists a logical problem of second language acquisition, unless they can justifiably be interpreted as evidence that the performance of these learners (frequently grammaticality judgements) reflects native-like grammatical knowledge. Yet just as in the debate on parameter setting in the preceding section of this chapter, the nature of the underlying knowledge remains largely unexplored. Even more importantly in the present context of a discussion of the Poverty of the Stimulus Hypothesis, we learn nothing about how this knowledge is obtained. In fact, the arguments offered here rarely go beyond insinuating that it is 'unlikely' that the relevant information could be found in the PLD, or that it is 'implausible' to assume that learners could induce the necessary generalizations from the input alone. This is clearly unsatisfactory (cf. Pullum and Scholz 2002). In fact, Lust (1988: 311), although ultimately supporting the Full Access to UG hypothesis, already pointed out that

> Many formal systems of knowledge which can be represented, no matter how bizarre, can be learned, e.g. by a machine of Turing machine capacity, especially if negative evidence is available . . . Thus arguments on the nature of a proposed language alone cannot conclusively argue the necessity for postulation of UG. In particular, they cannot in themselves argue for the role of UG in language acquisition.

She concludes, correctly, I believe, that 'an argument that UG was necessary to L2 learning must be based both on arguments for the nature of this knowledge plus arguments based on the rate and nature of L2 acquisition, and cannot be simply assumed on the basis of the end-state of attained language knowledge' (Lust 1988: 312).

The standard approach by proponents of the Full Access to UG and the Poverty of the Stimulus hypotheses is therefore not only unsatisfactory, it also suggests a deplorable lack of interest in learning mechanisms. Yet without an adequate theory of learning, any theory of (second) language acquisition will necessarily be incomplete. Not that the relevance of learning was not acknowledged, but one does not find serious attempts by these authors to deal with learning, possibly because it is – incorrectly – regarded as a comparatively trivial problem, or as one falling into the domain of psychology, thus not constituting a challenge for linguistic studies of L2 acquisition. Although nothing could be farther from the truth, as has been shown in considerable detail by Carroll (2001), it is fairly obvious that the empirical as well as the theoretical importance of learning mechanisms for a theory of second language acquisition is frequently underestimated.

Let me mention only one example, the Full Transfer/Full Access to UG hypothesis proposed by Schwartz and Sprouse (1994, 1996) (see section 4.2). According to these authors, grammatical development is 'failure driven', that is, input which cannot be assigned a mental representation by the initial grammar forces subsequent (UG-constrained) restructurings. Learners thus rely on three knowledge sources: the initial state largely determined by the L1 grammar, UG, and the input provided by the linguistic environment. Surprisingly, Schwartz and Sprouse (1996: 41) add 'learnability considerations' to this list, without, however, specifying to what this label is intended to refer. They acknowledge that L2 learners may never attain L1-like knowledge of the target languages, a fact for which they attempt to account by speculating that the information available to L2 learners might not be adequate, either because the triggering data necessary for the restructuring of approximative systems are not accessible, or they are too complex or infrequent to be used appropriately by the learners. As a result, transitional grammars may fossilize. Note that this scenario suggests that L2 learners do not go wrong (presumably because they are guided by UG), but that they may get stuck on their way to the target system. Note further that, in contrast to the differences between L1 and L2 grammars at the initial stage, the cognitive processes operative in the restructuring of initial grammars are postulated to be identical in L1 and L2 acquisition, an assumption which is by no means self-evident; I will return to this issue in section 6.3 of the following chapter. Note thirdly that this scenario does not explicitly assign specific tasks to learnability considerations.

How, then, can the restructuring of transitional grammars happen, and in what way are such changes 'failure driven'? Recall that Schwartz and Sprouse (1994, 1996) focused on the acquisition of verb placement by an L1 Turkish learner of L2 German (cf. section 4.2). At Stage 1 this learner already placed finite verbs in a position after the subject, rather than in clause-final position as predicted by the Full Transfer hypothesis. This is explained by a gap in the data ('Stage 0') and by the claim that the 'mismatch ... between the surface syntax of German and the surface syntax of Turkish' is particularly 'salient' (Schwartz and Sprouse 1996:

44), triggering a very early change in the initial grammar. We are not told, however, how the 'mismatch' translates into learning mechanisms, and I can only conclude that there is no point in pursuing this issue, although I find it unfortunate that second language acquisition research should not have anything to contribute to the inquiry into what causes the restructuring of grammars. After all, explaining changes in the course of acquisition is what acquisition research is all about, and if one wants to argue that this process is 'failure driven', one needs to explain what the cognitive processes are which enable learners to perceive the differences between particular properties of L1 and L2 grammars and how they become aware of them. Merely pointing to a 'salient mismatch' amounts to trivializing this core issue of L2 research, especially since the notion of 'saliency' adopted for this scenario is not made explicit. One may, in fact, doubt whether the mismatch is as salient as these authors believe it to be. Müller (1996: 10), for example, argues that this is not the case. She points out that NP V order coexists with V NP order in main clauses in colloquial German and that one finds preposed as well as postposed elements. Potentially conflicting evidence is also encountered in subordinate clauses since some subordinating conjunctions do not allow clause-final placement of finite verbs, for example *denn* 'since, for', and others like *weil* 'because' and *obwohl* 'although' allow both final and non-final order in colloquial speech.

Recall that the starting point of this discussion was to ask whether input-based learning can, in principle, serve as a compensatory mechanism enabling L2 learners to use constructions which in native language use reflect UG-related grammatical knowledge. The principal reason why this question needs to be addressed is that if one concludes that UG is not fully accessible to L2 learners, as is implied by the Partial Access to UG hypothesis, one must address the issue of what happens in such cases in L2 acquisition. Since it is hypothesized that in L1 development the linguistic knowledge concerned here is implemented in native grammars via triggering of knowledge available prior to experience, the issue at stake is whether inductive learning, that is, a substantially different acquisition mechanism, can indeed serve as a compensatory learning mechanism. My claim is that this question can be answered positively and that it is therefore possible to account for the observation that every surface property of any given language is learnable in L2 acquisition.

But this is not the only reason why inductive learning should be attributed an important role in L2 acquisition. It is indeed difficult to see how any theory of acquisition could do without it (cf. Carroll 2001, 2002a, 2002b). Note that even scholars like Schwartz and Sprouse (1996) who emphasize the role of UG and of L1-based knowledge in L2 acquisition concede that 'failure driven' learning must be taken into account. I interpret this as indirect support for my claim stressing the importance of inductive learning, even if researchers adopting the Full Access to UG hypothesis rarely ask how the knowledge which they attribute to L2 learners is actually acquired, let alone what inductive learning can achieve or not achieve. The reason for this lack of interest in the nature of the learning mechanisms may well be that full transfer from the L1 competence and full access to UG already provide such powerful explanatory mechanisms that no need is seen for an additional one, and other options are therefore not explored. This would also explain why studies based on the 'full access to UG' assumption invariantly follow the same line of argument: (i) a formal property of the target language not instantiated in the L1 grammar is shown to be perceived or produced by learners; (ii) it is stipulated, implicitly or explicitly referring to the Poverty of the Stimulus Hypothesis, that the L2 feature investigated could not have been extracted from the data, and (iii) it is concluded that the knowledge required for its use must have been made available by UG – *tertium non datur*! Learning rather than triggering is not even considered as an alternative explanation. This is undoubtedly a major shortcoming of this approach, for even if one accepts the possibility of full access to UG in L2, this does not necessarily preclude alternative options. As Felix (1987) suggested many years ago, the superior cognitive abilities of adult L2 learners might compete and interfere with UG-based learning mechanisms, and if authors like Carroll (2001) are correct in arguing that there is no Logical Problem in L2 acquisition, inductive learning should be expected to play a major role in L2 acquisition, irrespective of whether full access to UG is possible or not.

My conclusion from considerations such as the ones just mentioned is that inductive learning needs to be considered seriously as one of the mechanisms explaining the course and the attainable results of L2 acquisition. This includes the possibility of serving as a compensatory learning mechanism enabling L2 learners to acquire linguistic knowledge which allows them to use constructions equivalent to those generated by modules of grammars which in L1 development are the result of triggering of UG principles. Since I adopted a version of the Partial Access to UG hypothesis according to which parameterized principles are subject to maturational change and may therefore not remain accessible to L2 learners, the domains of grammar referring to grammatical parameters are again the ones to be examined. Note that the claim is not that compensatory mechanisms enable L2 learners to acquire identical linguistic knowledge as in L1 development. Rather, they are assumed to allow L2 learners to acquire a kind of linguistic knowledge sufficient to mimic the linguistic behaviour of native speakers. Consequently, the issue at stake is not whether L2 learners can produce particular constructions – this is a fact acknowledged by defendants of the Partial Access hypothesis as well as by proponents of the Full Access hypothesis. What is controversial is whether this type of linguistic performance in L2 reflects native-like grammatical knowledge and whether it is attained by parameter setting. This section is thus concerned with a similar issue to the previous one, but I will tackle it from the reverse angle. Having concluded in 5.2 that L2 research has not succeeded in providing evidence in support of the claim that parameters can be (re)set in L2 acquisition, I now want to ask whether the acquisition of constructions equivalent to those reflecting particular L1 parameter settings does indeed support the idea of inductive learning in L2. In doing so, I will have to refer mainly to my own observations because, as just mentioned, generative studies of L2 acquisition have rarely investigated inductive learning and especially not learning as a compensatory mechanism for parameter setting.

As in the preceding section, we are facing again the challenge of identifying types of empirical evidence which should allow us to distinguish between different kinds of knowledge underlying similar or apparently identical linguistic behaviour. Some of the arguments and empirical findings presented in 5.2 can indeed be carried over to the present discussion. If one finds, for example, that alleged cases of parameter setting lack the clustering effect and exhibit instead separate and partly different acquisition patterns for the various constructions related to a given parameter value, this finding is in tune with the assumption that we are looking at instances of data-driven learning. The same holds true for the observation that particular developmental patterns are not characterized by a dramatic increase in the frequency of use of the construction required by the target norm, but that target-conforming and target-deviant patterns are used interchangeably, suggesting a trial and error strategy of learning. A protracted period of acquisition is also an indication that inductive learning is happening. These arguments have been discussed at some length in the previous section, supported by references to empirical studies. They therefore need not be dwelt upon at length in this section. The following remarks are merely intended as a reminder of why findings of this type are likely to constitute evidence for inductive learning. I will also present some further empirical evidence supporting the claim that we are looking at results from this type of learning mechanism.

I hope to be able to demonstrate that it is indeed possible to distinguish empirically between the two learning mechanisms, either by analysing the *results* of the acquisition processes or by investigating these *processes* themselves, even if in some cases we have to rely on indirect evidence. The necessity of the hypothesized differences follows in a fairly straightforward manner from what has been said earlier about first and second language acquisition. Remember that one observation at the starting point of this search for parallels and differences between L1 and L2 acquisition has been that L1 children are always successful in acquiring the grammars of the ambient language(s) whereas few if any L2 learners attain native competence. This is such a fundamental and widely acknowledged fact that any approach to acquisition, in order to be seriously considered as an adequate theory of language acquisition, has to account for it. As for the approach taken in this book, I suggested that the LMC and especially UG, the central component of this capacity, can explain why L1 development is always successful, uniform and relatively fast. It necessarily follows that L2 acquisition will be more variable, more protracted in its course of development than L1, and never (or rarely) fully successful in those domains where parameter setting is no longer possible and where, consequently, L2 learners have to detect the structural properties of the corresponding constructions by analysing the PLD, as predicted by the Partial Access to UG hypothesis. In other words, since the learning mechanisms of L2 learners are not necessarily constrained by principles of UG, one should expect to find individual and learner-type dependent variation across L2 learners.

If all this is on the right track, it follows, for our search for parallels and differences between L1 and L2 acquisition, that L1 and L2 acquisition processes will strongly differ in those domains where parameter (re)setting would have been necessary, and that parallels will be found where this is not the case. Differences of this kind have indeed been observed and discussed in chapters 3 and 4 and also in the preceding section of the current chapter. My claim now is that these observable differences do not indicate merely that the two types of learners proceed in different ways but that they also develop different types of knowledge. In other words, my claim is that although the knowledge system acquired by L2 learners is in large part equivalent to that of the corresponding native speakers, subparts of the L2 knowledge are of a different kind, resulting from the fact that L2 learners have to compensate for the inaccessibility of certain UG constrained acquisition mechanisms by resorting to cognitive mechanisms not constrained by UG.

Before turning to the kind of evidence supporting the claim that different types of knowledge can be activated in using first and second languages, let me briefly illustrate again the differences between the acquisition processes, demonstrating that the L2 process is not only more protracted as compared to L1, it also lacks the abrupt changes characterizing parameter setting in L1, and it exhibits considerably more variation within and across learners. As an example I want to refer again to the analysis of a learner of the ZISA corpus, Bruno. I mentioned this learner already in the preceding section, especially pointing out the interindividual variation distinguishing him from other adult L2 learners, and also the lack of empirically detectable effects of triggering. Bruno's case can, however, also serve as an illustration of intra-individual variation and, most importantly, of item-by-item learning. We should expect to find this in instances of inductive learning, because it exemplifies a kind of inductive generalization which can enable learners to eventually use the target language adequately. Müller (1998) analysed the acquisition of German verb placement in an in-depth study of the longitudinal data from this Italian L1 learner who was recorded at week 7 after his arrival in Germany. She found that Bruno initially placed both finite and non-finite verbs, without exception, in a position preceding objects and adverbials (VX). Correct order, including XV patterns, emerged gradually. In fact, it took this learner approximately one year to acquire it, and during an extended period of time he used both VX and XV orders. Interestingly, the acquisition of XV order was learned in an item-by-item fashion. In other words, Bruno did not make a generalization referring to [±finite] verbs, but learned the target-like placement separately for each lexical item. This becomes evident when one looks at newly learned verbs which were at first placed before objects again, even as late as in week 75. In addition, when he began using subordinate clauses, verbs were placed once more in the original VX position, and, once again, he acquired the correct order in an item-by-item fashion. It took Bruno more than one year to arrive at the target order in German. Note that the observed pattern of lexically dependent learning of verb placement indicates that L2 acquisition, in this case, did not involve setting a parameter to a different value, but is rather the result of lexical learning. This is most obvious in the case of non-finite verbs in subordinate clauses where the VO/VAdv pattern reappeared even though it had already been abandoned in main clauses. These findings leave little doubt about the fact that Bruno acquired important parts of German word order regularities in a piecemeal fashion, generalizing over properties of individual lexical items.

Observations like these as well as the ones discussed in the preceding section give strong support, I contend, to the claim that L2 learners differ from L1 children not only in the way in which they proceed towards the goal of becoming able to use target-conforming utterances. More importantly, these findings reveal some differences which suggest that the nature of the operations applied and consequently also the nature of the ultimately attained knowledge differ from those in L1 development. To illustrate this point, let me remind you of the approach taken by Bruno in learning German word order. His relying on distributional properties of individual lexical items rather than generalizing over the syntactic feature [+V] or rather [±finite] is a first indication that L2 learners focus on less abstract and more superficial clues in the linguistic data than children developing native grammars.

My hypothesis is that this observation captures a core feature of second language acquisition. To avoid misunderstandings, the claim is not that this is consistently the case; it rather characterizes specific parts of L2 learners' linguistic knowledge corresponding to particular domains of native grammars. Let me explain this hypothesis and the ensuing claims in a little more detail. It is important to remember that structure dependency has been argued to be the crucial property characterizing human language (see chapter 2, section 2.2). From this it follows that native knowledge of any language contains abstract grammatical entities such as syntactic categories which, in turn, enter into structural relationships which necessarily involve hierarchical relationships and cannot be defined in linear terms alone. One of the fascinating properties of first language development is that children are able from very early on to focus on cues allowing them to discover abstract grammatical entities as well as structure-dependent relationships holding between them, although this information is not easily detectable in surface patterns. Now, there can be no doubt that the linguistic knowledge of L2 learners also refers to abstract grammatical units and to structural properties of constituents and clauses; it is shaped and constrained by UG as well as by their previously acquired grammatical competence. However, when facing acquisition tasks where the target grammars differ from the L1 and where the grammatical property in question is not accessible any more via UG, as in the case of certain parameterized options, they must rely on the cues provided by the PLD. This is where L2 acquisition crucially deviates from L1 development; in instances where child L1 learners unconsciously detect the structural triggers for specific parameter values by analysing the PLD, L2 learners have to make do with that kind of information about formal properties of the target system which can be extracted from the data by means of their parser fed by the transitional grammar and probably also the L1 grammar. Where this fails, they need to rely on generalizations based on observation. The latter, however, can only capture superficial reflections of parameter settings, but not their abstract underlying value as expressed, for example, by uninterpretable grammatical features.

In order to motivate and justify this line of argument, it suffices perhaps to recall the sketch of parameter theory outlined in section 2.4, including a discussion of how parameterized options are grammatically encoded. If, for example, a syntactic parameter refers to an abstract feature which is part of the featural makeup of a functional category and of the syntactic element to be moved to the functional head, a problem arises for the L2 learner whose grammar differs from the target system in that this feature is not instantiated in the same categories, or perhaps not at all. Now, setting the parameter to a specific value has been argued to license a number of different surface constructions (the clustering effect). Assuming then that L2 learners cannot detect the differences in the featural composition of the categories concerned, they may nevertheless be able to observe the various surface reflections of a given parametric value. Yet since they are not able to relate them to one and the same underlying grammatical property, thus failing to realize that the same logic caused them to emerge, they will focus on each of the surface properties of these constructions separately. Inductive learning thus enables them to generalize from the observable characteristics to more overarching formal characteristics without, however, being able to establish a connection between the various surface phenomena.

To sum up, the predictions entailed by the hypothesis proposed above assert that L2 learners, when dealing with certain grammatical (morphosyntactic as well as phonological) acquisition tasks, are not able to capture the full set of grammatical properties of an item or a constituent. But they can and will in these cases rely on properties detectable in the construction and which can serve as the basis for data-driven generalizations. These bits of information are less abstract in nature than the ones triggering parameter settings in L1, that is, they are more superficial and therefore more easily available for induction. Starting from this basis, one way to proceed is to rely on distributional properties, possibly only taking into account the linear order of surface strings, thus attributing structure-independent regularities to the data where native grammars establish structure-dependent relationships. But a less radical solution is also possible, namely by assigning partial structures to the construction in question, for example if DP-internal relationships are taken into account without referring to the structural position of this DP in clause structure. This is to say that L2 learners may focus on shallow structures, failing to complete the process of incremental structure building. The most radical option, the one which deviates most from native grammars, is that formal properties are interpreted as encoding functional ones, for example if L2 learners interpret grammatical gender as expressing biological sex (see Carroll 1999). Importantly, the scenario to be derived from the above hypothesis does not necessarily imply that the operations applied in the learning process or the resulting knowledge systems will *not* be domain-specific. After all, the learning processes in L2 acquisition implied here do refer to grammatical entities like verbs, even if they may fail to detect the full set of their grammatical properties. But as the examples involving purely linear order of elements in an utterance or functionally motivated formal regularities show, we cannot exclude the possibility of domain-general operations intervening in the organization of L2 utterances, either.

In the remainder of this section, I want to discuss very briefly some empirical observations which will hopefully clarify my hypothesis. The acquisition of *negative constructions* discussed in chapter 3 (see section 3.3) can serve as a first example. Remember that what is frequently referred to as the 'syntax of negation' primarily refers to the placement of finite verbs. Universally, one finds a close relationship between finiteness and the position of NEG. This is reflected in developmental facts in L1 acquisition: initially NEG is placed clause-externally, but as soon as finiteness is implemented in the developing grammar, that is, a distinction is made between [±finite] and finite verbal elements are raised to the appropriate functional heads, child utterances consistently exhibit target-conforming word order, and NEG appears clause-internally if this is required by the target language. The developmental sequence thus follows a grammatically determined logic, instantiated by head movement, a structure-dependent operation. In child as well as adult L2 acquisition, on the other hand, early learners of a variety of target languages tend to place NEG pre-verbally (rather than clause-externally). This, however, is not a pattern adopted by all learners; it varies rather according to learner types. For example, a longitudinal study with three L1 Romance (Portuguese, Spanish and Italian) learners of German, reported on in section 3.3, found that NEG was placed adjacent to the verb, but whereas it precedes both the finite and the non-finite verb in these Romance languages, each of the learners preferred different word order patterns, one of them using predominantly postverbal and even clause-final position, another one preferring pre-verbal position, and the third exhibiting variable usage, with NEG in both pre- and postverbal position, even after non-finite verbs. The latter order violates the requirements of both German and the three Romance languages. In other words, L2 acquisition of the 'syntax of negation' (i) differs from the developmental pattern in L1, (ii) exhibits considerable variation both across and within learners, (iii) is dissociated from the acquisition of finiteness and (iv) violates requirements of both the L1 and the L2 grammars.

In order to account for the observed facts, I suggested that L2 learners adopt a strategy which consists of placing the negator adjacent to the element to be negated, preferably preceding it. Once they become aware of the typologically unusual position of the German negator, frequently distant from the finite verb and close to the end of the clause, they may be induced to placing NEG string-finally. If this explanation is correct, the L2 knowledge system indeed differs fundamentally from that represented by the L1 grammar. (1) It follows a semantic rather than a syntactic logic in that the order of elements is partially determined in terms of the (narrow) scope of the negator (adjacent to the negated element). (2) The NEG +X strategy is linear in nature, rather than being constrained by structure-dependent properties like c-command which typically defines the scope of operators. (3) The positions referred to (clause-initial, clause-final, pre-verbal, etc.) are all defined in terms of linear order in a string rather than by hierarchically represented structural positions. (4) NEG placement does not depend on whether the verbal element is finite or not, allowing even for constructions where NEG follows the non-finite element. (5) NEG placement implies movement of the 'wrong' element, that is, NEG rather than the finite verb. (6) NEG placement involves movement to the right which, if this was a structure-dependent operation, would require lowering in the structure, a type of operation not tolerated by UG since it violates the Empty Category Principle, as explained in section 4.4.

What is worth noticing is that this NEG +X strategy may enable the learner to produce constructions which superficially conform to the target norm although the underlying knowledge is significantly different from that underlying native usage. This can be seen in the following examples from a fifteen-year-old Spanish learner of German, uttered after one year in Germany. Interestingly, the more complex construction in (i), containing a modal followed by a main verb, is superficially standard-like, whereas (ii), which only contains a main verb, deviates from the target norm. The explanation for this apparently paradoxical result is that the main verb is the negated element. The NEG +X strategy thus yields a result which superficially corresponds to a pattern where the modal is placed in a higher functional head and therefore precedes in linear order both NEG and the non-finite main verb. Only (3) (ii) reveals that finite elements are actually not placed in a structurally higher position.

(3) (i) Ich kann nich sprechen in Deutschlan (Rosemarie S)
Ich kann nicht Deutsch sprechen.[8]
I can not speak$_{\text{-fin}}$ in Germany
'I cannot speak German.'
(ii) Oder nich versteht ich auch Spanisch
Oder ich verstehe auch nicht Spanisch.
Or not understand$_{\text{3rd sg}}$ I also Spanish
'Or I don't understand Spanish either.'

Examples like these show very clearly that one cannot simply take surface patterns at their face value when the goal of our research is to discover the underlying knowledge of learners. In cases where the L2 learning strategies result in target-conforming uses of particular constructions, it is difficult to detect the fact that the linguistic knowledge of the learner is fundamentally different from the native grammatical competence. But this only emphasizes the necessity of searching for alternative explanations of observed facts rather than attributing apparent success invariantly to guidance by UG.

The same conclusion can be drawn from studies investigating the acquisition of constructions exhibiting postverbal subjects in German, that is, apparent subject–verb *inversion* or *verb-second* placement. In chapters 2 and 4, we saw that children discover quite early the specific features of German verb placement, and in 4.4 I discussed in some detail the different sequences characterizing the development of this domain of grammar. One of the striking differences between the two types of acquisition consists in the fact that children start placing finite verbal elements in front of subjects from very early on and *never* do so (incorrectly) with non-finite verbs, whereas L2 learners begin to use word order patterns of this type fairly late; see Table 4.4 in section 4.4. In fact, target-deviant *V3 patterns persist for an extended period of time, and they can even be detected in the speech of near-native speakers of German. This is all the more striking since this is equally the case if the first languages (e.g. English, French, Spanish) of these learners also allow for pre-subject position of finite verbs, if only in a more restricted range of contexts (e.g. in interrogatives, after some adverbs) than Germanic V2 languages. The crucial point is that such cases of 'subject–verb inversion' are commonly analysed as resulting from finite verb movement, irrespective of whether the constraints on this movement and the targeted landing sites are identical in these languages. In other words, contrary to what the term 'inversion' seems to suggest and to what appears to be assumed in traditional grammars, postverbal subject position does not imply that the two elements swap places or that the subject goes behind the verb. What L2 learners do, however, is apparently just that (cf. section 4.4).

My claim thus is that at least some L2 learners do not actually acquire inversion but rather learn to mimic the surface effects of this syntactic operation, placing the subject in a position behind the verb. A number of observations and of empirical facts support this idea. First of all, we find the same L1–L2 differences as in the acquisition of negative constructions: (i) as discussed in detail in section 4.4, the developmental patterns differ, and 'inversion' emerges late in L2 acquisition; (ii) although it is not possible to decide empirically whether all L2 learners resort to this ersatz solution, it can apparently persist for an extended period of time and be part of the linguistic knowledge of very advanced learners; (iii) the emergence of inversion in L2 speech is independent of the acquisition of finiteness, and contrary to what we observe in L1, non-finite as well as finite verbal elements are placed in pre-subject position; (iv) some of the resulting surface patterns are tolerated by neither the L1 nor the L2 grammar, as becomes evident from examples (10) (ii) in section 4.4 and (4) (i), quoted from a learner of the ZISA corpus (Clahsen, Meisel and Pienemann 1983) who at the time of recording was thirty-one years old and had lived in Germany for ten years.

(4) (i) Bestimmt liebe diese Frau ich nix (Franco I)
Definitely love this woman I not
'I definitely do not love this woman.'

(ii) Da hat sieben Kinder diese Frau.
There has seven children this woman
'So, this woman has seven children.'

Note that the subject is not placed immediately after the finite verb but in utterance-final position, after the complement and followed only by NEG which is competing for final position. This, however, means that its exact placement only becomes apparent when the verb is accompanied by a complement; it is therefore difficult to detect because constructions of this type are infrequent in the recordings with Franco and in those with other learners at this stage of L2 acquisition. The vast majority of their utterances consist of bare verb constructions without objects or adverbial expressions. In these cases, both operations, placing the subject in final position or raising the verb to clause second position, yield identical surface patterns. In other words, similarly as with the NEG +X strategy, placement of the subject in final position is a successful compensatory mechanism in most instances. Only in the infrequent cases where it results in a target-deviant surface pattern is it possible to find empirical evidence distinguishing it from native grammar operations.

What matters for the present discussion is that this type of inversion relies on information obtained by scanning the directly observable superficial properties of utterances, without referring to abstract structural properties. It resembles in more than one way the mechanism producing the negative constructions discussed above. (1) It is an operation applying to linear strings, rather than to hierarchical structural relationships. (2) The position identified as the landing site (utterance-final) is defined in terms of string order. (3) It does not distinguish between finite and non-finite verbs. (4) It obliges the 'wrong' element to move, that is, the subject rather than the finite verb. (5) It involves movement to the right. (6) The fact that some learners move the subject only over 'light' constituents (cf. Clahsen, Meisel and Pienemann 1983) suggests that this movement is constrained by processing restrictions rather than by grammatical principles. Quite clearly, inversion as postverbal placement of the subject is not an operation which could be described in grammatical terms conforming to principles of UG.

As has hopefully become apparent from these examples, learning mechanisms which cannot rely on abstract grammatical information underlying particular constructions can nevertheless enable learners to produce correct surface patterns, even if this may not be possible in all cases. In fact, no principled reasons speak against the possibility of fully successful surrogate solutions. If the target construction can be defined exhaustively in terms of characteristics displayed by surface strings, this might very well be possible. Let us assume, for example, just for the sake of the argument, that the Head Direction Parameter could be defined exclusively in terms of verb–complement order (OV/ VO); I see no reason why these properties could not be learned inductively, since they are revealed at the surface level by the linear order of the concerned elements. It goes without saying, however, that such construction types, whose grammatical properties can be fully detected by observing their superficial characteristics, are not appropriate test cases when it comes to deciding on the issue of access to UG in L2 acquisition – precisely because triggering of parameterized choices and inductive learning seem to yield superficially identical results here, thus making it impossible to distinguish empirically between the two types of learning.

An example of this sort is discussed by White (2003: 133), namely ADJ N order. The relative order of these two elements is commonly explained in terms of noun raising within DP, but very much the same effect can be obtained by applying linear principles of utterance organization. In languages like French which prefer N ADJ order, raising of the noun is said to be triggered by a strong feature in a higher functional head, yielding *le livre anglais*, as opposed to English *the English book* where the noun remains in the NP below the ADJP. White (2003: 133) argues that, if the corresponding parameter could not be reset, 'English-speaking learners of French should be unable to acquire N Adj order, whereas French-speaking learners of English should be unable to lose it'. Of course, this simple logic only holds up if learners were indeed restricted to the alternative of either resetting parameters or not learning anything at all. It is difficult to see why anybody would want to entertain such an idea, especially in a case where inductive learning is such an obvious possibility.

In all the examples presented so far, inductive learning mechanisms rely on information conveyed by the linear organization of utterances in order to arrive at generalizations enabling learners to produce constructions which superficially resemble those generated by structure-dependent operations in native grammars. But as mentioned at the beginning of this discussion, L2 learners not only refer to formal properties of a different kind (linear rather than hierarchical order), they also seem to resort to functional information in their attempts at discovering regularities of target systems which cannot easily be extracted from surface chains. This is likely to result in a kind of linguistic knowledge which differs more radically from native grammars than the ones mentioned so far, as should become obvious from the following example.

Verb inflection may serve a number of syntactic, semantic and pragmatic functions. These formal devices not only encode grammatical tense, modality, aspect, as well as subject–verb agreement in person, number and sometimes gender, they also serve semantic and pragmatic purposes, coding agentivity, transitivity, deixis and so forth. Acquisition research must therefore try to answer the question of whether the emergence of devices like inflectional morphology is determined by grammatical or by semantic-pragmatic principles. In Meisel (1991) I argued that, whereas in L1 development verb inflection expresses grammatical agreement from very early on, in L2 semantic-pragmatic considerations can override grammatical principles (see also the discussion in the preceding section and in section 2.4). The statement referring to L1 development is, in fact, fairly uncontroversial; monolingual as well as bilingual children (cf. Meisel 1990, 1994a) have been shown to acquire verb inflection fast, and person agreement develops virtually without errors.

A quite different picture emerges when we look at L2 acquisition. It has been shown repeatedly that the acquisition of these devices is slow, characterized by important individual differences, that ultimate success is often quite limited, and that the acquisition of verb inflection exhibits no developmental connection with grammatically related devices, either with verb placement or with the emergence of subjects; see Köpcke 1987 and Clahsen 1988b for results based on analyses of the longitudinal data of the ZISA corpus. The study of six of these learners (Meisel 1991) revealed that they represent four different learning approaches. There are those who do not make much progress toward the target system, those who seem to be able to use such forms from very early on, and those who make some progress – some slower, others faster. The crucial issue, however, is whether the inflection markers used by these learners indeed express target-like subject–verb agreement. My claim is that the usage of at least some learners is determined by semantic and pragmatic rather than morpho-syntactic principles. A number of facts support this claim. Notice, for example, that the verbal inflectional markers used by these learners do not necessarily agree with the corresponding subjects. Rather, these learners exploit different options as to how to use these devices:

(5) (i) *Only verb inflection*
0 kaufst ein Maschine — Giovanni IL (21)[9]
Buy$_{+2nd\ sg}$ a machine
'You buy a machine.'

(ii) *Only subject, no verb inflection*
Mein Bruder for Ferie komm$_{+0}$ in Sizilie — Bruno IL (7)
My brother for holidays come in Sicily
'My brother comes to Sicily for holidays.'

(iii) *Only subject pronoun*
Isch isch (= ich) auch gehen Naxos — Giovanni IL (8)
I, I also go$_{+inf}$ Naxos.
'I also go to Naxos'

(iv) *Scaffolding: the native speaker identifies the person; the learner omits the subject as well as inflection markings* — Giovanni IL (8)
N: Du hattest mal gesagt, dass du ab Januar nicht mehr samstags arbeitest.
'You once said you wouldn't work on Saturdays any more, as of January.'
Giovanni: vielleicht. jetz jetz viel arbeiten
perhaps. now now much work$_{+inf}$
'Perhaps. Right now I am working a lot.'

The crucial factor determining use or omission is not grammatical in nature but pragmatic. It cannot be excluded that this behaviour is partly determined by an indirect influence of the first languages of the six learners, all L1 speakers of Romance languages, that is, null-subject languages where subjects are only supplied when required by pragmatic constraints. Yet this would only account for option (i); other syntactic properties of null-subject languages are not transferred to German, and even with respect to the null-subject property German is not treated systematically as a null-subject language. Rather, some learners use subjects right from the start in all or almost all required contexts, but drop them occasionally later on. These observations are not compatible with the assumption that the observed facts reflect an influence of the L1 Null-Subject Parameter. A more plausible hypothesis is that the pattern of usage results from the learners' focus on expressing personal deixis and that nouns and pronouns in subject position as well as verb morphology all seem to serve a similar function, in this respect. It is therefore possible for the learners to omit one or the other – or even both if the context or the interlocutors provide the necessary information. And this is what some learners indeed do, at least temporarily, that is, they use *either* inflection *or* lexical subjects. Zita PL, for example, omits subjects fairly consistently when she uses personal inflection on the verb, whereas Giovanni IL, who only supplies few correct person markings anyway, never does so when using a subject together with the verb.

If this interpretation of the facts is on the right track, we may conclude that the logic underlying the use of identical surface forms is construed differently in the two acquisition types; whereas it is of a semantic-pragmatic nature in L2, it is predominantly grammatical in L1 acquisition. More specifically, subjects and subject–verb agreement in L1 encode grammatical relations, and they simultaneously carry semantic-pragmatic functions; but the same devices may be stripped of their grammatical values in L2 acquisition. A plausible interpretation of this difference in the underlying logic might be that L2 learners attribute functional values to grammatical devices in their attempt to get into a system whose more abstract formal logic is not easily transparent for them.

Before concluding this section, let me draw attention to one further domain where first and second language acquisition differ strongly, although I can only offer some tentative remarks on why this is the case. I am alluding to the difference in how bound and free morphology items are acquired in first and second language acquisition. Once again, the facts are fairly uncontroversial. Children acquiring their first languages focus on cues relating to formal properties of language well before they can grasp their semantic or pragmatic values, and also before they can assign grammatical values to these devices (see chapter 2). Once developing grammars contain functional elements and can thus be argued to be organized according to grammatical principles, elements encoding the structural relationships are acquired fast and successfully. As Jill de Villiers (1992: 425) put it (cf. quote at the end of section 2.3), one can observe 'functional categories popping out all over'. What matters in the present context is that these elements are frequently expressed by inflectional morphology which does not represent a particular challenge for L1 learners. This is true not only for Indo-European languages, the perhaps best-studied languages. Take Basque, for example, a highly inflecting language with a complex verbal agreement system encoded almost exclusively by means of verbal affixes. Children acquiring Basque as their L1 develop the target system at least as fast and easily as children learning English, and where they have been observed to deviate temporarily from the target norm, they introduced even more inflectional markings, arguably regularizing the target system, but at the cost of additional inflections (cf. Ezeizabarrena 1996; Meisel and Ezeizabarrena 1996).

A substantially different picture emerges when we look at how second language learners deal with bound morphology. We saw in chapter 3 (section 3.2) that this distinction is crucially relevant as an explanatory factor for the order of emergence of morphemes instantiating functional categories, as was shown by Andersen (1978b) and Zobl and Liceras (1994). In fact, Wode (1978) already argued that the bound–free distinction matters only in L2 but not in L1 acquisition. This is to say that if a particular grammatical function is expressed by an independent word rather than by an affix, L2 learners will acquire this faster and probably more successfully. A number of studies have corroborated this claim, for example Parodi (1998) in an in-depth analysis of L1 and L2 data. In fact, second language learners are known to substitute bound morphemes by independent words in cases where this results in target-deviant constructions, as, for example, when using adverbs rather than tense morphology, for instance introducing an utterance by an adverb, followed by an infinitival form of the verb (cf. von Stutterheim 1986 or Meisel 1987a). A reflection of this L1–L2 difference is found in pidgin and creole languages, confirming the idea that it is caused by fundamentally different learning processes which shape the various types of language development. Whereas pidgins are always second languages of their users, creoles are native languages. This is why pidginization shares crucial properties with second language acquisition and creolization with L1 development (see the contributions to Andersen 1983b). Concerning the specific example of TMA (tense–modality–aspect) markers, Bickerton (1981) pointed out that in creoles they are derived from verbal elements, in pidgins however from adverbial expressions. This suggests that L2 learners universally tend to replace inflectional markers by independent words, in this case verb inflection encoding TMA values by adverbs.

If the facts attesting to an L1–L2 difference with respect to bound versus free morphology are uncontroversial and have been confirmed in a series of data-based-studies, an explanation is more difficult to give and is, to my knowledge, still outstanding. One possibility which comes to mind immediately is that independent words should be easier to parse. But even if one can show that this is the case, it does not really solve the problem – unless one can explain why adults but not children need that kind of support in order to enhance the acquisition process. Part, at least, of the solution to this problem can perhaps be found in how learners segment the speech stream and extract lexical items at the initial state of acquisition. Perhaps they rely on specific types of acoustic cues to locate prosodic words (Carroll 2001, 2004), and a priori mapping strategies allow them to link such cues to word boundaries. Grammatical markers encoded as affixes can be predicted to represent a special acquisition task since these elements are 'prosodically cliticised onto other lexical items which can be realised as prosodic words' (Carroll 2001: 180). Child L1 learners are credited with a particular sensitivity to acoustic cues, and the fact that they are able to 'map specific semantic or morphosyntactic functions onto suffixes must also be explained by a priori correspondence strategies, which involve mapping specific concepts onto specific types of morphosyntactic categories' (Carroll 2001: 182). This is in tune with what we saw in chapter 2, concerning toddlers' and very young children's capacity to focus on formal cues which will bootstrap them into the grammatical system. As for L2 learners, little is known about how they proceed, but 'adults may not be sensitive at all to prosodic cues to morphosyntax, or be unable to compute prosodic cues in the presence of other types of cues' (2001: 183); see also Carroll (1999). Carroll (2001: 183) emphasizes, on the other hand that 'it has been demonstrated experimentally that *adults are sensitive to the distribution of forms in linearly ordered strings, and can readily locate particular forms relative to fixed positions in a string or relative to other forms in a string*'. One can thus hypothesize that second language learners are not able to make full use, any more, of the discovery procedures which allow children to bootstrap into the grammatical system of their first languages and that this has particularly detrimental consequences for the acquisition of inflectional morphology and of bound morphemes, more generally.

Segmentation of the speech stream may, however, only be part of the story. The other part relates to the structural integration of the previously identified elements. Whereas bound morphemes like tense or agreement markers inevitably enter into structure-dependent relationships within the word and within larger constituents of the clause, it may be possible to assign to free morphemes like adverbs a position in the surface string, relying exclusively on their distributional properties. This at least temporary avoidance of structural integration of newly acquired constituents is reminiscent of what Hoekstra and Jordens (1994) argued for L1 learners; when facing the task of integrating new grammatical material into the clause structure, they initially adjoin them to the structure in question. In other words, focusing on independent words rather than on bound morphemes might spare L2 learners difficult and perhaps insurmountable problems in segmenting as well as in structure building.

Second language acquisition thus seems to include a process, among others, which can be viewed as the reversal of grammaticalization, a mechanism of diachronic change already described by Meillet (1912) and which is currently one of the most frequently discussed phenomena in historical linguistics (cf. Heine and Kuteva 2002). Grammaticalization can be defined as a process by which a lexical element loses its referential properties over time and adopts a formal value, simultaneously losing its autonomy by being cliticized or attached as an affix to another lexical element. An example would be when personal pronouns develop diachronically into person agreement markers. As for the reverse process which can be observed in L2 acquisition, it consists of attributing a functional (semantic-pragmatic) value to a formal device. If, for example, the analysis of the data quoted in (5) is correct, agreement markers are interpreted as deictic elements which replace pronouns and subjects. This amounts to saying that grammaticalized formal devices are acquired and used by assigning to them functional interpretations.

To conclude this section, let me emphasize that there is solid evidence demonstrating that inductive learning enables L2 learners to acquire all surface manifestations of the target language. The knowledge acquired in order to use the respective L2 constructions may, however, differ fundamentally from the corresponding grammatical competence of native speakers. Not only do L2 learners have to resort to compensatory mechanisms in cases where parameterized principles of UG are not accessible to them any more, as shown in the preceding section of this chapter, they also have to make do without certain kinds of discovery principles which children can rely on when acquiring their L1 grammars. Moreover, L2 learners seem to rely on solutions for acquisition problems which facilitate parsing and structure building using L1-based resources. In all these cases, the acquired knowledge allows in some instances for the production of patterns which are superficially indistinguishable from those of L1 speech, but it sometimes results in uses deviating from the target norm. Since learners differ in the kind of learning mechanisms adopted and also in how successfully they use them, the course of L2 acquisition exhibits considerable variation across and within learners in those domains of grammar where they resort to inductive learning. Importantly, the acquired knowledge differs, in these cases, from that represented by native grammars, even in those instances where the L2 constructions are superficially identical to those used by native speakers. Whether this is permanently so or whether amendments are possible when individuals succeed in performing in a near-native fashion is a question which cannot be answered with any certainty, based on insights from currently available L2 research. My suspicion, however, is that these fundamental differences characterize the linguistic knowledge even of near-native speakers. Whatever the answer to this question may ultimately be, the crucial insight to be retained is that learners incorporate at least some operations into their L2 system which are not structure-dependent and are of a type which is not to be found in native competences. In other words, L2 knowledge contains these elements alongside others which are constrained by (non-parameterized) principles of UG as well as grammatical knowledge derived from the L1 grammar, and this may well be a permanent state of affairs. It follows from all this that L2 knowledge conforms only in part to principles of UG. This is why L2 knowledge can be characterized as a *hybrid system*, drawing on domain-specific grammatical knowledge (UG as well as not-UG constrained), and also on domain-general cognitive resources.

5.4 Some fundamental differences between L1 and L2 acquisition

Much of the discussion in this chapter has been dedicated to the question of whether the various parallels and differences between first and second language acquisition justify the claim that the two acquisition types differ in fundamental ways. The fact that important differences (and parallels) can be observed in L2 studies is generally acknowledged. What is controversial is whether they reflect mere superficial deviations from what is typically found in

L1 development or whether they are fundamental in that they indicate that the underlying knowledge systems are distinct. This controversy is of considerable significance because the latter claim arguably implies that the LAD is not playing the same role in L2 as in L1 acquisition.

As suggested at the beginning of the chapter, it is necessary to settle some specific problems, in order to be able to gain insights into the more basic ones, and I argued that the *restructuring* and *inertia* issues are crucial in this respect. Concerning restructuring, we can safely conclude that it is not a possibility in L2 acquisition if what is meant entails that parameters fixed in the course of L1 acquisition will be set to a different value. The least one can say is that proponents of the idea of parameter setting have so far failed to present empirical evidence in its support which would allow one to distinguish it from inductive learning. Studies allegedly demonstrating that L2 learners can reset parameters typically mistake (partially) correct use of surface constructions for evidence indicating changes of parameter values, and they fail to explore other explanations like inductive learning. Exactly the same situation presents itself when we examine the possibility of setting inert parameters, that is, instances where the L1 grammar does not require fixing of a given parameter on a specific value: L2 learners are able to learn – to various degrees – constructions related to a particular parameter setting, but nothing in the acquisition process suggests that this involves parameter setting. Non-parameterized principles of UG, on the other hand, do constrain L2 acquisition, and this seems always to be the case, irrespective of whether particular principles had previously been activated in the process of developing the L1 grammars.

Having answered the questions about grammatical restructuring and inertia in this fashion, the answer to the deeper question about the fate of the LAD can only be that it does not guide L2 acquisition in the same way as in L1. Crucial properties of child grammars and their developmental logic are constrained by principles of UG and can therefore be described and hopefully explained in grammatical terms. In L2 acquisition, this is true for many, but not for all domains of grammar. L2 learners' linguistic knowledge can thus not be accounted for exhaustively in grammatical terms, and the acquisition process is only partially determined by a grammatical logic. As a consequence, it is not possible to describe and explain L2 acquisition by means of identical principles, at least not without having recourse to a number of additional assumptions, many of which cannot be falsified by empirical findings.

As argued at the beginning of this chapter (section 5.1), negative answers to the questions on the restructuring and inertia issues necessarily entail the rejection of all variants of the Full Access hypothesis, but also of versions (a) and (b) of the Partial Access hypothesis (see Table 5.1). Since variant (C) (a) of the No Access hypothesis had already been eliminated for principled reasons, we are left with only one alternative, the one between version (C) (b) of the No Access hypothesis and variant (B) (c) of the Partial Access hypothesis. The former, however, is in conflict with the claim that non-parameterized principles are accessible in L2 acquisition. My conclusion therefore is that partial access to

UG is the most plausible explanation of the facts known about second language acquisition. It takes into consideration the many parallels between L1 and L2 acquisition, an achievement difficult to explain if one was to adopt the No Access hypothesis. But it also acknowledges the fact that the vast majority of L2 learners do not even come close to a near-native grammatical competence in the target language, and it may indeed be impossible to attain native-like competence in an L2 (see the following chapter for a discussion of related issues). One can only wonder how this limited success in the L2 is to be reconciled with the Full Access claim. A vague reference to the 'false start' at the initial state (e.g. due to L1 transfer) will certainly not suffice. Version (c) of the Partial Access hypothesis, the one which I have adopted, offers the further advantage of being able to explain in a non-ad hoc way which parts of the LAD or of UG, in this case, become inaccessible to L2 learners – a challenge which all-or-nothing approaches do not have to face. By stating that parameters cannot be newly set or reset in L2 acquisition, the distinction between accessible and non-accessible domains is theoretically motivated, and it can arguably be justified by neuropsychological findings (see chapter 6).

Let me finally answer explicitly the question formulated above as to whether the indisputable differences between L1 and L2 acquisition are fundamental ones. I contend that this is indeed the case, because the Partial Access hypothesis states that the underlying knowledge systems attainable in the two types of acquisition are distinct, even if they do not differ in grammatical domains determined by non-parameterized principles or by parameterized principles set to identical values in the L2 and the native grammars. Moreover, since I have argued that all surface manifestations of the target languages can in principle be learned in L2 acquisition but that the learning mechanisms as well as the attainable knowledge are partially different in nature from what is encountered in L1 development, the resulting L2 knowledge system can justly be qualified as a *hybrid* system and thus as being fundamentally different from an L1 competence. It comprises different types of knowledge, all feeding into L2 learners' performance systems:

- an approximative and incomplete version of the target grammar;
- learned linguistic knowledge which, although arguably domain-specific in nature, is not fully constrained by UG principles;
- knowledge attained by the learners having recourse to domain-general cognitive operations.

At this point, it may be useful to add some remarks on how this perspective on second language acquisition compares with other approaches to L2 acquisition which share the view that the two types of language acquisition exhibit fundamental differences. This argument has in fact been made as soon as the first L2 acquisition studies adopting the Principles and Parameter Theory appeared in print, and researchers working in this framework suggested implicitly or explicitly the possibility of full access to UG. Clahsen and Muysken (1986, 1989), in their seminal papers discussed in chapter 4, were among the first to argue against this claim, but also Schachter (1988, 1989, 1990) and Meisel (1988, 1991). Bley-Vroman's (1987, 1989, 1990) *Fundamental Difference Hypothesis* (FDH) deserves special mention in this context. Already the widely circulated pre-publication version (1987) of this paper attracted much attention and was exceptionally influential, and it continues to be widely cited.[10]

The earliest studies suggesting that L1 and L2 acquisition exhibit fundamental differences (e.g. Clahsen and Muysken 1986, Bley-Vroman 1987, 1989, 1990 and Schachter 1988) were interpreted as defending the view that L2 learners do not have access to UG; see White (1989a) for a summary and discussion of this literature. I am not concerned here with the question of whether this indeed captures the intentions of the various authors, although I believe that they were actually more careful in their claims than is generally acknowledged by their critics. For the present purpose it must suffice to state that this is how the Fundamental Difference Hypothesis has frequently been perceived and to summarize briefly what kinds of differences have been claimed to be fundamental ones. Bley-Vroman (1990) enumerated and discussed in some detail 10 differences between the two types of acquisition.

1. Lack of success
2. General failure
3. Variation in success, course, and strategy
4. Variation in goals
5. Correlation in age and proficiency
6. Fossilization
7. Indeterminate intuitions
8. Importance of instruction
9. Negative evidence
10. Role of affective factors.

Without going into much detail, one can say that many of the arguments discussed during the subsequent twenty years are already addressed here. In contrast to L1 development, L2 acquisition is characterized by its lack of success (1, 2 and 6) and lack of uniformity (3, 4 and 7), a protracted rate of acquisition (7), and by the fact that the Logical Problem of second language acquisition (8 and 9) does not present itself in the same way as in L1, because adult L2 learners can rely on native language knowledge and on a domain-general learning system. This, however, implies that even if UG is not accessible to learners, their L2 knowledge is shaped in important ways by UG principles via their L1 knowledge, and, moreover, *some* UG-related information may still 'be around'. Bley-Vroman (1990: 18) also argues that L1 parameters cannot be set to the L2 value in cases where the two are distinct but that the 'same range of facts' (1990: 42) can be learned. He concludes (1990: 44) that 'there is as yet no clear evidence for the continuing operation of a domain-specific acquisition system in adult foreign language learning'; L2 acquisition rather seems to be 'an instance of general adult problem-solving'. Importantly, Bley-Vroman (1990) explains these fundamental differences as resulting from age-related changes in the individual, referring to the *Critical Period Hypothesis* (CPH) as proposed by Lenneberg (1967) (5 and 6).

My intention here is not to engage in a philological analysis of the various versions of the FDH presented by Bley-Vroman (1987, 1989, 1990, 2009) but to acknowledge that the early FDH already addressed most of the crucial issues which have occupied the 'UG or not UG' debate since then and which are also at the core of the discussion of this volume. This is why I believe that the Partial Access hypothesis which I am defending can be seen as a variant of the Fundamental Difference Hypothesis, even if it disagrees in a couple of essential points with the early version and, in fact, even more with the most recent version (Bley-Vroman 2009). One of the points of divergence relates to age-dependent-changes of the LMC. Recent research has shown that the CPH cannot be maintained as originally suggested. Since this issue is discussed in some detail in chapter 6, I will merely mention here that maturational changes happen at a much earlier age than suggested by Lenneberg (1967), and this speaks against Bley-Vroman's (1990: 30) assumption that the LAD should still be accessible in the late teens.

The most important modification of the early FDH concerns the point designated by the very label of 'Partial' Access. What is claimed to become inaccessible is not UG in its totality but the parameterized principles. As should have become apparent in this and in the preceding chapter, the claim that parameters cannot be reset is not a recent modification of the FDH. Rather, this was already suggested by Clahsen and Muysken (1989: 23) who argued that 'L2 acquisition is neither parameter fixing . . . nor parameter resetting . . . It is rather language acquisition without access to parameter setting.' As for invariant principles of UG, however, they defended a view much like the one adopted by Bley-Vroman (1990), namely that these are only indirectly present in L2, that is, via the L1 grammar. Note that this does not entail L2 'wild grammars', not constrained by UG principles, but that UG operates via the previously acquired grammatical knowledge. Similar claims have been made by other authors, notably by Schachter (1989, 1990) in her Window-of-Opportunity Hypothesis. These approaches have sometimes been interpreted as postulating partial access to UG, but, as argued in section 5.1, this is misleading since it confounds UG effects (constraining L2 knowledge via L1 grammars) with access to UG. Although this may appear as a merely terminological quarrel, it really refers to a substantive difference between divergent theoretical stances.

This is why the Partial Access to UG hypothesis truly represents an innovation in theorizing about L2 acquisition, marking a turning point in the controversial debate about UG accessibility in that it acknowledges the validity of theoretical arguments and empirical findings by scholars arguing that UG principles do remain accessible. Moreover, the claim that parameterized but not invariant principles of UG are subject to maturational change refers in a non-ad hoc way to a theoretically founded distinction between different types of UG principles. It is plausible also from an evolutionary perspective in that parameters refer to an interface area where experience and innate knowledge interact – precisely the domain in which maturational changes are expected to happen if development is subject to critical period effects. To my knowledge, Tsimpli and Roussou (1991) were the first to propose that only parameterized principles of UG become inaccessible for L2 learners. In fact, Bley-Vroman (1990: 20) had also considered this possibility as a plausible alternative, but decided not to follow up on it. What is of particular importance is that Smith and Tsimpli (1995) reported on research from which they concluded that only parameterized principles are subject to maturation, thus establishing the relationship between linguistic and neural maturation which I also assume holds (see chapter 6).

Smith and Tsimpli (1995) hypothesized that features of functional categories are subject to critical period effects. This is in accordance with how we defined parametric variation. More specifically, it is argued that uninterpretable features become inaccessible in L2 acquisition (see Tsimpli 2004). Even if one does not exclude the possibility that macroparameters exist too (cf. Snyder 2001), uninterpretable features of functional heads are clearly crucial for the definition of parametric variation. Moreover, although some authors seem to be concerned only with feature accessibility, feature strength should also be taken into account (see Beck 1998). Viewed from this perspective, one can say that a number of different claims and hypotheses ultimately defend a similar position in that they agree with the above-mentioned studies in assuming that the 'parts' of grammar which according to the Partial Access hypothesis are inaccessible in L2 acquisition are the ones defined in terms of presence and strength of uninterpretable features of functional categories; see Hawkins 1994, Towell and Hawkins 1994 and Hawkins and Chan 1997 (Failed Functional Features Hypothesis), Clahsen and Hong 1995, Neeleman and Weerman 1997 or Beck 1997 (Local Impairment Hypothesis), to mention only some earlier publications on this issue. More recently, Ianthi Tsimpli and her colleagues suggested a recast of this hypothesis in the framework of the Minimalist Program (cf. Tsimpli 2005, Tsimpli and Dimitrakopoulou 2007 or Tsimpli and Mastropavlou 2007). This recast includes a revision of the original claims in that they argue that grammatical parameters might refer not only to uninterpretable but also to interpretable features (see, for example, Tsimpli and Mastropavlou 2007: 151). The crucial assumption concerning L2 acquisition, however, remains unchanged, that is, that uninterpretable features are inaccessible for L2 learners. If, then, parameters can indeed also refer to interpretable features, differences between L1 and L2 acquisition embrace not all parameterized options, since only the ones relating to uninterpretable features are affected by maturational changes.

All these approaches advocating partial access to UG agree in that they find substantial differences between L1 grammars and L2 knowledge, the latter frequently being qualified as impaired. They differ in how 'impairment' is interpreted, for example in that some refer to the presence or absence of formal features in a functional head whereas others allude to parameter setting in general. This has occasionally been represented as reflecting either more local or more global impairment; see White 2003: chapter 4 for a critical discussion of these views from the perspective of the Full Access to UG position. In reality, however, this merely reflects different notions of parameter due to changes in grammatical theorizing. If we adopt a parameter theory along the lines sketched out in chapter 2 and discussed in section 5.2, relating parameterization primarily or exclusively to uninterpretable features of functional heads, the differences in view boil down to the question of whether a given functional category in a transitional grammar lacks a particular feature altogether or whether the strength of the feature differs from what is required by the target grammar.

The more important difference between the various approaches subsumed under the label of the Partial Access to UG hypothesis concerns the two related questions of how the compensatory means are assessed and whether the impairment is considered to be temporary or permanent. As for the latter, the proponents of what was later called the Failed Functional Features Hypothesis (Hawkins and Chan 1997) entertain the idea of a temporary impairment. Hawkins, Towell and Bazergui (1993: 221), for example, suggest that parameters ‘may be highly resistant to resetting over long periods of exposure to primary data from an L2, but not necessarily immune to resetting’, and Towell and Hawkins (1994: 126) comment that parameterized principles become ‘progressively resistant to resetting’. Hawkins (2001: 302) summarizes his discussion of this issue by stating that the ‘no parameter resetting’ claim by Tsimpli and Roussou (1991) ‘may be too strong, and that “difficulty in establishing the correct parameter setting” may be a more appropriate characterization’. If these statements can be interpreted as suggesting that resetting becomes more difficult with increasing age of onset of L2 acquisition but that this merely amounts to an increased difficulty, not to an impossibility to change parameter values, this conclusion comes as a surprise given that Hawkins, Towell and Bazergui (1993: 219) stated very clearly that nativeness in L2 ‘is an illusion’ when it comes to acquiring knowledge in domains where L1 and L2 differ in parameter settings. ‘While subjects give the strong impression that they are native-like, they have rather different underlying grammatical representations from native speakers.’ In fact, just like Hawkins and Chan (1997), these authors had demonstrated that correct use of L2 surface patterns is not necessarily proof of L1-like grammatical knowledge. More importantly, it is not at all obvious how temporary impairment or resetting difficulty could possibly be explained. These ideas are in conflict with the assumption – shared by these authors – that it is due to maturational changes that parameterized options become inaccessible. It is difficult to see how impairment resulting from age-related changes could be attenuated or repaired as the age of learners increases. This is certainly not self-evident and would require theoretical and empirical support in order to gain in plausibility.

As for the nature of the compensatory mechanisms, there is also disagreement among the advocates of the Partial Access to UG hypothesis. As I have argued in the preceding section of this chapter, L2 learners may resort to strategies and mechanisms resulting in solutions not constrained by principles of UG. This is in line with the findings by Clahsen and Muysken (1986, 1989), Bley-Vroman (1987, 1989, 1990), Schachter (1988, 1989, 1990), Meisel (1988, 1991, 1998), Clahsen and Hong (1995), Beck (1997, 1998), Liceras (1997) or Neeleman and Weerman (1997), among others.

Tsimpli and colleagues, on the other hand, argue that only UG-constrained compensatory mechanisms are explored by L2 learners (cf. Tsimpli 2001, 2004, Tsimpli and Dimitrakopoulou 2007 or Tsimpli and Mastropavlou 2007). This proposal suggests that whenever parameter settings differ between an L1 and a target L2, inaccessibility of uninterpretable features is compensated for by the assignment of interpretable features. In other words, although parameters of UG relating to uninterpretable features cannot be accessed any more, L2 grammars are nevertheless said to be constrained by UG. In the words of Tsimpli and Mastropavlou (2007: 144), 'this compensatory strategy which involves the exploitation of interpretable features in L2 grammars is a UG-based possibility adopted by L2 grammars when faced with problematic (due to uninterpretability) L2 input'. The examples discussed by these authors indeed make a strong case for this claim. The question, however, is whether principled reasons determine that only UG-based compensatory strategies are available to L2 learners or whether this merely happens to be the case in these and possibly some other instances. Note that the Failed Functional Features Hypothesis, too, postulates that adult L2 learners can only opt for UG-constrained compensatory solutions. Hawkins and Chan (1997: 189), for example, argue that L2 learners either rely on compensatory mechanisms provided by L1 grammars or that 'once they have sufficient exposure to recognize that the L2 is different on the surface, they will adopt solutions which are different from those of their L1, but also different from those of native speakers of the target language. In the latter case the solutions will nevertheless be compatible with the principles of UG.'

Again, the rationale for this claim is not made explicit, but I think it is safe to assume that it emanates from the role as a core module of the human Language Making Capacity, attributed to UG by these authors. From the perspective of the theory of UG, it is indeed plausible to postulate that language learners (unconsciously) strive for solutions which avoid conflicts with UG principles. In other words, this is a theoretically motivated assumption. Yet the question remains as to whether it excludes the possibility of resorting to compensatory mechanisms not conforming to UG principles. I suspect that the (implicitly assumed) reason for rejecting this possibility is based on assumptions about the modularity of the human mind which stipulate that UG-based knowledge cannot interact with learned linguistic knowledge (Schwartz 1996). If this is indeed the case, these approaches, although defending the Partial Access to UG hypothesis, share this belief with proponents of the Full Access to UG hypothesis like Schwartz (1992, 1999), for example. The stipulated impossibility of interaction of these knowledge systems is, however, highly questionable, cf. the discussion of this issue by Carroll (2001: chapter 7). Moreover, in not considering the possibility of non-UG-conforming compensatory strategies, defendants of the idea of partial access to UG underestimate the importance of inductive learning, much like the advocates of the Full Access to UG hypothesis who exclude it as an alternative explanation of target-like use of L2 surface constructions. The vague reference to the role of the input in the quote from Hawkins and Chan (1997: 189) is indeed reminiscent of the view of learning expressed by the quote from Schwartz and Sprouse (1996) on the mismatch between surface syntax of the two languages, cited in the preceding section. I believe instead that the discussion of inductive learning above has shown that L2 learners in search of compensatory mechanisms do go beyond what proponents of the Full Access to UG or the Failed Functional Features hypotheses can imagine. This is to say that although it may well be true that UG-conforming solutions are preferred, further options are also explored. This is what has led me to hypothesize that L2 knowledge is a hybrid system; I will return to this question in chapter 7.

The question of whether L2 learners can resort, if necessary, to compensatory mechanisms not conforming to principles of UG should ultimately be an empirical issue. Irrespective of the final verdict on this case, the discussion of this chapter has demonstrated, I believe, that the assumption of fundamental differences between first and second language acquisition is theoretically plausible and empirically adequate. It captures the fact that the Language Acquisition Device does not determine second language acquisition in the same way it shapes the development of first languages. Since this has been claimed to be due to the fact that parameterized knowledge becomes inaccessible as a result of maturational changes, chapter 6 will examine how neural maturation and possibly other age-related changes affect the LAD.

5.5 Suggested readings and topics for discussion

Suggested readings

The discussion of parameter setting in section 5.2 refers to reaction time experiments as a means to supplement data collection relying exclusively on grammaticality judgements. Eubank (1993) offers a more detailed description of this method and discusses its relevance for L2 research.

Eubank, L. 1993. 'Sentence matching and processing in L2 development', *Second Language Research* 9: 253–80.

In order to be able to assess the role of inductive learning embedded in a formal theory of learning, it is crucial to gain a better understanding of what induction can achieve.

Carroll, S. E. 2002b. 'Induction in a modular learner', *Second Language Research* 18: 224–49.

The original version of the paper in which the Fundamental Difference Hypothesis was introduced will give a better idea of what the notion of 'fundamental difference' refers to.

Bley-Vroman, R. 1990. 'The logical problem of foreign language learning', *Linguistic Analysis* 20: 3–49.

Since uninterpretable features are claimed to result in fundamental differences between first and second language acquisition, it should be useful to examine a specific example demonstrating how this effect can be accounted for.

Tsimpli, I.-M. and M. Mastropavlou 2007. 'Feature-interpretability in L2 acquisition and SLI: Greek clitics and determiners' in J. M. Liceras, H. Zobl and H. Goodluck (eds.), *The role of formal features in second language acquisition*, pp. 143–83. London: Routledge.

Topics for discussion

- In section 5.1, it was argued that the term 'indirect access to UG' is inappropriate because it refers to instances where principles of UG constrain learner grammars indirectly via the grammar of the first language. In other words, the L2 learner can access only previously acquired grammatical knowledge (but not UG). In your opinion, is this merely a quarrel about terminology or does it reflect a conceptual distinction? Search for arguments to support your answer to this question in introductions (of your choice) to L2 acquisition research, and try to find additional arguments of your own.
- Parameter (re)setting has been identified as the crucial issue to be solved if one wants to decide on the question of whether L2 acquisition is fundamentally similar to or different from L1 development. In this chapter, it is claimed that the available empirical evidence does not support the idea of (re)setting. This claim is based on the fact that analyses of L2 acquisition data found no evidence for phenomena which in L1 distinguish the triggering of parameter settings as opposed to inductive learning, like the 'clustering effect' or abrupt changes in developmental patterns. Can you find other types of empirical evidence in L2 research, either in textbooks, handbook articles or empirically based research articles? Could you think of additional types of empirical evidence in support of the (re)setting assumption?
- The observation of a discrepancy between experience and knowledge in language acquisition has played a crucial role in the tradition of the generative theory of Universal Grammar. It constitutes a central argument in favour of the claim that a core part of grammatical knowledge

is innate (genetically transmitted). The question of whether there also exists a Logical Problem in second language acquisition is not answered unanimously among acquisition researchers working in the UG framework. Spell out the arguments in favour of and against the idea of a Logical Problem of second language acquisition, focusing on the Poverty of the Stimulus Hypothesis. Use the discussion in section 5.3 as a starting point and search for additional arguments in the literature referred to in this section and/or in introductory textbooks to L2 research.

- Input-based learning is a crucial aspect of language acquisition. An adequate theory of acquisition will therefore have to specify the role it attributes to this type of learning. A UG-based theory must specifically address the question of what kinds of grammatical knowledge can or cannot be acquired in this fashion. As for second language acquisition, one crucial issue is whether inductive learning can serve as a compensatory mechanism in grammatical domains in which children acquiring their L1 can rely on parameter setting. Search for answers to these questions in textbooks and handbooks on psycholinguistics and language acquisition, examine them critically, and discuss.

6 Neural maturation and age: Opening and closing windows of opportunities

6.1 Sensitive phases for language acquisition

> (Language) differs . . . widely from all ordinary arts, for man has an instinctive tendency to speak . . . while no child has an instinctive tendency to brew, bake, or write . . . (Language) is an instinctive tendency to acquire an art.
>
> Charles Darwin (1874). *The descent of man, and selection in relation to sex.*

Scrutinizing parallels and differences between first and second language acquisition has led us to the conclusion that some of the observable differences between these two acquisition types reflect different kinds of knowledge about formal properties of the respective target systems and result from different learning processes. These fundamental differences between L1 and L2 acquisition, I have argued, are due to the fact that the LAD does not operate in quite the same way in the two types of acquisition. It goes without saying that a complex and multifaceted process like language acquisition cannot be explained in terms of one factor or even one bundle of factors alone. In fact, variability within and across learners has been argued to be a defining characteristic of L2 acquisition, and this can be variability of knowledge as well as of how the knowledge is used (cf. Meisel, Clahsen and Pienemann 1981). Although the working of the LAD cannot be held accountable for all observed L1–L2 differences, there are good reasons to believe that it is the single most important cause for both similarities and differences. It is precisely when the LAD ceases to strictly constrain acquisition that other determining factors gain in importance. This is just another way of describing the fact that L2 acquisition exhibits less uniformity than L1 development. As has been argued in chapter 2, the LAD, and especially UG, are responsible for this uniformity in the emergence of L1 grammar. Once their influence on grammatical development wanes, the importance of other factors increases. Social-psychological factors, for example, have been shown to form different types of L2 learners who vary considerably in their approach to acquisition, as well as in the kind of use they make of the acquired knowledge about the target language (see Clahsen, Meisel and Pienemann 1983).

However, since the diminution of the role of UG seems to be due primarily to an age-dependent partial inaccessibility of the LAD, I will focus on age-related changes as possible explanations of fundamental differences between first and second language acquisition. More specifically, following Smith and Tsimpli (1995), who hypothesized that the accessibility of parameterized principles is subject to maturational changes, I will be concerned mainly with the question of whether maturation can indeed offer a plausible explanation for the noted L1–L2 differences. I should hasten to add again that the role of age is not limited to aspects of neural maturation, and the latter obviously entails first of all an increase of cognitive capacities. If the Critical Period Hypothesis (CPH) is correct, neural maturation is hypothesized to open and close windows of opportunities during which certain learning tasks – in our case grammatical development – can be achieved with relative ease and maximal success. It is the claim that the windows of opportunities close over time which I intend to discuss here, and although this discussion focuses on the negative aspects of a possible loss of opportunities, the overall message is not: 'There's nothing but bad news for older learners'. Maturation and age-related changes also bring positive effects. But it is precisely the question of why older learners with a mature and more powerful cognitive system do worse, in some respects at least, than toddlers learning one or more first language(s) which needs to be addressed.

Postulating a causal relationship between maturational changes and changes in the language making capacity is not a novel idea. It takes up claims made by the Critical Period Hypothesis which have already been referred to in the preceding chapter. The CPH was proposed by Penfield and Roberts (1959), and, due to the seminal work by Lenneberg (1967), it gained much attention in the language sciences. Although he was mainly concerned with the development of a first language, Lenneberg (1967: 176) himself suggested that the CPH could be extended to L2 acquisition.

> [A]utomatic acquisition from mere exposure to a given language seems to disappear [after puberty], and foreign languages have to be taught and learned through a conscious and labored effort. Foreign accents cannot be overcome easily after puberty. However, a person *can* learn to communicate at the age of forty. This does not trouble our basic hypothesis.

Note that the question of whether L2 acquisition is indeed subject to critical period effects is independent of the problem of the validity of the CPH in L1 development. In other words, if we assume that the CPH makes the correct predictions for L1 in stating that a first language must be acquired during the age period indicated, in order for the attainment of native competence to be possible, this need not necessarily be true for the subsequent acquisition of further languages. One could, in fact, imagine a scenario according to which the activation of the LAD in the course of the acquisition of *one* language would make the acquisition device permanently accessible. Yet if the claim by Lenneberg can be maintained and the LAD is subject to maturational changes in spite of the fact that it has been activated previously in first language development, this will lend strong support to the Partial Access to UG hypothesis because it not only provides independent evidence for the L1–L2 differences observed in the linguistic behaviour of learners, it even offers the possibility of explaining *why* these differences emerge.

In what follows I will argue that the Critical Period Hypothesis can indeed be extended to second language acquisition, but that findings stemming from more recent research call for modifications of the original version developed by Lenneberg (1967). The first necessary change concerns us only indirectly. Lenneberg had concluded, based on a state-of-the-art review of previous research, that the critical period for language acquisition was causally connected to the process of lateralization which results in the functional specialization of the two hemispheres of the human brain (see Obler and Gjerlow 1999: 66 for a summary of some of his arguments). Although much of what Lenneberg wrote about lateralization has been confirmed by subsequent research, we now know that it happens much earlier than at around puberty, and there does not seem to be a causal relationship between this process and critical period effects in language acquisition. What matters for the present discussion is that, in both cases, the originally suggested age ranges are definitely not correct. I will immediately return to this issue, if only briefly (see Long 1990 and Hyltenstam and Abrahamsson 2003 for state-of-the-art discussions of the age question from the perspective of acquisition research). Let me first emphasize that these revisions of the CPH do not affect the basic concept of the hypothesis, and it ought to surprise us that it has met with much scepticism among L2 researchers.[1] Contrary to what is asserted by some of its critics, the Critical Period Hypothesis is supported by a wealth of empirical evidence, some of which I will summarize below, and it contributes significantly to an explanation of L1–L2 differences. Many of the criticisms directed against the CPH can be accounted for by the observation by Eubank and Gregg (1999) that they are based on insufficiently precise definitions of the CPH. In fact, as Birdsong (1999) correctly observed, the conceptualization of the CPH on which these studies are based tends to be heterogeneous and covers several distinct hypotheses. This also explains why various empirical studies have come up with conflicting findings.

In order to avoid this fallacy, it is useful to define the critical period more strictly. First of all, it must be kept in mind that it is not 'language' which is affected by such changes but certain *domains of grammar*. Lexical knowledge, for example, is predicted not to be concerned at all. In fact, in view of what we know about critical periods in the animal world, it appears to be a reasonable assumption that the development of knowledge which is genetically transmitted but which needs to be triggered by experience is most likely to be subject to maturational constraints. Parameterized principles are thus prime candidates because they are conceptualized as innate principles of grammar whose open values need to be fixed by experience, that is, by exposure to the ambient languages.

Secondly, it is not reasonable to expect that all grammatical domains will be affected simultaneously, during a single age period. Past research rather suggests that the subcomponents of grammar – syntax, phonology and morphology – do not follow the same developmental agenda, as has been pointed out by Eubank

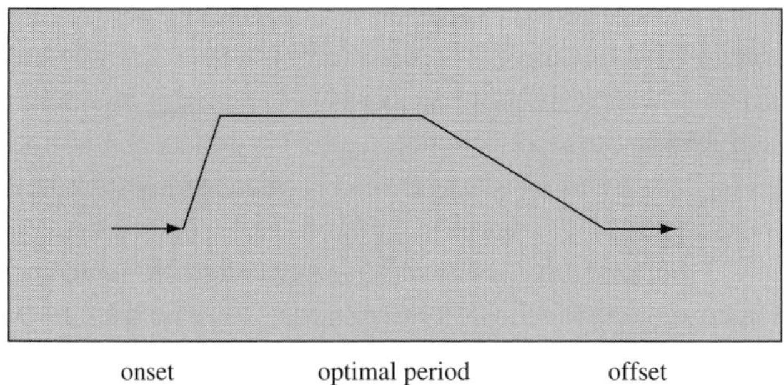

Figure 6.1: *Schematic representation of sensitive phases*

and Gregg (1999). In fact, even within these subcomponents we may expect to find asynchronous developments each tied to specific grammatical phenomena. Consequently, the critical period is better understood as a *cluster of sensitive phases* during which the LAD is optimally prepared to integrate new information into developing grammars.[2] In other words, various grammatical phenomena are predicted to be affected by maturational changes at different points in development. Thirdly, these phases should not be understood as offering categorical yes/no options, as if biological switches were flipped to 'on' and later again back to 'off'. Instead, critical periods are viewed 'as periods of heightened sensitivity or responsiveness to specific types of environmental stimuli or input, bounded on both sides by states of lesser sensitivity' (Schachter 1996: 165). Finally, notions like 'critical period' or 'sensitive phase' do not imply abrupt changes. Rather, we may assume that, after a relatively short onset, each phase is characterized by an optimal period, followed by a gradual offset, as is illustrated by Figure 6.1.

Let me now turn to the modification of Lenneberg's version of the CPH which is directly relevant for our purposes, concerning the *age range* during which crucial changes happen. I want to refer again to Hyltenstam and Abrahamsson 2003 as a careful and thorough discussion of this topic. As should be apparent from the remarks above, we are dealing with multiple sensitive periods which do not end abruptly and which are subject to individual variation. In view of these considerations, it should be obvious that the age ranges of critical periods for successive language acquisition, defined as clusters of sensitive phases for grammatical development, can only be determined approximately, referring for each of the phases to the end of the optimal period, that is, the time when an optimal period begins to fade out.

Hyltenstam and Abrahamsson (2003: 575) conclude from their review of the literature that 'At least up to AOs [age of onset, JMM] 6 or 7, all learners will automatically reach levels that allow them to pass as native speakers – provided that there is sufficient input and that the learning circumstances are not deficient'. Judging on the basis of the evidence presented, this seems to be an optimistic but perhaps not impossible conclusion, and the ages of onset are roughly in line with what Long (1990) suggested. After this age, social-psychological factors play an increasingly important role in L2 acquisition, whereas their influence is negligible during early childhood. In other words, although the kind of knowledge attainable in successive language acquisition does not depend on a single factor, maturation plays the crucial role during the first years of childhood. In fact, Hyltenstam and Abrahamsson (2003: 570) 'suggest that maturational effects can be detected much earlier, perhaps as early as 12 months' referring to phonological development, and they observe that such effects on language development are noticeable from birth and up to approximately age fifteen, the age period when, according to them, the maturational period ends.

The picture emerging here implies that native-like grammatical knowledge may never be attainable in L2 acquisition, although the differences, when we compare L2 learners to native speakers, may be subtle and confined to particular aspects of grammar if the onset of acquisition occurs during early childhood; see section 6.4, below, for some further remarks on this issue. We can further conclude that changes do not happen in a continuous fashion over the entire maturational period. Rather, during specific age periods certain grammatical domains are affected in more decisive ways. The time at around age 6–7 appears to be one such crucial phase. As for earlier ages of onset of acquisition (AOA), Hyltenstam and Abrahamsson (2003) are rather careful and do not single out specific age spans, although they do suggest that changes may happen earlier. If, however, we take into account findings by neurolinguistic studies, to which I will turn immediately, it is possible to identify the period at around age 4 as one which is also of special importance, and recent research on child second language acquisition (see the following section 6.2) corroborates this suspicion. Even if these are necessarily tentative approximations, it is possible to suggest age ranges which are crucial for the development of morphosyntax. Noticeable differences as compared to L1 development emerge in this domain as early as age of onset between 3;6 and 4 years. It is therefore justified to refer to successive acquisition with first exposure to the second language after this age as child second language (cL2) acquisition. If age of onset happens after the age of approximately 6–7 years, the course of acquisition as well as the acquired grammatical knowledge increasingly resembles adult L2 acquisition, even if one can undoubtedly detect differences among learners, depending on whether their first exposure to the L2 occurred sooner or later after this age. In sum, although the exact age ranges are still a matter of speculation, there can hardly be any doubt that the optimal periods for grammatical development occur significantly earlier than is commonly assumed by those who follow Lenneberg's (1967) idea that the age around puberty is the crucial one. In fact, Krashen (1973) already posited that crucial changes happen around age 5, and McLaughlin (1978) set the cut-off point between first and second language acquisition at age 3, and although he admitted that this was a somewhat arbitrary decision, it was based on empirical evidence.

Since I adopted the hypothesis that age of onset of acquisition is the major cause of L1–L2 differences, primarily because neural maturation brings about changes in the LMC, I should give at least an idea of what kind of evidence supports the claim that changes in the functional organization of the brain are responsible for the differences between acquisition types. Although this can only be done in a cursory fashion, a brief summary of findings by neuroimaging studies may be useful for this purpose (cf. Meisel 2008b). Neuroimaging studies start from the idea that changes over time in the functional organization of the brain result in different activation patterns, as well as in a different spatial organization of the brain in language processing when the onset of exposure to a language does not fall within the optimal period. However, no such differences are expected to emerge if first exposure to a language falls within this period. Supporting evidence for this assumption has indeed become available through studies using electrophysiological as well as various haemodynamic methods (e.g. functional magnetic resonance imaging, fMRI, positron emission tomography, PET). The predicted changes primarily concern activation in areas of the brain which are typically involved in language processing, most importantly *Broca's area* corresponding to Brodmann areas[3] (BA) 44–45 and *Wernicke's area* (BA 22) (see Friederici 2002). In the present context, Broca's area, encompassing the *pars opercularis* of the left inferior frontal gyrus (BA 44) and the posterior portion of *pars triangularis* (BA 45), is particularly relevant, for it is assumed to play a crucial role in syntactic processing during sentence comprehension.

Electrophysiological research uses electroencephalography (EEG), a non-invasive method by which electrical variations induced by neural activity are recorded at the surface of the scalp. From these recorded variations event-related brain potentials (ERPs) are derived. EEG makes it possible to locate electrical activity of the brain in different critical regions. The major advantage of ERP studies is their high temporal resolution (even if they do not reach the higher spatial resolution of haemodynamic methods). A number of ERP studies, for example Weber-Fox and Neville 1996, 1999, have demonstrated that the spatial distribution of activation patterns in the left hemisphere changes at later ages of onset of acquisition, that is, specialization in the left hemisphere is reduced, and the right hemisphere is increasingly activated. The critical age range seems to be the ages around 4 years and again around 7 years, that is, if age of onset happens at age 4 or later, this effect of more diffuse spatial distribution and increasing right hemispheric processing becomes increasingly stronger. Importantly, Weber-Fox and Neville (1999) and others observed differences not only in spatial distribution but also in the quality of ERP-responses as a result of later ages of onset. The most crucial finding is that such differences between L1 and L2 learners are only detectable if subjects are exposed to syntactically deviant sentences, whereas exposure to semantically ill-formed ones does not produce this type of effect. Weber-Fox and Neville (1999: 35) concluded that 'later learners utilize altered neural systems and processing of English syntax'.

A functional dissociation within the neural basis of auditory sentence processing has, in fact, been observed in a number of ERP studies; see Friederici (2002) for a critical review and for an outline of a 'syntax-first model' of processing.

Hahne and Friederici (2001), for example, confirm the finding by Weber-Fox and Neville that first and second language learners differ primarily in their processing of syntax. In native speakers, semantic processes are reflected in a centro-posterior bilateral negativity between 300 and 500 ms, the so-called N400. Syntactic processing is correlated with two ERP components, a left-anterior negativity (LAN), which occurs early, between 100 and 500 ms, and a later centro-parietal positivity, P600, between 500 and 1000 ms. The subjects of this study, Japanese speakers who had learned German as adults, were exposed to grammatical and ungrammatical as well as semantically correct and deviant German sentences. No differences between L1 and L2 learners could be detected with respect to semantically ill-formed stimuli, that is, both evidenced the N400 effect. In processing grammatical and ungrammatical stimuli, however, the activation patterns of L2 learners are clearly distinct from those of L1 speakers in that neither early LAN nor P600 effects could be detected in the L2 learners. This can be interpreted as indicating that formal, syntactic aspects of language are subject to maturational changes; see also Isel (2005) for a review of ERP studies investigating L1 and L2 acquisition.

Studies using haemodynamic methods of investigation corroborate these results. They find differences with respect to spatial differentiation as well as intensity of brain activation between native speakers and L2 learners, and this refers again to morphosyntactic, not to semantic or pragmatic processing. In functional magnetic resonance imaging, variations of cerebral activity are recorded as tomograms, that is, slices through the brain measuring the regional cerebral blood flow. This, in turn, is interpreted as reflecting regional brain activation. Kim, Relkin, Lee and Hirsch (1997) contrasted in their fMRI study six children acquiring two languages from ‘early infancy’ with six bilingual children who acquired their languages successively (11;2 average age of onset). They found that in early bilinguals both languages are processed in largely overlapping regions in Broca’s area, whereas in successive bilingualism processing of the two languages is spatially separated. Also in an fMRI study, Dehaene, Dupoux, Mehler, Cohen, Paulescu, Perani, van de Moortele, Lehéricy and Le Bihan (1997) found that processing of L2 relies on larger and spatially more diffuse networks than of L1, and they concluded that ‘first language acquisition relies on a dedicated left-hemispheric cerebral network, while late second language acquisition is not necessarily associated with a reproducible biological substrate’. They reported on more brain activation in the temporal lobe and in the right hemisphere and generally more individual variation in L2 learners when compared to native speakers.

I should mention that these studies have been criticized for methodological shortcomings. Since ‘stories’ were played to the subjects, or they had to produce ‘inner language’, there is virtually no control of the stimulus material or of the elicited mental activity. It is therefore difficult to determine whether group differences are due to AOA or to differences in the stimuli or the mental activity. Another weakness is that these studies either did not consider the possibility that proficiency in a particular language might be the cause of observed neurolinguistic differences between groups, or they did not assess the linguistic proficiency of the learners adequately. Even if not all details of these findings should ultimately turn out to be correct, there can be no doubt that these investigations strongly support the claim according to which differences exist between acquisition types depending on age of onset of acquisition. In fact, crucial aspects of the results obtained by these studies have subsequently been corroborated.

Wartenburger, Heekeren, Abutalebi, Cappa, Villringer and Perani (2003), for example, elicited brain responses to syntactically and semantically well-formed and ill-formed sentences in their fMRI study. They too found that brain activities vary with age of onset of acquisition (critical age around 6 years), but only in grammatical processing (including agreement), not in processing semantic information. They controlled the stimuli as well as the proficiency of participants, and, interestingly enough, proficiency did not play a role in syntactic processing, whereas stronger effects of proficiency were detected in processing semantically deviant sentences. Comparing highly proficient late L2 learners with L1 speakers, they found additional bilateral activation in the inferior frontal gyrus (BA 44, 47), anterior insula, putamen, thalamus, mesial frontal cortex (BA 8), in the left frontal operculum (BA 44/6), left inferior parietal lobe (BA 40), left caudate nucleus, and in the right middle frontal gyrus (BA 46/9) (see Wartenburger *et al.* 2003: 160). They concluded that AOA influences syntactic processing, whereas proficiency influences semantic processing.

Most of the studies mentioned so far contrasted monolingual L1 speakers and L2 learners. The fMRI study by Saur, Baumgärtner, Möhring, Büchel, Bonnesen, Rose, Musso and Meisel (2009) compared 2L1 subjects who acquired French and German simultaneously to French L2 learners of German and German L2 learners of French, all highly proficient in both languages, age of onset ten years or older. Special attention was paid to testing linguistic proficiency in order to be able to distinguish potential effects of proficiency from effects caused by age of onset of acquisition. Stimuli included grammatical and ungrammatical sentences in both languages, both sets exhibiting word order variation, including ungrammatical orders. This analysis revealed similar patterns of activation in the two L2 groups. They showed higher activation during syntactic sentence processing than in L1 in the left inferior frontal gyrus (including the *pars opercularis* and *triangularis*), the basal ganglia and the left inferior temporal gyrus. Early bilinguals, however, did not exhibit differences in activation between the two languages in these areas. This suggests that syntactic processing in the second language triggers stronger activation in the language network than in the L1 and activation in areas beyond those primarily associated with syntactic processing of word order. Since no such effect is detected in early bilinguals, age of onset of acquisition can be argued to cause these differences. Moreover, processing sentences containing verb–subject order, a pattern common in the V2 language German but encountered infrequently in colloquial

French, triggered significantly higher changes in functional activation in L2 German than in L1 German speakers. This constitutes a first piece of evidence relating a specific syntactic phenomenon to changes in brain activation.

In sum, these neuroimaging studies speak in favour of the claim of functional differentiation, with syntax being dissociated from semantics and pragmatics. They furthermore support strongly the hypothesis that age of onset of acquisition is a major cause for the observed differences in processing grammatical information. They also confirm that important changes happen around age 6–7, and some ERP results further show that crucial changes occur at around age 4. This kind of research cannot, however, offer more detailed insights about which grammatical domains within the area of morphosyntax are primarily affected by the changes caused by neural maturation. Most importantly, no direct let alone causal relationship has as yet been established between specific differences in the linguistic behaviour distinguishing first and second language learners and the changes in brain activation detected by neuroimaging research. In fact, the claims and hypotheses defended in linguistic studies are so much more detailed than what can currently be tested by neuropsychological and neurophysiological research that it would be unrealistic to search for one-to-one correlations and clearly established causal connections between the two types of research findings. Yet the parallels in the findings of linguistic and neurological research are sufficiently suggestive to allow us to entertain the hypothesis that causal relations do indeed exist, even if, for the time being, conclusive evidence is not available.

However, the two disciplines can and do stimulate each other. Neuroimaging studies, for example, suggest that not only the age period around AOA 6–7 is of particular importance, but also the one around 4 (see also Johnson and Newport 1989). This has inspired L2 research to examine more closely early child L2 acquisition, and as I will show in the following section of this chapter, the results of this work seem to confirm this claim. As for the questions of which domains of grammar are affected by maturational changes or whether it is possible to draw up a developmental schedule indicating which grammatical phenomena are concerned first in early childhood, neurological research has currently little to contribute. As we have seen in the preceding chapters, linguistic theory and acquisition research identified parameterized principles of UG as the most likely domain of grammar to be affected by maturation. Although this hypothesis is supported by empirical evidence, as reported by Smith and Tsimpli (1995), we definitely need more information on the neuropsychological basis on which this claim rests. Independently of what this will teach us, there is no reason to believe that only mental representations of (UG-constrained) grammatical knowledge should be subject to such changes. Rather, the summary of research findings on child L2 acquisition in section 6.2 suggests that discovery procedures may also be affected, and the discussion in section 6.3 shows that this seems to apply to processing mechanisms, as well.

6.2 Child second language acquisition

The overwhelming majority of the research results providing evidence for the Fundamental Difference Hypothesis are based on analyses of adult second language acquisition and on comparisons of adult L2 (aL2) with monolingual L1 acquisition. Yet if these differences are primarily the result of changes related to maturation and age, and if what has been argued in the preceding section is on the right track, we need to account for more than simply a distinction between first and second language acquisition, for we should expect that successive language acquisition in childhood differs from both L1 and aL2 acquisition – and that it resembles both. The most plausible hypothesis is indeed that the grammatical knowledge acquired by cL2 learners will resemble aL2 knowledge in some of its properties, but that it should share others with the respective L1 grammars. This prediction follows quite straightforwardly from the revision of the CPH according to which alterations of the acquisition device happen over an extended period of time, caused by subsequent sensitive phases which may bundle during critical periods but which do not all fall into a single age period. Consequently, cL2 acquisition may be expected to resemble aL2 acquisition (and inversely also L1 development) to variable degrees, depending on the age of onset of acquisition. After all, the Partial Access to UG hypothesis asserts that even aL2 learners typically acquire a kind of L2 knowledge which is only partially distinct from that of native speakers. If, then, certain domains of grammar become gradually inaccessible with increasing age of onset, early cL2 acquisition can be predicted to share fewer properties with aL2 acquisition than cL2 at a later age of onset.

The obvious questions to ask at this point are: During which age periods do the crucial changes happen? Which domains of grammar are first affected by them? Concerning the latter question, grammatical theory allows us to predict that parameterized principles of UG should certainly be affected, as has been argued at quite some length in the preceding chapters. Notice, however, that this does not exclude the possibility of other aspects of the LMC being concerned as well. More importantly perhaps, neither grammatical nor neurocognitive theories make specific predictions about a maturational schedule which would help us to identify the grammatical phenomena which are likely to be the earliest or the latest ones to be subject to maturational changes. Since our current knowledge does not enable us to propose a theoretically motivated sequence of inaccessibility, I suggest proceeding inductively and scrutinizing findings from research on cL2 acquisition in order to determine empirically the areas where cL2 learners first resemble aL2 learners. In this way, the results of investigation may eventually lead to a better understanding of the logic underlying these developments.

If we want to proceed in this more pragmatic fashion, how can we decide on the age range which needs to be investigated? This is where we can refer to the discussion of the preceding section where I reported that major maturational effects have been observed at around ages 4 and 7, and I concluded that this age range is most likely to qualify as the one during which we can identify cL2 acquisition as a type of language acquisition (partially) distinct from both L1 and aL2. In my view, the evidence in support of AOA around age 7 as a critical phase for L2 acquisition is solid enough to be accepted as such without further discussion (cf. the state-of-the-art summaries by Long 1990 or by Hyltenstam and Abrahamsson 2003). I will therefore focus in the following discussion on the earlier period at around AOA 4. But let me first have a brief look at what happens before that age.

Notice that referring to cL2 acquisition as the type of acquisition covering the age range starting at around AOA 4 seems to imply that we are dealing with a qualitatively different type of acquisition if age of onset happens at an earlier time in the life of a learner. Yet this is not necessarily correct. What is fairly uncontroversial is that the simultaneous acquisition of two or more languages from birth is of a different type. There is indeed a broad consensus in the research literature on bilingualism that acquisition in this setting can be qualified as an instance of bilingual first language (2L1) development (see de Houwer 1995 for a summary). 2L1 children differentiate from early on the linguistic systems of the languages to which they are exposed (Genesee 1989; Meisel 1989; 1993; Genesee, Nicoladis and Paradis 1995; Köppe 1996; 1997), they proceed through the same developmental phases as the respective monolinguals (see, for example, Paradis and Genesee 1996; Meisel 2007b), and they are able to attain native competence in each of their languages (see Meisel 2001, 2004 for state-of-the-art summaries of the relevant research). It therefore seems to be justified to assert that the human LMC constitutes an endowment for multilingualism.

The question whether successive acquisition of languages during the first three years of life can still be considered as an instance of bilingual first language acquisition is, however, much more difficult to answer. Some authors (e.g. de Houwer 1995) have claimed that successive acquisition of bilingualism will necessarily differ from bilingual and monolingual first language development, even if age of onset happens during the first year. In fact, Hyltenstam and Abrahamsson (2003) also concluded that maturational effects can be detected as early as AOA 1;0, at least as far as phonological development is concerned. Since the productive use of grammatical morphology and of multi-word utterances emerges only during the second year, mostly during the second half of the second year, it is particularly difficult to determine whether age of onset during the second year can result in qualitative differences in the morphosyntactic competence of these learners as compared to (2)L1 (monolingual and bilingual first language) development. Certainly this possibility cannot be excluded a priori, and it is even possible that the effects of late onset of acquisition become detectable only at a later time; see also the remarks on ultimate attainment in section 6.4, below. The problem, however, is that we know very little about morphosyntactic development in children first exposed to the other language during their second or third year of life (but see Nicholas 1987 or Pfaff 1992). If their grammatical competence is indeed different from that of (2)L1 children, these differences will probably be rather subtle ones. Although I think that it is plausible to assume that differences of this sort exist, I prefer to refrain from speculating about which grammatical phenomena are most likely to be concerned.

In other words, by limiting the following discussion to research investigating cL2 learners who were first exposed to the second language at age 3;0 or later, I do not necessarily want to imply that successive language acquisition starting at an earlier age qualifies as an instance of bilingual first language acquisition. Rather, I am simply acknowledging the fact that we lack the necessary information about learners of this type which might enable us to decide whether successive acquisition at a very early age of onset differs in at least some subtle ways from 2L1. The following brief summary of research findings thus focuses on successive acquisition starting at AOA 3, with the goal of determining the approximate age range as of which similarities between cL2 and aL2 learners begin to emerge which distinguish both from (2)L1. Moreover, I will attempt to identify some of the grammatical properties affected by early maturational changes, for they characterize cL2 acquisition (cf. Meisel 2008a, 2009).

Notice that assuming such a perspective in comparing different types of acquisition has methodological implications, concerning, most importantly, the criteria for what can count as similarity or difference across types of acquisition. Since the FDH refers to underlying knowledge systems which may be partially different in the three types of acquisition under consideration, we will be looking for constructions shared by two acquisition types, that is, cL2 and aL2, but not (2)L1. The rationale behind this procedure is that shared construction types are likely to reflect identical underlying mechanisms. Counting error frequencies, on the other hand, is unlikely to provide insights of this sort for, if I am correct in assuming that every surface property is learnable, every target-deviant construction can obviously be replaced by the one required by the target norm. The fact that the frequency of an incriminated device decreases and might eventually even disappear altogether from the speech of an L2 learner does not necessarily mean that the underlying system has been reorganized and that the target grammar is now in place – rather, the ersatz system may have become more efficient in producing the required surface forms.

In comparison to the prolific research activities investigating aL2 acquisition, the number of studies focusing on cL2 learners is rather limited, even if one includes all learners who were first exposed to the L2 before age 10, since this age limit had long been considered as crucial, following Lenneberg (1967). Interestingly enough, cL2 learners had been actively investigated in the 1970s (see Lakshmanan 1994: 19 for a brief summary of this research), but were largely ignored later on, and the question of how they compare to aL2 learners, on the one hand, and to L1 children, on the other, attracted very little attention. This has changed recently, as is evidenced by the summary of current knowledge about cL2 acquisition presented by Unsworth (2005) and by publications like the volume edited by Haznedar and Gavruseva (2008). Note that Unsworth (2005) concluded, based also on her own analysis of cL2 syntax, that cL2 resembles aL2 in some respects (L1 transfer, presence of functional categories), but that findings concerning developmental sequences are still inconclusive.

Let me therefore turn to the question of which domains of grammar are acquired by cL2 learners in a fashion resembling aL2 more than (2)L1, that is, bilingual or monolingual L1 development. In the preceding chapters I argued that inflectional morphology instantiating uninterpretable features of functional heads presents a major problem for aL2 learners. In fact, there is widespread consensus that 'inflectional morphology in the verbal domain poses major acquisition problems for adult L2 acquirers' (Parodi, Schwartz and Clahsen 2004: 670), and it has been observed repeatedly that aL2 is characterized by the dissociation of morphology and syntax, for example non-finite verb forms are raised into finite positions, a phenomenon not attested in L1 speech. Irrespective of whether one interprets this as an instance of missing surface inflections (cf. Haznedar and Schwartz 1997) or as indicating deficient representations of grammatical knowledge, it undoubtedly represents a crucial difference between L1 and L2 acquisition. Whether this also applies to cL2 learners, however, is a more controversial issue. Schwartz (2004: 121), for example, gives a negative answer to this question, claiming that cL2 acquisition is like aL2 acquisition (and both are distinct from child L1 acquisition) in the domain of syntax, but that cL2 acquisition is like L1 acquisition (and distinct from aL2 acquisition) in the domain of inflectional morphology.

Although our knowledge about cL2 acquisition is fairly limited, this claim comes as a surprise, especially with respect to the alleged ease of acquisition of inflectional morphology for cL2 learners. Let us therefore examine the available evidence. The first observation is that older children have been reported not to differ from aL2 learners, either in their syntactic or in their morphological development; cf. Pienemann 1981 who analysed the acquisition of German by three Italian children at the age of onset of 8 years. The question is whether this is also the case if AOA happens earlier, and one does find evidence speaking in favour of this possibility. Interestingly, many of the more recent studies dealing with these problems report that syntactic phenomena like VO/OV, V2 placement and subject–verb inversion do not represent major acquisition problems if AOA happens between ages 3 and 5. Evidence of this type is provided by Blom (2006), among others, in an experimental study of cL2 acquisition of Dutch (AOA 4), Rothweiler (2006) analysing the course of development of three Turkish children acquiring German (AOA 2;10–4;5), Thoma and Tracy (2006) studying four learners (L1 Arabic, Russian and Turkish, AOA 3;0–3;7) of German, as well as Haznedar (2003) investigating the acquisition of English by a Turkish boy (AOA 4;3), and Hulk and Cornips (2006) studying children raised in immigrant families in the Netherlands, considered to be L2 learners because they are believed not to have been exposed to Dutch in their homes. The latter two studies also confirm the dissociation of syntax and morphology in that these learners used target syntactic constructions, for example verb placement in Dutch or English subordinate clauses, during a phase when they still had not mastered the morphological system. Rothweiler and her associates, on the other hand, explicitly state that a dissociation of this type is not found in the Turkish learners of German in their corpus; see Rothweiler 2006 or Kroffke, Rothweiler and Babur 2007. The latter, for example, find no differences between syntax and inflectional morphology in their study of two Turkish children (AOA 3 and 6) acquiring German. The acquisition of both subject–verb agreement and verb placement resembles aL2 acquisition in the older child, whereas in the younger one both develop much as in L1 children. Kroffke and Rothweiler (2006) obtained identical results for five children at AOA 3 and two at AOA 6.

With respect to the apparent invulnerability of syntax in early cL2, the results obtained by Sopata (2008) are of particular interest. She analysed the acquisition of German by three Polish boys (AOA 3;8–4;7) whose families had moved to Germany. In the domain of inflectional morphology they exhibit considerable interindividual variation; but although two of them acquired verbal inflections fast and with low error rates, whereas the third one behaved much like aL2 learners, the type of errors made qualifies all of them as cL2 learners. This is evidenced most clearly by the fact that they exhibit a striking dissociation in the development of verb morphology and related verb placement regularities. For example, none of the three uses predominantly German OV word order. Whether their use of VO patterns can be attributed to the influence of their L1 is an open question (see the discussion of the Romance learners in chapter 4). However, they clearly behave like aL2 learners in this respect. Moreover they initially place finite verbs frequently in a target-deviant *V3 position, while at the same time moving non-finite verbs to the V2 position, an unambiguous feature of L2 acquisition.

Research findings like the ones mentioned here constitute an important body of evidence in favour of the claim that crucial changes in the LMC occur well before age 6. As for the problem of whether the optimal periods for syntactic developments fade out earlier than those for inflectional morphology, as postulated by Schwartz (2004), the results of these studies do not allow us to draw a clear picture. We can retain, however, that syntax and morphology are reported either to undergo changes simultaneously, or inflectional morphology is affected earlier. Recent research focusing on cL2 acquisition corroborates the hypothesis that at least some areas in the domain of inflectional morphology are subject to fundamental changes even during very early developmental phases, cL2 learners thus resembling aL2 in this domain.

Some of these findings stem from a longitudinal study at the University of Hamburg investigating the acquisition of French by thirty-five German children in an immersion setting at the Lycée Français de Hambourg attended mostly by children coming from French-speaking families. They enter preschool at around age 3 where they normally spend six hours per day. The medium of instruction is French, except for five weekly lessons intended to foster the knowledge of German of the children from French homes. Recordings were conducted approximately every three to five months over a period of about two years. The children were interviewed individually by French native speakers, each recording lasting twenty to thirty minutes (see Meisel 2008a for further details).

The acquisition of finiteness by ten children of the Hamburg cL2 corpus was the object of a study by Meisel (2008a). It revealed that six of them resembled aL2 learners in their use of non-finite and finite verb forms. Most importantly, they analysed subject clitics (SCLs) as maximal projections rather than as clitics, following a pattern familiar from aL2 learners of French observed by Granfeldt (2000) and Granfeldt and Schlyter (2004). This implies combining SCLs with non-finite verb forms, a pattern not encountered with (2)L1 learners. Granfeldt, Schlyter and Kihlstedt (2007), who compared Swedish cL2 and 2L1 children with French monolinguals, report similar findings. They observed that cL2 learners (AOA 3;5–6;7) resemble adult learners of French not only in combining SCLs with non-finite verbs, but also in their use of tense forms and of gender agreement and in placing object clitics postverbally. Note that in their syntactic development, the ten children of the Hamburg cL2 corpus did not behave like aL2 learners. This was confirmed by Bonnesen (2007), who contrasted the acquisition of interrogative constructions by adult and child German L2 learners of French with monolingual and bilingual L1 learners. The cL2 learners behaved much like L1 children in that they did not use the kind of target-deviant constructions which characterize aL2 speech but are not attested in L1 (see also Bonnesen and Chilla forthcoming).

Bonnesen (2008) returned to the acquisition of finiteness by the learners of the Hamburg cL2 corpus, focusing on French negative constructions. Since target word order in negated French clauses requires finite verbs to move across the negative element *pas*, inflectional morphology and verb placement are again closely related (see chapter 3, section 3.3). His analysis of a larger group of seventeen children studied over a longer period of time corroborated the finding (Meisel 2008a) that some of them behave like aL2 learners in their acquisition of finiteness, but not with respect to verb placement regularities. Riedel (2009), too, analysed the acquisition of finiteness by this group of learners, focusing on the occurrence of root infinitives (RI), that is, main clauses violating the adult norm in that the verb appears in a non-finite form (Rizzi 1993/94). RIs are attested in the speech of L1 children of many languages, and although researchers disagree on whether they indicate a grammatical deficit as compared to mature grammars or whether they reflect processing problems, it is important to note that they occur in specific syntactic contexts, for example they typically do not appear in negated clauses, nor are they used in wh-questions or in embedded clauses. This is of crucial importance, for similar constructions in the speech of L2 learners are not subject to the same type of grammatical constraints. L1 and L2 thus differ with respect to the structural distribution of main clause infinitival constructions. The emergence of RIs can therefore serve as a criterion distinguishing the two types of acquisition. Based on her analysis of eighteen children first exposed to French between AOA 3 and 4, Riedel (2009) concluded that most of them behaved like aL2 learners, thus corroborating the claim that cL2 learners differ significantly from (2)L1 children in their acquisition of verb morphology.

Finally, let us take a look at the acquisition of grammatical gender, a frequently studied phenomenon in research on cL2 acquisition. Whereas it represents a notoriously difficult problem for aL2 learners (see Andersen 1984 or Carroll 1999, among others), conflicting results have been reported for cL2 learners. This is possibly due to the fact that most studies do not distinguish between gender assignment and concord, an issue to which I will return immediately. Still, in view of the evidence presented by some authors, there can be no doubt that even very young cL2 learners encounter problems with gender. Pfaff (1992), for example, concluded in her analysis of Turkish L1 children acquiring German in early childhood, AOA around 2;0, that some children in a bilingual daycare centre failed to acquire anything remotely resembling the target system. Möhring (2001), analysing the acquisition of French by German children, noted problems with gender assignment as of approximately AOA 3;7. Recall also that Granfeldt, Schlyter and Kihlstedt (2007) observed that Swedish cL2 learners (AOA 3;5–6;7) looked like aL2 learners of French in their use of gender agreement. Hulk and Cornips (2006), finally, found quantitative and qualitative differences in gender markings by successive learners of Dutch, as compared to L1 children; note that at that point of development, the cL2 learners did not exhibit problems with verb placement in subordinate clauses. These and similar research results corroborate the claim that gender acquisition represents a challenge for cL2 learners as well. What is unclear, however, is which aspects of the acquisition task are most problematic for them.

A major reason why grammatical gender is a particularly interesting problem for acquisition research is that it requires morphological as well as syntactic knowledge. Whereas gender *assignment* refers essentially to morphological properties of nominal elements in languages like French and German, gender *concord* (or agreement) is a syntactic operation. Hawkins and Franceschina (2004: 175) analyse grammatical gender as 'a morphological reflex of the "checking" of uninterpretable gender features during the construction of derivations by the syntactic-computational component'. According to these authors, nouns contain a [±fem] and determiners the uninterpretable [*u*gender] feature. Irrespective of the technical details of this analysis, we can retain that the *acquisition* of gender markings involves *three tasks*: (1) The parameterized option of specifying categories for gender features; in L1 development, this typically happens before age 2;0. (2) Gender assignment to lexical items, determining for every one of them to which of the classes of the target system it belongs. Depending on how these classes are marked in the respective languages, this is a more or less difficult task for learners. In languages like French (*masculine* and *feminine*) and German (*neuter*, *masculine* and *feminine*), it is a rather complex process since gender is neither fully motivated by semantics, nor is it unambiguously marked on nouns, determiners and so on. For complex nouns, suffixes frequently indicate reliably the correct gender. But with simple nouns, learners have to rely on phonological, morphological or semantic cues which allow them to assign the correct gender with a variable degree of reliability. In French the most important cue for gender assignment is the final sound of a noun (cf. Tucker *et al.* 1977). In cases where these properties give conflicting evidence, formal cues tend to override functional ones (cf. Karmiloff-Smith 1979). (3) Gender concord needs to be established. In (2)L1, this is achieved at around age 3:0 for languages like French and German. Note that children may assign the wrong gender to a given noun, but demonstrate mastery of concord. In this case, all determiners and modifiers systematically carry the 'wrong' markings. If, for example, *maison* 'house' is assigned *masculine gender, successful acquisition of concord results in combinations like *le maison*, *un maison*, *petit maison* and so on.

When trying to determine whether cL2 learners resemble L1 or aL2 learners, all three tasks offer criteria for distinguishing between acquisition types. Concerning the first one, it has been argued that learners whose L1 lacks grammatical gender should encounter more difficulties in acquiring gender than those whose L1 resembles the L2 in this respect (see Hawkins and Franceschina 2004). As for gender assignment, what is of particular interest is that L1 children focus on formal properties of nouns and on distributional properties (e.g. Art + N combinations). In doing so, they rely not on principles of UG but on discovery mechanisms. These are domain-specific in that they refer to abstract linguistic entities (morphemes, words, etc.) and to formal properties of such units (e.g. sound quality of the ending). In aL2 acquisition, on the other hand, learners seem to rely primarily on functional properties (semantic, contextual, etc.) and on lexical learning, overemphasizing functional to the detriment of formal cues (see Carroll 1999). With respect to the acquisition of gender concord, finally, we should predict that L2 learners cannot activate this syntactic process if the L1 lacks the [*u*gender] feature on D, because parameter (re)setting has been argued not to be possible (see section 5.2 in the preceding chapter).

Meisel (2009) investigated gender acquisition by the same ten children of the Hamburg cL2 corpus whose acquisition of finiteness had been studied by Meisel (2008a). Note that French marks gender overtly on singular forms of articles (*le/la* 'the', *un/une* 'a'), on adjectives and pronouns. If the definite article is followed by a noun with an initial vowel, the article will be elided (e.g. *l'idée* 'the idea (fem)' instead of **la idée*), and with possessive pronouns a form ending in a consonant, identical to the masculine one, replaces the feminine form (e.g. *mon idée* 'my idea' instead of **ma idée*). As mentioned above, gender on simple nouns is typically not marked overtly in a transparent way, except for some nouns where sex differences are coded overtly, as in *chien/chienne* 'dog (masc/fem)'.

The analysis of the speech of the ten German cL2 learners of French (five recorded after 16 months of exposure to French, five after 27–29 months of exposure) revealed that all of them omitted articles frequently, that is, those items on which gender is typically marked overtly. Considering the three learning tasks, it appears at first sight as if the *first* one, discovering that French makes use of noun classification according to [±gender], does not represent a major problem since all children with the exception of one did use different gender-marked forms. A closer look at the data revealed, however, that eight (8/10) children made gender errors and that none of them used the full set of masculine and feminine forms for both definite and indefinite articles. In other words, only two of those with 27–29 months of exposure seem to have been successful, and one from the group with less exposure can be argued to be on the right track. The main reason, however, for why seven of them are classified as L2 learners is not the frequency of errors but the kind of errors they make. It turns out that they differ substantially from L1 learners with respect to the *second* task, gender assignment. They systematically violate the generalizations referring to formal properties of nouns which are used as cues by L1 learners. They thus do not seem to be able to make use of the discovery principles which guide L1 acquisition. More seriously, it is not at all obvious whether these children are adhering to any kind of system. Semantic criteria clearly do not play a decisive role, as is evidenced by such uses as *mon Schwester* 'my + masc sister', *le madame* 'the + masc lady', *une frère* 'a + fem brother', *le maman* 'the + masc mommy', nor do the learners transfer gender assignment from the L1 German: a survey of incorrect gender markings revealed that transfer can maximally account for 24% of them. It thus seems that gender assignment is the result of lexical learning rather than of gender attribution to noun classes. This definitely makes these children look like aL2 learners.

In order to determine whether cL2 learners cannot rely on the discovery principles referring to formal properties of nouns, nine additional children from the same school in Hamburg were tested for gender assignment to French-type nonce words. Hoping to discover the initial strategies of young learners, we included three children with three months or less of exposure to French at the time of testing. The experimental design followed Karmiloff-Smith's (1979) study of French monolingual children. The experimenter presents a card with two pictures of an unknown item in different colours or different sizes and refers to the object using the plural form of a nonce word in such a way as to stimulate a response containing a (gender-marked) singular form. The nonce words ended in sounds typically indicating masculine or feminine nouns in French according to Tucker *et al.* (1977). Eight different word endings were selected, four intended to trigger masculine and four feminine gender assignment. For each ending three examples were presented, for a total of twenty-four stimuli, twelve masculine and twelve feminine. The stimuli further included six French nouns, three examples each for two endings (see Table 6.2). They were all high-frequency items likely to be familiar to children of this age. The feminine ones ended in sounds typical of masculine nouns and vice versa, in order to allow us to distinguish between lexical familiarity and effects of formal cues in assigning gender. In other words, if they are assigned the target gender, we may assume that they have been learned by experience.

The overall results (Table 6.1) show that with the exception of Pascal (18/24), the children correctly assigned the predicted gender in only 10 to 14 out of 24 cases. This corresponds to chance distribution. Anton after one month of exposure (ME) does not fare worse than Emma with 26 ME or most of the others with 14 to 15 ME. Four children seem to have adopted a strategy of trying to stick to one gender: Eike (*un* on all 24), Dennis (17 *une*), Nico (22 *le*, and 2 correct *la*) and Emma (18 *le*, 2 *un*, thus 20 masculine forms). Notice further that they show no preference for one of the two genders; instead, some are doing better with

Table 6.1: *Overall results of the gender assignment test*

Name	AOA	ME	Results: correct/total	
Eike	2;11	3		**un** (×24)
Gina	3;07	2	m: 2/12 f: 5/12	**le la un une**
Anton	3;08	1	m: 6/12 f: 5/12	**le la un une**
Conny	2;11	15	m: 5/12 f: 9/12	**le la une**
Janina	3;01	14	m: 10/12 f: 4/12	**le un une**
Dennis	3;04	15	m: 3/12 f: 9/12	**un une** (×17)
Nico	3;08	15	m: 12/12 f: 2/12	**le** (×22) **la**
Pascal	3;08	15	m: 10/12 f: 8/12	**le la**
Emma	2;11	26	m: 9/12 f: 1/12	**le** (×18) **un** (×2) **une**

Table 6.2: *Gender assignment test*

Ending	nonce words	Reliability	Conny	Janina	Dennis	Nico	Pascal	Emma
[ɛ]	nodrais	90% m	1/3	**3/3**	1/3	**3/3**	2/3	**3/3**
[ʒ]	plichage	94% m	2/3	2/3	1/3	**3/3**	2/3	2/3
[o]	golcheau	97% m	2/3	**3/3**	0/3	**3/3**	**3/3**	2/3
[ɛ̃]	brougin	99% m	0/3	2/3	1/3	**3/3**	**3/3**	2/3
[s]	podaisse	68% f	2/3	1/3	**3/3**	0/3	**3/3**	0/3
[n]	fasène	68% f	**3/3**	2/3	1/3	0/3	1/3	1/3
[i]	tartis	75% f	**3/3**	1/3	2/3	0/3	2/3	0/3
[z]	bravaise	90% f	1/3	0/3	**3/3**	2/3	2/3	0/3
French nouns								
Masc. soleil			2/3	1/3	**3/3**	**3/3**	2/3	1/3
Fem. main			1/3	**3/3**	1/3	**3/3**	1/3	**3/3**

masculine (e.g. Janina) and others with feminine stimuli (Conny). In sum, only Pascal can perhaps be argued to rely on the formal cues which L1 children refer to when assigning gender to unknown nouns. For the other children it is not possible to discern a general pattern of gender assignment.

Let us therefore examine the success rate for the various endings of nonce and of existing nouns as displayed in Table 6.2 in order to see whether cross-individual patterns can be detected. Again, we find that some learners do better with masculine and others with feminine endings, that is, masculine nouns do not systematically yield better results although they attain higher rates of reliability in terms of the predictability of gender for existing French nouns. It is also *not* the case that specific endings are used correctly by all or by none of the children. Remember, finally, that some of the positive results are due to the overgeneralization of a gender form, for example Nico who uses *le* almost exclusively.

Interestingly, Pascal, who used formal cues most successfully, does relatively poorly with existing nouns, possibly because their endings are in conflict with their actual gender, as explained above. Nico, on the other hand, who does not make use of the formal cues, is the most successful child with existing French nouns. This suggests that for most of these children formal cues do not play a significant role in assigning gender; they rather rely on an item-by-item learning process when exposed to lexical material. This, of course, is in accordance with the conclusions drawn from the analysis of the spontaneous data. Needless to say that this is a preliminary result which needs to be re-examined once a larger database is available.

Concerning the *third* task, establishing gender concord, it is frequently impossible to decide on the basis of spontaneous production data whether errors result from wrong gender assignment or from a failure to establish concord. Note that in the spontaneous data one and the same noun can appear with feminine *and* masculine articles in the speech of the same child, for example *le/la souris* 'the mouse', *un/la maison* 'a/the house', and when it is resumed by a pronoun, gender conflict is again possible as in *la souris il fait* . . . 'the mouse + fem, he does . . .', *la fenêtre il est cassé* 'the window + fem, he is broken'. These uses suggest that concord has not been established successfully. In fact, it appears that these learners have not even activated the [*u*gender] feature on D in their L2 system, although this should not be a problem for L1 German learners, given that German is a gender marking language (cf. Hawkins and Franceschina 2004). Quite obviously, both gender assignment and concord represent major acquisition problems, even for learners who should be able to rely on their L1 grammatical knowledge.

My conclusion from the foregoing discussion and from the available research results more generally is that cL2 acquisition is indeed a type of acquisition in its own right. We have seen that it shares crucial features with aL2 acquisition. By implication this means that it also shares properties with first language development. The grammatical domains in which cL2 resembles aL2 and in which they both differ from (2)L1 include at least some areas of inflectional morphology. The extent to which the computational system is also subject to maturational changes is a matter of more controversy, but we have seen that specific aspects of syntax are affected during early phases of development. As for the question of which linguistic properties are concerned, empirical studies corroborate the hypothesis that parameterized principles should be prime candidates. More surprisingly, perhaps, discovery and learning principles too seem to become inaccessible in the course of linguistic development.

But this finding should really not be all that surprising, for it should be obvious from the discussion in the previous chapters that the LMC comprises not only *representational knowledge* (UG principles) guiding language development but also domain-specific *discovery* and *processing* mechanisms, referring to abstract grammatical entities and structural properties of sentences, that is, grammatical categories and relations. In fact, Bley-Vroman (1989, 1990) had made a similar distinction referring to Universal Grammar and to a set of learning procedures as subcomponents of the language acquisition system. However, the 'UG or not UG' debate over the past twenty-five years or so largely ignored this distinction and has been concerned exclusively with grammatical principles. Recall the discussion in chapter 2 where I summarized findings showing that children during the first year of their lives focus on just those aspects of linguistic units which are crucial for the discovery of formal properties of languages. This is why I referred to the principles guiding them as discovery principles, distinguishing them from principles of UG. My claim has been that both types of principles are part of the human LMC. Whether we are dealing here with a homogeneous set or whether quite different principles and mechanisms have been subsumed under the term of 'discovery' principles is a question which cannot be answered on the basis of our current knowledge. Once generative research on language acquisition is ready to broaden its scope of investigation beyond the domain of UG, it should become possible to give a more comprehensive answer which can also account for learning mechanisms.

My hypothesis is that processing and discovery mechanisms are also affected by maturational changes. Whether the same causes are at work in these cases too, as with representational knowledge, is still a matter of speculation. A perhaps plausible guess is that in the case of these principles we are not looking at a decrease of the accessibility of modules but at the consequences of the fact that other cognitive modules have developed which are now competing with the domain-specific ones. This is reminiscent of the hypothesis proposed by Felix (1984) (see section 5.3).

Returning to the problem of a possible agenda explaining the inaccessibility sequence, we have to acknowledge that our current knowledge does not enable us to formulate specific predictions about which grammatical phenomena are likely to be affected by maturational changes at such an early age. As a tentative hypothesis, I propose that those properties which are acquired very early in L1 development will be well entrenched at the time of onset of cL2 acquisition and can therefore be expected to cause problems if the L2 differs from the L1 option. Note that work on attrition suggests that after parameter setting the newly acquired grammatical knowledge requires a period of stabilization in order to remain available permanently (see Flores 2008, 2010). It is not implausible to assume, contrary to Clahsen and Muysken (1996), that alternative parameter values continue to remain accessible during this period. This would also help to explain the fact that bilingual children acquiring two languages simultaneously develop two first languages not differing in their grammatical knowledge from the respective monolinguals.

Finally, concerning the age ranges during which sensitive periods bundle, the study of cL2 acquisition confirmed the hypothesis that crucial changes happen not only at AOA 6–7, but also at around AOA 4. In fact, all but one of the children in the Hamburg cL2 corpus who were classified as cL2 learners based on their acquisition of finiteness and gender markings were first exposed to French at age 3;7 or later. Whether this approximate age can indeed be regarded as a dividing line between cL2 and 2L1 learners will have to be determined in further studies based on larger groups of individuals, but the age period between 3;6 and 4;0 may well qualify as such. Still, given the kind of individual differences mentioned in the preceding section, it is possible that some of the children who begin to acquire another language during this age range will resemble L1 learners whereas others will behave like aL2 learners.

6.3 Syntactic processing in the second language

In the previous chapters, properties of language processing have been evoked repeatedly as possible explanations for parallels and differences between various types of language acquisition. It is therefore time to examine this point more closely. Let me begin with what may appear to be a trivial statement but one which I believe serves as a reminder. As has been emphasized repeatedly, a primary interest of our endeavour is to gain insights into the linguistic knowledge (I-language) underlying the language use by individuals who acquired the particular language as their mother tongue, as one of several native languages, or as a second language either in childhood or at a later age. Yet as in all areas of linguistic investigation, acquisition research has direct access only to speech data (E-language) produced either in spontaneous speech or in experimental settings. Since these data are shaped by grammatical principles as well as by mechanisms determining how this knowledge is put to use in production or comprehension, properties of acquisition data are determined not only by grammar but also by these processing mechanisms, in addition to discovery procedures and learning strategies. When attributing properties to grammatical representations we must therefore subtract those which are due to performance factors. This, however, is only feasible if we have at least a basic understanding of the strategies and mechanisms of language use, of how they interact with grammatical principles, and how they affect the nature of the data. In chapter 5 I argued that L2 learners' use of target-like constructions does not necessarily imply that they have activated the same acquisition mechanisms and attained identical grammatical knowledge as L1 children. Rather, inductive learning can substitute UG-guided development, and this may result in surface patterns which do not differ from those employed by native speakers. In this section I intend to show that the course of acquisition and the formal properties of L2 utterances are not determined by principles of UG alone, but that they are also shaped by production and comprehension mechanisms.

As a first example, let me remind you of the acquisition sequences discussed in the previous chapters. We saw that both first and second language acquisition proceed through invariant developmental sequences in a number of core areas of morphosyntax but that these sequences are not identical in the two acquisition types contrasted here. This observation may be interpreted as reflecting fundamental differences between L1 and L2 acquisition only if it can be shown that the sequence-internal orders are determined by distinct knowledge sources. In sections 2.2 and 2.3 of chapter 2 I argued that in L1 acquisition the underlying logic determining the order of phases within the invariant developmental sequences is constrained by principles of UG and is thus grammatical in nature. In L2 acquisition, on the other hand, grammar can account only partially for the observed acquisition orders. The discussion in chapter 3, for example, demonstrated beyond reasonable doubt that the Morpheme Order Studies of the 1970s had not been able to offer a satisfactory explanation for why morphemes emerged in just the order detected (section 3.2) and that later attempts at remedying this deficit were only partially successful, since they concluded that 'category-specific development' as observed in L1 does not hold for L2 acquisition (Zobl and Liceras 1994). Note that grammatical criteria like the differentiation between nominal and verbal elements enabled researchers to reduce variability in L2 sequences, but morphemes dependent on different functional categories appeared simultaneously whereas others related to the same functional domain were scattered over the acquisition sequence. This stands in clear contrast to L1 development where the order of acquisition of morphemes can be accounted for by distinguishing between elements learned as lexical items as opposed to those dependent on the accessibility of functional categories; the emergence of the latter can be interpreted as an instance of incremental development. Although in L2 acquisition the lexical–functional distinction is also relevant, the acquisition order of elements related to functional categories does not follow a logic determined by properties of functional heads. Add to this that the bound–free distinction plays a significant role in L2 but not in L1 acquisition and that L1 but not L2 acquisition order in the domain of propositional negation can be explained by grammatical developments relating to verb placement (see section 3.3).

The overall conclusion to be drawn from these and similar observations is that the course of L2 acquisition is undoubtedly influenced by grammatical properties of the target constructions but that structure-independent placement strategies contribute to its explanation too. Importantly, even if we ignore those L1–L2 differences which have been argued to result from L1 transfer or from inductive learning, there remain others which cannot be fully accounted for in grammatical terms, let alone by principles of UG. This is all the more intriguing given that both acquisition types exhibit invariant developmental sequences defined by the grammatical properties emerging in the course of the sequence. Typical examples are the sequences in which German word order emerges in L1 and in L2 acquisition, as discussed in chapter 4 (section 4.4); the L2 sequence proposed by Meisel *et al.* (1981) and Clahsen *et al.* (1983) is reproduced here for convenience as Table 6.3. Empirically, this order represents an unusually robust finding. The explanation of why these phenomena emerge in just this order in L2 German, however, is a matter of some controversy.

It is quite obvious that syntactic structure building is not an adequate explanation (see Meisel *et al.* 1981 or Clahsen and Muysken 1986, 1989). Transfer from the L1 does not fare any better as an explanation. At this point, I do not want to

Table 6.3: *Developmental sequence of word order in L2 German*

1. SVO/ADV	invariant order: subject–verb–object/adverbial
2. ADV–PRE	adverbials appear in initial position
3. PART	non-finite verbal elements (including particles) are placed in final position
4. INV	subject–verb inversion, e.g. after preposed adverbials
5. ADV–VP	adverbials are inserted between the verb and its complement
6. V–END	finite verbs in subordinate clauses appear in final position

return to this issue in more detail. In section 4.3 I argued against the claim that initial SVO order can be accounted for in this way (cf. Meisel 1983b, 1983c). As for subsequent phases, let me merely point out that the phenomena defining phases 4 (pre-subject position of finite verbs) and 5 (pre-adverbial position of finite verbs) are familiar from the (Romance) first languages of the learners studied by Meisel *et al.* (1981), whereas phase 3 is defined by the emergence of non-finite verbal elements in clause-final position, a phenomenon not encountered in Romance languages. If syntactic transfer played a crucial role here, we should have expected phases 4 and 5 to precede phase 3. Clahsen *et al.* (1983) therefore hypothesized that L2 acquisition sequences reflect an increasing complexity in the processing of the constructions involved (see also Meisel 1987b). In other words, constructions which are less difficult to process seem to be acquired or used earlier than those involving greater processing complexity.

This suspicion was subsequently confirmed and explained in much more detail by Manfred Pienemann (1998a, 1998b) and his associates who developed the Processability Theory (see Pienemann and Håkansson 1999, Glahn, Håkansson, Hammarberg, Holmen, Hvenekilde and Lund 2001, Pienemann, Di Biase, Kawaguchi and Håkansson 2005 or Pienemann 2005). The basic insight on which this theory builds is that one can predict the structural properties which learners are able to process at a given point in development if one can determine how language processing mechanisms develop in the learner. Note that the theory focuses on production and on what has been referred to as the formulator in models of language production (cf. Levelt 1989). It is also crucial to note that the processor comprises computational routines operating on the linguistic knowledge of a speaker but that these are not part of this knowledge. From this perspective, acquiring a language implies the acquisition of the necessary *procedural skills* for the processing of the target language. If learners are initially constrained by the lack of adequate processing routines, the subsequent course of acquisition can be seen as a process of constraint shedding (cf. Pienemann and Håkansson 1999). Processability Theory thus provides a plausible solution for the developmental problem. Its general design is based on the architecture of the language processor as developed by Levelt (1989) and by Kempen and Hoenkamp (1987) and others. Importantly, it suggests a universal hierarchy of processing resources, and it maintains (Pienemann 1998b: 2) that

1. processing components are relatively autonomous specialists which operate largely automatically;
2. processing is incremental;
3. the output of the processor is linear;
4. grammatical processing has access to a grammatical memory store.

The hierarchy of processing resources comprises at least six levels, starting at the word/lemma level and proceeding via category, phrasal, clausal (S-procedure, involving either salient or non-salient stimuli) through subordinate clause procedures. Notice that this ordering implies that 'the resource of each lower level is a prerequisite for the functioning of the higher level' (Pienemann 1998b: 8). At every level processing resources are implemented which are specific to the target language, for example target word order properties at the S-procedure level. This is crucial for L2 acquisition in that it entails that L2 learners have to create new, language-specific processing routines in addition to the universal resources on which they can rely from the beginning, just like native speakers of the target language.

Within this theoretical framework, Pienemann (1998a, 1998b) is able to argue convincingly that the acquisition sequence for German L2 word order[4] given in Table 6.3 corresponds indeed to the hierarchy of processing resources established by Processability Theory. Rather than recapitulating his arguments here, I refer to Pienemann 1998b: 11–12 for details. Suffice it to say that canonical SVO can be dealt with at the category level where grammatical functions are assigned; ADV–PRE does not require cross-constituent exchange of grammatical information either, although it deviates from the canonical order. PART does make exchange of information across constituent boundaries necessary and must therefore be handled at a higher level of the processability hierarchy, the first of two 'S-procedure' levels; INV then requires processing at the second of the 'S-procedure' levels because it involves non-salient placement of an element; processing of V–END, finally, occurs at the next higher level of the hierarchy where subordinate clause procedures become available.

The Processability Theory can thus indeed contribute significantly to a solution of the developmental problem. The question, however, is whether it can also help us to account for the L1–L2 differences. In view of the fact that it claims that the hierarchy of processing resources is universal and identical in first and second language acquisition (cf. Pienemann 1998a, 1998b), this does not seem to be the case. We should not expect processing mechanisms to take over altogether and to replace grammatical considerations. Rather, as I said at the beginning of this section, one can plausibly expect to find that both contribute to the shaping of the course of language acquisition. Interestingly, Pienemann 1998b: 14, addressing the concern that according to Processability Theory certain constructions should be acquired simultaneously because they rely on processing resources of the same hierarchical level, stated that the theory 'does not predict that whatever can be processed will indeed be acquired. Instead, the theory predicts that what cannot be processed will not be acquired. In other words, processability acts as a constraint on development . . .' This is to say that processing mechanisms do not override grammatical principles and select the structural phenomena to be acquired at a given point of development. The claim that processing resources constrain the course of L1 development therefore does not conflict with the idea of a grammatically determined logic of development, like, for example, structure building guided by properties of functional heads. Only if this logic resulted in a developmental sequence violating the constraints imposed by processability considerations would a conflict arise.

Concerning the specific example of German word order, the essential difference between L1 and L2 relates to the hypothesis about underlying word order. L1 children, guided by principles of UG (see the discussion in chapter 4), opt for the target SOV order right from the beginning. The L1 developmental sequence presented in section 4.4 results from the unfolding of grammatical structure under the guidance of UG principles. What matters in the present context is that this order of phases is not in conflict with the hierarchy of processing routines (see Pienemann 1998b: 13). L2 learners, on the other hand, erroneously analyse German as an SVO language. I have tried to show in chapters 4 and 5 that the available empirical evidence suggests that even very advanced learners of German operate on the basis of this assumption, and I argued that they cannot change it by resetting the OV/VO parameter. This is not the occasion to recapitulate the possible reasons why L2 learners opt for SVO order, but remember that one plausible explanation (see section 4.2) is that SVO may be easier to parse. If this is correct, processing constraints do override grammatical requirements in L2, but not in L1 acquisition. The subsequent L2 acquisition sequence is not only in accordance with the processing hierarchy, just like the L1 sequence, it is in fact primarily determined by the processing routines. Thus, although both types of learners rely on grammatical knowledge as well as on processing mechanisms, the latter shape L2 acquisition in a more substantive fashion than L1 development.

However, starting with the assumption that German exhibits underlying SVO order is clearly not the optimal solution, as is evidenced by the fact that the L2 sequence contains a larger number of phases, not to mention that some of the operations defining such phases violate principles of UG if Clahsen and Muysken (1986) are correct (see section 4.4). Yet if canonical SVO order is a sub-optimal solution for German, one wonders why L2 learners do not revise this hypothesis – by inductive learning if necessary, assuming that resetting of the OV/VO parameter is ruled out. Interestingly, this hypothetical alternative is not viable for reasons related to processing constraints, as is demonstrated by Pienemann (1998a, 1998b) who explains this fact as a result of *generative entrenchment*. What this means is that early structural choices are determining factors for later developments, and subsequent development of structural options, one feeding into the next, can be cut off. This is said to happen in the acquisition of German word order as a consequence of the non-optimal initial hypothesis and of generative entrenchment. Just as I argued in chapter 4, Pienemann (1998b: 17) concluded that there is no evidence supporting the claim that L2 learners of German switch from VO to OV in the course of acquisition, and he demonstrates that this would be computationally very costly, because several structural assumptions would have to be revised. In other words, a change from VO to OV, which would enhance L2 learners' chances to move closer to near-native knowledge of German, is impossible to achieve by means of parameter (re)setting, as I have tried to show in chapter 5 (section 5.2), and it is extremely difficult to perform by other means because of generative entrenchment and the ensuing additional computational costs.

To sum up, research results obtained by investigating processing mechanisms in language production support the hypothesis according to which first and second language acquisition exhibit fundamental differences. In addition to the differences in grammatical knowledge detected in the preceding chapters, we also find differences due to effects of grammatical processing. Production resources play a significantly more important role in determining the course of L2 acquisition than they do in L1 development. Note that this is the case in spite of the fact that the processing routines themselves as well as the hierarchy of processing resources are identical in the two types of acquisition, if proponents of the Processability Hypothesis are correct. This, however, must not necessarily be the case. If future research revealed that production mechanisms do change over age, after all, this would obviously widen the gap between first and second language acquisition even further. Let me add that the particular importance of processing requirements for L2 acquisition is also evidenced by the fact that even learners at advanced stages of acquisition seem to be under pressure to reduce the processing complexity of their utterances (cf. Clahsen *et al.* 1983). One effect of this is that it prevents some learners from proceeding further through the acquisition sequence and from attaining near-native grammatical knowledge. Moreover, those who do approach the target tend not to use the acquired knowledge consistently in all required contexts.

The research on syntactic processing to which I have referred so far has been concerned exclusively with language production. Let me now turn to comprehension and more specifically to the role of morphosyntactic parsing in language acquisition. Remember that the major reason why I think that we need to take grammatical processing into account is that we cannot hope to reveal the nature of learners' developing linguistic knowledge unless we succeed in distinguishing between, on the one hand, the contributions of mechanisms of language use and of mental representations of grammatical knowledge, on the other, when it comes to deciding on what causes specific properties of learner utterances to emerge.

Unfortunately, research on second language acquisition has long neglected the systematic study of parsing mechanisms, largely ignoring results from psycholinguistic research on mature speakers or on L1 development (see Carlson and

Tanenhaus 1989, Berwick, Abney and McCarthy 1991 or Pritchett 1992, among many others). This is all the more regrettable since to the extent that L2 research did take this into account, it suggested strongly that parsing is likely to contribute in important ways to an explanation of L2 acquisition (see Chaudron 1985, Juffs 1998a, 1998b, 2005, Juffs and Harrington 1995, 1996, Klein 1999, Carroll 2001, Hulstijn 2002, Fernández 2003, Papadopoulou and Clahsen 2003 or Sabourin 2003, among others). In fact, it is not an exaggeration to state that it is impossible to assess the role of learning in L2 acquisition without an adequate understanding of parsing – a point emphasized by Carroll (2001: 10) whose Autonomous Induction Theory explicitly addresses the role of parsing in L2 acquisition. She states that

> Intake from the speech signal is . . . not input to learning mechanisms. Rather, it is *input to speech parsers*. Parsers are mechanisms designed to encode the signal in various representational formats.

Learning happens when parsing of the input fails; in this sense it is input driven. Parsing, in turn, fails when no available parsing procedure is capable of analysing the input data. Crucially, parsing failure in second language acquisition does not necessarily entail that no interpretation is assigned to the unanalysed and unparsed stimuli. Rather, 'transferred parsing routines will map interpretations onto the stimuli and ignore unanalysable parts of speech' (Carroll 2001: 305). This is a crucial point since total failure of the parser would make it impossible for the L2 learner to detect the problematic part and to trigger learning. Importantly, it is hypothesized that initial phases of L2 acquisition are characterized by the transfer of L1 parsing and production procedures.

Recall that I outlined a similar scenario in chapter 4 (section 4.3), arguing that we need to distinguish between transfer of grammatical knowledge where properties of the native grammar are integrated into the target grammar, as opposed to cross-linguistic influence resulting from the fact that L1 grammatical knowledge is fed into the processing routines applied to the L2 data. From this perspective it is plausible to assume massive transfer of parsing mechanisms during an initial phase of L2 acquisition. Particularly in naturalistic L2 acquisition, learners exposed to input comprising speech at rapid speed may not have any other option than to use the L1 parser in their attempt to recognize parts of L2 speech. This is not to say, however, that their L2 grammar initially contains parts of their native grammar. Considering the kind of problems resulting from generative entrenchment if target-deviant structural choices are made in production routines at an early point of acquisition, it is more plausible and also more in line with the known empirical facts about early phases of L2 acquisition to assume that learners initially apply L1 strategies of language use, allowing them to communicate successfully while at the same time enabling them to build up a body of knowledge about the L2. The grammatical knowledge thus acquired is fed into the parser and the formulator, gradually adapting them to the requirements of the target norm. This scenario avoids the problem alluded to in chapter 4 (section 4.2) according to which it would not be possible for learners to assign structural interpretations to constructions in which source and target grammars differ; consequently, exposure to such constructions cannot trigger learning if learners are not able to detect the grammatical particularities of the target language. The apparent paradox is avoided by attributing the necessary flexibility to the systems of language use. In case of parsing failure, alternative solutions can be tested by scanning surface chains and by allowing parsers to interact with other modules, for example semantic knowledge. The decisive point is that if grammatical learning primarily relies on alterations of parsing mechanisms rather than on restructuring of mental representations of grammatical knowledge, the entrenchment problem is avoided, and the apparent paradox concerning input-driven learning disappears.

As for the similarities and differences between first and second language acquisition, the hypothesized transfer of parsing procedures implies that processing mechanisms in language comprehension are of the same nature as in L1 development, just as has been claimed above for production routines. Carroll (2001: 190) emphasizes this idea in formulating the Uniform Parsers Hypothesis according to which not only are L1 parsing procedures initially applied systematically to L2 stimuli, but the same parsers process stimuli of both sources, L1 and L2. The latter claim does speak in favour of fundamental parallels between L1 and L2 acquisition. The differences would then be due primarily to the fact that the procedures fed by the L1 grammar must eventually be replaced by novel ones attuned to the specific requirements of L2 stimuli. This involves re-weighting of cues or learning of new cues according to the requirements of the L2 system. If this scenario describes correctly the role of processing mechanisms in L2 acquisition, one may assume that the process of reorganizing the parsing system will take time but that the system is fundamentally identical in first and second language acquisition.

This question of whether L2 learners can indeed acquire native-like parsing routines, once the mechanisms transferred from the L1 have been substituted by those attuned to the L2 grammar, can only be answered if experimental research methods are applied in studying L2 processing. Only fairly recently has the number of this type of investigation increased, applying a variety of research methods like self-paced reading, ERP, or eye-tracking; cf. the special issue of *Second Language Research*, edited by Felser (2005), triggering an animated debate of this issue. The growing interest in this problem is also evidenced by the discussions of the keynote article in *Applied Psycholinguistics* by Clahsen and Felser (2006a) and by the state-of-the-art summary presented by Clahsen and Felser (2006b).

These studies employing online techniques in investigating L2 processing seem to agree that L2 speakers are slower than native speakers in language processing (Papadopoulou 2005), a fact repeatedly observed before; see also White and Genesee 1996 who reported significantly slower processing even by highly proficient L2 learners who achieved near-nativeness in some aspects of grammar.

Moreover, and more importantly for the present discussion, most of these studies also agree in concluding that L2 learners develop different processing routines, as compared to L1 native speakers, although this claim is more controversial, requiring further research investigating a larger variety of morphosyntactic phenomena in a broader range of learners with varying linguistic backgrounds. But in spite of this caveat one can say that Clahsen and Felser (2006a, 2006b) succeed in presenting a convincing line of argument when they conclude that in some domains of grammar even very advanced and highly proficient L2 learners cannot perform natively in processing the L2. This is claimed to be the case, for example, when parsing constructions containing non-local structural dependencies as in wh-questions where the wh-phrase has been fronted (*Which book did Mary think John believed the student has borrowed?*) (see also Felser and Roberts 2007). What is particularly interesting in view of the results obtained in brain imaging studies (ERP as well as fMRI), mentioned in section 6.1 above, is that this research also detected L1–L2 differences in operations relying on structure-dependent relations but not in parsing lexical-semantic information (see Papadopoulou and Clahsen 2003). More specifically, Felser, Roberts, Gross and Marinis (2003) found that learners use non-structural information in processing L2 sentences and that they rely more than native speakers do on lexical-semantic information.

Clahsen and Felser (2006a) attempt to explain these findings in terms of the Shallow Structure Hypothesis (SSH) which goes back to Townsend and Bever (2001) who distinguish between *full parsing* and *shallow parsing* in sentence processing by mature native speakers. Shallow parsing is hypothesized to rely on lexical-semantic information and on surface cues to interpretation rather than on the complete hierarchical structure for the strings to be parsed. Clahsen and Felser (2006b: 565) summarize that 'the SSH claims that the L2 grammar does not provide the type of syntactic information required to process non-local grammatical phenomena in native-like ways . . . even though the basic architecture of the processing system is the same in the L1 and L2'. L2 learners are thus claimed to rely more heavily on semantic, associative and surface information than on syntactic cues. This, obviously, parallels what I believe to be happening in inductive learning, see chapter 5 (section 5.3), and, as just mentioned (see also section 6.1 above), brain imaging studies suggest that L2 processing does not differ substantially from the L1 in lexical-semantic processing (no difference in N400 effects) whereas it exhibits fundamental differences in morphosyntactic processing (no LAN effects in L2 learners). Since LAN and P600 effects arguably reflect distinct phases in processing (cf. Friederici 2002), LAN indicating automatic first-pass parsing processes and P600 reanalysis and repair, the absence of LAN can be interpreted as an indication of reduced automaticity. Note that although the latter seems to vary according to proficiency in the L2, there is broad consensus that L2 processing is less automatic than L1. This is in line with the finding of increased cortical activation in L2 processing (see Saur *et al.* 2009 and other studies referred to in section 6.1). Importantly, these L1–L2 differences can plausibly be attributed to maturational changes (see section 6.1).

To summarize, the various insights gained by psycholinguistic studies using online research techniques allow us to conclude that L2 processing of morphosyntactic information differs from L1 processing in that it relies more heavily on non-structural and on lexical-semantic information. To be precise, this happens when structure-dependent relations are involved, and possibly only when attempting to parse non-local structural relationships. At any rate, no such differences emerge in L2 processing of semantic or pragmatic information. According to Clahsen and Felser and their associates, the observed differences provide strong evidence in support of the claim that L2 speakers rely on different parsing routines in these cases. At least when dealing with advanced learners other possible explanations can be ruled out. They do not exhibit transfer effects any more, and slower speed of processing cannot account for the detected differences either. Moreover, since these differences are also found in highly proficient L2 learners, proficiency can arguably be ruled out as a possible explanation. Finally, the L1–L2 differences under discussion have been observed with learners who can be shown to have acquired the grammatical knowledge required in the specific constructions. In other words, the particularities attributed to L2 speakers cannot be explained as being caused by incomplete grammatical knowledge, by a lack of proficiency, the slower speed of processing, or transfer of L1 processing mechanisms. According to the Shallow Structure Hypothesis, the L2-specific parsing routines rely on lexical-semantic information and on surface cues rather than on the complete hierarchical structural information. It has also been observed that L2 parsing, as opposed to L1 sentence processing, does not happen fully automatically; for a discussion of this issue, see Segalowitz 2003. All these facts are in line with what we know about L2 processing of morphosyntactic information in the brain. This refers to the fact that only morphosyntactic but not lexical-semantic processing is concerned by the observed changes, to the reduced automaticity, and also to the observation that learners resort to resources not typically involved in the processing of grammatical information.

As argued in section 6.1, I view these parallels between behavioural and neuropsychological and neurophysiological research as particularly strong support for the claim that L1 and L2 acquisition are characterized by fundamental differences in some domains of grammar. The findings referred to here suggest that such differences concern not only the mental representation of grammatical knowledge, but grammatical processing as well. Quite obviously, the parallels between results from linguistic and neuroimaging studies do not solve the problem once and for all. But they do provide reciprocal support, and they add plausibility to the idea that the observed L1–L2 differences in linguistic behaviour are caused at least to a significant degree by maturational changes which, in turn, seem to be age-related. In fact, this line of argument is further strengthened by the observation that neurolinguistic theorizing concurs with these findings and interpretations, thus bridging the gap between neural and behavioural results. I am alluding here to the distinction between *declarative* and *procedural* systems (cf. Paradis 1994, 2004, 2009 and Ullman 2001). These terms refer to distinct cognitive systems subserving language processing, and they are claimed to rely on distinct neural bases. More specifically, the declarative/procedural model posits for mature native speakers that the so-called 'declarative memory system' is primarily implicated in the learning and processing of lexical-semantic information whereas the 'procedural memory system' underlies the learning and use of grammatical information. This model has been extended to second language acquisition, arguing that L2 learners over-rely on the declarative system, even for grammatical processing where native speakers rely on the procedural system (cf. Ullman 2001). This difference is argued to be caused by maturational changes, and although increasing proficiency reduces the differentiating effects, '[e]ven learners who were indistinguishable from L1 speakers in offline tasks . . . failed to show indications of native-like procedural processing of morphosyntactic phenomena' (Clahsen and Felser 2006b: 568).

To conclude this section and in an attempt to answer the questions raised at the beginning, we can say that we have seen solid evidence suggesting that processing mechanisms indeed shape the course of L2 acquisition and the form of learner utterances. Although the 'basic architecture of the processing system' seems to be identical in L1 and L2 acquisition, substantive differences have emerged. If parsing routines are different, it follows that some observed differences between these two types of acquisition are not due to differences in the mental representations of grammatical knowledge but to these processing differences. Yet if learning happens when parsing of the input fails (Carroll 2001), 'non-optimal parsing' (Papadopoulou 2005) will also result in representational differences, and the fact that L2 learners tend to treat German as an SVO language may well be an instance of non-optimal learning due in part to L2-specific parsing. Once such an option is adopted, it is difficult and in some cases even impossible to revise it because of processing constraints which have been demonstrated to determine the further course of acquisition. Ultimately, certain formal properties of L2 acquisition may thus be the result of processing requirements rather than being shaped by principles of Universal Grammar as in L1 development. Importantly, these fundamental differences between first and second language acquisition are caused by age-related maturational changes.

6.4 A note on ultimate attainment in second language acquisition

In place of a concluding summary to this chapter, I want to end by addressing at least briefly an issue which I have hardly mentioned so far, although second language acquisition research has dealt with it extensively. I am referring here to the question of what kind of grammatical knowledge can ultimately be attained by L2 learners. The focus in this chapter and, indeed, in the entire volume has been on parallels and differences between first and second language acquisition, as they can be detected in the course of acquisition. We have seen that both similarities and differences exist, and I have argued that some of the observed differences are fundamental ones in that they reflect a different kind of underlying linguistic knowledge. I have further argued that every surface property of a given language is, in principle, learnable for L2 learners. But since different learning mechanisms are involved in some instances of learning of L2 forms and constructions (see sections 5.3 and 5.4), as compared to grammatical development in L1, it is unlikely that L2 learners will ever be able to attain native grammatical competence in the target language. Instead, L2 knowledge has been characterized as a hybrid system because parts of it are not constrained by principles of Universal Grammar even if others – possibly most of them – represent a native-like grammatical system. Yet if this scenario suggests that it is highly unlikely that the type of knowledge which L2 learners can ultimately attain will converge with the kind of knowledge characterizing L1 grammatical competence, the question ultimately is whether this possibility is excluded altogether for principled reasons, or whether very advanced and highly proficient L2 'perfect' or 'expert' learners are able to substitute the alien parts of their near-native L2 knowledge by genuinely grammatical ones and thus attain native competence, after all. In view of what we have seen in the present chapter, the answer to this question will have to be negative. If it is correct that some of the observed L1–L2 differences are caused by maturational and other age-related changes, by far the most plausible prediction is that they do not have access any more to all the modules of the Language Acquisition Device which would enable them to achieve this goal. In fact, we have seen evidence suggesting that not only parameterized principles of UG become inaccessible as a consequence of maturational changes; rather, discovery procedures and processing mechanisms can also be affected by age-dependent changes.

Notice that the findings from neurolinguistic and psycholinguistic research do not merely lend support to the Fundamental Difference Hypothesis, they actually favour a stronger version of this approach to L2 acquisition in that they justify the claim that principled reasons speak against the assumption that L2 learners can ultimately attain native grammatical competence. That the vast majority of L2 learners never come close to native-like use of the target languages is too obvious to merit further discussion, and although one could speculate that many or all of them do have native-like knowledge but are not able to perform adequately, such an assumption is, to my knowledge, not seriously entertained in the literature on L2 acquisition. As mentioned above, the issue really is whether native-likeness is impossible to attain and whether even the so-called 'expert learners' who apparently behave like native speakers have not, in fact, attained native competence. At first sight, this appears to be an empirical question which would easily be answered by investigating these apparently perfect learners. For a number of reasons, however, it is particularly difficult to obtain empirical evidence which might yield a convincing answer. First of all, it will not suffice to analyse spontaneous speech, for learners might (consciously or unconsciously) avoid certain constructions; at any rate, comprehension also needs to be assessed. Secondly, since all surface manifestations of languages are learnable, expert learners can come very close to the target if they are particularly good at inductive learning. The issue, however, is whether their underlying grammatical knowledge converges with that of the respective native speakers. Thirdly, and most importantly, even subtle tests which assess comprehension as well as production and which aim at the underlying knowledge of speakers cannot be interpreted in a straightforward way in the absence of a set of valid criteria which would allow us to decide on native-likeness. Since languages are not homogeneous objects but are characterized by variation along a number of dimensions – regional (dialects), social (sociolects), situational (registers), and individual (idiolects), to mention only the most obvious ones – it is no simple matter to decide whether a particular result may be interpreted as falling within the variation space characterizing native knowledge. Not to mention the fact that individuals (mature native speakers as well as learners) do not necessarily behave in tests as they do in spontaneous speech.

Note that all this does not amount to saying that it is impossible to assess native-likeness, but it certainly requires carefully designed research methods, and it must cover multiple aspects of grammatical knowledge. The latter remark refers to the fact that, in contrast to native speakers, even particularly successful L2 learners tend to excel in only *some* areas (phonology *or* syntax *or* morphology, etc.); see Herschensohn (2000: 47) for a brief summary of such findings. This is to be expected if they are not guided by the LAD but are learning inductively, because learning in the traditional sense of the term typically yields variable degrees of success, depending on the learner, on the task and so on. Yet when we scrutinize the research literature for empirical evidence suggesting that expert learners really exist, that is, learners who excel across the board in multiple domains of grammar, the result is rather disappointing. Selinker (1972: 212) speculated that 5% of L2 learners might be qualified as perfect learners, and although he made it quite clear that this was merely an educated guess on his behalf, this figure has subsequently been referred to as if it had been established on the basis of scientific investigation. In reality, systematic empirical research on this issue only began to be carried out in the 1980s.

Coppieters (1987), for example, argued in his seminal paper that even exceptionally successful second language learners can be shown to differ from native speakers if carefully examined. He studied L1 English learners who had acquired French as adults and contrasted them to French native speakers, investigating various morphosyntactic phenomena. Coppieters (1987) concluded that the grammars of these exceptional learners differed from native grammars. Birdsong (1992b), however, after a critical in-depth discussion and a replication of this study reached substantially different conclusions; see also Birdsong (1992a, 1994), Hyltenstam and Abrahamsson (2000), Sorace (2003) or Birdsong (2004) who presents a state-of-the-art summary of some of the extensive literature on this topic. At this point I do not want to recapitulate this debate or review the arguments presented. Suffice it to say that Birdsong (1992b) is undoubtedly correct in his criticism of some methodological weaknesses of the study by Coppieters (1987). More importantly, as Birdsong (1992b) pointed out, Coppieters failed to distinguish between constructions reflecting principles of UG as opposed to language-specific regularities. Quite obviously, judgements concerning the latter are irrelevant when it comes to deciding whether native versus non-native-differences indeed reflect fundamental differences in the underlying grammatical knowledge. Birdsong's (1992b) study also revealed that L2 learners differed significantly from native speakers in at least some aspects. In fact, as is stated by Herschensohn (2000: 176), these as well as subsequent studies seem to demonstrate that expert learners are better qualified as 'near-native' than as 'native-like' speakers. In other words, expert learners are merely vastly more successful in some domains of grammars than even very advanced learners; they nevertheless still exhibit differences when compared to native speakers. Paradis (2009: 135) phrases a similar result somewhat more bluntly when he writes

> Some authors emphasize overall deficiencies in ultimate attainment, others focus on cases of high achievement on several tasks – but whether one considers the late second language implicit competence to be half-full or half-empty, the implication is that it is not full.

It is only very recently that the issue of ultimate attainment in second language acquisition has begun to be studied in a fashion which meets most of the requirements listed above. Up to now the most comprehensive and sophisticated research enterprise of this sort has been carried out at the University of Stockholm, directed by Kenneth Hyltenstam and Niclas Abrahamsson. They investigated native-likeness in 195 self-identified native-like speakers of Swedish whose first language was Spanish, age of onset of acquisition (AOA) ranging from <1 to 47 years. Abrahamsson and Hyltenstam (2009) grouped them according to AOA:

1. ≤ 5, early childhood;
2. 6–11, late childhood;
3. 12–17, adolescence;
4. 18–23, early adulthood;
5. ≥ 24, later adulthood.

These subjects as well as a control group of Swedish native speakers were then judged by ten native Swedish judges. Since two of the twenty participants of the control group were judged as native speakers by only nine of the judges (average score 9.9), equivalent ratings for the L2 learners (nine or ten judges) were considered as sufficient for classification as native-likeness. The average scores for the five groups amounted to:

1. 8.3,
2. 7.6,
3. 5.1,
4. 1.6,
5. 0.4.

The difference between early and late childhood learners and adolescents on the one hand and adolescents and early and later adulthood learners on the other were statistically significant. Only a small minority (6%, all of them adolescents) of those who had acquired Swedish at age 12 or later, but a majority (62%) of those with AOA before that age were perceived as native speakers. A group of forty-one (thirty-one childhood and ten adolescent learners, AOA 1–19), a subset of those who were judged as native speakers by six or more judges, were selected to be scrutinized in linguistic detail with a cognitively demanding battery of twenty highly complex tasks. Abrahamsson and Hyltenstam (2009) reported on the results obtained on the basis of ten of these tasks, relating to speech production and perception (partly in noise, either increasing babble or white noise), grammaticality judgements (written and auditory, referring to subject–verb inversion, reflexive possessive pronouns, placement of sentence adverbs in relative clauses, gender and number agreement), grammatical, lexical and semantic inferencing, and formulaic language use (idioms and proverbs).

Only two (AOA 3 and 7) or three[5] participants of these tests scored within the range of the fifteen native speakers of a control group on all ten tests. On the other hand, native-likeness was attained for each of the features tested by several of the learners. This confirms the claim that every surface property of a language is learnable. At the same time these results cast doubts on the assumption that onset of acquisition during early childhood will necessarily result in native-likeness. In fact, the probability of achieving overall linguistic native-likeness is extremely low even for childhood learners and zero for late learners (AOA 13 or later). It should also be kept in mind that Abrahamsson and Hyltenstam (2009) were primarily concerned with the linguistic performance of the self-identified native-like learners of Swedish, including their grammaticality or rather acceptability judgements. Even so, the more subtle differences in comparison to native speakers may be extremely difficult to detect; Abrahamsson and Hyltenstam (2009: 291) mention the possibility of 'non-perceivable non-nativeness'. At any rate, as we have seen repeatedly throughout this volume, native-like performance need not reflect native grammatical competence. Moreover, in order to answer the question of whether maturational changes make it impossible for L2 learners to attain native competence, it would be necessary to reinterpret the findings by Abrahamsson and Hyltenstam (2009) in terms of the more constrained version of the Critical Period Hypothesis and its possible consequences for grammatical development (see section 6.1). Not all the phenomena scrutinized in the Stockholm study are predicted to be subject to maturational changes, for example semantic inferencing or formulaic language use. On the other hand, not all core syntactic properties have as yet been examined. Note that grammaticality judgements proved to be one of the domains where native-likeness seems to be most difficult to attain. Only 65% (written presentation) and 58% (auditory presentation) of the childhood learners and merely 50% of the adolescent learners obtained results in this domain which fell within the range of the native control group.

This is undoubtedly an area in which more research along the lines of the Stockholm study is required; as Abrahamsson and Hyltenstam (2009: 293) observe, 'research on nativelikeness has only begun'. But in view of the fact that so few of the learners studied are able to perform in native-like fashion, the only possible conclusion at this point in time is that the available evidence does not support the claim that native grammatical competence can be attained by L2 learners and that our prediction has thus not been falsified and can therefore be maintained – until further notice.

6.5 Suggested readings and topics for discussion

Suggested readings

The discussion of child second language acquisition is based on the assumption that the simultaneous acquisition of two or more languages from birth qualifies as an instance of bilingual first language acquisition. For more information on this issue:

Meisel, J. M. 2004. 'The bilingual child', in T. K. Bhatia and W. C. Ritchie (eds.), *The handbook of bilingualism*, pp. 91–113. Oxford: Blackwell.

Language processing is an essential aspect of first and second language acquisition, although not as thoroughly researched as the properties of learners' linguistic knowledge. The following two papers provide valuable information on L2 production and parsing routines.

Pienemann, M. 1998b. 'Developmental dynamics in L1 and L2 acquisition: Processability theory and generative entrenchment', *Bilingualism: Language and Cognition* 1: 1–20.

Clahsen, H. and C. Felser 2006b. 'How native-like is non-native language processing?', *TRENDS in Cognitive Sciences* 10: 564–70.

The problem of whether L2 learners can attain native-like success in using the second language is carefully investigated in a large-scale study on which the following paper reports.

Abrahamsson, N. and K. Hyltenstam 2009. 'Age of onset and nativelikeness in a second language: Listener perception versus linguistic scrutiny', *Language Learning* 59: 249–306.

Topics for discussion

- Try to gather as much information about critical period effects in other species. Most importantly, summarize the criteria which define the domains in which behaviour is subject to such effects. Based on such insights from the life sciences, assess critically the claims to be found in this chapter in favour of multiple sensitive phases in the course of grammatical development.
- The decision whether child second language acquisition resembles adult L2 acquisition rather than monolingual or bilingual first language development hinges on which criteria are employed in order to identify similarities and differences between types of acquisition. Order of emergence, frequency of use, frequency of target-deviant forms or constructions, or types of constructions attested in the speech of learner types are some of the criteria used in the research literature. Compare different studies on child L2 acquisition, for example those in the volume edited by Haznedar and Gavruseva (2008), and determine which criteria are used and how they correlate with the respective authors' conclusions on similarities and differences between cL2 on the one hand and aL2 and L1 on the other.
- According to the Processability Hypothesis presented in section 6.3, acquisition sequences can be explained in terms of L2 learners' ability to process structural properties at a given point in development. Contrast the analysis by Pienemann (1998) of the acquisition of German word order (see Table 6.3 in section 6.3) with attempts to explain this sequence in grammatical terms, referring to the studies discussed in chapter 3 and/or with the explanation offered by duPlessis, Solin, Travis and White (1987) discussed in chapter 4 (section 4.4).
- The most comprehensive and most detailed study currently available investigating ultimate attainment by second language learners, the Stockholm study on which Abrahamsson and Hyltenstam (2009) report, suggests that the most important changes happen at around age 12 (onset of acquisition). If this is confirmed by further research, it could be interpreted as corroborating the proposal by Lenneberg (1967), according to which the critical age range is the one at around puberty. Since the findings by Abrahamsson and Hyltenstam (2009) refer primarily to the performance of L2 learners, one could argue instead that the ability to develop native-like grammatical knowledge fades out earlier but that child L2 learners can still acquire native-like performance during the subsequent period of stabilization mentioned towards the end of section 6.2. Do you view this as a plausible explanation? Try to present arguments in favour of or against one of these two lines of argument.

7 A (tentative) theory of language acquisition – L1, 2L1 and L2

Language acquisition is something that happens to children. It is not a task which they need to actively or consciously pursue, nor do they require special training, and they do not have to rely on coaching efforts from their caretakers. Mere exposure to their linguistic environment in interaction with their caretakers and peers suffices for them to acquire the language, and if they are exposed to more than one language, they are able to acquire each one without much apparent effort. The same cannot be said, however, about second language acquisition, as myriads of L2 learners who have failed to acquire native competence in the languages they were exposed to in either naturalistic or classroom settings can testify. These and similar observations suggest that children acquiring their languages from birth can rely on a Language Making Capacity which seems to become partially or totally inaccessible in the course of subsequent development. In fact, this consideration was the starting point of our discussion, defined in chapter 1 as a quest for the LAD. Our goal has been to discover essential properties of the LAD as they are revealed in first language development and to inquire about its fate as it is evidenced by child and adult second language acquisition. This enterprise aspires to a deeper and more comprehensive understanding of the human Language Making Capacity and ultimately of the language faculty.

The purpose of this final chapter is to highlight the major results obtained in the discussion of the previous chapters and to ask whether these goals have indeed been reached. I will first summarize very briefly findings concerning parallels and differences between acquisition types. Interestingly, there exists little controversy about these facts. The questions of how they should be interpreted and what they tell us about the fate of the LAD, however, touch upon highly controversial issues. In section 7.2 I will outline the picture which emerges from the discussion in this volume. In section 7.3, in lieu of a conclusion, I offer some thoughts and raise some questions about the nature of L2 knowledge and indirectly about the human Language Making Capacity.

7.1 Similarities and differences across types of language acquisition

The view of first language development as a process through which children engaged in communicative interaction acquire the language to which they are exposed in a seemingly effortless fashion is strongly confirmed by a vast amount of research investigating the acquisition of numerous languages. Focusing on grammatical development, it has been demonstrated that children unfailingly attain full knowledge of the grammatical system and that the developmental process exhibits important similarities across individuals and across languages. This is all the more remarkable since significant differences undoubtedly exist in what children bring to the task of acquisition (intelligence, personality, attitudes and so forth) and in the acquisition settings. L1 acquisition is, furthermore, believed to happen at a fast rate. Although the empirical underpinnings of this claim are somewhat shaky because a reliable yardstick against which to measure the overall pace of L1 development is not available, specific grammatical phenomena are indeed acquired rapidly, as is evidenced by abrupt changes in children's linguistic behaviour. Success, uniformity and fast acquisition rates have thus been identified as defining characteristics of grammatical development in the first language. Since the discussion in this volume focuses on the *process* of language acquisition, it has mainly been concerned with the uniformity of that process. One of the most important insights of language acquisition research during the past decades is the finding that grammatical development proceeds through invariant developmental sequences, that is, that the acquisition of crucial grammatical properties follows an order which is largely the same across individuals (cf. Brown 1973). These sequences can therefore serve as the most important, albeit not the sole, criterion defining developmental uniformity.

What has been said so far about L1 acquisition refers to monolingual acquisition. As suggested in chapter 1 (section 1.3), important insights are likely to be gained by contrasting L2 and monolingual L1 with a third type of acquisition, the simultaneous acquisition of two or more languages. If, for example, bilingual children exhibit the same developmental sequences as the monolingual children in their respective languages, this constitutes strong evidence in support of the claim that the two types of acquisition are not qualitatively different, in spite of the fact that more than one language is present in bilingual learners' environment and in their minds. Findings by the large and steadily increasing number of studies on child bilingualism carried out over the past thirty years indeed support the conclusion that simultaneous acquisition of languages from birth can be qualified as bilingual first language acquisition (Meisel (1989)); cf. de Houwer (1995) or Meisel (2001, 2004) for state-of-the-art summaries of this research. The term 'bilingual L1 acquisition' emphasizes the fact that the development of each language of the bilingual child proceeds in the same way and leads to the same kind of grammatical competence as in monolingual children.

Two issues must be distinguished when searching for evidence supporting these claims: firstly, whether bilinguals differentiate the grammatical systems of their ambient languages from early on and, secondly, whether these systems develop independently during subsequent phases. The former is of particular importance, for if it was the case that bilinguals initially develop a single mental system for the languages they acquire, such a *fusion* of grammars might later on be difficult to disentangle and could thus have long-lasting effects in that learners might follow developmental paths different from those of the monolinguals.

Empirical support for the differentiation hypothesis became available in the late 1980s (see Genesee 1989 or Meisel 1989), and it has led to a broad consensus on this issue (cf. summaries of this research by de Houwer 1995 and Köppe 1997). As an example, we can briefly look again at the acquisition of phenomena reflecting the verb-second (V2) effect, the structural property found, for example, in Germanic languages, dealt with repeatedly in this volume. Remember that in V2 languages the finite verb is placed in the second structural position of the sentence, that is, if some constituent other than the subject is placed clause-initially, the subject follows the finite verb. Given that young children frequently use constructions beginning with a deictic expression like 'there', German *da*, French *là*, or with some other type of adverbial, examples of this sort appear at early points of acquisition. A number of studies investigated this phenomenon in different corpora documenting the acquisition of German simultaneously with a non-V2 language like French, Italian, Portuguese, or English. The results show unambiguously that children place the finite verb in second position in such constructions in German main clauses and in third position in the other languages. Moreover, already during the earliest period of multi-word utterances, one finds that bilingual children use clause-final position of verbs in German, an OV language, but not in VO languages like French or Portuguese. We can therefore conclude that parameterized properties of the functional heads T and COMP as well as the settings of the OV/VO and the Verb Movement Parameter have all been acquired very early, and, more importantly, that these parameters are set to their appropriate values although these languages differ in this respect. In addition, in French, where the relative order of verbs and objects depends on the clitic/non-clitic status of the object, this distinction is also made from early on, but it is never carried over to the other language. Finally, it has been shown that word order patterns specific to child usage in these languages, and commonly attested in monolingual corpora, are never used in German; for example VOS order appears in monolingual child L1 French and in French utterances of French–German bilinguals, but not in their German utterances.

What matters for the present discussion is that the differences in word order patterns used in the two languages of bilingual children emerge as soon as these start using multi-word utterances, usually around age 1;10 when their MLU attains a value of approximately 1.75. In other words, the average utterance, at this point of development, contains less than two words. For obvious reasons, it is not possible to establish an earlier moment in linguistic development at which reasonable generalizations could be made concerning the acquisition of syntax. One may thus conclude that the differentiation of grammatical systems happens very early.

In summary then, the available evidence favours very strongly the differentiation hypothesis. Morphosyntactic systems can be shown to be differentiated by children acquiring two languages simultaneously as soon as the earliest pieces of empirical evidence for a productive use of syntax and morphology become available. Note that most of the studies dealing with these questions are based on data from the production of spontaneous speech. It is very likely that more extensive research on language comprehension will be able to show that differentiation of grammatical systems occurs even earlier than towards the end of the second year. Moreover, although more research is needed, analyses of phonological development in bilinguals suggest that differentiation of phonological systems happens with similar ease and that it precedes chronologically the separation of syntactic systems. In fact, it is not implausible to assume that language differentiation is initiated and enhanced by phonological bootstrapping into two distinct systems.

The claim that the simultaneous acquisition of two or more languages can be qualified as first language development in more than one language is, however, also based on the assumption that the course of development in each of the languages of bilingual children does not differ qualitatively from the acquisition of the respective languages by monolinguals. If this is correct, bilinguals should proceed through the same developmental sequences as monolinguals in their respective languages. Early differentiation of grammars suggests that this should be possible since it implies that parameters are set to the values required by the different target languages. The necessity of parameter 'resetting' therefore does not arise. But this insight does not yet settle the issue conclusively, because it does not rule out the possibility of interdependent developments during subsequent acquisition phases. In other words, cross-linguistic influence might determine the course of acquisition in the two languages of bilingual children. Paradis and Genesee (1996) raised this issue of interdependent versus autonomous grammatical development, pointing out that interdependence can manifest itself in three ways: as transfer, acceleration or delay. It could thus cause grammatical phenomena of one language to be implemented in the grammar of the other one, or it could cause them to be acquired earlier or later than in the course of acquisition by monolinguals. If acceleration or delay of this type is indeed possible, it could lead to a reordering of otherwise invariant developmental sequences, and this would count as a qualitative change.

The possibility of interdependent developments triggered a heated and ongoing debate in the literature on child bilingualism. Note that Paradis and Genesee (1996) themselves did not find evidence supporting the idea that the grammars of bilinguals are subject to effects of cross-linguistic influence, either as transfer or as acceleration or delay. Others, however, like Döpke (1992) or Hulk and Müller (2000), did find effects of cross-linguistic interaction. It is important to note that these authors confirmed the hypothesis of early grammatical differentiation and that, to my knowledge, defendants of the interdependence hypothesis do not question the claim that children acquiring two languages simultaneously attain native grammatical competence identical to that of the respective monolinguals in both languages.[1] In other words, interdependency effects seem to emerge only temporarily, and they appear to be quantitative rather than qualitative in nature (cf. Meisel 2007b for a more detailed discussion of these issues). If this is correct, possible interdependent developments do not constitute evidence against the claim that the simultaneous acquisition of two languages qualifies as first language development in each language. At any rate, I am not aware of any study arguing that the developmental sequences familiar from monolingual L1 acquisition are substantially altered in bilingual development as a result of cross-linguistic influence. In fact, although developmental acceleration or delay may occur, the overall rate of acquisition is comparable to that of monolinguals, that is, it falls within the range of what is generally regarded as 'normal' for monolinguals (see Meisel 2004). We may thus conclude that bilingual acquisition is not qualitatively different from monolingual first language development and leads to the same kind of grammatical competence.

Adult second language acquisition differs in all these respects from both monolingual and bilingual first language development. This statement should not be a matter of much controversy. It reflects the experience of countless second language learners, and it is in tune with the wealth of facts amassed by many years of L2 research. The moot point concerns the question of which conclusions may be drawn from these observations, viz. how they can be explained. Before I return to this debate in the following section, let me mention again the facts which need to be accounted for by any theory of language acquisition aiming at their explanation. This can be done in a concise fashion since all the relevant points have been addressed in the preceding chapters.

If successful attainment of native grammatical knowledge is a defining characteristic of L1, this is certainly not true of L2 acquisition. That the vast majority of L2 learners never come close to native-like use of the target languages is too obvious to merit further discussion, and although one could speculate that some or many of them do have native-like knowledge but are not able to perform adequately, such an assumption is highly implausible and, to my knowledge, not entertained in the literature on L2 acquisition. The only point of disagreement concerns the question of whether it is impossible for principled reasons to acquire native grammatical knowledge in the L2, as I argued in chapter 6 (section 6.4), or whether this is 'only' true of the vast majority of L2 learners. Defendants of the latter claim will have to offer a non-ad hoc explanation of what distinguishes the happy few from the others.

The rate of acquisition is, as I have argued repeatedly, the least revealing property when searching for parallels and differences between acquisition types. This is mainly due to the fact that it is difficult, if not impossible, to identify an independent scale which would allow us to measure the pace of overall grammatical development. Nevertheless, if we limit our discussion to particular grammatical phenomena, we find that some are acquired very rapidly in L1 acquisition, as is evidenced by abrupt changes in the use of finite verb forms, agreement markers, subjects, word order and so on. In L2 acquisition we witness a much more protracted process. What children achieve in days or weeks may take adult L2 learners months or years. These striking differences in the rate of emergence of grammatical devices definitely require an explanation.

The uniformity of the acquisition process is, in my view, the most impressive feature of both monolingual and bilingual L1 acquisition, and it is what distinguishes sharply (2)L1 and L2 acquisition. As we saw in chapters 3 to 6, L2 acquisition may also exhibit uniformity in the course of acquisition. I believe, in fact, that the discovery of invariant developmental sequences in untutored L2 acquisition is a particularly important insight, and some of these findings, for example the acquisition sequence for German word order (cf. chapter 4), count among the most robust empirical facts to be explained by L2 theories. Importantly, however, such invariant L2 sequences have not been detected in all the grammatical domains where they are attested in L1 development, for example not for the acquisition of inflectional morphology, and those which have been established in L2 differ in important ways from the ones encountered in L1 acquisition of the same languages.

There is consensus that first and second language acquisition differ in what characterizes the 'initial state'. The exact nature of these differences is, however, a matter of controversy again, but researchers working within the UG framework seem to agree that L2 learners start out, generally speaking, with 'more structure', arguably relying on functional categories where L1 utterances lack them. This can undoubtedly be attributed to L1 influence, even if the idea of 'full' transfer is not warranted by empirical findings. Importantly, L1 transfer entails the necessity of reanalysis and restructuring of grammars. I have argued that the differences between L1 and L2 sequences cannot be fully explained by the hypothesis that the point of departure is different, but this is, of course, a statement which goes beyond the description of facts. It is certainly an issue to be addressed when attempting to explain L1 and L2 acquisition. The same holds true for the problem of what role one wants to attribute to transfer at the initial state. More transfer not only requires more restructuring, it also means less uniformity across L2 learners overall, and similarities between those sharing the same L1 – a questionable point, not sufficiently documented by advocates of massive transfer.

Another possibility to establish parallels or differences between types of acquisition is to search for erroneous or target-conforming constructions which are either shared across the acquisition types or which surface in only some of them. I have discussed a number of these throughout this volume, for example German analysed as underlying VO by (some?) L2 learners, but not in L1; raising of non-finite verbs in L2 but not in L1; L2 item-by-item learning in cases where L1 children generalize over classes of items; different treatment of bound versus free morphemes in L2, but not in L1. Independently of how we attempt to account for such differences – as transfer effects, missing surface inflections, inductive learning and so forth – an adequate theory of acquisition must have a story to tell about them, and it needs to explain why acquisition types differ in these respects.

It is important to keep in mind that the observed differences do not merely indicate a lack of uniformity in L2 relative to L1 acquisition; they also show that certain domains of grammar develop differently in adult second language acquisition; crucially, we find significantly more variation across individuals within

L2 than within L1. The latter observation refers to all aspects mentioned above: ultimate attainment, rate of acquisition and uniformity, that is, the course and success of the acquisition of particular phenomena.

Let us finally have a brief look at child L2, the fourth acquisition type. If we include only learners who were first exposed to the L2 before age 7, as suggested in chapter 6 (section 6.2), it is difficult to make firm claims about the issues discussed here, for we still lack the research necessary to answer our questions. We have seen that cL2 grammatical knowledge differs in a number of crucial properties from that of (2)L1 learners, but although there are reasons to believe that the respective domains of grammar will be affected permanently (see chapter 6), the empirical evidence is too scant to confirm this assumption with confidence. If, however, age of onset of acquisition happens after age 7, learners resemble adult L2 learners in most relevant aspects, and increasingly so with later AOA. Their use of the L2 at the initial state as well as the acquisition sequences detectable in the data of these learners are largely identical to what we know from aL2 (see, for example, Pienemann 1981). This is why they were grouped with aL2 learners in section 6.2. Only their faster rate of overall acquisition distinguishes them from adults. This is also true of young cL2 learners at AOA between 4 and 7. Yet in acquiring some domains' grammatical properties, even young cL2 learners tend to behave like aL2 learners and proceed through protracted learning periods. Consequently, we can conclude that, in the acquisition of at least some features, cL2 and aL2 resemble each other more than they resemble (2)L1 children. Importantly, cL2 and aL2 learners also resemble each other in the considerable amount of cross-individual and intra-individual variation in their use of L2 knowledge. In sum, cL2 shares crucial properties with aL2, although perhaps to variable degrees, depending on the age of onset of acquisition of the L2.

7.2 Exploring the limits of the LAD

Language is a species-specific endowment of humans. Few would contradict this statement, and what we know about the properties of human languages – not least due to insights gained by linguistic research carried out in the framework of Universal Grammar – strongly confirms this view. The minds of children are not *tabulae rasae*. Investigations of language development, like the ones reported on in chapter 2, leave little doubt that children are predisposed to acquire language; rather, they have access to knowledge which determines how they analyse the data to which they are exposed. Linguistics tries to capture the essence of this a priori knowledge about formal properties of languages in a theory of Universal Grammar, comprising grammatical principles and parameters. The comment at the beginning of this chapter that language acquisition 'happens' to children was meant to convey that exposure to the data suffices to trigger linguistic development constrained by UG. It is in this sense that UG can be conceived as a crucial component of the LAD, the language acquisition device, yet UG should not be equated with the LAD (see Carroll 2001: 113).

In order to be able to account for the observable facts in linguistic development, any theory of language acquisition must distinguish between what shapes possible linguistic objects (UG) and what enables the child to acquire, process and store these objects as parts of the grammar of the language to be acquired. This includes what I have referred to as discovery principles (section 2.2), as well as processing mechanisms, to the extent that these are universal in nature (cf. section 6.3), and also learning mechanisms required for the acquisition of non-UG-constrained properties of particular languages. What these principles and mechanisms have in common is that they are domain-specific, referring to abstract grammatical properties of linguistic objects. My suggestion has been to define the LAD in such a way as to include all language-specific principles and mechanisms, that is, the ones just mentioned as well as the ones in UG. The human Language Making Capacity, in turn, comprises not only the LAD (including UG), but also domain-general cognitive operations which subserve language acquisition. What matters here is not the particular terminological choice but that this tripartite distinction is made. If, therefore, the quest for the LAD has been singled out as a major goal of the discussion in this volume, it attributes a crucial role to UG without limiting its scope to the UG-or-not-UG alternative.

As for L1 development, the importance of the LAD as a guiding force can hardly be overestimated. All the characteristics presented in chapter 2 and addressed repeatedly in the subsequent ones – most importantly ultimate success in attaining native grammatical competence and uniformity of development from the initial through the steady, mature state of grammatical knowledge – follow naturally from the assumption that this process is guided by a universal acquisition device. Because of its universal nature, one should not expect individuals or groups of learners to behave in substantially different ways. The very limited variability of the developmental process across learners confirms this expectation. Moreover, abrupt changes in the use of a number of grammatical devices corroborate the hypothesis that these are instances where a priori knowledge is triggered, that is, that this is the result of parameter setting rather than of learning new, previously unavailable knowledge. Most importantly for the current line of argument, the observed invariant developmental sequences can be accounted for in grammatical terms, thus confirming that the acquisition process follows an underlying logic which is grammatical in nature – as was to be expected, given the hypothesized nature of the LAD with UG as its core component. Let me add that my claim is not that only an acquisition theory comprising a device like the LAD can account for the facts referred to above. Rather, I am arguing that this approach is capable of dealing with the observed facts and can therefore be regarded as an adequate component of an acquisition theory.

The LAD really is a rather robust device, as is evidenced by the fact that it enables all children to develop full grammatical knowledge of their target languages, irrespective of considerable differences in their cognitive and social capacities and despite the heterogeneity of the settings in which acquisition happens. This robustness becomes even more evident when considering that the simultaneous acquisition of two or more languages is equally successful and exhibits no qualitative differences in comparison to monolingual L1 acquisition. Having to deal with several grammatical systems simultaneously clearly does not represent a serious challenge for the LAD. Moreover, in multilingual acquisition the amount of exposure to each of the languages is necessarily reduced as compared to monolingual L1. But this is not problematic for the acquisition device, either. Even in settings where one of the languages is clearly dominant, bilinguals are capable of developing native grammatical competence in the 'weaker' language (see Meisel 2007a for a detailed discussion of this phenomenon). Only if exposure to one language is drastically reduced does the LAD reach its limits, not surprisingly, one might add.

Although neither the task of dealing with more than one grammatical system simultaneously nor unfavourable acquisition settings or reduced exposure to the target languages prevent the LAD from operating fully successfully, maturational changes do. This, at least, is the hypothesis defended in this book. Following Smith and Tsimpli (1995), who claimed that the accessibility of parameterized principles is subject to maturational changes, I adopted a version of the Partial Access to UG hypothesis, according to which L1–L2 differences can be explained as resulting from the fact that parameter (re)setting is not possible for L2 learners. I should hasten to add that not all observable differences can necessarily be traced back to this one fundamental difference, although I do think that one can account for most of the ones discussed in this volume. I would also like to emphasize again that partial inaccessibility of UG principles does not imply that constructions related to these principles cannot be learned. Rather, my claim is that all surface properties of languages are learnable. This can be achieved by means of inductive learning, an option offered by the LAD anyway. Yet L2 learners have to resort to it in instances where children acquiring their first language attain the underlying knowledge as a result of parameter setting, triggered by the detection of the relevant structural cues in the input data. Finally, these L2 learning processes may fail to take into account the complete structural information characterizing the surface construction in question, relying instead on shallow structures – or merely on linear organization principles. In these cases, the resulting interlanguage construction is likely not to conform to principles of UG.

I believe that this approach to second language acquisition can account for the L2 properties discussed in the preceding chapters, and it can offer answers to the questions raised in the preceding section 7.1. The ideas briefly summarized here should therefore be incorporated into any theory of language acquisition which aims to explain first as well as second language acquisition. This is not to say that the explanations offered by this approach are the only possible ones, just as the LAD need not be the only way to explain L1 development. But I do think that the approach advocated here fares better in dealing with the observable facts of L2 acquisition than theories based on the assumption that principles of UG remain fully accessible over a learner's lifespan. In the remainder of this section, I will try to show briefly how this claim can be justified.

One basic fact which needs to be accounted for is that L2 acquisition also exhibits invariant aspects across learners, for example developmental sequences, although they differ from those in L1 acquisition. This suggests that even naturalistic, non-tutored L2 acquisition is guided by some kind of underlying mechanism, rather than proceeding in an erratic fashion. The question, however, is whether the noted differences justify the claim that the guiding acquisition mechanism is different. Since these differences concern invariant properties of grammatical development, that is, phenomena ascribed to the operating of principles of UG, first doubts are justified as to whether L2 acquisition follows completely the same developmental logic, and although it would be too simplistic to conclude that partial identity of surface phenomena must be due to partial access to the acquisition device, this congruity is in accordance with our assumptions, whereas an approach postulating full access would have to provide additional arguments explaining the differences.

A further and particularly significant fact which any theory of acquisition needs to account for is that few or no second language learners are fully successful in acquiring a native grammatical competence. They certainly do not acquire the full knowledge of the target grammar without effort and by 'mere exposure' (Lenneberg 1967) in the course of communicative interaction. There can thus be no doubt that the language learning capacity is subject to age-related changes. In fact, cL2 acquisition also shows very clearly such effects when compared to (2)L1 acquisition on the one hand and aL2 on the other. I adopted the view that they are primarily due to maturational changes in the brain. Quite obviously, this does not exclude the possibility of other causes for age-dependent changes. On the contrary, social-psychological characteristics of individuals are known to change over the life-span and affect the person's approach to language acquisition (see, for example, Clahsen, Meisel and Pienemann 1983). In the present context, the crucial point is that the LAD is subject to maturational changes, a claim which leaves little room for doubt, given that it is supported not only by linguistic analyses but also by what we know about linguistic processing of L1 and L2 in the brain; cf. chapter 6 (section 6.1). What requires further discussion and more research is the question of what are the exact effects for the LAD, caused by maturation. Although this also applies to the hypothesis that the accessibility of parameterized principles dwindles during the course of maturation, it does cover the facts revealed by behavioural as well as neuroimaging studies.

Importantly, the claim that parameter setting becomes impossible in L2 acquisition is strongly supported by empirical findings concerning the course of development in the two types of acquisition. As I have argued at some length in chapter 5, the entire debate about UG accessibility only makes sense if it can be based on empirical evidence allowing us to distinguish between UG-guided development as opposed to learning in the traditional sense of the term. The differentiating criteria which I defined, most importantly the clustering of superficially unrelated phenomena depending on specific parameter settings and the rapid and abrupt emergence of grammatical devices indicating successful acquisition of grammatical knowledge, unambiguously distinguish between monolingual and bilingual first language development on the one hand and second language acquisition on the other. Further and perhaps other criteria can and should indeed be considered. But for the time being, only the Partial Access to UG hypothesis is compatible with the currently available knowledge whereas the Full Access hypothesis requires modifications of the notion of parameter, for example 'gradual' or 'partial resetting' (Herschensohn 2000), which effectively renders it indistinguishable from inductive learning.

Moreover, lack of uniformity is also a consequence following from the impossibility of new parameter settings in L2. Uniformity in L1 was explained as resulting from guidance by the LAD, most importantly by being constrained by principles of UG. Where this is impossible, learners can resort to other means of learning the surface properties detected in the primary linguistic data, inductive learning being an obvious choice. Non-UG-constrained learning, however, is shaped by a variety of learning and processing strategies, and this is precisely what explains the considerable amount of interlanguage variability across and even within learners. I have shown that the resulting linguistic expressions do not necessarily conform to UG principles. Neither this range of variability nor the occurrence of constructions violating UG principles are in accordance with the assumption of full access to UG, not even if it could be shown that the initial state of L2 acquisition was indeed characterized by full transfer from the L1 grammar, for the theory of UG predicts that in case of competing principles, UG will prevail. The Full Access to UG hypothesis is thus incompatible with the attested cases in which processing mechanisms or, more generally, performance factors override grammatical principles determining formal properties of linguistic expressions encountered in L2 speech or their order of emergence in the language use of L2 learners.

In my view, there can be no doubt that such instances do occur in L2 interlanguage, and I discussed some of them in this volume, for example German verb placement in negative constructions (section 3.3) or in relation to objects and adverbial expressions (section 4.4), or more generally raising of non-finite verbs to the head of TP or of CP. The empirical facts are generally agreed upon. Yet defendants of the Full Access to UG hypothesis argue in these cases that violations of UG principles can be avoided by adopting a different analysis of the phenomenon in question or by assigning to the observable surface properties a different interpretation on a more abstract level (cf. the Missing Surface Inflection Hypothesis). I do not find these alternative analyses convincing; see, for example, the discussion in section 4.4 of chapter 4. Irrespective of the plausibility of such solutions, the fact remains that L2 acquisition differs in these respects from L1 development and that only L2 learners exhibit the kinds of constructions which oblige researchers to construe special treatments of the incriminated phenomena. An example is the case of German verb placement where L2 learners analyse

German as an SVO language whereas L1 children never entertain this hypothesis; they rather treat German and other languages of this type as OV as soon as they use multi-word utterances. Recall that transfer from the first language grammar is not a satisfactory explanation for these facts, as the discussion in section 4.3 demonstrated. At any rate, even in cases where surface properties of the L2 or knowledge possibly transferred from the L1 appear to instigate L2 learners to adopt options deviating from the ones of target grammar, UG principles should prevail – and this is what happens in L1. It does not occur in L2. This speaks forcefully against the alleged full accessibility of UG principles for L2 learners.

In conclusion, all the observations about the course of second language acquisition which I summarized and reviewed in this chapter are in accordance with the assumptions of partial access to UG, and they confirm the predictions following from this hypothesis. According to the arguments presented in section 5.1 where I discussed various scenarios representing the possible role of UG in L2, it follows from this conclusion that full access to UG does not offer plausible explanations for the relevant facts. Let me add that I believe that Flynn (1996: 122) is undoubtedly right in rejecting approaches which 'interpret *any* differences that emerge between L1 and L2 acquisition to mean that the two must be fundamentally different and therefore *cannot* be accounted for within the same theoretical framework'. Conversely, however, it is equally implausible to assume that similarities necessarily indicate that the same type of knowledge base is drawn upon and that this can only be accounted for in terms of UG principles.

7.3 The hybrid nature of second language knowledge

Language is a species-specific endowment of humans, distinguishing them from other living beings, and mental grammars (I-language) are specific to the human mind. Phrased in terms of the theory of Universal Grammar, this means that these knowledge systems conform to the principles of UG, designed to capture all and only those properties which human languages have in common and which can therefore explain the nature of this species-specific faculty. If a grammar, in the technical sense of the term, is the UG-constrained knowledge which children develop of a natural language, and if children's Language Acquisition Device becomes partially inaccessible in successive language acquisition, the question necessarily arises whether the knowledge acquired by second language learners qualifies as a grammar of a natural language. In what follows I will argue that this question should be answered positively and that L2 learners' *hybrid systems* are indeed natural grammars.

It may be useful to recall at this point that the discussion of parallels and differences between first and second language acquisition revealed substantial similarities which can be argued to reflect identical types of grammatical knowledge. The fact that the discussion focused on differences between populations of learners should not deflect attention from this finding. The differences are claimed to be fundamental in nature, given that an acquisition mechanism which is of prime importance in L1 development, parameter setting, is not available to L2 learners. It also follows naturally from this approach that non-parameterized UG principles and processing mechanisms not adapted to a particular language apply to L2 acquisition in much the same way as to L1 development. The same applies to properties of approximative L2 systems derived from previously acquired grammatical knowledge. Consequently, L2 knowledge and acquisition processes are in large part domain-specific and share with native grammars the crucial property of structure dependency.

The potentially problematic parts of L2 learners' linguistic knowledge are the ones resulting from inductive learning of features of the target language which in L1 contain structural information triggering the setting of parameters to their appropriate values. The problem is not that acquisition happens via inductive learning, involving considerable effort, item-by-item learning, trial and error, and so forth. After all, input-based learning also occurs in L1 acquisition, and it is a necessary part of acquisition theory even under the assumption of full access to UG. However, if inductive learning produces in some instances mental representations of formal properties of the target language which involve only shallow structures or even outright flat ones relying merely on linear organization principles, the question arises as to whether the result of this learning process still qualifies as a mental grammar rather than as some kind of an ersatz solution. The delicate point concerns the implementation of constraints which do not refer to the (full) hierarchical structure in which the respective linguistic objects appear. Structure dependency is, however, the constitutive property of human language. In fact, recursion generating hierarchical configurations is what Hauser, Chomsky and Fitch (2002: 1569) defined in their seminal paper as the 'only uniquely human component of the faculty of language', characterizing what they call the 'faculty of language in the narrow sense'. If grammars generating human languages necessarily comprise grammatical principles exhibiting sensitivity to structural principles in non-local contexts, this does not entail the necessity that every linguistic expression shares this kind of structural property. In fact, Hauser *et al.* (2002: 1573) emphasize that the faculty of language 'in the broad sense' contains a wide variety of cognitive mechanisms, and this is undoubtedly also true of the LMC and, of course, of the specific mental grammars instantiated when this faculty is activated in the course of first language development. Moreover, these authors do not exclude the possibility that children use domain-general mechanisms in L1 acquisition (2002: 1576) or that local dependencies (2002: 1577) play a role in grammars. What matters is that systems of this sort alone do not suffice to capture any human languages. But there is no reason why principles contained in linguistic systems should not refer to both, local as well as hierarchical relationships – rather, it is implausible to assume that they would not do so since precedence, succession, adjacency, initialization, finalization and the like, are essential ordering principles of language.

I would like to add, on a more speculative note, that a number of observations suggest that local dependencies precede hierarchical ones ontogenetically as well as phylogenetically. Remember that the discussion in chapter 2 led to the conclusion that during early phases of L1 development child language does not yet show evidence of a structure-dependent hierarchical organization of utterances. Rather, children can be argued to compute linear properties of language, for example prosodic cues related to linear segmentation, early multi-word utterances as linear concatenations of elements and so forth. This may be reminiscent of the idea of grammaticalization of an ontogenetically preceding pragmatic mode (Givón 1979). As argued in chapter 2 (section 2.2), no convincing argument has been presented so far, demonstrating that the developmentally earlier mode of organizing speech actually disappears. Similarly, we can assume that principles relying on local dependencies remain available once hierarchical organization has become available. If this is correct, organizing the speech chain without taking into account the complete set of hierarchical dependencies is not as alien a solution as one might have thought; moreover, it is perhaps not implausible to assume that L2 learners may in some cases fall back to the early L1 mechanisms.

A similar scenario has, in fact, been developed for the phylogenetic evolution of language. Jackendoff (2001: 569), in his review of a book by Calvin and Bickerton, writes that

> Derek Bickerton is responsible for what I consider one of the few good ideas in the literature on evolution of language: his proposal (Bickerton 1990) that language evolved in two stages, the second of which is the modern language faculty. The first stage is what he calls 'protolanguage' ... What makes B's proposal of interest is his claim that protolanguage did not go away when modern language evolved. Rather, it still surfaces in situations when full language is either not yet developed (as in early child language) or disrupted ... Thus, these situations function as sort of living fossils of earlier stages of human evolution.
>
> (A somewhat similar proposal appears in Givón 1979.)

Bickerton (1990b) refers indeed to early child language as one illustration of protolanguage (see section 2.2) which is argued to make use of linear order. Jackendoff points out that modern language uses linear order intersententially and that it is directly accessible in the surface signal and therefore learnable. 'Hence there is no reason evolution should throw it away as a source of structure inside the sentence. That is, we should see phrasal hierarchy as *supplementing* linear order rather than *supplanting* it' (Jackendoff 2001: 571). Hierarchical phrase structure is, according to Bickerton's approach, the innovation which distinguishes modern syntax from protolanguage. In the present context I am not concerned with the details of this proposal concerning linguistic evolution. What matters here is that ontogenetic and phylogenetic considerations support the idea of language learners being able to resort to means of organizing the units of their language which do not make use of the full hierarchical structure of the phrase or the clause.

This glance at what has been proposed in studies of linguistic evolution – another type of language development – provides perhaps further evidence or at least plausibility for my claim that L2 learners rely not only on principles conforming to UG but also on domain-specific ones which, however, refer to shallow or flat structures, and even non-domain-specific ones. This, however, leads to another aspect of the question concerning the nature of the knowledge acquired by these learners, namely whether the various types of principles and mechanisms just alluded to constitute a single system or whether L2 learners should be assumed to switch between different knowledge systems. In claiming that L2 knowledge is a hybrid knowledge system,[2] I opted for the former idea which represents a more parsimonious hypothesis and which is in tune with the notion of the faculty of language 'in the broad sense', containing a wide variety of cognitive mechanisms (Hauser *et al.* 2002). As far as I can see, the only possible reason to assume distinct systems is the modularity hypothesis postulating a grammatical module comprising knowledge resulting exclusively from parameter setting. Yet such a view can, at best, capture core properties of grammars; it fails to account for the fact that the grammatical competence of L1 as well as L2 learners comprises knowledge of language-specific grammatical phenomena, about which UG has nothing to say (see section 2.1 in chapter 2). Recall that we saw in chapter 5 (section 5.3) that even proponents of the Full Access to UG Hypothesis must rely on inductive learning when arguing that L2 acquisition is 'failure driven'. In her detailed discussion of modularity in language acquisition,[3] Carroll (2001: chapter 7) argued convincingly that the view according to which linguistic cognition is *modular* and all acquisition results from parameter setting is conceptually and empirically untenable. Importantly, for the issue at stake here, there is no empirical evidence demonstrating that inductive learning in L2 acquisition results in knowledge different from that encountered in L1 mental grammars (Carroll 2001: 258).

All this necessarily leads to the conclusion that an adequate theory of language acquisition must capture the fact that the underlying logic of the process of grammatical development and the resulting grammatical competence are shaped by different acquisition mechanisms, inductive learning being one of them, and Universal Grammar, the 'only uniquely human component of the faculty of language' (Hauser *et al.* 2002: 1569), arguably representing the crucial one. This is what I have tried to account for by distinguishing between the Language Making Capacity, comprising domain-specific as well as domain-general operations, the Language Acquisition Device, comprising various domain-specific mechanisms, and Universal Grammar, the core component of the LAD. Importantly, the language acquisition faculty thus designed is put to work in first as well as in second language acquisition. The fundamental difference between the two acquisition types results from the fact that a subcomponent of one of the components of the LMC, namely parameterized principles of UG, becomes inaccessible with increasing age of onset of acquisition as a result of neural maturation. All surface properties of the target language can, nevertheless, still be acquired. L2 learners can and will then resort to the other acquisition mechanisms provided by the LMC, including non-domain-specific ones. This, however, does not always lead to target-conforming results, and, most importantly, the acquired knowledge differs in these particular instances from the one attained in L1 development. It is thus a *hybrid system* which can nevertheless be qualified as a natural grammar.

Glossary

access to UG: children are innately equipped with a **LAD**. The availability of the same kind of **Language Making Capacity** in L2 acquisition is a matter of controversy, relating primarily to the question of whether L2 learners have *full access*, *partial access* or *no access* to **UG**.

acquisition criterion: needed in order to decide whether a linguistic device is used **productively** rather than resulting from *rote learning* or *imitation*. L1 research frequently relies on a quantitative criterion according to which a form has been acquired at the time of 'the first speech sample of three, such that in all three [it] . . . is supplied in at least 90 percent of the contexts in which it is clearly required' (Cazden 1968). It has not been possible to establish a reliable *quantitative* criterion for L2 acquisition.

acquisition sequence: see **developmental sequence**.

adequacy: theories can aim at observational, descriptive and explanatory adequacy. *Observational adequacy* is met when all facts encountered in a given set of data are accounted for. *Descriptive adequacy* is met when a data set is described in terms of a given theory, e.g. all grammatical sentences of a language must be generated by a syntactic theory. *Explanatory adequacy* is achieved if a theory can account for the reasons causing certain phenomena to appear, e.g. why grammars have specific properties and how children can acquire them.

adjunct: a constituent attached (adjoined) to another one to create a larger constituent of the same type. An adverbial phrase, for example, can be adjoined to a VP, resulting in a larger VP. Adjuncts are thus hierarchically outside the phrase containing a **specifier** and **complement**; they may precede or follow the **projection** to which they are adjoined.

affix: a grammatical morpheme which cannot appear as an independent word but must be attached to a host word, preceding (*prefix*) or following (*suffix*) it, or incorporated into it (*infix*).

agreement: a formal relationship linking constituents of a sentence, e.g. subjects and verbs may share grammatical properties like *person*, *number* or *gender*. The syntactic operation of agreement makes sure that the relevant **features** in the constituents concerned are assigned identical values.

anaphoric negation: a form of negation typically expressing refusal of an offer, rejection of an opinion or statement uttered by another speaker in an immediately preceding utterance of a conversation. It normally occurs at the left edge of an utterance and links the current utterance to prior discourse; see also **non-anaphoric negation**.

approximative system: transitional competence of learners, defined as a structured knowledge base. Introduced by Nemser (1971), the term is primarily used in L2 research; see also **interlanguage**.

argument: refers to the relationship between particular types of expression (e.g. DP) and the *predicate* (typically a verb) of a *proposition* (sentence) in describing the semantic structure of sentences. In syntax, complements are referred to as *internal arguments*, because they originate within V', and subjects as *external arguments*, since they are placed outside V'.

aspect: originally the opposition between *perfective* or *non-perfective*, expressing the speakers' perspective on events or actions. In many languages, aspect is encoded by means of verbal **affixes**, frequently fused with *tense* markings. Often, the type of activity expressed by the meaning of the verb (*aktionsart*) is subsumed under the term 'aspect'.

attrition: deterioration or **interference** (from the L2) effects on the ability to use an L1 as a result of non-use or dramatically limited use, e.g. by immigrants to a country where they predominantly use the L2. Grammatical knowledge is affected to a lesser degree than lexical access.

autonomous development: independent development of **mental grammars** in multilingual children, without **interference** from the other language(s). To the extent that **cross-linguistic interaction** happens, it affects **performance**. If the underlying knowledge is affected, this is referred to as **interdependent development**.

canonical word order: the typical or neutral order in declarative sentences, e.g. Subject – Verb – Object in English, when no constituent is emphasized or highlighted by means of particular word order options, e.g. by placing it in clause-initial position.

c-command: a structural relationship within a clause structure: category α c-commands category β if the first branching node dominating α also dominates β.

clitic: an item which is neither an independent word nor an **affix**. It is '*cliticized*' to ('leans on') other words. French subject and object pronouns, for example, are placed next to verbs to which they are cliticized.

competence: native speakers' knowledge of the grammar of their language(s), as opposed to their **performance** when using this knowledge. This knowledge is understood as being internal to the human mind/brain. It is therefore also referred to as **I-language**. Acquisition studies refer to the changing knowledge of learners as their transitional competence; see also **approximative system** or **interlanguage**.

complement: a constituent selected and combined with a **head** to form an intermediate **projection**, e.g. a V and a DP form a V' as part of a VP (see **X'/X-bar (theory)**). The complement may precede or follow the head; cf. the **OV/VO Parameter**.

complementizer (C, Comp): **functional category** of clause-introducing elements, comprising, e.g., conjunctions and relative clauses. In generative syntax, it is commonly assumed that main clauses as well as subordinate clauses are introduced by C. It is therefore also understood as the position preceding the subject. Verbal elements can occupy this position in instances of subject–verb **inversion**.

continuity (assumption): referring to the nature of grammatical knowledge, it implies that children have access to the same kind of linguistic knowledge as adults, making use of the same grammatical entities and relations.

cross-linguistic influence (interaction): structural changes in a language caused by another language of multilingual individuals. Commonly used as a neutral term which leaves open the question of whether the influence affects **mental grammars** or **performance** mechanisms.

cross-sectional study: a methodological choice entailing that data are collected from a large number of subjects, recording each of them once. If the study investigates the course of development, variation across subjects must be interpreted chronologically; cf. **longitudinal study**.

declarative/procedural model: posits distinct cognitive systems subserving language processing, relying on distinct neural bases. The declarative system is implicated in the learning and processing of lexical-semantic information; the procedural system underlies learning and use of grammatical information (Paradis 2004, 2009; Ullman 2001). L2 learners are claimed to over-rely on the declarative system for grammatical processing.

default (-value of parameter): the option which prevails if no specific one is explicitly required. It has been argued that in L1 development **parameters** come pre-set to a default value, i.e. prior to the child's exposure to primary linguistic data.

determiner (Det): **functional category**, elements modifying nouns, e.g. definite or indefinite *articles* or *demonstratives*, or replacing noun phrases, e.g. *der* 'that one/ he' in *der kommt heute nicht* 'he won't come today' in reply to 'Where is X?'

developmental sequence: a sequence of grammatically related and chronologically strictly ordered phases or stages, each defined in terms of the properties of the target system acquired during this phase. 'Strictly ordered' refers to the fact that the order of phases is not reversible; i.e. learners are predicted not to violate this ordering, although a particular phenomenon may not appear at all in the speech of some learners.

differentiation (of languages): the development of separate **mental grammars** in children acquiring two or more languages simultaneously; see also **fusion** of grammars.

discovery principles: the **LAD** comprises discovery principles guiding children towards the cues which enable them to discover formal properties of languages.

domain-general, -specific: some mental faculties are assumed to process only information of a specific kind, applying, for example, exclusively to language-specific mental objects. In contrast to these domain-specific mental subsystems, others are domain-general, operating in multiple domains. These assumptions follow from the **modularity** hypothesis.

E-language: 'external', i.e. overt products of language use or **performance**, as opposed to the underlying knowledge, internal to the human mind, also termed **I-language** or **competence**.

Empty Category Principle (ECP): a principle of **UG** stating that a lexically empty category must be *properly governed*, i.e. the governing element must be a *lexical category* or it must be *coindexed* with the governed category, and it must **c-command** the governed category.

EPP (Extended Projection Principle): originally a principle of **UG** stating that every category T has to project to a TP containing a **specifier**. According to recent syntactic theorizing, T bears an uninterpretable **feature** [EPP] forcing a nominal element to appear in its specifier.

Event-Related Brain Potentials (ERP): a non-invasive method to study brain activities, using *electroencephalography* (EEG). Electrical variations induced by neural activity are recorded at the surface of the scalp; from the recorded variations event-related brain potentials (ERPs) are derived.

expletive: a pronoun with no semantic content, serving as the overt subject in non-null-subject languages where phonetically empty subjects are not allowed. Example: the '*it*' in '*it seems . . .*'

feature (grammatical): the most basic device to encode grammatical properties. Syntactic categories can be represented as bundles of features encoding their morphosyntactic properties. Syntactic theory distinguishes between *interpretable* and *uninterpretable* features. Interpretable features contribute to the semantic interpretation of the category; uninterpretable features play a crucial role in syntax; they are responsible for parametric variation.

feature specification: the set of features defining the properties of a syntactic category. The feature specification of a given category can vary across languages, e.g. a feature can be allocated to distinct categories in various languages (*distribution* of features) or it may be strong in one language and weak in another (**feature strength**).

feature strength: syntactic features can be *strong* or *weak*. Strength motivates **movement** to take place. Feature strength of functional heads varies across grammars. It can therefore not be specified at the onset of acquisition; it must rather be determined in the course of acquisition. Initially, uninterpretable features may either all be weak or **inert**, i.e. not specified for strength.

feature underspecification: since feature specification of categories varies across languages, the featural content of categories must be determined in the course of acquisition. Initially, categories may be underspecified, i.e. they may lack features required by the target grammar.

final state: the endpoint of successful L1 development, i.e. the mature competence.

Finiteness Parameter: see **Verb Movement Parameter**.

formulator: the central component of Levelt's (1989: 11) model of language production which 'translates conceptual structures into a linguistic structure'.

functional category: an element conveying *grammatical information*, in contrast to **lexical** categories which carry *referential* or *descriptive content*. Examples are C(OMP), D(ET) or T(ENSE). They are realized as **affixes** or as independent words. Traditional grammars make a similar distinction between 'empty' *versus* 'content' words, or 'closed' classes, containing a limited number of elements, and 'open classes'. **Parameter** theory refers to functional categories as the source of parametric variation.

functional Magnetic Resonance Imaging (fMRI): a *haemodynamic* method of investigating brain activity. Variations of cerebral activity are recorded as tomograms, i.e. images of slices through the brain measuring the *regional cerebral blood flow* reflecting brain activation.

fusion (of grammars): the development of a unitary **mental grammar** in children acquiring two or more languages simultaneously. Research on child bilingualism has shown that grammars are typically **differentiated** during very early phases of bilingual acquisition.

head: a **lexical** or **functional category** functioning as the basic element of a phrase which, in terms of *Principles and Parameters Theory*, is its maximal **projection**; e.g. the verb is the head of a VP. Heads determine the grammatical properties of the phrase. In *minimalist* terms, a head selects in **merge** operations and projects its **features** to the newly created syntactic object.

Head (Direction) Parameter: see **OV/VO Parameter**.

hierarchical order, structure: the constitutive property of human language is that linguistic expressions exhibit not only a **linear order** but also an abstract hierarchical structure where elements may contain others. This **structure dependency** is captured by representing sentence structures as tree diagrams defining hierarchical relationships between the components of sentences, e.g. dominance or path relations, in addition to the linear ones.

I-language: the theory of **UG** understands knowledge of language as being internal to the human mind, as an *internal* entity of the individual, as opposed to **E-language**. I-language or **competence** is viewed as the primary object of grammatical theory.

inductive learning: the kind of learning mechanism commonly implied by the notion of 'learning'. It involves procedures scrutinizing **primary linguistic data** to discover regular patterns. Learners generalize from specific observable properties to more general characteristics. Alternatively, L1 learners can rely on **UG**-guided deductive procedures, i.e. **parameter setting**.

inert, inertia: at the **initial state**, parts of the grammatical knowledge provided by **UG** have not yet been activated; uninterpretable **features** are inert, they are neither specified as <strong> nor as <weak> and require subsequent specification of strength. **Parameters** referring to these features can therefore also be considered as inert and need to be **set** to the appropriate value.

initial state: the starting point of linguistic development, in L1 characterized by the child's a priori knowledge about linguistic structures, i.e. **Universal Grammar**.

interdependent development: when development of **mental grammars** in multilingual children is affected by **interference** from the other language(s); see also **autonomous development**.

interference: influence of one language on another in bilinguals. The term is frequently used ambiguously, referring to either **competence** or **performance**; see also **transfer**.

interlanguage: transitional competence of learners, defined as a structured knowledge base. The term was first introduced by Reinecke (1935) but became popular in L2 research due to the paper by Selinker (1972); see also **approximative system**.

interpretable feature: see **feature**.

inversion (subject-verb-): constructions where the subject follows the finite verb although it appears preverbally in **canonical word order**. This reordering results from verb **raising** to C.

LAD (Language Acquisition Device): the centrepiece of the human *language faculty*. Chomsky (2000a: 4) argues that it 'takes experience as "input" and gives the language as an "output"'. Although it is frequently equated with **UG**, the LAD must comprise, in addition to UG, **discovery principles**, bootstrapping children into grammatical systems, and *learning mechanisms*, allowing them to acquire non-universal properties of their target grammars. The LAD comprises all **domain-specific** principles and mechanisms.

Language Making Capacity (LMC): human beings are equipped with an innate language faculty. It comprises **domain-specific** principles and mechanisms provided by the **LAD** as well as **domain-general** problem-solving capacities.

lateralization: the functional specialization of the two hemispheres of the human brain.

lexical category: an element carrying *referential* or *descriptive content*, in contrast to **functional** categories which convey grammatical information. Examples are nouns, verbs, adjectives or prepositions. Traditional grammars distinguish between 'content' *versus* 'empty' words, or 'closed' and 'open' classes comprising a large and in principle unlimited number of items.

linear order: utterances are organized *sequentially* as concatenations of linguistic elements. But this linear order does not define sentences exhaustively; rather, they are defined by their underlying **hierarchical structure**.

Logical Problem of language acquisition: termed *Plato's Problem* by Chomsky (1986), refers to the discrepancy between experience and knowledge in grammatical development: native grammars comprise knowledge which is not encoded in the **primary linguistic data**, so it must have been in the system prior to experience (it represents innate knowledge).

longitudinal study: a methodological choice entailing that data are collected from a normally small number of subjects, recording each of them repeatedly over a certain period of time; see also **cross-sectional study**.

mental grammar: the theory of **UG** understands knowledge of language as being *internal* to the human mind/brain. The object of linguistic theory is therefore the mental grammar or **competence** of the individual, also referred to as **I-language**.

merge: a syntactic operation by which two constituents are combined to form a larger constituent, e.g. a V and a DP form a V' or a VP (see **X'/X-bar (theory)**).

modularity: the modularity hypothesis postulates that the mind consists of various information processing components that are informationally encapsulated. A processing component is informationally encapsulated when it accepts only inputs of a particular sort, e.g. acoustic representations of speech, and outputs only representations of a particular sort, e.g. meanings. Modules might also be autonomous or **domain-specific**, e.g. specific to language.

movement: a *computational* operation by which a constituent is moved from one structural position to another. Since principles of **UG** (cf. the **ECP**) require that elements are normally moved to a higher structural position, this type of movement is also referred to as *raising*.

multi-dimensional model: distinguishes between a *developmental dimension* defining the invariant **developmental sequence** through which all learners of a specific L2 proceed, and a *dimension of variability* characterizing the variation space explored by different types of L2 learners when using the knowledge acquired at a given point of development.

NEG+X strategy: many L2 learners tend to rely on **linear** rather than **hierarchical ordering** principles. Example: they place the negative element in a position preceding the verb, rather than **moving** the finite verb to a higher **functional head**.

negative evidence: refers to the non-occurrence of certain structures and the problem of how one can learn that they are not generated by the target grammar. Children acquiring their L1 only have access to *positive evidence*, the information conveyed by the **primary linguistic data**. To the extent that they receive negative evidence at all, e.g. through corrections, they do not seem to make use of it.

non-anaphoric negation: negates the proposition expressed by the sentence in which the negator appears, or parts of this sentence (*constituent negation*); see also **anaphoric negation**.

Null-Subject Parameter: specifies whether the grammar of a language requires the subject position of a finite main clause to be lexically filled or not. Since the null subject is syntactically analysed as a pronominal element (*pro*), the parameter is also referred to as the *Pro-Drop Parameter*. Other surface properties associated with null-subject languages include 'free' **inversion** and the fact that **expletive** subjects are ruled out. The exact set of properties pertaining to the *cluster* of properties related to this parameter is a matter of controversy.

OV/VO Parameter: specifies the relative ordering of **heads** and their **complements** in the **canonical word order** of a language; also referred to as the *Head (Direction)*

Parameter. The surface *cluster* related to this parameter refers to the position of adverbs and of verbal **particles**.

parameter: principles of **UG** do not account exhaustively for the grammatical properties to which they refer. They offer several options, encoding properties in which grammars differ across languages or across time in the processes of acquisition or diachronic change. Since they are defined at an abstract level of grammar, **setting** parameters to specific values causes *clusters* of superficially unrelated grammatical properties to appear. In recent theorizing, parameters refer exclusively to uninterpretable **features** of **functional categories**.

parameter setting/resetting: parameterized principles are initially unspecified and must be set to one of their values in L1 development. Learners need to identify the **triggering** evidence, i.e. structural properties of the input data. The *clustering* effect implies that learners need to discover only *one* of the surface properties indicating the target value of the parameter. In L2 acquisition, parameter settings may be **transferred** from the L1 and changed to the L2 value, '*reset*', if UG is fully **accessible** to L2 learners, as some authors claim to be the case.

parsing: assignment of grammatical structure in processing the **primary linguistic data** in language comprehension.

partial access to UG: see **access to UG**.

particle: a pretheoretical term referring to elements which cannot be assigned easily to traditional syntactic categories. Example: the non-finite part of separable verbs, like *an* in *sie sieht ihn an* (she looks him at) 'she is looking at him' or *out* in *put the dog out*.

perceived similarity: shared structural properties of languages, as perceived intuitively by learners, as opposed to similarities attributed to language pairs by linguistic analyses.

performance: the use native speakers or L2 learners make of their **competence**. Linguistic behaviour is also referred to as **E-language**, denoting the products of language use.

Plato's Problem: see the **Logical Problem**.

pregrammatical phase: refers to the hypothesis that very early child language is shaped by non-grammatical principles and that **UG** kicks in only later in the course of linguistic development. Bickerton (1990b) termed this *protolanguage*.

primary linguistic data (PLD): the utterances of the ambient language(s) from which learners extract structural information about the target grammar. Also referred to as *positive evidence*.

procedural (knowledge) system: see **declarative/procedural model**.

Pro-Drop Parameter: see **Null-Subject Parameter**.

productive use: when learners have acquired grammatical knowledge which enables them to use forms or constructions.

projection: **functional** as well as **lexical heads** can be combined with other syntactic objects to form *intermediate* and *maximal* projections, e.g. a verb expands into V' (see **X'/X-bar (theory)**) by combining with a **complement** and into VP by combining V' with a **specifier**. In terms of the *Minimalist Program*, this is the result of the operation **merge**. A *minimal* projection is an element which is not a projection of another element; a *maximal* projection is an element not contained in a larger projection of the same head.

protolanguage: see **pregrammatical phase**.

raising: see **movement**.

resetting of parameters: see **parameter**.

root infinitives: refers to the observation that in many languages children use infinitival forms of main verbs alongside finite ones in declarative matrix (or *root*) clauses during early phases of L1 development. Also referred to as *optional infinitives*.

sensitive phase: neural maturation is hypothesized to open and close *windows of opportunities* during which certain learning tasks can be achieved with relative ease and maximal success. The *critical period* for language acquisition is best understood as a cluster of sensitive phases during which the LAD is optimally prepared to integrate new information into developing grammars.

setting of parameters: see **parameter**.

SOV: word order pattern, Subject–Object–Verb, usually referring to the **canonical word order** of a language, a major criterion for its typological classification.

specifier (SPEC): a constituent which combines with an *intermediate* **projection** to form a *maximal* projection or phrase; e.g. a DP can function as the specifier of a VP. Specifiers precede the heads of their phrases.

steady state: see **final state**.

structure-dependent: sentences exhibit not only **linear order** but also a **hierarchical structure**. This fact is referred to as the *structure dependency* of human language.

SVO: word order pattern, Subject–Verb–Object, usually referring to the **canonical word order** of a language, a major criterion for its typological classification.

thematic/non-thematic verb: verbs assigning/not assigning *thematic roles* (the semantic roles of verbal arguments). Whereas main verbs assign thematic roles, e.g. AGENT to the subject of *eat*, auxiliaries and modals do not.

transfer: influence of one language on another in bilinguals. Like **interference**, the term is frequently used ambiguously, referring to either **competence** or **performance**.

trigger, triggering: the structural information extracted from the **primary linguistic data** which causes a **parameter** to be set to its appropriate value; the acquisition process involved in **parameter setting**. Compared to **inductive learning**, triggering happens faster, requires more simple and less frequent input, and is always successful.

underspecification: see **feature underspecification**.

uninterpretable feature: see **feature**.

Universal Grammar (UG): a set of constraints on formal properties of all human languages. UG comprises invariant principles, formulating constraints which no grammar may violate, and **parameters**, defining the range of variation across grammars. Children are hypothesized to be innately endowed with implicit knowledge about UG. It is therefore a core component of the human **Language Making Capacity**, and the principles of UG determine the properties of grammars at each point of L1 development.

Verb Movement Parameter: specifies whether the *finite* verb must move out of its base position in VP and, if it does, which **functional head** is the appropriate landing site, T or C; this is why it is also referred to as the *Finiteness Parameter*. Depending on which option is chosen, different *clusters* of properties concerning the linearization of elements will surface. In French, for example, **movement** to T affects the relative ordering of finite verbs and the negator *pas*, quantifiers and certain adverbs.

verb-second (V2): the grammars of some languages, e.g. most Germanic languages, require the finite verb to be consistently placed in second position (*V2 effect*), i.e. the subject follows the verb if another element appears sentence-initially. Structurally, this means that the finite verb is **raised** to **Comp**, and a maximal **projection**, the subject or another one, **moves** to the specifier position of CP.

wh: *wh* is commonly used as an *interrogative* **feature**. Originally referring to *interrogative* or *relative* pronouns beginning with *wh*, the term *wh-word* now applies to all elements serving similar syntactic functions, e.g. *how*.

wh-movement: a type of **movement**, moving a **wh**-word or a **wh**-phrase to the specifier position of CP. Some languages, like French, allow for *wh* to remain *in situ*, i.e. the constituent containing *wh* remains in its base position.

X'/X-bar (theory): originally developed in order to constrain possible phrase structures. It stated that every syntactic **head** (X) must **project** twice, to X' and to XP. According to more recent syntactic theorizing, this is only the case if the head **merges** with a **complement** and a **specifier**. If it lacks one or both of these, it is nevertheless analysed as a phrasal constituent.

Notes

1. The quest for the LAD

1. As Selinker (1992: 17) points out, quite correctly, this statement is inadequate in yet another sense: 'How could NL [native language] forms be transferred (even when shown beyond a doubt that they have been transferred) to the TL [target language]? In Andersen's (1983a) terms, the transfer must be to "somewhere" and the TL, as spoken by native speakers of that language, is something other than what learners transfer to . . . Inherent in the sentence just quoted from Lado, for me, is the notion of a third system in addition to the NL of learners and the TL to be learned – what in 1969 I first called "interlanguage" (Selinker 1969: fn 4).'
2. Larsen-Freeman and Long (1991:74) inform us that the term was actually first used by Reinecke (1935), published 1969, 'to refer to a non-standard variety of a first or second language, used as a means of intergroup communication, gradually approximating the norms of the standard language of some economically and politically dominant group'.

2. First language development

1. For a recent discussion of a number of criteria which must be met in order for variation to count as parametric rather than accidental, see Smith and Law 2009.
2. Minimal exposure to the data should indeed be sufficient for parameter setting. It has in fact been claimed that, ideally, even a single example encountered in the input could suffice. While this strong idealization cannot be maintained (see note 4), not much is known as to how to define the minimal threshold.
3. As for what may act as a trigger, see the summarizing discussion in Meisel (1995: section 3.5.4). It is desirable to define triggers narrowly with respect to the kind of structural information that may count as a triggering element. Lightfoot (1989), for example, argues that a triggering element must appear in main-clauses (including the front of the subordinate clause, his 'degree-0 learnability'), whereas Roeper and Weissenborn (1990) suggest that it should be contained in the subordinate clause.
4. It is likely that for each parameter and for every possible setting there exists a unique trigger, as has been suggested by Roeper and Weissenborn (1990), Valian (1990b) and others. This is to say that one specific bit of information contained in the input data invariably triggers the setting of the parameter to a specific value. Importantly, however, not every form present in the input should be allowed to automatically trigger the parameter; cf. Fodor (1998, 1999) for an insightful discussion of the triggering problem.
5. See White (2003: 9) for a brief presentation of a similar view of grammatical parameters.

3. Obvious (observable) similarities and differences between first and second language acquisition

1. See also Hawkins (2001: sections 2.4 and 2.5) for a discussion of these studies.
2. J. D. Brown (1983) replicated Andersen's study, analysing sixty-six learners, 18 to 20 years of age, from a variety of language backgrounds, and was able to corroborate Andersen's results.
3. This leads to a different order of nominal morphemes as a result of which differences between L1 and L2 sequences are concealed. A further problem is that variation within each group is necessarily reduced if one considers only eight morphemes which are, furthermore, distributed over three groups.
4. This role might, however, be defined negatively, in the sense that these lexical morphemes are semantically transparent in a way in which the functional elements are not. At this point, I do not want to speculate further about this issue. But there is, in fact, more evidence supporting the idea of a semantic-pragmatic approach to L2 acquisition; see, for example, the discussion of negation in the following section.
5. In Colloquial French, the use of *ne* has only survived in a limited number of contexts.
6. Zweitspracherwerb italienischer, portugiesischer und spanischer Arbeiter – Second language acquisition by Italian, Portuguese and Spanish workers. The ZISA research group was established at the University of Wuppertal in 1974, under the direction of the present author. The cross-sectional study was funded by the Minister für Wissenschaft und Forschung des Landes Nordrhein-Westfalen (1977–78) and the longitudinal study by the Volkswagen Foundation (1978–82). Additional funding was granted by the Deutsche Forschungsgemeinschaft (1992–95) for a study comparing first and second language acquisition, based partly on the same corpus. All research grants were awarded to Jürgen M. Meisel and are hereby gratefully acknowledged. In 1980, when I took up a position at the University of Hamburg, the group was transferred to Hamburg. A description of the research methodology is given by Meisel, Clahsen and Pienemann (1981) and, in more detail, by Clahsen, Meisel and Pienemann (1983).
7. Jordens (1980) addresses the respective roles of the main verb/auxiliary distinction and of finiteness in L2 negative structures, but he views the former as a semantic problem and the latter merely as a morphological difference.

4. The initial state and beyond

1. This type of research was initiated in the 1980s by Flynn (1983, 1987, 1989), Liceras (1986, 1989), Mazurkevich (1984), White (1985, 1989a, 1989b) and others.
2. See White (1989a: 80, 2003: chapter 3) or Hawkins (2001: 67, 335) for similar discussions.
3. Similar ideas were already entertained by White (1985, 1989a, 1989b) and by Flynn (1987), although their discussion does not explicitly focus on the initial state of L2 acquisition.
4. Hawkins' (2001: 32) modulated structure building approach adopts a slightly attenuated version of the MTH.
5. As an explanation of stage I, Eubank (1996) suggests an XP-only structure, e.g. a VP, to which NEGP is adjoined; since verbs always precede their complements, he has to claim, just like the Minimal Trees Hypothesis, that a switch in headedness to head-left has occurred. The objections against this assumption raised above obviously apply here too. There is, in fact, no need to refer to switch-headed VPs in order to explain the facts encountered at stage I; see Meisel (1997a, 1997b).
6. There is some controversy concerning a small number of these languages. Russenorsk, for example, is claimed to be SOV by some, whereas others classify it as SVO. Russenorsk emerged in a Russian–Norwegian contact situation with some possible influence from Uralic languages. See the postings by M. Parkvall on CreoLIST (creolist@ling.su.se) in February, 1997.

7. It is, of course, possible that natural languages do not, in fact, vary with respect to underlying word order but are all uniformly SVO; cf. Kayne 1994. Note that this assumption does not allow for transfer of head directionality as an explanation, either.
8. Possible data sources of this type are the ZISA corpora (Zweitspracherwerb italienischer, spanischer und portugiesischer Arbeiter – Second language acquisition by Italian, Spanish and Portuguese workers) and the ESF (European Science Foundation) corpus. The latter is presented in Perdue 1993a; see also Klein and Perdue 1992. The ZISA corpora were collected in a cross-sectional and in a longitudinal study; see chapter 3, section 3.3. The data and the methods of data collection and analysis are described by Clahsen, Meisel and Pienemann (1983).
9. See Pienemann and Håkansson (2007) for further clarification and for a rejection of the claim by Bohnacker (2006) that this lack of V2 transfer is due to knowledge of the previously learned L2 English.
10. This study was carried out as part of the research project 'Simultaneous and successive acquisition of bilingualism' which I directed in the Collaborative Research Center on Multilingualism at the University of Hamburg, funded by the DFG (Deutsche Forschungsgemeinschaft). The financial support by the DFG is gratefully acknowledged.
11. I want to thank the author who graciously permitted me to reproduce this poem here. The following approximative translation does not render the meaningful ambiguities of the original: 'one must do something, must one do something, what must one do, do something one must – one would have done something, had one done something, what would one have done, done something one would have – do what one must, what one must do, do something one must, what must one do.'
12. The putative target sentences are presented below the original utterances, preceding the English translation.
13. The argument is still valid if one adopts a more recent version of UG theory, e.g. the Minimalist Program; see Hornstein *et al.* (2005) for an introductory text. To mention just one point, the same conclusions are attainable by attributing to the children knowledge about Merge and principles constraining head movement.
14. Radford, for example, discusses these issues in Radford (1997: chapters 6–8).
15. Of the three children studied by Meisel and Müller (1992), one used these constructions only twice during the entire period investigated; in the recordings of the other two children, the frequency of final position of finite verbs in main clauses never exceeded 4% of the utterances containing finite verbs.
16. The letters I, P, S obviously indicate the learners' first language, as in (8), above; L is added to the pseudonyms of the learners recorded longitudinally.

5. Developing grammatical knowledge

1. Setting a parameter in the L2 grammar to a value distinct from that of the L1 grammar is commonly though misleadingly called parameter 'resetting' in the L2 research literature; see for example Hawkins (2001) or White (2003). In reality, no change of settings is said to occur since this term does not imply that the L1 grammar is altered. Rather, the term is intended to refer to a process in successive language acquisition by which a given UG parameter is set once again, but to a different value, as compared to the previously acquired language(s). If 'resetting' was meant merely to indicate repetitive settings of a parameter, this would also apply in cases when it is set to the same value in either simultaneous or successive acquisition of two or more languages, but this is not how the term is used. I have decided to adopt this inappropriate terminological choice, although reluctantly, because it is firmly established in the L2 research literature.
2. A feature-based analysis adopting full transfer and attempting to refine the Full Access to UG hypothesis has been developed by Lardiere (1998b, 2000, 2008, 2009). She abandoned, however, the idea of relating the featural composition of functional heads to grammatical parameters.

3. These results and their interpretation by Clahsen and Hong (1995) explicitly contradict Vainikka and Young-Scholten (1994) who in their analysis of L2 German by Turkish and Korean learners claimed to have found a clustering effect for just these phenomena, i.e. the emergence of subject–verb agreement and the setting of the Null-Subject Parameter. Clahsen and Hong (1995: 68) convincingly demonstrate that this conclusion is not warranted by the analysis offered by Vainikka and Young-Scholten (1994).
4. The tests carried out with the latter revealed that a number of construction types which are frequently judged as grammatical in the syntactic literature are rejected by many or most native speakers. This concerns primarily infinitival constructions like *Souvent choisir bien, ce n'est pas facile* (rejected by 92% of the eighty-five native speakers) which are not discussed here, but also some sentences involving quantification at a distance as in *Paul a beaucoup lu de livres* (rejected by 62%) where the quantifier precedes the non-finite verb. It thus seems that the grammaticality judgements on which part of Pollock's (1989) theory is based are highly problematic. Somewhat surprisingly, these were nevertheless included in the test materials presented to the L2 learners who had to carry out a grammaticality judgement and a production task. It is not obvious why the proficiency of L2 learners is not assessed in comparison to native speakers but in relation to highly problematic judgements by linguists.
5. See also Bley-Vroman and Chaudron (1990) for critical comments on Flynn's approach.
6. The data analysed in this study are part of a corpus collected and analysed by the research group DuFDE (Deutsch und Französisch: Doppelter Erstspracherwerb – German and French: bilingual first language acquisition) investigating the simultaneous acquisition of French and German at the University of Hamburg since 1981. This longitudinal study was funded by the Deutsche Forschungsgemeinschaft (German Research Foundation) from 1986 through 1992. These research grants were awarded to Jürgen M. Meisel and are hereby gratefully acknowledged.
7. Schwartz (1996) also addresses the clustering issue, arguing that the absence of the clustering effect does not constitute evidence against access to UG whereas evidence for clustering would provide strong support for the correctness of this approach. She discusses the Head Direction Parameter ('Headedness of VP') but does not list, let alone explain, the clustering properties of this parameter. Instead, she argues, referring to the observation by Meisel, Clahsen and Pienemann (1981) and Clahsen, Meisel and Pienemann (1983) that target-like placement of non-finite verbs and of verbal particles emerge at the same acquisition stage in the cross-sectional data of the ZISA corpus, that this constitutes a cluster of the required sort. Apart from the fact that this is at best true for two of the properties related to the parameter, the longitudinal data do not confirm this assumption, not even for these two phenomena.
8. The putative target sentences are presented below the original utterances, preceding the English translation.
9. Figures indicate weeks of exposure to German at the time of recording.
10. This is acknowledged by the fact that *Studies in Second Language Acquisition* dedicated a special issue to 'The Fundamental Difference Hypothesis twenty years later', including a 'recasting' of the FDH by Bley-Vroman (2009). Surprisingly, all other contributions to this issue are authored by scholars who, in their previous work, had argued against the FDH and who, not so surprisingly, continue to be critical of this approach to L2 acquisition. In fact, the only contribution which discusses the revised FDH in some detail is the one by Herschensohn (2009).

6. Neural maturation and age

1. In the present context it is not possible to recapitulate the arguments put forth in this debate. Let me merely refer to the discussion by Herschensohn (2000: chapter 2) and to the contributions to the volumes edited by Singleton and Lengyel (1995) and by Birdsong

(1999), as well as to the following publications addressing this controversy: Oyama (1973); Harley (1986); Scovel (1988); Johnson and Newport (1989, 1991); Singleton (1989); Johnson (1992); Flynn and Martohardjono (1994); Ioup *et al.* (1994); Pulvermüller and Schumann (1994); Eubank and Gregg (1995); Jacobs (1995); Schumann (1995); Pulvermüller (1995); Slavoff and Johnson (1995); Epstein *et al.* (1996); White and Genesee (1996); Locke (1997); DeKeyser (2000); Herschensohn (2007).
2. The idea of multiple critical periods had been suggested already by Seliger (1978) and adopted by Schachter (1996: 166).
3. The brain map presented by the neuropathologist Korbinian Brodmann is based on cell types; cf. Brodmann (1909).
4. Pienemann does not include phase 5 (ADV–VP) in his version of the sequence; it is thus not considered here.
5. Due to technical problems, some results from one participant (AOA 8) were incomplete.

7. A (tentative) theory of language acquisition

1. This is not to say that incomplete acquisition could not occur when children are exposed to two or more languages from birth. It is claimed to happen only in cases of drastically reduced input (Silva-Corvalán 2003) or if exposure to a language is completely interrupted. In the latter case, attrition of the grammatical knowledge acquired in childhood may also occur. For a recent discussion of these and related issues, see Montrul 2008.
2. Herschensohn (2000) makes very similar observations about the L2 knowledge system and about how L2 learners proceed. 'They use a coalition of strategies to build the L2 grammar: general cognitive skills . . . social and motivational particularities related to individual learning styles . . . linguistically focused instruction . . . negative feedback . . . the innate constraints provided by UG . . .' She thus regards L2 knowledge as instantiating natural grammars, despite the observed differences as compared to L1 grammars. Moreover, although she acknowledges (Herschensohn 2009: 281) that 'Second language learners can never be native speakers', she attempts to explain L1–L2 differences in her Gradient Differences Hypothesis as gradient and not categorical in nature. If I understand this correctly, gradient differences refer to properties of entire grammars which, as I have also argued, exhibit important parallels when comparing L1 and L2 acquisition. But I do not see how specific differences, e.g. the acquisition of a particular property either via parameter setting or by inductive learning, can possibly be gradient in nature.
3. See Schwartz (1992, 1993).

References

Abrahamsson, N. and K. Hyltenstam 2009. 'Age of onset and nativelikeness in a second language: Listener perception versus linguistic scrutiny', *Language Learning* 59: 249–306.

Adger, D. 2003. *Core syntax: A minimalist approach*. Oxford: Oxford University Press.

Al-Kasey, T. and A. T. Pérez-Leroux 1998. 'Second language acquisition of Spanish null subjects', in S. Flynn, G. Martohardjono and W. O'Neil (eds.), *The generative study of second language acquisition*, pp. 161–85. Mahwah, N J: L. Erlbaum.

Allen, S. 2001. 'The importance of discourse-pragmatics in acquisition', *Bilingualism: Language and Cognition* 4: 23–5.

Andersen, R. W. 1978a. 'The impoverished state of cross-sectional morpheme acquisition/ accuracy methodology', in C. Henning (ed.), *Proceedings of the Los Angeles second language research forum*, pp. 308–20. Los Angeles: UCLA.

1978b. 'An implicational model for second language research', *Language Learning* 28: 221–82.

1983a. 'Transfer to somewhere', in S. Gass and L. Selinker (eds.), *Language transfer in language learning*, pp. 177–201. Rowley, MA: Newbury House.

(ed.) 1983b. *Pidginization and creolization as language acquisition*. Rowley, MA: Newbury House.

1984. 'What's gender good for, anyway?', in R. W. Andersen (ed.), *Second languages: A cross-linguistic perspective*, pp. 77–99. Rowley, MA: Newbury House.

Atkinson, M. 1992. *Children's syntax: An introduction to Principles and Parameter Theory*. Oxford: Blackwell.

Ayoun, D. 1999. 'Verb movement in French L2 acquisition', *Bilingualism: Language and Cognition* 2: 103–25.

Bailey, N., C. Madden and S. D. Krashen 1974. 'Is there a "natural sequence" in adult second language learning?', *Language Learning* 24: 235–43.

Baker, M. 1996. *The polysynthesis parameter*. Oxford. Oxford University Press.

1982. 'A landing site theory of movement rules', *Linguistic Inquiry* 13: 1–38.

Barbosa, P. 2009. 'Two kinds of subject *pro*', *Studia Linguistica* 63: 2–58.

Barreña, A. 1994. 'Sobre la adquisición de la categoría funcional Comp en niños vascos', in J. M. Meisel (ed.), *La adquisición del vasco y del castellano en niños bilingües*, pp. 231–84. Madrid/Frankfurt: Vervuert.

Beck, M.-L. 1997. 'Regular verbs, past tense, and frequency: Tracking down one potential source of NS/NNS syntactic competence differences', *Second Language Research* 13: 93–115.

1998. 'L2 acquisition and obligatory head movement: English-speaking learners of German and the Local Impairment Hypothesis', *Studies in Second Language Acquisition* 20: 311–48.

Belletti, A. (ed.) 2004. *Structures and beyond: The cartography of syntactic structures*, Vol. 3. New York: Oxford University Press.
Berwick, R. C., S. P. Abney and C. Tenny (eds.) 1991. *Principle-based parsing: Computation and psycholinguistics*. Dordrecht: Kluwer.
Biberauer, Th. (ed.) 2008. *The limits of syntactic variation*. Amsterdam: John Benjamins.
Bickerton, D. 1981. *Roots of language*. Ann Arbor: Karoma Publishers.
1990a. *Language and species*. Chicago: The University of Chicago Press.
1990b. 'Syntactic development: The brain just does it'. University of Hawai'i at Manoa: Unpublished paper.
Birdsong, D. 1992a. *Metalinguistic performance and interlinguistic competence*. New York: Springer.
1992b. 'Ultimate attainment in second language acquisition', *Language* 68: 706–55.
1994. 'Asymmetrical knowledge of ungrammaticality in SLA theory', *Studies in Second Language Acquisition* 16: 463–73.
(ed.) 1999. *Second language acquisition and the Critical Period Hypothesis*. Mahwah, NJ: Erlbaum.
2004. 'Second language acquisition and ultimate attainment', in A. Davies and C. Elder (eds.), *The handbook of applied linguistics*, pp. 82–105. Oxford: Blackwell.
Bley-Vroman, R. 1987. 'The logical problem of foreign language learning'. University of Hawai'i at Manoa: Manuscript.
1989. 'What is the logical problem of foreign language learning?', in S. M. Gass and J. Schachter (eds.), *Linguistic perspectives on second language acquisition*, pp. 41–68. Cambridge: Cambridge University Press.
1990. 'The logical problem of foreign language learning', *Linguistic Analysis* 20: 3–49.
2009. 'The evolving context of the Fundamental Difference Hypothesis', *Studies in Second Language Acquisition* 31: 175–98.
Bley-Vroman, R. and C. Chaudron 1990. 'Second language processing of subordinate clauses and anaphora – first language and universal influences: A review of Flynn's research', *Language Learning* 40: 245–85.
Bley-Vroman, R., S. W. Felix and G. L. Ioup 1988. 'The accessibility of Universal Grammar in adult language learning', *Second Language Research* 4: 1–32.
Blom, E. 2006. 'Agreement inflection in child L2 Dutch', in A. Belletti, E. Bennati, C. Chesi, E. DiDomenico and I. Ferrari (eds.), *Language acquisition and development (Proceedings of GALA 2005)*. Cambridge: Cambridge Scholars Press.
Bobaljik, J. D. and H. Thráinsson 1998. 'Two heads aren't always better than one', *Syntax* 1: 37–71.
Bohnacker, U. 2006. 'When Swedes begin to learn German: From V2 to V2', *Second Language Research* 22: 443–86.
Bonnesen, M. 2007. 'The acquisition of questions in L1, adult L2 and child L2 in French'. University of Hamburg, Research Center on Multilingualism: Unpublished paper.
2008. 'The acquisition of subject–verb-agreement and negation in early child L2 of French and German'. University of Hamburg, Research Center on Multilingualism: Unpublished paper.
Bonnesen, M. and S. Chilla forthcoming. 'The acquisition of questions in L2 German and French by children and adults', *Studies in Second Language Acquisition*.
Borer, H. 1984. *Parametric syntax*. Dordrecht: Foris.

Brodmann, K. 1909. *Vergleichende Lokalisationslehre der Großhirnrinde in den Principien dargestellt auf Grund des Zellenbaues*. Leipzig: J.A. Barth.

Brown, J. D. 1983. 'An exploration of morpheme-group interactions', in K. M. Bailey, M. H. Long and S. Peck (eds.), *Second language acquisition studies*, pp. 25–40. Rowley, MA: Newbury House.

Brown, R. 1973. *A first language*. Cambridge, MA: Harvard University Press.

Burt, M. K., H. C. Dulay and E. Hernández 1973. *Bilingual syntax measure*. New York: Harcourt Brace Jovanovich.

Cancino, H., E. J. Rosansky and J. H. Schumann 1978. 'The acquisition of English negatives and interrogatives by native Spanish speakers', in E. Hatch (ed.), *Second language acquisition*, pp. 207–30. Rowley, MA: Newbury House.

Carlson, G. N. and M. K. Tanenhaus (eds.) 1989. *Linguistic structure in language processing*. Dordrecht: Kluwer.

Carroll, S. E. 1989. 'Language acquisition studies and a feasible theory of grammar', *Canadian Journal of Linguistics* 34: 399–418.

1996. 'Le point de départ: La notion d'input dans une théorie de l'acquisition d'une langue seconde'. Paper presented at the *Journée 'Processus d'acquisition en dialogue'*, Université de Paris III – Sorbonne Nouvelle.

1999. 'Input and SLA: "Adults" sensitivity to different sorts of cues to French gender', *Language Learning* 49: 37–92.

2001. *Input and evidence: The raw material of second language acquisition*. Amsterdam: John Benjamins.

2002a. 'I-learning', in S. Foster-Cohen, T. Ruthenberg and M.-L. Poschen (eds.), *EUROSLA Yearbook*, Vol. 2, pp. 7–28. Amsterdam/Philadelphia: Benjamins.

2002b. 'Induction in a modular learner', *Second Language Research* 18: 224–49.

2004. 'Segmentation: Learning how to "hear words" in the L2 speech stream', *Transactions of the Philological Society (Special issue: Empirical evidence and theories of representation in current research into second language acquisition)* 10: 227–54.

forthcoming. 'Input processing in second language acquisition', in M. Gullberg and J. Williams (eds.), *Encyclopedia of Applied Linguistics*. New York: Wiley.

Cazden, C. B. 1968. 'The acquisition of noun and verb inflection', *Child Development* 39: 433–48.

Cazden, C. B., H. Cancino, E. J. Rosansky and J. H. Schumann 1975. *Second language acquisition sequences in children, adolescents and adults*. Harvard University: Final Report, U.S. Department of Health, Education and Welfare.

Chaudron, C. 1985. 'Intake: On models and methods for discovering learners' processing of input', *Studies in Second Language Acquisition* 7: 1–14.

Chomsky, N. 1959. 'Review of B. F. Skinner's "Verbal Behavior"', *Language* 35: 26–58.

1965. *Aspects of the theory of syntax*. Cambridge, MA: MIT Press.

1968. *Language and mind*: New York: Harcourt Brace Jovanovich.

1981a. *Lectures on government and binding*. Dordrecht: Foris.

1981b. 'Principles and parameters in syntactic theory', in N. Hornstein and D. Lightfoot (eds.), *Explanation in linguistics: The logical problem of language acquisition*, pp. 32–75. London: Longman.

1986. *Knowledge of language: Its nature, origin and use*. New York: Praeger.

1988. 'On the nature, use and acquisition of language'. Lecture given at Kyoto University.

1989. 'Some notes on economy of derivation and representation', *MIT Working Papers in Linguistics* 10: 43–74.

1995. *The Minimalist Program*. Cambridge, MA: MIT Press.

2000a. *New horizons in the study of language and mind* (with a foreword by N. Smith). Cambridge: Cambridge University Press.

2000b. 'Minimalist inquiries: The framework', in R. Martin, D. Michaels and J. Uriagereka (eds.), *Step by step: Essays on minimalist syntax in honor of Howard Lasnik*, pp. 89–155. Cambridge, MA: MIT Press.

2001. 'Derivation by phase', in M. Kenstowicz (ed.), *Ken Hale: A life in language*, pp. 1–52. Cambridge, MA: MIT Press.

Cinque, G. 1999. *Adverbs and functional heads*. New York: Oxford University Press.

(ed.) 2002. *Functional structure in DP and IP: The cartography of syntactic structures*, Vol. 1. New York: Oxford University Press.

2006. *Restructuring and functional heads: The cartography of syntactic structures*, Vol. 4. New York: Oxford University Press.

Clahsen, H. 1982. *Spracherwerb in der Kindheit: Eine Untersuchung zur Entwicklung der Syntax bei Kleinkindern*. Tübingen: Narr.

1983. 'Some more remarks on the acquisition of German negation', *Journal of Child Language* 10: 465–9.

1984. 'The acquisition of German word order: A test case for cognitive approaches to L2 development', in R. W. Andersen (ed.), *Second languages: A cross-linguistic perspective*, pp. 219–42. Rowley, MA: Newbury House.

1986. 'Verb inflection in German child language: Acquisition of agreement markings and the functions they encode', *Linguistics* 24: 79–121.

1988a. 'Kritische Phasen der Grammatikentwicklung: Eine Untersuchung zum Negationserwerb bei Kindern und Erwachsenen', *Zeitschrift für Sprachwissenschaft* 7: 3–31.

1988b. 'Parameterized grammatical theory and language acquisition: A study of the acquisition of verb placement and inflection by children and adults', in S. Flynn and W. O'Neil (eds.), *Linguistic theory in second language acquisition*, pp. 47–75. Dordrecht: Reidel.

1988c. *Normale und gestörte Kindersprache: Linguistische Untersuchungen zum Erwerb von Syntax und Morphologie*. Amsterdam: John Benjamins.

1991. 'Constraints on parameter setting: A grammatical analysis of some acquisition stages in German child language', *Language Acquisition* 1: 361–91.

Clahsen, H. and C. Felser 2006a. 'Grammatical processing in language learners', *Applied Psycholinguistics* 27: 3–42.

2006b. 'How native-like is non-native language processing?', *TRENDS in Cognitive Sciences* 10: 564–70.

Clahsen, H. and U. Hong 1995. 'Agreement and null subjects in German L2 development: New evidence from reaction-time experiments', *Second Language Research* 11: 57–87.

Clahsen, H., J. M. Meisel and M. Pienemann 1983. *Deutsch als Zweitsprache: Der Spracherwerb ausländischer Arbeiter*. Tübingen: Narr.

Clahsen, H. and P. Muysken 1986. 'The availability of universal grammar to adult and child learners: A study of the acquisition of German word order', *Second Language Research* 2: 93–119.

1989. 'The UG paradox in L2 acquisition', *Second Language Research* 5: 1–29.
1996. 'How adult second language learning differs from child first language development', *Behavioral and Brain Sciences* 19: 721–23.

Clahsen, H. and M. Penke 1992. 'The acquisition of agreement morphology and its syntactic consequences: New evidence on German child language from the Simone-corpus', in J. M. Meisel (ed.), *The acquisition of verb placement: Functional categories and V2 phenomena in language acquisition*, 181–223. Dordrecht: Kluwer.

Clahsen, H., M. Penke and T. Parodi 1994. 'Functional categories in early child German', *Language Acquisition* 3: 395–429.

Coppieters, R. 1987. 'Competence differences between native and near-native speakers', *Language* 63: 544–73.

Corder, S. P. 1967. 'The significance of learner's errors', *International Review of Applied Linguistics* 5: 161–70.
1971. 'Idiosyncratic dialects and error analysis', *International Review of Applied Linguistics* 9: 147–59.

Culicover, P. and R. Jackendoff 2005. *Simpler syntax*. Oxford: Oxford University Press.

Curtiss, S. 1977. *Genie: A linguistic study of a modern-day 'wild child'*. New York: Academic Press.

Dahl, Ö. 1979. 'Typology of sentence negation', *Linguistics* 17: 79–106.

Darwin, C. 1874. *The descent of man, and selection in relation to sex*, 2nd edn. London: John Murray.

Dehaene, S., E. Dupoux, J. Mehler, L. Cohen, E. Paulescu, D. Perani, P.-F. van de Moortele, S. Lehéricy and D. Le Bihan 1997. 'Anatomical variability in the cortical representation of first and second language', *NeuroReport* 8: 3809–15.

DeKeyser, R. 2000. 'The robustness of critical period effects in second language acquisition', *Studies in Second Language Acquisition* 22: 499–533.

Dekydtspotter, L., R. Sprouse and B. Anderson 1997. 'The interpretive interface in L2 acquisition: The process–result distinction in English–French interlanguage grammars', *Language Acquisition* 6: 297–332.

Déprez, V. and A. Pierce 1993. 'Negation and functional projections in early grammar', *Linguistic Inquiry* 24: 25–67.

de Villiers, J. 1992. 'On the acquisition of functional categories: A general commentary', in J. M. Meisel (ed.), *The acquisition of verb placement: Functional categories and V2 phenomena in language acquisition*, pp. 423–43. Dordrecht: Kluwer.

de Villiers, J. and P. de Villiers 1973. 'A cross-sectional study of the acquisition of grammatical morphemes in child speech', *Journal of Psycholinguistic Research* 2: 267–78.

Döpke, S. 1992. *One parent – one language: An interactional approach*. Amsterdam: John Benjamins.

Dulay, H. C. and M. K. Burt 1972. 'Goofing: An indicator of children's second language learning strategies', *Language Learning* 22: 235–52.
1973. 'Should we teach children syntax?', *Language Learning* 23: 245–58.
1974. 'Natural sequences in child second language acquisition', *Language Learning* 24: 37–54.
1975. 'A new approach to discovering universals of child language acquisition', in D. Dato (ed.), *Developmental psycholinguistics*, pp. 209–33. Washington, DC: Georgetown University Press.

Dulay, H. C., M. K. Burt and S. Krashen 1982. *Language two*. Oxford: Oxford University Press.

duPlessis, J., D. Solin, L. Travis and L. White 1987. 'UG or not UG, that is the question: A reply to Clahsen and Muysken', *Second Language Research* 3: 56–75.

Ellis, R. 1989. 'Are classroom and naturalistic acquisition the same? A study of the classroom acquisition of German word order rules', *Studies in Second Language Acquisition* 11: 305–28.

Emonds, J. 1976. *A transformational approach to English syntax*. New York: Academic Press.

1978. 'The verbal complex V' – V in French', *Linguistic Inquiry* 9: 151–75.

Epstein, S. D., S. Flynn and G. Martohardjono 1996. 'Second language acquisition: Theoretical and experimental issues in contemporary research', *Behavioral and Brain Sciences* 19: 677–758.

Ervin-Tripp, S. M. 1974. 'Is second language learning like the first?', *TESOL Quarterly* 8: 111–27.

Eubank, L. 1993. 'Sentence matching and processing in L2 development', *Second Language Research* 9: 253–80.

1993/94. 'On the transfer of parametric values in L2 development', *Language Acquisition* 3: 183–208.

1994. 'Optionality and the initial state in L2 development', in T. Hoekstra and B. D. Schwartz (eds.), *Language acquisition studies in generative grammar*, pp. 369–88. Amsterdam: John Benjamins.

1996. 'Negation in early German–English interlanguage: More valueless features in the L2 initial state', *Second Language Research* 12: 73–106.

Eubank, L., J. Bischof, A. Huffstutler, P. Leek and C. West 1997. '"Tom eats slowly cooked eggs": Thematic-verb raising in L2 knowledge', *Language Acquisition* 3: 171–99.

Eubank, L. and K. R. Gregg 1995. '"Et in Amygdala Ego"?: UG, (S)LA, and neurobiology', *Studies in Second Language Acquisition* 17: 35–57.

1999. 'Critical periods and (second) language acquisition: Divide et impera', in D. Birdsong (ed.), *Second language acquisition and the Critical Period Hypothesis*, pp. 65–99. Mahwah, NJ: Lawrence Erlbaum.

Eubank, L. and B. D. Schwartz (eds.) 1996. *Second Language Research: Special Issue on the L2 Initial State*. London: Arnold.

Ezeizabarrena, M.-J. 1996. *Adquisición de la morfología verbal en euskera y castellano por niños bilingües*. Bilbao: Servicio Editorial de la Universidad del País Vasco.

Felix, S. W. 1978. 'Some differences between first and second language acquisition', in N. Waterson and C. Snow (eds.), *The development of communication*, pp. 469–79. Chichester: Wiley.

1982. *Psycholinguistische Aspekte des Zweitsprachenerwerbs*. Tübingen: Narr.

1984. 'Maturational aspects of Universal Grammar', in A. Davies, C. Criper and A. Howatt (eds.), *Interlanguage*, pp. 133–61. Edinburgh: Edinburgh University Press.

1987. *Cognition and language growth*. Dordrecht: Foris.

Felser, C. (ed.) 2005. 'Experimental psycholinguistic approaches to second language acquisition', *Second Language Research* 21: 95–7.

Felser, C. and L. Roberts 2007. 'Processing wh-dependencies in a second language: A cross-modal priming study', *Second Language Research* 23: 9–36.

Felser, C., L. Roberts, R. Gross and T. Marinis 2003. 'The processing of ambiguous sentences by first and second language learners of English', *Applied Psycholinguistics* 24: 453–89.

Ferdinand, A. 1996. *The development of functional categories: The acquisition of the subject in French*. The Hague: Holland Academic Graphics.

1997. 'The development of phrase structure in child French', in J. A. Coerts and H. de Hoop (eds.), *Linguistics in the Netherlands 1997* 14, pp. 85–96. Amsterdam: John Benjamins.

Fernández, E. 2003. *Bilingual sentence processing*. Amsterdam: John Benjamins.

Flores, C. 2008. *A competência sintáctica de falantes bilingues luso-alemães regressados a Portugal: Um estudo sobre erosão linguística*. Universidade do Minho, Braga: PhD dissertation.

2010. 'The effect of age on language attrition: Evidence from bilingual returnees', *Bilingualism: Language and Cognition* 13(4): 533–46.

Flynn, S. 1983. 'Similarities and differences between first and second language acquisition: Setting the parameters of universal grammar', in D. Rogers and J. Sloboda (eds.), *Acquisition of symbolic skills*, pp. 485–500. New York: Plenum Press.

1987. *A parameter-setting model of L2 acquisition: Experimental studies in anaphora*. Dordrecht: Reidel.

1989. 'The role of the head-initial/head-final parameter in the acquisition of English relative clauses by adult Spanish and Japanese speakers', in S. M. Gass and J. Schachter (eds.), *Linguistic perspectives on second language acquisition*, pp. 89–108. Cambridge: Cambridge University Press.

1996. 'A parameter-setting approach to second language acquisition', in W. C. Ritchie and T. K. Bhatia (eds.), *Handbook of second language acquisition*, pp. 121–58. San Diego: Academic Press.

Flynn, S. and G. Martohardjono 1994. 'Mapping from the initial state to the final state: The separation of universal principles and language-specific properties', in B. Lust, M. Suñer and J. Whitman (eds.), *Syntactic theory and first language acquisition: Cross-linguistic perspectives*. Vol. 1*: Heads, projections and learnability*, pp. 319–35. Hillsdale, NJ: Lawrence Erlbaum.

Flynn, S. and W. O'Neil 1988. 'Introduction', in S. Flynn and W. O'Neil (eds.), *Linguistic theory in second language acquisition*, pp. 1–24. Dordrecht: Kluwer.

Fodor, J. D. 1998. 'Unambiguous triggers', *Linguistic Inquiry* 29: 1–36.

1999. 'Learnability theory: Triggers for parsing with', in E. C. Klein and G. Martohardjono (eds.), *The development of second language grammars: A generative approach*, pp. 336–407. Amsterdam: John Benjamins.

Friederici, A. D. 2002. 'Towards a neural basis of auditory sentence processing', *TRENDS in Cognitive Sciences* 6: 78–84.

Fries, C. C. 1945. *Teaching and learning English as a foreign language*. Ann Arbor: University of Michigan Press.

Gass, S. 1996. 'Second language acquisition and linguistic theory: The role of language transfer', in W. C. Ritchie and T. K. Bhatia (eds.), *Handbook of second language acquisition*, pp. 317–45. San Diego: Academic Press.

Genesee, F. 1989. 'Early bilingual development, one language or two?', *Journal of Child Language* 16: 161–79.

Genesee, F., E. Nicoladis and J. Paradis 1995. 'Language differentiation in early bilingual development', *Journal of Child Language* 22: 611–31.

Givón, T. 1979. *On understanding grammar*. New York: Academic Press.

Glahn, E., G. Håkansson, B. Hammarberg, A. Holmen, A. Hvenekilde and K. Lund 2001. 'Processability in Scandinavian second language acquisition', *Studies in Second Language Acquisition* 23: 389–416.

Goldbach, M. 1999. *Spezifische und arbiträre leere Objekte*. Frankfurt am Main: Vervuert Verlag.

Granfeldt, J. 2000. 'The acquisition of the determiner phrase in bilingual and second language French', *Bilingualism: Language and Cognition* 3: 263–80.

Granfeldt, J. and S. Schlyter 2004. 'Cliticisation in the acquisition of French as L1 and L2', in P. Prévost and J. Paradis (eds.), *The acquisition of French in different contexts*, pp. 333–70. Amsterdam: John Benjamins.

Granfeldt, J., S. Schlyter and M. Kihlstedt 2007. 'French as cL2, 2L1 and L1 in pre-school children', *Petites Études Romanes de Lund* 24: 5–42.

Gregg, K. 1984. 'Krashen's monitor and Occam's razor', *Applied Linguistics* 5: 79–100.

1996. 'The logical and developmental problems of second language acquisition', in W. C. Ritchie and T. K. Bhatia (eds.), *Handbook of second language acquisition*, pp. 49–81. San Diego: Academic Press.

Grondin, N. and L. White 1996. 'Functional categories in child L2 acquisition of French', *Language Acquisition* 5: 1–34.

Grosjean, F. 2001. 'The bilingual's language modes', in J. L. Nicol (ed.), *One mind, two languages: Bilingual language processing*, pp. 1–22. Oxford: Blackwell.

Guasti, M. T. 2002. *Language acquisition: The growth of grammar*. Cambridge MA: MIT Press.

Guasti, M. T., M. Nespor, A. Christophe and B. van Ooyen 2001. 'Pre-lexical setting of the head complement parameter through prosody', in B. Höhle and J. Weissenborn (eds.), *Approaches to bootstrapping: Phonological, syntactic and neurophysiological aspects of early language acquisition*, Vol. 1, pp. 229–48. Amsterdam: John Benjamins.

Guilfoyle, E. and M. Noonan 1992. 'Functional categories and language acquisition', *Canadian Journal of Linguistics* 37: 241–72.

Hahne, A. and A. D. Friederici 2001. 'Processing a second language. Late learners' comprehension mechanisms as revealed by event-related potentials', *Bilingualism: Language and Cognition* 4: 123–41.

Haider, H. 1991. 'Die menschliche Sprachfähigkeit – exaptiv und kognitiv opak', *Kognitionswissenschaft* 2: 11–26.

1994. '"(Un-)heimliche Subjekte: Anmerkungen zur Pro-drop Causa", im Anschluß an die Lektüre von Osvaldo Jaeggli und Kenneth J. Safir (eds.), *The Null Subject Parameter*', *Linguistische Berichte* 153: 372–85.

Håkansson, G. 1997. *Against Full Transfer in SLA: Evidence from the acquisition of German word order by Scandinavian learners*. Lund University, Department of Linguistics: Unpublished manuscript.

2001. 'Against Full Transfer: Evidence from Swedish learners of German', *Lund University: Department of Linguistics, Working Papers* 48: 67–86.

Håkansson, G., M. Pienemann and S. Sayehli 2002. 'Transfer and typological proximity in the context of second language processing', *Second Language Research* 18: 250–73.

Harley, B. 1986. *Age in second language acquisition*. Clevedon: Multilingual Matters.
Hatch, E. 1974. 'Second language learning – universals?', *Working Papers on Bilingualism* 3: 1–17.
Hauser, M. D., N. Chomsky and W. T. Fitch. 2002. 'The faculty of language: What is it, who has it, and how did it evolve?', *Science* 298: 1569–79.
Hawkins, R. 1994. 'French accusative case assignment and second language acquisition', *Essex Research Reports in Linguistics* 4: 37–69.
2001. *Second language syntax: A generative introduction*. Oxford: Blackwell.
Hawkins, R. and C. Y. Chan 1997. 'The partial availability of Universal Grammar in second language acquisition: The "failed functional features hypothesis"', *Second Language Research* 13: 187–226.
Hawkins, R. and F. Franceschina 2004. 'Explaining the acquisition and non-acquisition of determiner-noun gender concord in French and Spanish', in P. Prévost and J. Paradis (eds.), *The acquisition of French in different contexts: Focus on functional categories*, pp. 175–205. Amsterdam: John Benjamins.
Hawkins, R., R. Towell and N. Bazergui 1993. 'Universal Grammar and the acquisition of French verb movement by native speakers of English', *Second Language Research* 9: 189–233.
Haznedar, B. 1997. 'L2 acquisition by a Turkish-speaking child: Evidence for L1 influence', in E. Hughes, M. Hughes and A. Greenhill (eds.), *Proceedings of the 21st Annual Boston University Conference on Language Development*, pp. 245–56. Somerville, MA: Cascadilla Press.
2003. 'The status of functional categories in child second language acquisition: Evidence from the acquisition of CP', *Second Language Research* 19: 1–41.
Haznedar, B. and E. Gavruseva (eds.) 2008. *Current trends in child second language acquisition: A generative perspective*. Amsterdam: John Benjamins.
Haznedar, B. and B. D. Schwartz 1997. 'Are there optional infinitives in child L2 acquisition?', in E. Hughes, M. Hughes and A. Greenhill (eds.), *Proceedings of the 21st Annual Boston University Conference on Language Development*, pp. 257–268. Somerville, MA: Cascadilla Press.
Heine, B. and T. Kuteva 2002. *World lexicon of grammaticalization*. Cambridge: Cambridge University Press.
Hemforth, B. 1993. *Kognitives Parsing: Repräsentation und Verarbeitung sprachlichen Wissens*. Sankt Augustin: Infix.
Herschensohn, J. 2000. *The second time round: Minimalism and L2 acquisition*. Amsterdam: John Benjamins.
2007. *Language development and age*. Cambridge: Cambridge University Press.
2009. 'Fundamental and gradient differences in language development', *Studies in Second Language Acquisition* 31: 259–89.
Hilles, S. 1986. 'Interlanguage and the pro-drop parameter', *Second Language Research* 2: 33–52.
1991. 'Access to Universal Grammar in second language acquisition', in L. Eubank (ed.), *Point-counterpoint: Universal Grammar in the second language*, pp. 305–38. Amsterdam: John Benjamins.
Hinzelin, M.-O. 2003. 'The acquisition of subjects in bilingual children: Pronoun use in Portuguese–German children', in N. Müller (ed.), *(In)vulnerable domains in multilingualism*, pp. 107–37. Amsterdam: John Benjamins.

Hoekstra, T. and P. Jordens 1994. 'From adjunct to head', in T. Hoekstra and B. D. Schwartz (eds.), *Language acquisition studies in generative grammar: Papers in honor of Kenneth Wexler from the 1991 GLOW workshop*, pp. 119–49. Amsterdam: John Benjamins.

Holmberg, A. (ed.) 2009. 'Partial pro-drop', Special issue of *Studia Linguistica* 63.

Hong, U. 1995. *Null-Subjekte im Erst- und Zweitspracherwerb des Deutschen: Eine vergleichende Untersuchung im Rahmen der Prinzipien- und Parametertheorie*. Tübingen: Narr.

Hornstein, N., J. Nunes and K. Grohmann 2005. *Understanding Minimalism*. Cambridge: Cambridge University Press.

Houwer, A. de 1995. 'Bilingual language acquisition', in P. Fletcher and B. MacWhinney (eds.), *The handbook of child language*, pp. 219–50. Oxford: Blackwell.

Hulk, A. 1991. 'Parameter setting and the acquisition of word order in L2 French', *Second Language Research* 7: 1–34.

2000. 'Non-selective access and activation in child bilingualism: The syntax', in S. Döpke (ed.), *Cross-linguistic structures in simultaneous bilingualism*, pp. 57–78. Amsterdam: John Benjamins.

Hulk, A. and L. Cornips 2006. 'Between 2L1 and child L2 acquisition', in C. Lleó (ed.), *Interfaces in multilingualism*, pp. 115–37. Amsterdam: John Benjamins.

Hulk, A. and N. Müller 2000. 'Bilingual first language acquisition at the interface between syntax and pragmatics', *Bilingualism: Language and Cognition* 3: 227–44.

Hulstijn, J. 2002. 'Towards a unified account of the representation, processing, and acquisition of a second language', *Second Language Research* 18: 193–232.

Hyams, N. 1986. *Language acquisition and the theory of parameters*. Dordrecht: D. Reidel.

1989. 'The null subject parameter in language acquisition', in O. Jaeggli and K. J. Safir (eds.), *The null subject parameter*, pp. 215–38. Dordrecht: Kluwer.

Hyltenstam, K. 1977. 'Implicational patterns in interlanguage syntax variation', *Language Learning* 27: 383–411.

1978. 'A framework for the study of interlanguage continua', *Working Papers: Phonetics Laboratory/Department of Linguistics* 16, University of Lund.

Hyltenstam, K. and N. Abrahamsson 2000. 'Who can become native-like in a second language? All, some, or none?', *Studia Linguistica* 54: 150–66.

2003. 'Maturational constraints in second language acquisition', in C. Doughty and M. H. Long (eds.), *Handbook of second language acquisition*, pp. 539–88. Oxford: Blackwell.

Iatridou, S. 1990. 'About Agr(P)', *Linguistic Inquiry* 21: 551–77.

Ingram, D. 1989. *First language acquisition: Method, description and explanation*. Cambridge: Cambridge University Press.

Ioup, G., E. Boustagui, M. El Tigi and M. Moselle 1994. 'Reexamining the critical period hypothesis: A case study of successful adult SLA in a naturalistic environment', *Studies in Second Language Acquisition* 16: 73–98.

Isel, F. 2005. 'First- and second-language processing: Cross-linguistic neurophysiological evidence', *Le langage et l'homme* 40: 79–95.

Jackendoff, R. 2001. 'Review of W. H. Calvin and D. Bickerton, *Lingua ex machina: Reconciling Darwin and Chomsky with the human brain*. Cambridge, MA: MIT Press, 2000', *Language* 77: 569–73.

Jacobs, B. 1995. 'Dis-integrating perspectives of language acquisition: A response to Eubank and Gregg', *Studies in Second Language Acquisition* 17: 65–71.

Jaeggli, O. and K. J. Safir (eds.) 1989. *The null subject parameter.* Dordrecht: Kluwer.

Jansen, B., J. Lalleman and P. Muysken 1981. 'The alternation hypothesis: Acquisition of Dutch order by Turkish and Moroccan foreign workers', *Language Learning* 31: 315–36.

Johnson, J. 1992. 'Critical period effects in second language acquisition: The effect of written versus auditory materials on the assessment of grammatical competence', *Language Learning* 42: 217–48.

Johnson, J. and E. Newport 1989. 'Critical period effects in second language learning: The influence of maturational state on the acquisition of English as a second language', *Cognitive Psychology* 21: 60–99.

1991. 'Critical period effects on universal properties of language: The status of subjacency in the acquisition of a second language', *Cognition* 39: 215–58.

Jordens, P. 1977. 'Rules, grammatical intuitions and strategies', *Interlanguage Studies Bulletin* 2: 5–76.

1980. 'Interlanguage research: Interpretation or explanation', *Language Learning* 30: 195–207.

Jordens, P. and E. Kellerman 1981. 'Investigations into the strategy of transfer in second language acquisition', in J. J. Savard and L. Laforge (eds.), *Actes du Vième Congrès International de Linguistique Appliquée*, pp. 195–215. Quebec: Les Presses de l'Université Laval.

Juffs, A. 1998a. 'Main verb vs. reduced relative clause ambiguity resolution in second language sentence processing', *Language Learning* 48: 107–47.

1998b. 'Some effects of first language argument structure and morphosyntax on second language processing', *Second Language Research* 14: 406–24.

2005. 'The influence of first language on the processing of wh-movement in English as a second language', *Second Language Research* 21: 121–51.

Juffs, A. and M. Harrington 1995. 'Parsing effects in second language sentence processing', *Studies in Second Language Acquisition* 17: 483–516.

1996. 'Garden path sentences and error data in second language processing research', *Language Learning* 46: 286–324.

Jusczyk, P. W., A. D. Friederici, J. M. I. Wessels, V. Y. Svenkerud and A. M. Jusczyk 1993. 'Infants' sensitivity to the sound patterns of native language words', *Journal of Memory and Language* 32: 402–20.

Kaltenbacher, M. 2001. *Universal Grammar and parameter resetting in second language acquisition.* Frankfurt am Main: Peter Lang.

Karmiloff-Smith, A. 1979. *A functional approach to child language.* Cambridge: Cambridge University Press.

Kayne, R. 1994. *The antisymmetry of syntax.* Cambridge, MA: MIT Press.

Kellerman, E. 1977. 'Towards a characterisation of the strategy of transfer in second language learning', *Interlanguage Studies Bulletin* 2: 58–145.

1979. 'Transfer and non-transfer: Where are we now?', *Studies in Second Language Acquisition* 2: 37–58.

1987. *Aspects of transferability in second language acquisition.* Nijmegen: PhD thesis.

Kempen, G. and E. Hoenkamp 1987. 'An incremental procedural grammar for sentence formulation', *Cognitive Science* 11: 201–58.

Kim, K. H., N. R. Relkin, K.-M. Lee and J. Hirsch 1997. 'Distinct cortical areas associated with native and second languages', *Nature* 388: 171–4.

Klein, E. 1999. 'Just parsing through: Notes on the state of L2 processing research today', in E. Klein and G. Martohardjono (eds.), *The development of second language grammars: A generative approach*, pp. 197–216. Amsterdam: John Benjamins.

Klein, W. and C. Perdue (eds.) 1992. *Utterance structure: Developing grammars again*. Amsterdam: John Benjamins.

1993. 'Utterance structure', in C. Perdue (ed.), *Adult second language acquisition: The results*, pp. 3–40. Cambridge: Cambridge University Press.

1997. 'The Basic Variety (or: Couldn't natural languages be much simpler?)', *Second Language Research* 13(4): 301–47.

Klima, E. and U. Bellugi 1966. 'Syntactic regularities in the speech of children', in J. Lyons and R. Wales (eds.), *Psycholinguistic papers*, pp. 183–208. Edinburgh: Edinburgh University Press.

Köpcke, K.-M. 1987. 'Der Erwerb morphologischer Ausdrucksmittel durch L2-Lerner am Beispiel der Personalflexion', *Zeitschrift für Sprachwissenschaft* 6: 186–205.

Köppe, R. 1996. 'Language differentiation in bilingual children: The development of grammatical and pragmatic competence', *Linguistics* 34: 927–54.

1997. *Sprachentrennung im frühen bilingualen Erstspracherwerb: Französisch/Deutsch*. Tübingen: Narr.

Kouwenberg, S. 1992. 'From OV to VO: Linguistic negotiation in the development of Berbice Dutch Creole', *Lingua* 88: 263–99.

Krashen, S. D. 1973. 'Lateralization, language learning and the critical period: Some new evidence', *Language Learning* 23: 63–74.

1977. 'Some issues relating to the Monitor Model', in H. Brown, C. Yorio and R. Crymes (eds.), *On TESOL '77*, pp. 144–58. Washington, DC: TESOL.

Krashen S. D., C. Madden and N. Bailey 1975. 'Theoretical aspects of grammatical sequencing', in M. K. Burt and H. C. Dulay (eds.), *On TESOL '75: New directions in second language learning, teaching and bilingual education*, pp. 44–54. Washington, DC: TESOL.

Krems, J. 1984. *Erwartungsgeleitete Sprachverarbeitung: Computersimulierungen von Verstehensprozessen*. Frankfurt am Main: Peter Lang.

Kroffke, S. and M. Rothweiler 2006. 'Variation im frühen Zweitspracherwerb des Deutschen durch Kinder mit türkischer Erstsprache', in M. Vliegen (ed.), *Variation in Sprachtheorie und Spracherwerb: Akten des 39. Linguistischen Kolloquiums in Amsterdam*, pp. 145–54. Frankfurt am Main: Peter Lang.

Kroffke, S., M. Rothweiler and E. Babur 2007. 'Turkish-German successive bilingual children: Age of onset and the development of German V2'. Paper presented at the 6th International Symposium on Bilingualism, Hamburg, May 2007.

Lado, R. 1957. *Linguistics across cultures*. Ann Arbor: University of Michigan Press.

Lakshmanan, U. 1991. 'Morphological uniformity and null subjects in child second language acquisition', in L. Eubank (ed.), *Point-counterpoint: Universal Grammar in the second language*, pp. 389–410. Amsterdam: John Benjamins.

1994. *Universal Grammar in child second language acquisition*. Amsterdam: John Benjamins.

1995. 'Child second language acquisition of syntax', *Studies in Second Language Acquisition* 17: 301–29.

Lardiere, D. 1998a. 'Dissociating syntax from morphology in a divergent end-state grammar', *Second Language Research* 14: 359–75.

1998b. 'Parameter-resetting in morphology: Evidence from compounding', in M.-L. Beck (ed.), *Morphology and its interfaces in second language knowledge*, pp. 283–305. Amsterdam: John Benjamins.

2000. 'Mapping features to forms in second language acquisition', in J. Archibald (ed.), *Second language acquisition and linguistic theory*, pp. 102–29. Oxford: Blackwell.

2008. 'Feature assembly in second language acquisition', in J. M. Liceras, H. Zobl and H. Goodluck (eds.), *The role of formal features in second language acquisition*, pp. 106–40. London: Routledge.

2009. 'Some thoughts on the contrastive analysis of features in second language acquisition', *Second Language Research* 25: 173–227.

Lardiere, D. and B. D. Schwartz 1997. 'Feature-marking in the L2 development of deverbal compounds', *Journal of Linguistics* 33: 327–53.

Larsen-Freeman, D. 1975. *The acquisition of grammatical morphemes by adult learners of English as a second language*. University of Michigan: PhD thesis.

Larsen-Freeman, D. and M. H. Long 1991. *An introduction to second language acquisition research*. London: Longman.

Lebeaux, D. 1988. *Language acquisition and the form of the grammar*. University of Massachusetts, Amherst, MA: PhD thesis.

Lenneberg, E. 1967. *Biological foundations of language*. New York: Wiley.

Levelt, W. J. M. 1989. *Speaking: From intention to articulation*. Cambridge, MA: MIT Press.

Liceras, J. M. 1986. *Linguistic theory and second language acquisition*. Tübingen: Narr.

1989. 'On some properties of the "pro-drop" parameter: Looking for missing subjects in non-native Spanish', in S. M. Gass and J. Schachter (eds.), *Linguistic perspectives on second language acquisition*, pp. 109–33. Cambridge: Cambridge University Press.

1997. 'The now and then of L2 growing pains', in L. Díaz and C. Pérez-Vidal (eds.), *Views on the acquisition and use of a second language*, pp. 65–85. Barcelona: Universitat Pompeu Fabra.

Liceras, J. M., L. Díaz and D. Maxwell 1999. 'Null subjects in non-native grammars', in E. C Klein and G. Martohardjono (eds.), *The development of second language grammars: A generative approach*, pp. 109–45. Amsterdam: John Benjamins.

Lightfoot, D. 1989. 'The child's trigger experience: Degree-0 learnability', *Behavioral and Brain Sciences* 12: 321–34.

1991. *How to set parameters: Arguments from language change*. Cambridge, MA: MIT Press.

Locke, J. L. 1995. 'Development of the capacity for spoken language', in P. Fletcher and B. MacWhinney (eds.), *The handbook of child language*, pp. 278–302. Oxford: Blackwell.

1997. 'A theory of neurolinguistic development', *Brain and Language* 58: 265–326.

Long, M. H. 1990. 'Maturational constraints on language development', *Studies in Second Language Acquisition* 12: 251–68.

Long, M. H. and C. J. Sato 1984. 'Methodological issues in interlanguage studies: An interactionist perspective', in A. Davies, C. Criper and A. Howatt (eds.), *Interlanguage*, pp. 253–79. Edinburgh: Edinburgh University Press.

Lust, B. 1988. 'Universal Grammar in second language acquisition: Promises and problems in critically relating theory and empirical studies', in S. Flynn and W. O'Neil (eds.), *Linguistic theory in second language acquisition*, pp. 1–24. Dordrecht: Kluwer.

Martohardjono, G. and J. Gair 1993. 'Apparent UG inaccessibility in second language acquisition: Misapplied principles or principled misapplications?', in F. Eckman (ed.), *Confluence: Linguistics, second language acquisition and speech pathology*, pp. 79–103. Amsterdam: John Benjamins.

Mazurkevich, I. 1984. 'The acquisition of the dative alternation by second language learners and linguistic theory', *Language Learning* 49: 91–109.

McLaughlin, B. 1978. *Second-language acquisition in childhood*. Hillsdale, NJ: Lawrence Erlbaum.

McNeill, D. 1966. 'Developmental psycholinguistics', in F. Smith and G. Miller (eds.), *The genesis of language*, pp. 15–84. Cambridge, MA: MIT Press.

McNeill, D. and N. B. McNeill 1968. 'What does a child mean when he says "no"?', in E. M. Zale (ed.), *Proceedings of the conference on language and language behavior*, pp. 51–62. New York: Appleton, Century, Crofts.

Meillet, A. 1912. 'L'évolution des formes grammaticales', *Scientia* 12: 384–400.

Meisel, J. M. 1977. 'Linguistic simplification: A study of immigrant workers' speech and foreigner talk', in S. P. Corder and E. Roulet (eds.), *The notions of simplification, interlanguages and pidgins and their relation to second language pedagogy*, pp. 88–113. Geneva: Droz.

1983a. 'Strategies of second language acquisition: More than one kind of simplification', in R. W. Andersen (ed.), *Pidginization and creolization as language acquisition*, pp. 120–57. Rowley, MA: Newbury House.

1983b. 'An encounter of the third kind: Will the non-real interfere with what the learner does?', in R. W. Andersen (ed.), *Pidginization and creolization as language acquisition*, pp. 198–205. Rowley, MA: Newbury House.

1983c. 'Transfer as a second-language strategy', *Language and Communication* 3: 11–46.

1985. 'Les phases initiales du développement des notions temporelles, aspectuelles et de modes d'action', *Lingua* 66: 321–74.

1986. 'Word order and case marking in early child language: Evidence from simultaneous acquisition of two first languages: French and German', *Linguistics* 24: 123–83.

1987a. 'Reference to past events and actions in the development of natural second language acquisition', in C. W. Pfaff (ed.), *Cross-linguistic studies of language acquisition*, pp. 206–24. Rowley, MA: Newbury House.

1987b. 'A note on second language speech production', in H. W. Dechert and M. Raupach (eds.), *Psycholinguistic models of production*, pp. 83–90. Norwood, NJ: Ablex.

1988. 'Second language learners' (limited) access to Universal Grammar'. Paper presented at the Eighth Second Language Research Forum. University of Hawai'i at Manoa, 3–6 March.

1989. 'Early differentiation of languages in bilingual children', in K. Hyltenstam and L. Obler (eds.), *Bilingualism across the lifespan: Aspects of acquisition, maturity, and loss*, pp. 13–40. Cambridge: Cambridge University Press.

1990. 'INFL-ection: Subjects and subject-verb agreement', in J. M. Meisel (ed.), *Two first languages: Early grammatical development in bilingual children*, pp. 237–98. Dordrecht: Foris.

1991. 'Principles of Universal Grammar and strategies of language use: On some similarities and differences between first and second language acquisition', in L. Eubank (ed.), *Point-counterpoint: Universal Grammar in the second language*, pp. 231–76. Amsterdam: John Benjamins.

1993. 'Simultaneous first language acquisition: A window on early grammatical development', *DELTA* 9 (No. Especial): 353–85.

1994a. 'Getting FAT: Finiteness, Agreement and Tense in early grammars', in J. M. Meisel (ed.), *Bilingual first language acquisition: French and German grammatical development*, pp. 89–129. Amsterdam: John Benjamins.

1994b. 'La adquisición de la negación en euskera y castellano', in J. M. Meisel (ed.), *La adquisición del vasco y del castellano en niños bilingües*, pp. 151–80. Madrid/ Frankfurt am Main: Vervuert.

1995. 'Parameters in acquisition', in P. Fletcher and B. MacWhinney (eds.), *The handbook of child language*, pp. 10–35. Oxford: Blackwell.

1997a. 'L'acquisition de la négation en langue première', in C. Martinot (ed.), *Actes du Colloque international sur l'acquisition de la syntaxe en langue maternelle et en langue étrangère*, pp. 190–222. Besançon: Annales Littéraires de l'Université de Franche-Comté.

1997b. 'The acquisition of the syntax of negation in French and German: Contrasting first and second language development', *Second Language Research* 13(3): 227–63.

1997c. 'The Basic Variety as an i-language', *Second Language Research* 13: 374–85.

1998. 'Parametric change in language development: Psycholinguistic and historical perspectives on second language acquisition', in J. Fernández González and J. de Santiago Guervós (eds.), *Issues in second language acquisition and learning*, pp. 18–36. Valencia: Servei de Publicacions.

2000a. 'Revisiting Universal Grammar', *DELTA* 16 (No. Especial): 129–40.

2000b. 'On transfer at the initial state of L2 acquisition', in C. Riemer (ed.), *Kognitive Aspekte des Lehrens und Lernens von Fremdsprachen – Cognitive aspects of foreign language learning and teaching. Festschrift für Willis J. Edmondson*, pp. 186–206. Tübingen: Narr.

2001. 'The simultaneous acquisition of two first languages: Early differentiation and subsequent development of grammars', in J. Cenoz and F. Genesee (eds.), *Trends in bilingual acquisition*, pp. 11–41. Amsterdam: John Benjamins.

2004. 'The bilingual child', in T. K. Bhatia and W. C. Ritchie (eds.), *The handbook of bilingualism*, pp. 91–113. Oxford: Blackwell.

2007a. 'The weaker language in early child bilingualism: Acquiring a first language as a second language?', *Applied Psycholinguistics* 28: 495–514.

2007b. 'On autonomous syntactic development in multiple first language acquisition', in H. Caunt-Nulton, S. Kulatilake and I.-H. Woo (eds.), *Proceedings of the 31st Annual Boston University Conference on Language Development*, pp. 26–45. Somerville, MA: Cascadilla Press.

2008a. 'Child second language acquisition or successive first language acquisition?', in B. Haznedar and E. Gavruseva (eds.), *Current trends in child second language acquisition: A generative perspective*, pp. 55–80. Amsterdam: John Benjamins.

2008b. 'Âge du début de l'acquisition successive du bilinguisme. Effets sur le développement grammatical', in M. Kail, M. Fayol and M. Hickman (eds.), *Apprentissage des langues premières et secondes*, pp. 245–72. Paris: Editions du CNRS.

2009. 'Second language acquisition in early childhood', *Zeitschrift für Sprachwissenschaft* 28: 5–34.

forthcoming. 'Bilingual language acquisition and theories of diachronic change: Bilingualism as cause and effect of grammatical change', *Bilingualism: Language and Cognition* 14.

Meisel, J. M., H. Clahsen and M. Pienemann 1981. 'On determining developmental stages in natural second language acquisition', *Studies in Second Language Acquisition* 3: 109–35.

Meisel, J. M. and M.-J. Ezeizabarrena 1996. 'Subject-verb and object-verb agreement in early Basque', in H. Clahsen (ed.), *Generative perspectives on language acquisition: Empirical findings, theoretical considerations, crosslinguistic comparisons*, pp. 201–39. Amsterdam: John Benjamins.

Meisel, J. M. and N. Müller 1992. 'Finiteness and verb placement in early child grammars: Evidence from the simultaneous acquisition of two first languages: French and German', in J. M. Meisel (ed.), *The acquisition of verb placement: Functional categories and V2 phenomena in language acquisition*, pp. 109–38. Dordrecht: Kluwer.

Mills, A. 1985. 'The acquisition of German', in D. I. Slobin (ed.), *The crosslinguistic study of language acquisition,* Vol. 1*: The data*, pp. 141–254. Hillsdale, NJ: Lawrence Erlbaum.

Milon, J. 1974. 'The development of negation in English by a second language learner', *TESOL Quarterly* 8: 137–43.

Möhring, A. 2001. 'The acquisition of French by German pre-school children: An empirical investigation of gender assignment and gender agreement', in S. Foster-Cohen and A. Nizegorodcew (eds.), *EUROSLA Yearbook*, Vol. 1, pp. 171–93. Amsterdam: John Benjamins.

2005. 'Against full transfer during early phases of L2 acquisition: Evidence from German learners of French', *Working Papers in Multilingualism 63*. Hamburg: Research Center on Multilingualism.

Möhring, A. and J. M. Meisel 2003. 'The verb-object parameter in simultaneous and successive acquisition of bilingualism', in N. Müller (ed.), *(In)vulnerable domains in multilingualism*, pp. 293–332. Amsterdam: John Benjamins.

Montrul, S. 2008. *Incomplete acquisition: Re-examining the age factor*. Amsterdam: John Benjamins.

Müller, N. 1993. *Komplexe Sätze: Der Erwerb von COMP und Wortstellungsmustern bei bilingualen Kindern (Französisch–Deutsch)*. Tübingen: Narr.

1994a. 'Gender and number agreement within DP', in J. M. Meisel (ed.), *Bilingual first language acquisition: French and German grammatical development*, pp. 53–88. Amsterdam: John Benjamins.

1994b. 'Parameters cannot be reset: Evidence from the development of COMP', in J. M. Meisel (ed.), *Bilingual first language acquisition: French and German grammatical development*, pp. 235–69. Amsterdam: John Benjamins.

1996. 'Subordinate clauses in second and first language acquisition: A case against parameters'. University of Hamburg: unpublished manuscript.

1998. 'Die Abfolge OV/VO und Nebensätze im Zweit- und Erstspracherwerb', in H. Wegener (ed.), *Eine zweite Sprache lernen: Empirische Untersuchungen zum Zweitspracherwerb*, pp. 89–116. Tübingen: Narr.

Neeleman, A. and F. Weerman 1997. 'L1 and L2 word order acquisition', *Language Acquisition* 6: 125–70.

1999. *Flexible syntax: A theory of case and arguments*. Dordrecht: Kluwer.

Nemser, W. 1971. 'Approximative systems of foreign language learners', *International Review of Applied Linguistics* 9: 115–23.

Nicholas, H. 1987. *A comparative study of the acquisition of German as a first and as a second language*. Melbourne, Monash University: Unpublished thesis.

Noyau, C. 1982. 'French negation in the language of Spanish-speaking immigrant workers: Social acquisition/variability/transfer/individual systems', European–North American Workshop on Cross-linguistic Second Language Acquisition Research, Lake Arrowhead, 1981.

Obler, L. K. and K. Gjerlow 1999. *Language and the brain*. Cambridge: Cambridge University Press.

Ouhalla, J. 1991. *Functional categories and parametric variation*. London: Routledge.

Oyama, S. 1973. *A sensitive period for the acquisition of a second language*. Harvard University: PhD thesis.

Papadopoulou, D. 2005. 'Reading-time studies of second language ambiguity resolution', *Second Language Research* 21: 98–120.

Papadopoulou, D. and H. Clahsen 2003. 'Parsing strategies in L1 and L2 sentence processing: A study of relative clause attachment in Greek', *Studies in Second Language Acquisition* 24: 501–28.

Paradis, J. and F. Genesee 1996. 'Syntactic acquisition in bilingual children: Autonomous or Interdependent?', *Studies in Second Language Acquisition* 18: 1–25.

Paradis, M. 1994. 'Neurolinguistic aspects of implicit and explicit memory: Implications for bilingualism and SLA', in N. Ellis (ed.), *Implicit and explicit language learning*, pp. 393–419. London: Academic Press.

2004. *A neurolinguistic theory of bilingualism*. Amsterdam: John Benjamins.

2009. *Declarative and procedural determinants of second languages*. Amsterdam: John Benjamins.

Park, T. Z. 1979. 'Some facts on negation: Wode's four-stage developmental theory of negation revisited', *Journal of Child Language* 6: 147–51.

Parodi, T. 1998. *Der Erwerb funktionaler Kategorien im Deutschen. Eine Untersuchung zum bilingualen Erstspracherwerb und zum Zweitspracherwerb*. Tübingen: Narr.

Parodi, T., B. D. Schwartz and H. Clahsen 2004. 'On the L2 acquisition of the morphosyntax of German nominals', *Linguistics* 42: 669–705.

Penfield, W. and L. Roberts 1959. *Speech and brain mechanisms*. New York: Athenaeum.

Perdue, C. (ed.) 1993a. *Adult second language acquisition: Crosslinguistic perspectives*. Vol. 1*: Field methods*. Cambridge: Cambridge University Press.

(ed.) 1993b. *Adult second language acquisition: Crosslinguistic perspectives*. Vol. 2: *The results*, Cambridge: Cambridge University Press.

1996. 'Pre-basic varieties: The first stages of second language acquisition', *Toegepaste Taalwetenschap in Artikelen* 55: 135–50.

Pfaff, C. W. 1992. 'The issue of grammaticalization in early German second language', *Studies in Second Language Acquisition* 14: 273–96.

Pfaff, C. W. and R. Portz 1979. 'Foreign children's acquisition of German: Universals versus interference'. Paper presented at the LSA Annual Meeting, Los Angeles, 27–29 December.

Phinney, M. 1987. 'The pro-drop parameter in second language acquisition', in T. Roeper and E. Williams (eds.), *Parameter setting*, pp. 221–38. Dordrecht: Reidel.

Pienemann, M. 1981. *Der Zweitspracherwerb ausländischer Arbeiterkinder*. Bonn: Bouvier.

1984. 'Psychological constraints on the teachability of languages', *Studies in Second Language Acquisition* 6: 186–214.

1998a. *Language processing and second language development: Processability theory*. Amsterdam: John Benjamins.

1998b. 'Developmental dynamics in L1 and L2 acquisition: Processability theory and generative entrenchment', *Bilingualism: Language and Cognition* 1: 1–20.

(ed.) 2005. *Cross-linguistic aspects of processability theory*. Amsterdam: John Benjamins.

Pienemann, M., B. Di Biase, S. Kawaguchi and G. Håkansson 2005. 'Processability, typological constraints and L1 transfer', in M. Pienemann (ed.), *Cross-linguistic aspects of processability theory*, pp. 86–116. Amsterdam: John Benjamins.

Pienemann, M. and G. Håkansson 1999. 'A unified approach towards a theory of the development of Swedish as L2. A processability account', *Studies in Second Language Acquisition* 21: 383–420.

2007. 'Full transfer versus developmentally moderated transfer: A reply to Bohnacker', *Second Language Research* 23: 105–14.

Pierantozzi, C. 2009. 'The acquisition of word order: Comparing first language acquisition, (2)L1, child L2 and adult L2 acquisition'. University of Hamburg: Unpublished paper.

Pierce, A. E. 1992. *Language acquisition and syntactic theory: A comparative analysis of French and English child grammars*. Dordrecht: Kluwer.

Pinker, S. 1984. *Language learnability and language development*. Cambridge, MA: Harvard University Press.

1994. *The language instinct*. New York: William Morrow and Company.

Platt, E. 1993. 'Parameter-resetting in second language acquisition: A study of adult Spanish and Vietnamese learners of English', in F. R. Eckman (ed.). *Confluence: Linguistics L2 acquisition and speech pathology*, pp. 105–34. Amsterdam: John Benjamins.

Platzack, C. 1996. 'The initial hypothesis of syntax: A minimalist perspective on language acquisition and attrition', in H. Clahsen (ed.), *Generative perspectives on language acquisition: Empirical findings, theoretical considerations, crosslinguistic comparisons*, pp. 369–414. Amsterdam: John Benjamins.

Platzack, C. and A. Holmberg 1989. 'The role of AGR and finiteness in Germanic VO languages', *Scandinavian Working Papers in Linguistics* 43: 51–76.

Poeppel, D. and K. Wexler 1993. 'The full competence hypothesis of clause structure in early German', *Language* 69: 1–33.

Pollock, J.-Y. 1989. 'Verb movement, universal grammar, and the structure of IP', *Linguistic Inquiry* 20: 365–424.

Powers, S. M. 1999. '(E)merging functional structure'. University of Potsdam: Unpublished paper.

2001. 'A minimalist account of phrase structure acquisition', in G. M. Alexandrova and O. Arnaudova (eds.), *The minimalist parameter*, pp. 33–50. Amsterdam: John Benjamins.

Prévost, P. and L. White 2000a. 'Accounting for morphological variation in second language acquisition: Truncation or missing inflection?', in M.-A. Friedemann and L. Rizzi (eds.), *The acquisition of syntax: Studies in comparative developmental linguistics*, pp. 202–35. London: Longman.

2000b. 'Missing surface inflection or impairment in second language acquisition? Evidence from tense and agreement', *Second Language Research* 16: 103–33.

Pritchett, B. L. 1992. *Grammatical competence and parsing performance.* Chicago: Chicago University Press.

Pullum, G. K. and B. C. Scholz 2002. 'Empirical assessment of stimulus poverty arguments', *The Linguistic Review* 19: 9–50.

Pulvermüller, F. 1995. 'What neurobiology can buy language theory: A response to Eubank and Gregg', *Studies in Second Language Acquisition* 17: 73–7.

Pulvermüller, F. and J. H. Schumann 1994. 'Neurobiological mechanisms of language acquisition', *Language Learning* 44: 681–734.

Radford, A. 1986. 'Small children's small clauses', *Bangor Research Papers in Linguistics* 1: 1–38.

1990. *Syntactic theory and the acquisition of syntax.* Oxford: Blackwell.

1997. *Syntactic theory and the structure of English: A minimalist approach.* Cambridge: Cambridge University Press.

2004. *Minimalist syntax.* Cambridge: Cambridge University Press.

Randall, J. 1990. 'Catapults and pendulums: The mechanisms of language acquisition', *Linguistics* 28: 1381–406.

Ravem, R. 1968. 'Language acquisition in a second language environment', *International Review of Applied Linguistics* 6: 165–85.

Reinecke, J. 1935/1969. *Language and dialect in Hawaii.* Honolulu: University of Hawaii Press.

Richards, J. 1971. 'Error analysis and second language strategies', *Language Sciences* 17: 12–22.

Riedel, A.-K. 2009. 'Root infinitives in child L2 acquisition of French'. Working Paper 4, University of Hamburg, Research Center on Multilingualism.

Rizzi, L. 1982. *Issues in Italian syntax.* Dordrecht: Foris.

1986. 'Null objects and the theory of pro', *Linguistic Inquiry* 17: 501–57.

1993/94. 'Some notes on linguistic theory and language development: The case of root infinitives', *Language Acquisition* 3 (4): 371–93.

1997. 'The fine structure of the left periphery', in L. Haegeman (ed.), *Elements of grammar*, pp. 281–337. Dordrecht: Kluwer.

(ed.) 2004. *The structure of CP and IP: The cartography of syntactic structures*, Vol. 2. New York: Oxford University Press.

Roeper, T. 1992. 'From the initial state to V2: Acquisition principles in action', in J. M. Meisel (ed.), *The acquisition of verb placement: Functional categories and V2 phenomena in language acquisition*, pp. 333–70. Dordrecht: Kluwer.

1996. 'Merger theory and formal features in acquisition', in H. Clahsen (ed.), *Generative perspectives on language acquisition: Empirical findings, theoretical considerations, crosslinguistic comparisons*, pp. 415–50. Amsterdam: John Benjamins.

2007. *The prism of grammar: How child language illuminates humanism.* Cambridge, MA: MIT Press (A Bradford Book).

Roeper, T. and J. Weissenborn 1990. 'How to make parameters work: Comments on Valian', in L. Frazier and J. de Villiers (eds.), *Language processing and language acquisition*, pp. 147–62. Dordrecht: Kluwer.

Roeper, T. and E. Williams (eds.) 1987. *Parameter setting*. Dordrecht: Reidel.

Rosansky, E. 1976. *Second language acquisition research: A question of methods*. Harvard University: PhD thesis.

Ross, J. R. 1967. *Constraints on variables in syntax*. MIT: PhD dissertation.

Rothweiler, M. 1993. *Der Erwerb von Nebensätzen im Deutschen: Eine Pilotstudie*. Tübingen: Niemeyer.

2006. 'The acquisition of V2 and subordinate clauses in early successive acquisition of German', in C. Lleó (ed.), *Interfaces in multilingualism*, pp. 91–113. Amsterdam: John Benjamins.

Rutherford, W. 1983. 'Language typology and language transfer', in S. Gass and L. Selinker (eds.), *Language transfer in language learning*, pp. 358–70. Rowley, MA: Newbury House.

Sabourin, L. 2003. *Grammatical gender and second language processing: An ERP study*. University of Groningen: PhD dissertation.

Saur, D., A. Baumgärtner, A. Möhring, C. Büchel, M. Bonnesen, M. Rose, M. Musso and J. M. Meisel 2009. 'Word order processing in the bilingual brain', *Neuropsychologia* 47: 158–68.

Saussure, F. de 1916/1975. *Cours de linguistique générale*, published by Charles Bally and Albert Sechehaye, ed. T. de Mauro, Paris: Payot.

Say, T. 2001. *Feature acquisition in bilingual child language development*. University of Hamburg, Research Center on Multilingualism: Working Papers in Multilingualism.

Schachter, J. 1988. 'Second language acquisition and its relation to universal grammar', *Applied Linguistics* 9: 219–35.

1989. 'Testing a proposed universal', in S. Gass and J. Schachter (eds.), *Linguistic perspectives on second language acquisition*, pp. 73–88. Cambridge: Cambridge University Press.

1990. 'On the issue of completeness in second language acquisition', *Second Language Research* 6: 93–124.

1996. 'Maturation and the issue of Universal Grammar in second language acquisition', in W. C. Ritchie and T. K. Bhatia (eds.), *Handbook of second language acquisition*, pp. 159–93. San Diego: Academic Press.

Schachter, J. and M. Celce-Murcia 1977. 'Some reservations concerning error analysis', *TESOL Quarterly* 11: 441–51.

Schlyter, S. 1990. 'The acquisition of tense and aspect', in J. M. Meisel (ed.), *Two first languages: Early grammatical development in bilingual children*, pp. 87–121. Dordrecht: Foris.

Schumann, J. 1978. *The pidginization process: A model for second language acquisition*. Rowley, MA: Newbury House.

1979. 'The acquisition of English negation by speakers of Spanish: A review of the literature', in R. Andersen (ed.), *The acquisition and use of Spanish and English as first and second languages*, pp. 3–32. Washington, DC: TESOL.

Schumann, J. H. 1995. 'Ad Minorem Theoriae Gloriam: A response to Eubank and Gregg', *Studies in Second Language Acquisition* 17: 59–63.

Schwartz, B. D. 1992. 'Testing between UG-based and problem-solving models of L2A: Developmental sequence data', *Language Acquisition* 2: 1–20.

1993. 'On explicit and negative data effecting and affecting competence and linguistic behavior', *Studies in Second Language Acquisition* 15: 147–63.

1996. 'Parameters in non-native language acquisition', in P. Jordens and J. Lalleman (eds.), *Investigating second language acquisition*, pp. 211–35. Berlin: Mouton de Gruyter.

1999. 'Let's make up your mind: "Special nativist" perspectives on language, modularity of mind, and nonnative language acquisition', *Studies in Second Language Acquisition* 21: 635–55.

2004. 'On child L2 development of syntax and morphology', *Lingue e Linguaggio* 3: 97–132.

Schwartz, B. D. and R. A. Sprouse 1994. 'Word order and nominative case in non-native language acquisition: A longitudinal study of (L1 Turkish) German interlanguage', in T. Hoekstra and B. D. Schwartz (eds.), *Language acquisition studies in generative grammar: Papers in honor of Kenneth Wexler from the 1991 GLOW workshop*, pp. 317–68. Amsterdam: John Benjamins.

1996. 'L2 cognitive states and the Full Transfer/Full Access model', *Second Language Research* 12: 40–77.

Schwartz, B. D. and A. Tomaselli 1990. 'Some implications from an analysis of German word order', in W. Abraham, W. Kosmeijer and E. Reuland (eds.), *Issues in German syntax*, pp. 251–74. Berlin: de Gruyter.

Scovel, T. 1988. *A time to speak: A psycholinguistic inquiry into the critical period for human speech*. Cambridge, MA: Newbury House.

Segalowitz, N. 2003. 'Automaticity and second languages', in C. Doughty and M. H. Long (eds.), *Handbook of second language acquisition*, pp. 382–408. Oxford: Blackwell.

Seliger, H. 1978. 'Implications of a multiple critical period hypothesis for second language learning', in W. Ritchie (ed.), *Second language acquisition research: Issues and implications*, pp. 11–19. New York: Academic Press.

Selinker, L. 1969. 'Language transfer', *General Linguistics* 9: 67–92.

1972. 'Interlanguage', *International Review of Applied Linguistics* 10: 209–31.

1992. *Rediscovering Interlanguage*. London: Longman.

Serratrice, L., A. Sorace and S. Paoli 2004. 'Crosslinguistic influence at the syntax–pragmatic interface: Subjects and objects in English–Italian bilingual and monolingual acquisition', *Bilingualism: Language and Cognition* 7: 183–205.

Sharwood-Smith, M. and E. Kellerman 1986. 'Crosslinguistic influence in second language acquisition: An introduction', in E. Kellerman and M. Sharwood-Smith (eds.), *Crosslinguistic influence in second language acquisition*, pp. 1–9. Oxford: Pergamon.

Silva-Corvalán, C. 2003. 'Linguistic consequences of reduced input in bilingual first language acquisition', in S. Montrul and F. Ordóñez (eds.), *Linguistic theory and language development in Hispanic languages*, pp. 375–97. Somerville, MA: Cascadilla Press.

Silverstein, M. 1972. 'Chinook jargon: Language contact and the problem of multi-level generative systems', Part I, *Language* 48: 378–406, Part II, *Language* 48: 596–625.

Singleton, D. 1989. *Language acquisition: The age factor*. Clevedon: Multilingual Matters.

Singleton, D. and Z. Lengyel (eds.) 1995. *The age factor in second language acquisition: A critical look at the Critical Period Hypothesis*. Clevedon: Multilingual Matters.

Skinner, B. F. 1957. *Verbal behavior*. Acton, MA: Copley.

Slavoff, G. R. and J. S. Johnson 1995. 'The effects of age on the rate of learning a second language', *Studies in Second Language Acquisition* 17: 1–16.

Slobin, D. I. 1985. 'Crosslinguistic evidence for the Language-Making Capacity', in D. I. Slobin (ed.), *The crosslinguistic study of language acquisition*. Vol. 2: *Theoretical issues*, pp. 1157–1256. Hillsdale, NJ: Lawrence Erlbaum.

Slobin, D. I. and T. G. Bever 1982. 'Children use canonical sentence schemas: A cross-linguistic study of word order and inflections', *Cognition* 12: 229–65.

Smith, N. V. 1999. *Chomsky: Ideas and ideals*. Cambridge: Cambridge University Press.

2000. Foreword to N. Chomsky, *New horizons in the study of language and mind*. Cambridge: Cambridge University Press, vi–xvi.

Smith, N. V. and A. Law 2009. 'On parametric (and non-parametric) variation', *Biolinguistics* 3: 332–43.

Smith, N. V. and I.-M. Tsimpli 1995. *The mind of a savant: Language learning and modularity*. Oxford: Blackwell.

Snyder, W. 2001. 'On the nature of syntactic variation: Evidence from complex predicates and complex word-formation', *Language* 77: 324–42.

2007. *Child language: The parametric approach*. Oxford: Oxford University Press.

Sopata, A. 2008. 'Finiteness in child second language acquisition'. Paper presented at the *Colloquium on language acquisition and change: Across the lifespan and across generations*. University of Hamburg, June 2008.

Sorace, A. 2000. 'Differential effects of attrition in the L1syntax of near-native L2 speakers', in C. Howell, S. Fish and T. Keith-Lucas (eds.), *Proceedings of the 24th Annual Boston University Conference on Language Development*, pp. 719–25. Somerville, MA: Cascadilla Press.

2003. 'Near-nativeness', in C. Doughty and M. H. Long (eds.), *Handbook of second language acquisition*, pp. 130–51. Oxford: Blackwell.

Speas, M. 1991. *Phrase structure in natural language*. Dordrecht: Kluwer.

Stauble, A.-M. 1978. 'The process of decreolization: A model for second language development', *Language Learning* 28: 29–54.

1984. 'A comparison of a Spanish–English and a Japanese–English second language continuum: Negation and verb morphology', in R. W. Andersen (ed.), *Second languages: A cross-linguistic perspective*, pp. 323–53. Rowley, MA: Newbury House.

Stockwell, R., J. Bowen and J. Martin 1965. *The grammatical structures of English and Spanish*. Chicago: Chicago University Press.

Stowell, T. 1981. *Origins of phrase structure*. MIT: PhD dissertation.

Stutterheim, C. von 1986. *Temporalität in der Zweitsprache: Eine Untersuchung zum Erwerb des Deutschen durch türkische Gastarbeiter*. Berlin: de Gruyter.

Svenonius, P. (ed.) 2000. *The derivation of VO and OV*. Amsterdam: John Benjamins.

Thoma, D. and R. Tracy 2006. 'Deutsch als frühe Zweitsprache: Zweite Erstsprache?', in B. Ahrenholz (ed.), *Kinder mit Migrationshintergrund: Spracherwerb und Fördermöglichkeiten*, pp. 58–79. Freiburg i.B.: Fillibach.

Tomaselli, A. and B. D. Schwartz 1990. 'Analyzing the acquisition stages of negation in L2 German: Support for UG in adult SLA', *Second Language Research* 6: 1–38.

Towell, R. and R. Hawkins 1994. *Approaches to second language acquisition*. Clevedon: Multilingual Matters.

Townsend, D. and T. Bever 2001. *Sentence comprehension: The integration of habits and rules*. Cambridge, MA: MIT Press.

Trahey, M. and L. White 1993. 'Positive evidence and preemption in the second language classroom', *Studies in Second Language Acquisition* 15: 181–204.

Travis, L. 1984. *Parameters and effects of word order variation*. MIT: PhD dissertation.

Travis, L. deMena 1991. 'Parameters of phrase structure and verb-second phenomena', in R. Freidin (ed.), *Principles and parameters in comparative grammar*, pp. 339–64. Cambridge, MA: MIT Press.

Trévise, A. and C. Noyau 1984. 'Adult Spanish speakers and the acquisition of French negation forms: Individual variation and linguistic awareness', in R. W. Andersen (ed.), *Second languages: A cross-linguistic perspective*, pp. 165–89. Rowley, MA: Newbury House.

Tsimpli, I.-M. 2001. 'LF-interpretability and language development: A study of verbal and nominal features in Greek normally developing and SLI children', *Brain and Language* 77: 432–48.

2004. 'Interprétabilité des traits et acquisition des langues maternelles et secondes: Clitiques et déterminants en grec', *AILE* 20: 87–128.

2005. 'Peripheral positions in Early Greek', in M. Stavrou and A. Terzi (eds.), *Advances in Greek generative syntax*, pp. 178–216. Amsterdam: John Benjamins.

Tsimpli, I.-M., and M. Dimitrakopoulou 2007. 'The Interpretability Hypothesis: Evidence from wh-interrogatives in second language acquisition', *Second Language Research* 23: 215–42.

Tsimpli, I.-M., and M. Mastropavlou 2007. 'Feature-interpretability in L2 acquisition and SLI: Greek clitics and determiners', in J. M. Liceras, H. Zobl and H. Goodluck (eds.), *The role of formal features in second language acquisition*, pp. 143–83. London: Routledge.

Tsimpli, I.-M., and A. Roussou 1991. 'Parameter resetting in L2?', *UCL Working Papers in Linguistics* 3: 149–69.

Tucker, G. R., W. E. Lambert and A. G. Rigault 1977. *The French speaker's skill with grammatical gender: An example of rule-governed behavior*. The Hague/Paris: Mouton.

Ullman, M. 2001. 'The neural basis of lexicon and grammar in first and second language: The declarative/procedural model', *Bilingualism: Language and Cognition* 4: 105–22.

Unsworth, S. 2005. *Child L2, adult L2, child L1: Differences and similarities. A study on the acquisition of direct object scrambling in Dutch*. Utrecht: LOT.

Uriagereka, J. 2007. 'Clarifying the notion "parameter"', *Biolinguistics* 1: 99–113.

Vainikka, A. and M. Young-Scholten 1994. 'Direct access to X'-Theory: Evidence from Korean and Turkish adults learning German', in T. Hoekstra and B. D. Schwartz (eds.), *Language acquisition studies in generative grammar: Papers in honor of Kenneth Wexler from the 1991 GLOW workshop*, pp. 265–316. Amsterdam: John Benjamins.

1996a. 'Gradual development of L2 phrase structure', *Second Language Research* 12: 7–39.

1996b. 'The early stages in adult L2 syntax: Additional evidence from Romance speakers', *Second Language Research* 12: 140–76.

2006. 'The roots of syntax and how they grow: Organic grammar, the basic variety and processability theory', in S. Unsworth, T. Parodi, A. Sorace and M. Young-Scholten (eds.), *Paths of development in L1 and L2 acquisition: In honor of Bonnie D. Schwartz*, pp. 77–106. Amsterdam: John Benjamins.

Valian, V. 1990a. 'Logical and psychological constraints on the acquisition of syntax', in L. Frazier and J. de Villiers (eds.), *Language processing and language acquisition*, pp. 119–45. Dordrecht: Kluwer.

1990b. 'Null subjects: A problem for parameter-setting models of language acquisition', *Cognition* 35: 105–22.

VanPatten, B. 1984. 'Processing strategies and morpheme acquisition', in F. R. Eckman, L. H. Bell and D. Nelson (eds.) 1984, *Universals of second language acquisition*, pp. 88–98. Rowley, MA: Newbury House.

Vincent, M. 1982. 'Les transferts: Une stratégie acquisitionnelle provisoire dans l'acquisition d'une langue seconde', *Encrages* 9: 28–32.

Wartenburger, I., H. R. Heekeren, J. Abutalebi, S. F. Cappa, A. Villringer and D. Perani 2003. 'Early setting of grammatical processing in the bilingual brain', *Neuron* 37: 159–70.

Weber-Fox, C. M. and H. J. Neville 1996. 'Maturational constraints on functional specializations for language processing: ERP and behavioral evidence in bilingual speakers', *Journal of Cognitive Neuroscience* 8: 231–56.

1999. 'Functional neural subsystems are differentially affected by delays in second language immersion: ERP and behavioral evidence in bilinguals', in D. Birdsong (ed.), *Second language acquisition and the Critical Period Hypothesis*, pp. 23–38. Mahwah, NJ: Lawrence Erlbaum.

Weinreich, U. 1953. *Languages in contact.* New York: Publication of the Linguistic Circle of New York, 1. Reprint; The Hague: Mouton 1963.

Wexler, K. 1998. 'Maturation and growth of grammar', in T. K. Bhatia and W. C. Ritchie (eds.), *Handbook of child language acquisition*, pp. 51–109. New York: Academic Press.

Weyerts H., M. Penke, T. Münte, H. J. Heinze and H. Clahsen 2002. 'Word order in sentence processing: An experimental study of verb placement in German', *Journal of Psycholinguistic Research* 31: 211–68.

White, L. 1985. 'The "pro-drop" parameter in adult second language acquisition', *Language Learning* 35: 47–62.

1989a. *Universal grammar and second language acquisition*. Amsterdam: John Benjamins.

1989b. 'The adjacency condition on case assignment: Do L2 learners observe the subset principle?', in S. M. Gass and J. Schachter (eds.), *Linguistic perspectives on second language acquisition*, pp. 134–58. Cambridge: Cambridge University Press.

1990. 'Second language acquisition and Universal Grammar', *Studies in Second Language Acquisition* 12: 121–34.

1991a. 'Adverb placement in second language acquisition: Some effects of positive and negative evidence in the classroom', *Second Language Research* 7: 133–61.

1991b. 'The verb movement parameter in second language acquisition', *Language Acquisition* 1: 337–60.

1992. 'Long and short verb movement in second language acquisition', *Canadian Journal of Linguistics* 37: 273–86.

1996. 'Universal Grammar and second language acquisition: Current trends and new directions', in W. C. Ritchie and T. K. Bhatia (eds.), *Handbook of second language acquisition*, pp. 85–120. San Diego: Academic Press.

2003. *Second language acquisition and Universal Grammar.* Cambridge: Cambridge University Press.

White, L. and F. Genesee 1996. 'How native is near-native? The issue of ultimate attainment in adult second language acquisition', *Second Language Research* 11: 233–65.

Whitman, R. and K. Jackson 1972. 'The unpredictability of contrastive analysis', *Language Learning* 22: 29–41.

Wode, H. 1976. 'Developmental sequences in naturalistic L2 acquisition', *Working Papers in Bilingualism* 11: 1–31.

1977. 'Four early stages in the development of L1 negation', *Journal of Child Language* 4: 87–102.

1978. 'Free vs. bound forms in three types of language acquisition', *Interlanguage Studies Bulletin* 3: 6–22.

1981. *Learning a second language: An integrated view of language acquisition.* Tübingen: Narr.

Wode, H., J. Bahns, H. Bedey and W. Frank 1978. 'Developmental sequence: An alternative approach to morpheme order', *Language Learning* 28: 175–85.

Yuan, B. 2001. 'The status of thematic verbs in the second language acquisition of Chinese: Against inevitability of thematic-verb raising in second language acquisition', *Second Language Research* 17: 248–72.

Zanuttini, R. 1989. *The structure of negative clauses in Romance.* University of Pennsylvania: Unpublished manuscript.

Zobl, H. 1979. 'Nominal and pronominal interrogation in the speech of adult francophone ESL learners: Some insights into the workings of transfer', *SPEAQ Journal* 3: 69–93.

1980. 'The formal and developmental selectivity of L1 influence on L2 acquisition', *Language Learning* 30: 43–57.

Zobl, H. and J. Liceras 1994. 'Functional categories and acquisition orders', *Language Learning* 44: 159–80.

Index